CW00958696

WISDOM'S WORKSHOP

OTHER TITLES BY JAMES AXTELL

The Educational Writings of John Locke: A Critical Edition (1968)

The School Upon a Hill: Education and Society in Colonial New England (1974)

Indian Missions: A Critical Bibliography (with James P. Ronda, 1978)

The Indian Peoples of Eastern America: A Documentary History of the Sexes (1981)

The European and the Indian: Essays in the Ethnohistory of Colonial North America (1981)

The Invasion Within: The Contest of Cultures in Colonial North America (1985)

After Columbus: Essays in the Ethnohistory of Colonial North America (1988)

Beyond 1492: Encounters in Colonial North America (1992)

The Indians' New South: Cultural Change in the Colonial Southeast (1997)

The Pleasures of Academe: A Celebration & Defense of Higher Education (1998)

Natives and Newcomers: The Cultural Origins of North America (2001)

The Making of Princeton University: From Woodrow Wilson to the Present (2006)

The Educational Legacy of Woodrow Wilson (2012)

WISDOM'S WORKSHOP

The Rise of the Modern University

JAMES AXTELL

PRINCETON UNIVERSITY PRESS
Princeton & Oxford

Published by Princeton University Press
41 William Street, Princeton, New Jersey 08540

In the United Kingdom: Princeton University Press
6 Oxford Street, Woodstock, Oxfordshire OX20 1TR

press.princeton.edu

Jacket art: Bodleian Library, Oxford: interior, showing study desks.
Line engraving by J. le Keux after F. Mackenzie, 1836

Library of Congress Cataloging-in-Publication Data

Axtell, James.
Wisdom's workshop: the rise of the modern university / James Axtell.
pages cm
Includes bibliographical references and index.
ISBN 978-0-691-14959-2 (hardcover : alk. paper)
1. Education, Higher—History. I. Title.
LA174.A98 2016
378—dc23
2015020495

British Library Cataloging-in-Publication Data is available

This book has been composed in Adobe Caslon Pro

Printed on acid-free paper. ∞

Printed in the United States of America

1 3 5 7 9 10 8 6 4 2

Parent of sciences . . . wisdom's special workshop

POPE GREGORY IX (1231)

FOR SUSAN

Better Half, Best Friend, and Wicked-Good Editor

CONTENTS

ILLUSTRATIONS

CREDITS

Figures 1, 4, 5, 17, 20, 23–24, and 28 courtesy of Wikimedia Commons; figures 9, 10, 12–14, 14, 21, and 27 courtesy of Paul Venable Turner; figure 2 courtesy of Sonia O'Connor and Dominic Tweddle; figure 3 from Burnett Hillman Streeter, *The Chained Library* (Macmillan, 1931); figure 6 from John Foxe, *Acts and Monuments of the Christian Church* (London, 1563); figure 7 courtesy of the Welcome Institute; figure 8 from Samuel Eliot Morison, *The Founding of Harvard College* (Harvard University Press, 1935); figure 11 courtesy of the Princeton University Library; figure 15 "The Student" by Porte Crayon from *Harper's New Monthly Magazine*, 13:75 (Aug. 1856); figure 16 from F. G. Atwood, *Manners and Customs of Ye Harvard Studente* (1877); figure 18 by permission of the Virginia Historical Society (1989.27.1); figure 19 courtesy of Special Collections, Earl G. Swem Library, College of William & Mary; figure 22 by permission of Plexuss.com; figure 25 from Milton Greenberg, *The GI Bill* (Lickle, 1997); figure 26 by permission of *The New Yorker.*

PROLOGUE

There are few earthly things
more splendid than a university.

JOHN MASEFIELD

Some books beg to be written; a smaller number even appear to choose their authors. My long history of *The Making of Princeton University: From Woodrow Wilson to the Present* (2006) did both. Its conspicuous pleas (even to a Yale man's ears) apparently had not been heard or heeded by the Princeton community to mark the university's 250th anniversary in 1996. This is another of those books. But I didn't realize it until Peter Dougherty, my now-editor, friend, and press director, brought it to my attention after I had sounded him out on another topic. Given the alacrity with which I abandoned the latter, that idea did *not* beg to be written. This one did.

Why it chose me as its amanuensis is, in retrospect, not all that mysterious. I had begun my scholarly publishing career at Yale in the history of education, with a particular interest in higher education; there I taught an introductory seminar on the subject for two years. My first two books were on the one-time Oxford don John Locke's educational career and writings (1968) and on the full range of education in colonial New England, including Harvard and Yale (1974). Then, after the 100th anniversary of the massacre at Wounded Knee and during the long lead-up to the Columbus Quincentenary, I was drawn to the ethnohistory of Indian-European relations in the colonial Americas, which resulted in eight books. When I'd said my piece on a variety of processes, events, and issues, I realized that it was time to return to my first love, the history and current state of American higher education.

For the last twelve years of my tenure at William & Mary, I had taught a freshman seminar on that history, beginning—as this book does—in medieval Europe. But I needed to write about it as well, to see what I really thought and to connect the pieces. An article "What's Wrong—and Right—with American Higher Education" and a book of personal essays on what I have long considered to be the satisfactions of the academic life and reports from the field (*The Pleasures of Academe* 1998) preceded the Princeton history. After I retired in 2008, a semester teaching Princeton freshmen the history of their college and university (and graduate students, colonial ethnohistory) brought me into closer contact with Peter Dougherty and his engaging spokesmanship for this book. Once I had completed editing a volume of essays, *The Educational Legacy of Woodrow Wilson* (2012), the result of a conference I had organized at Princeton in 2009, I began to answer the persistent call of the book you now hold (or scan on a screen of some sort).

What I found most arresting about the recent history of U.S. higher education was that in the first global rankings in 2003 and ever since in others, the United States has dominated the top ranks. In the five major global rankings for 2014–15, U.S. universities claimed 7 (or 8, depending on the ranking) of the top 10, 11–16 of the top 20, and (with one British outlier at 17) 28–32 of the top 50 places. Moreover, the leading American research universities that crowd those lists also top our own national rankings, whether they are conducted by the *U.S. News and World Report "Best Colleges"* staff or by the National Research Council. I have never believed in "manifest destiny"—that U.S. universities were preordained to command the global-ranking heights—so this book inductively searches for understanding and explanation.

It also seeks to trace historically the particular and conspicuous rise of America's elite research universities, which dominate the global lists. It does so, I like to think, not because I've experienced, studied at, and had a lifelong interest in such institutions, but because those are the prevailing models that aspiring nations and competitive universities largely wish to emulate. As the world's standard- and pace-setters, our elite universities deserve to be understood not as unique, *sui generis*, creations, but as variable, contingent products of specific times, places, and conditions in a long lineage of similar, though never identical, institutions.

To be clear, we need to distinguish the elite research universities from the profuse rest of the institutions of higher education in the decentralized American (non-)system, which totaled 4,634 in the most recent Carnegie Foundation for the Advancement of Teaching classification in 2010. The most numerous institutions—1,920 of them—offer two-year associate degrees in a wide variety of subjects (mostly occupational and applied) and settings. Predominantly public (1,054) and private for-profit (752), they constitute 41 percent of the total, enroll more than a third of American students, and graduate more than a million annually. Smaller numbers of baccalaureate colleges—808—constitute only 17 percent of the institutional mix. Institutions that award master's degrees as well as bachelor's—728 (15.7 percent)—trail the 883 (19.1 percent) "special-focus" schools, such as religious seminaries, medical and nursing schools, other professional schools, and tribal colleges.

The smallest category—6.4 percent of the total—contains the 295 Research Institutions. Eighty-nine are combination Doctoral/Research Universities, but the rest—206 (4.4 percent)—are classified as Research Universities, having either "high" or "very high" research activity.[1] The most productive group of 108 is the main focus at the end of this book, in the last two chapters and the epilogue. But since the research university didn't begin to emerge as a species until the last quarter of the nineteenth century, our genealogical pursuit must of necessity track them from their European ancestors through their American antecedents, who were more distant or country cousins than lineal forebears. It is simply impossible to leap from early-seventeenth-century Oxford and Cambridge across the Atlantic and land in the second half of twentieth-century America without severe loss of historical understanding and consciousness. It may be attempted in commencement addresses, but you can't expect a dues-paying historian, even a former long-jumper, to risk it.

Thus, our genealogical tale begins in twelfth-century Europe with the slow growth and eventual formalization of the institutions that we, too, recognize as universities. But because, as L. P. Hartley famously said, "The past is a foreign country; they do things differently there," we must treat universities and their evolution on their own terms—in their own institutional, social, intellectual, and

1 *Chronicle of Higher Education Almanac 2014–15* (Aug. 22, 2014), 7, 73.

cultural contexts—and not simply assume that modern Berkeley or Yale is a carbon-copy of medieval Paris or Bologna. They *did* do things differently there and then, and I want to suggest just how different from—as well as similar to—us they were.

But we must also follow the *specific* genealogical path of America's elite universities, not from *all* of Europe's alma maters, but chiefly from Tudor and early-Stuart Oxford and Cambridge (Oxbridge), with a *few* Scottish features and faculty lent in the second half of the eighteenth century. For once Oxbridge alumni settled the New England colonies, they could hardly wait to plant, not the full, mature universities they had known as students, but the smaller constituent *colleges* where they had resided, studied, and prayed. By comparison with the *universities* of Oxford and Cambridge, Harvard *College* (1636) and Yale *College* (1701) were no larger—and often smaller—than a typical Oxbridge residential college, even though they arrogated to themselves the essential university right of awarding degrees.

With the single exception of the Royal College of William & Mary in Virginia (1693), the nine colonial colleges operated legally with charters granted solely by colonial governors or legislatures. When the colonies won their independence in the 1780s, the colleges easily and legally became American colleges through state charters. They were joined by a flood of home-grown institutions as the new nation spread across the continent. Most were small colleges, many denominational and some disguised as multipurpose "academies," but all resembled their colonial cousins and, before those, their Oxbridge progenitors. By European lights, there were few if any bona fide universities in America. But America was still young, proud, and not afraid to borrow from the Old World to make the New equal or superior to it.

Then, largely in the second half of the nineteenth century, we pick up a trail of influence that flowed not directly from Europe in the cultural baggage of emigrants, but as educational cuttings and scholarly souvenirs collected by American postgraduate students and professors who sought in Germany what the United States so keenly lacked, namely the graduate school, the Ph.D., and the research imperative (perhaps a less draconian version of our own "publish or perish"). They did not always find specific German solutions, so they cherry-picked and adapted when they returned home. They reconfigured the only German degree, the Ph.D., into an advanced research degree, and created the graduate school to build upon the very different American undergraduate experience, which in turn was built upon secondary preparation that was shorter and less thorough than that afforded by the classical German *Gymnasium.*

Although separate liberal-arts colleges for undergraduates continued to multiply, a number of new, true universities for both undergraduates and research-minded faculty and graduate students were founded, and a number of older elite colleges were enlarged and upgraded to university status. Both types soon rivaled Europe's more venerable (if no longer agile) archetypes, down to their Gothic, Georgian, or neoclassical fabrics.

By the opening decades of the twentieth century, U.S. universities had become ambitious, competitive, and largely standardized. They grew in number, faculty, facilities, and enrollments, but they all understood their key functions to be the production and application of new knowledge, transmission of the known, and public service in a variety of forms. When World War II broke out, they enlisted their intellectual, technological, and pedagogical services in the war effort and, with substantial federal funding, emerged energized and retooled for even more ambitious service through the Cold War and into the twenty-first century. It was these well-funded, autonomous, supercharged, postwar research universities that rose to the top of both national and global rankings and show no sign of relinquishing their position. In the epilogue I bring together my and other scholars' best guesses as to what accounts for that signal American success.

None of this story should suggest that higher education in the United States is perfect. Far from it. It is too large, too heterogeneous, unequally funded, too dependent on a flawed secondary system, and serves too many gods. But its *elite* universities, public and private, are in a small class of the world's best and set a powerful example for those that rank below them at home and abroad. It's the elite universities' (often-surprising) lineage that I've tried to trace wherever it led: to tough Tennessee river-towns, enterprising Midwestern cities, or flush-and-plush Silicon Valley.

Nor have I dealt with all that troubles the elite and other universities' existence and tranquility. The news media and other scholars and writers have treated such issues as academic freedom for students, faculty, and invited speakers; student protests (from the late 1960s forward); academic cheating and plagiarism; grade inflation; the complexities of growing minority, first-generation, lower-income, and foreign enrollments; sexual assault; excessive drinking; lack of fraternity couth and control; hazing; hydra-headed professional education; excessive time-to-graduate-degrees; wan markets for new Ph.D.s; sharply rising costs (particularly in public universities whose state funding has been reduced by recession or politics); student debt; privatization and corporatization; "administrative bloat"; and the rise of utilitarian (or conservative) thinking that regards higher education as a private rather than a public good, to name just a few.

As I chose not to write another "crisis" book or critique of American higher education, I also eschewed giving even indirect advice to high-school students seeking an edge in the fierce competition for admission to the nation's Harvards, Princetons, and Stanfords. As a historian, the best service I thought I could perform was to suggest some of the ways the elite research universities came into being and what energizes and sustains them in the high-stakes "brain race" they now run on the world stage.

ACKNOWLEDGMENTS

IN A LONG career of asking, I've found that experts of any kind don't mind—they even welcome—being asked for advice and assistance. I've also found, when they accept, as they usually do readily, that they are not easy to thank sufficiently for their time, patience, and talents. But it is one of the pleasant final tasks of writing a book such as this to strive not only for grateful sufficiency but also full justice. If there's any place for purplish prose, it's in acknowledging the generosity of all those experts who helped me track down sources, hone arguments, clarify prose, tame the computer, transform a manuscript to codex, and provide inspiration and encouragement when they were most needed.

First, the librarians whose professionalism, efficiency, and good humor kept me inundated with sources local and national: Cynthia Mack and her persistent staff in the Interlibrary Loan Department and Dave Morales and his accommodating crew in the Circulation Department of the Swem Library at William & Mary. Jay Gaidmore, director of Special Collections, indispensably digitized all of the illustrations. As a partner in supply, Anja Becker (now Werner) shared her dissertation on the Americans in nineteenth-century German universities before it became a book. Similarly, Fred M. Newmann gave me a personal copy of his Amherst senior thesis on the college's German influences. Jim McLachlan graciously lent me his trove of unpublished data on the colonial American colleges, as well as sage advice on the colonial chapter. Bill Bowen kept me supplied with his many influential books and even a reclusive Princeton monograph. His example was even more valuable.

Once chapters were written, friends, former William & Mary colleagues, and other authorities responded readily and helpfully to my requests for critical readings. Paul Needham, Tony Grafton, and Phil Daileader took on the medieval chapter. Dale Hoak, Bob Fehrenbach, and Moti Feingold improved the Oxbridge chapter. Chris Grasso and Carol Sheriff took the antebellum chapter in hand. Tony Grafton, Steve Turner, Jim Turner (no relation), and Nadine Zimmerli materially assisted the German chapter in transit.

Three people have provided the most help over the course of the book's writing. Jim Turner, whose *Philology* led the way through Princeton University Press, has been a friend, model, and ace improver of the whole book. Bruce Leslie, an even older friend, read and improved every chapter as they came out of the printer, and again when he and Jim read the completed manuscript for PUP with eagle-eyed attention to matters small and large. Even when he was not reading a chapter, he and two other long-term friends in higher education studies—John Thelin and Stan Katz—supplied frequent reading suggestions, collegial encouragement, and wise, often witty, commentary throughout.

The third person, my wife Susan, English major and inveterate reader, has read nearly every published word I've written since we met. She is the Ideal Reader I always encouraged my students to choose for their own work: a very intelligent nonspecialist who's interested in what you have to say but demanding and persuasive enough to make you say it clearly and with some style. For that service—and countless other tolerances and ministrations—she appears in the dedication.

The role of Peter Dougherty, my wise and demanding editor/publisher can be glimpsed in the prologue. But it extends well beyond putting the manuscript through its paces. His faith that this book and I were meant for each other—and his readiness to take me to lunch to talk trash about college basketball—are indelible high points in our long relationship.

I am, it may go without but needs saying, grateful for the skills of other, often anonymous, PUP professionals who edited, designed, and produced *Wisdom's Workshop*. Four I do know and wish to thank by name are Debbie Tegarden, production editor, and Gail Schmitt, former PUP production editor and now freelance copyeditor. Both perfectionists held me to PUP's famously high standards and taught an old dog several new tricks of the trade, for which I am grateful. Dimitri Karetnikov demanded and got from my illustrations the best possible clarity and most informative angles. And Chris Ferrante's skill and artistry in text, binding, and jacket design were a true pleasure to behold.

Last but not least, Tom Broughton-Willet's index is worth more than words can say but speaks eloquently in and of them.

WISDOM'S WORKSHOP

CHAPTER ONE

Foundings

The institutions which the Middle Age has bequeathed to us are of greater and more imperishable value even than its cathedrals.

HASTINGS RASHDALL

UNIVERSITIES, LIKE CATHEDRALS and parliaments, were unique creations of Western Europe and the Middle Ages.[1] They arose in the twelfth century in the midst of propitious change. The "barbarian" and "infidel" invasions from the north, south, and east had finally been thwarted, and the Crusades had even begun to direct Europe's martial energies outward. The resulting political stability, increased agricultural productivity, and new and improved roads fostered the growth of population, towns, trade, and the Roman Catholic Church.

As the Papacy extended its reach, it became clear that the inward-looking monasteries and even the newer cathedral schools

1 Although it developed a few curricular features in common with the madrasa and owed a deep intellectual debt to Islamic scholarship, "the university, as a form of organization, owes nothing to Islam." It was "a new product . . . utterly foreign to the Islamic experience." George Makdisi, *The Rise of Colleges: Institutions of Learning in Islam and the West* (Edinburgh: Edinburgh University Press, 1981), ch. 4, at 224, 225. See also Toby E. Huff, *The Rise of Early Modern Science: Islam, China, and the West*, 2nd ed. (New York: Cambridge University Press, 2003 [1993]), 149–59, 179–89, on the prevailing scholarly consensus. Darleen Pryds suggests that madrasas shared some key features and functions with *southern* European universities, such as the royally founded University of Naples and other Iberian universities, which differed significantly from their northern counterparts in Bologna, Paris, and Oxford. But she demonstrates neither influence nor causation in either direction. "*Studia* as Royal Office: Mediterranean Universities of Medieval Europe," in William J. Courtenay and Jürgen Miethke, eds., *Universities and Schooling in Medieval Society* (Leiden: Brill, 2000), 83–99, at 95–98.

could not provide the advanced training needed by the Church's growing ranks of priests, missionaries, and administrators. Nor could the rudimentary town schools prepare the personnel required by the burgeoning civil bureaucracies, particularly royal and imperial, that sought to preserve the fragile peace and to promote the social welfare. Those schools taught only the Seven Liberal Arts of antiquity and the early Middle Ages, and not the influx of "new" Greco-Roman and Arabic learning—in philosophy, mathematics, science, medicine, and law—that arrived after 1100 through Italy and Sicily but chiefly via Arab scholars and translators in Spain.[2] These conditions stimulated the advent of the university, one of the very few European institutions that have preserved their fundamental patterns and basic social roles and functions over the course of history.[3]

The earliest universities and even a few later ones have no firm birthdates. This causes no end of trouble when their older selves wish to celebrate major milestones. Cambridge has it easy in the ninth year of every new century because it was established—and well documented—in 1209 by professors and scholars fleeing

2 Olaf Pedersen, *The First Universities*: Studium generale *and the Origins of University Education in Europe*, trans. Richard North (Cambridge: Cambridge University Press, 1997), ch. 4; A. B. Cobban, *The Medieval Universities: Their Development and Organization* (London: Methuen, 1975), ch. 1; Gordon Leff, *Paris and Oxford Universities in the Thirteenth and Fourteenth Centuries: An Institutional and Intellectual History* (New York: John Wiley & Sons, 1968), 127–37; Charles Homer Haskins, *The Renaissance of the Twelfth Century* (Cambridge, Mass.: Harvard University Press, 1927); Robert L. Benson and Giles Constable, eds., *Renaissance and Renewal in the Twelfth Century* (Cambridge, Mass.: Harvard University Press, 1982); R. N. Swanson, *The Twelfth-Century Renaissance* (Manchester: Manchester University Press, 1999).

3 In 1982 Clark Kerr, a former chancellor of the University of California, noted that "about eighty-five institutions in the Western world established by 1520 still exist in recognizable forms, with similar functions and with unbroken histories, including the Catholic church, the Parliaments of the Isle of Man, of Iceland, and of Great Britain, several Swiss cantons, and seventy universities." *The Uses of the University*, 3rd ed. (Cambridge, Mass.: Harvard University Press, 1982 [1963]), 152. Walter Rüegg exaggerates the university's uniqueness in the foreword to *Universities in the Middle Ages*, Hilde de Ridder-Symoens, ed., vol. 1 of *A History of the University in Europe* [*HUE*], gen. ed. Walter Rüegg, 4 vols.(Cambridge: Cambridge University Press, 1992), xix.

Oxford after a legal and literal battle with the city and king over the discipline of the university's members.[4] But the earliest bona fide universities have had to be more arbitrary in selecting commemorative dates. In the latest and most comprehensive history of European universities, Bologna's founding is located sometime at the "end of the twelfth century," while Paris, Oxford, and Montpellier secured their corporate existence in the "beginning of the thirteenth century."[5]

The earliest founding dates are hard to pin down because those institutions were not created by royal, papal, or imperial decree but instead grew slowly and incrementally, leaving thin paper or parchment trails. Like most twelfth- and thirteenth-century universities, they began as schools belonging to monasteries, towns, or cathedral chapters. Some schools featured only a single charismatic teacher, such as Peter Abelard, who attracted clerics and the occasional layman interested in education higher than they could find locally. But the gathering of critical numbers soon led to the need for physical enlargement, faculty specialization, and new organization.[6] These

4 Damian Riehl Leader, *The University to 1546*, vol. 1 of *A History of the University of Cambridge* [*HUC*], gen. ed. Christopher Brooke (Cambridge: Cambridge University Press, 1988), 16–19; Alan B. Cobban, *The Medieval English Universities: Oxford and Cambridge to c. 1500* (Berkeley: University of California Press, 1988), 44–45, 53–54.

5 Jacques Verger, "Patterns," *HUE* 1:62–65. The Wikipedia entry "Medieval University" is much more confident in assigning (mostly fictitious) birthdates to the earliest universities. En.wikipedia.org/wiki/Medieval_university.

6 Pedersen, *First Universities*, ch. 4; Helene Wieruszowski, *The Medieval University: Masters, Students, Learning* (Princeton, N.J.: D. Van Nostrand, 1966), 15–26, 119–28; John W. Baldwin, *Paris, 1200* (Stanford, Calif.: Stanford University Press, 2010), ch. 5; C. Stephen Jaeger, *The Envy of Angels: Cathedral Schools and Social Ideals in Medieval Europe, 950–1200* (Philadelphia: University of Pennsylvania Press, 1994), chs. 5, 8–11; Stephan C. Ferruolo, *The Origins of the University: The Schools of Paris and Their Critics, 1100–1215* (Stanford, Calif.: Stanford University Press, 1985); Astrik L. Gabriel, "The Cathedral Schools of Notre-Dame and the Beginning of the University of Paris," in Gabriel, *Garlandia: Studies in the History of the Medieval University* (Notre Dame, Ind.: The Mediaeval Institute, University of Notre Dame, 1969), ch. 2; R. W. Southern, "From Schools to University," in *The Early Oxford Schools*, ed. J. I. Catto, vol. 1 of *The History of the University of Oxford* [*HUO*], gen. ed. T. H. Aston, 8 vols. (Oxford: Clarendon Press, 1984), ch. 1.

nascent universities only later received legal sanction, often piecemeal, from the powers-that-were, whereas later institutions largely did so in full at their starts.

Many *studia*, or advanced schools, functioned effectively as universities before they received privileges or full recognition from the pope, or even before they drafted statutes by which to govern themselves. Bologna, Paris, and Oxford were operating as genuine *studia generalia* no later than 1215. That is, their guild-like organizations of masters and students exercised a high degree of legal autonomy, elected their own officers, controlled their own finances, attracted students from a wide area (*generale*), offered instruction in one or more of the higher faculties of law, medicine, or theology as well as the seven foundational liberal arts, and conferred degrees and teaching licenses that were, in theory at least, honored by other universities.[7] Bologna's first statutes were not written until 1252, and its status as a *studium generale* was not confirmed until 1291, when the pope gave its graduates the privilege of *ius ubique docendi*, "the right to teach anywhere" papal power reached. Paris received the same privilege the following year, although it had statutes on the books in 1215 and 1231. For reasons unknown, Oxford—across the English Channel—never received the pope's confirmation as a *studium generale*, despite the pleas of two kings. Cambridge and Edward II were successful in 1318.[8]

In addition to their urban settings, universities were characterized by their formal privileges, which distinguished them from other social institutions. These grants, rights, and immunities sprang from Roman precedents that protected teachers and scholars of the liberal arts, particularly grammar and rhetoric. The medieval Church extended this protection because the arts were necessary to read and interpret Scripture. Even lay scholars without the tonsure enjoyed clerical status, subject to ecclesiastical law, and were immune from the jurisdiction of feudal and local civil courts. In 1155 Emperor Frederick I (Frederick Barbarossa) issued the Authentic *Habita* to guarantee protection and safe conduct to all teachers

7 Cobban, *Medieval Universities*, 32–33.

8 Verger, "Patterns," *HUE* 1:36, 45; Cobban, *Medieval Universities*, 29, 59, 61.

and students traveling to and from seats of learning throughout the Holy Roman Empire.[9]

As soon as faculty and students began to organize into their respective guilds and confraternities for academic effectiveness and self-protection, those in high authority gave them yet more written *privilegia*. These they carefully preserved in bound volumes and resorted to when local, church, or royal officials sought to ignore or deny them.[10] Clergymen with church benefices, or "livings," were allowed to draw their salaries while they were absent pursuing university degrees or teaching.[11] All students, faculty, and even university booksellers enjoyed deferment from military drafts and municipal obligations, such as night watch, guard duty, and roadwork. Scholars were not to be physically assaulted or their premises invaded. If they were arrested, they could choose their judges. Qualified M.A. and doctoral degree candidates were to be issued the *licentia docendi* (the license to teach) without fee, promise, or condition.[12] Customs duties could not be laid on scholars' books, nor could those volumes be seized for debt. Rents were to be fair and premises clean; study-disturbing noise and noisome smells emanating from the work of neighbors were prohibited. The quality and price of food, drink, books, and writing parchment were regulated. In Paris at least,

9 Pearl Kibre, "Scholarly Privileges: Their Roman Origins and Medieval Expansion," *American Historical Review* 59:3 (April 1954), 543–67; Pearl Kibre, *Scholarly Privileges in the Middle Ages: The Rights, Privileges, and Immunities of Scholars and Universities at Bologna, Padua, Paris, and Oxford* (Cambridge, Mass.: Mediaeval Academy of America, 1962); Paolo Nardi, "Relations with Authority," *HUE* 1:78.

10 In 1262 Pope Urban IV appointed two prelates from outside Paris as Conservators of Apostolic Privileges to preserve intact the privileges granted to the University of Paris. Kibre, *Scholarly Privileges*, 119 and 119n150.

11 Walter Rüegg, "Themes," *HUE* 1:17, 18; Aleksander Gieysztor, "Management and Resources," *HUE* 1:109; Jacques Verger, "Teachers," *HUE* 1:151; Kibre, *Scholarly Privileges*, 33, 63, 93n27, 96n40; Lynn Thorndike, *University Records and Life in the Middle Ages*, Columbia University Records of Civilization (New York: Columbia University Press, 1944), 250–53; Cobban, *Medieval Universities*, 26–27.

12 Gaines Post, "Alexander III, the *Licentia docendi*, and the Rise of the Universities," in *Anniversary Essays in Mediaeval History, by Students of Charles Homer Haskins, Presented on His Completion of Forty Years of Teaching*, ed. Charles H. Taylor (Boston: Houghton Mifflin, 1929), 255–77.

scholars' houses were tax exempt. Needless to say, the favoritism shown to the scholars often exacerbated town-gown tensions, which frequently burst into violence.[13]

The most essential privileges were two. The first was the *studium*'s right to incorporate as a legal entity and to run its own affairs, much like a craftsmen's guild. The second was the right, once so organized, to offer degrees and teaching licenses after examination and according to the faculty's sole judgment. The larger corporation of scholars (*universitas magistrorum et scholarium*) created its own subunits, enacted and enforced statutes, designed seals, elected officers, and controlled modest coffers. The professors, or "masters" (*magistri*), were organized into disciplinary faculties—of arts or one of the three learned professions—each with its own dean, a rotating rector to administer the entire university, and often a chancellor to represent royal or papal as well as university interests. Particularly in the southern universities, the students, initially vulnerable strangers from many parts of Europe, formed themselves into "nations," congregations based roughly on natal regions and headed by elected proctors. Bologna had as many as sixteen nations in the dominant law faculty at one time. For convenience's sake, they soon coalesced into two larger configurations, *cismontane* and *ultramontane*, based on the students' origins south or north of the Alps.

Paris, where only the masters and senior scholars of the arts faculty formed nations, had four primary groups: French, Norman, Picard, and English. The latter enrolled scholars from the British

13 Thorndike, *University Records*, 19–20, 38, 123–24, 215, 391; Wieruszowski, *Medieval University*, 136–37, 157–58, 168–69, 181, 183; *The Medieval Student*, ed. Dana Carleton Munro, vol. 2, no. 3 of *Translations and Reprints from the Original Sources of European History* (Philadelphia: Dept. of History, University of Pennsylvania, 1899), 2–10; Cobban, *Medieval English Universities*, 257–74; Hastings Rashdall, *The Universities of Europe in the Middle Ages*, rev. and ed. F. M. Powicke and A. B. Emden, 3 vols. (Oxford: Oxford University Press, 1936 [1895], 3:427–35; Joan B. Williamson, "Unrest in Medieval Universities," in Douglas Radcliff-Umstead, ed., *The University World: A Synoptic View of Higher Education in the Middle Ages and Renaissance*, vol. 2 of Medieval and Renaissance Studies Committee (Pittsburgh: University of Pittsburgh, 1973), 56–83; Rowland Parker, *Town and Gown: The 700 Years' War in Cambridge* (Cambridge: P. Stephens, 1983).

Isles, Flanders, Holland, the Germanies, Scandinavia, Hungary, and Slavic lands.[14] In less cosmopolitan Oxford, like Paris a faculty-dominant *studium*, the sovereign congregation of regent (teaching) masters in arts was divided into northern (*boreales*) and southern (*australes*) islanders. University governance was administered by a chancellor, two proctors (one from each nation), and a half-dozen bedels with bailiff-like powers.[15]

The first four major universities—Bologna and Montpellier in southern Europe, Paris and Oxford in the north—soon found imitators in large towns and cities seeking intellectual prestige, trained personnel, and, not least, income from student populations.[16] Eighteen universities that got their start in the twelfth century survive today. By 1400 the number of viable universities nearly doubled, due in part to several established in Central Europe after the Great Papal Schism in the Church began in 1378. The total grew to at least sixty-three by 1500, covering the continent from Catania (1444) in Sicily to Uppsala (1477) in eastern Sweden, from Lisbon (1290) in coastal Portugal to Cracow (1364) in southern Poland.[17]

❁ ❁ ❁

The sequence of *studium*-founding was much the same, but the process was often compressed and speeded up. Heidelberg, for one, received full university status in 1386 after a trio of Bavarian dukes pleaded with Pope Urban VI to grant the city permission to establish a university "with all faculties included on the model of the *studium*

14 Gray Cowan Boyce, *The English-German Nation in the University of Paris in the Middle Ages* (Bruges: Saint Catherine Press, 1927); Astrik L. Gabriel, "The English-German Nation at the University of Paris: 1425–1483," in Gabriel, *Garlandia*, ch. 8.

15 Pearl Kibre, *The Nations in the Mediaeval Universities* (Cambridge, Mass.: Mediaeval Academy of America, 1948), ch. 1, 160–66; Cobban, *Medieval English Universities*, 90–92, 103–106; A. B. Emden, "Northerners and Southerners in the Organization of the University to 1509," in *Oxford Studies Presented to Daniel Callus*, Oxford Historical Society, n.s., 16 (Oxford: Clarendon Press, 1964 [for 1959–1960], 1–30.

16 On the economic gains to be had from student and faculty migrations, see Thorndike, *University Records*, 310, 334.

17 Verger, "Patterns," *HUE* 1:62–65, 69–74.

of Paris and with all the privileges granted to this latter." Eight months later, after conveying to the pope an honorarium for his bull, the dukes and their council completed the foundation by promising to "endow and protect it with privileges." Good to their word, a new rector hired away from a church in Cologne and two other Paris masters were immediately given "a large stipend" to hire faculty in the arts and theology. In less than a year, the university was legally founded on a solid basis and lectures began on logic, the Bible, and Aristotle's *Physics*.[18]

Despite their juridical presence, the earliest universities were not easy to identify or to locate. For many decades, they were "disembodied," largely anonymous except to near neighbors, because they operated out of rented quarters and were conspicuously lacking in signage.[19] A prospective student coming to town in search of "the university" would not find what a modern American student would—highway exit signs, a central administration building, an office of admissions, a big library, or a landmark clock or bell tower, much less an imposing sports stadium or gymnasium. In a crowded urban setting, he would find no "campus" at all. He would have better luck seeking out a well-known, sartorially identifiable faculty member or master, who not only might explain the institution's hows if not whys but also would likely probe the lad's academic qualifications: was he born male and free, a baptized Christian, at least fourteen years of age, able to read and understand spoken Latin and, preferably, to write it as well? If he passed, the master might have him sign a parchment *matricula* and take him under his wing as a member of his academic *familia* and supervised inmate of his rented multiroom quarters.[20] An oath before the rector to obey the

18 Wieruszowski, *Medieval University*, 186–87.

19 W. A. Pantin, "The Halls and Schools of Medieval Oxford: An Attempt at Reconstruction," in *Oxford Studies Presented to Daniel Callus*, 31–100, at 31–32.

20 Unfortunately, no individual masters' matriculae have been found. The oldest extant *rector*'s matriculation register is that of the Prague law faculty, beginning in 1372. Rainer Christoph Schwinges, "Admission," *HUE* 1:177–80, at 180. At some universities, prospective students had up to 15 days to choose their master. Thorndike, *University Records*, 274 (Bologna, 1404); Alan Cobban, *English University Life in the Middle Ages* (Columbus: Ohio State University Press, 1999), 8 (Cambridge).

university's statutes and the payment of a fee adjusted to his social status completed his admission and earned him clerical status and its legal protections, although he might have to treat his new master and a few friends to food and drink as the first of several costly rites of academic passage.[21]

A century or so later, new students would have discovered the *beginnings* of an identifiably academic landscape. A number of residential halls, hostels, and colleges sprang up to house, feed, protect, and govern students, initially only a privileged minority of older graduate students but later younger arts students and even preparatory students as well.[22] From the early fourteenth century, the halls of Oxford and hostels of Cambridge were rented houses each overseen by a mature faculty *domus*, or principal. The principal assumed not only the regent master's disciplinary duties—confiscating weapons, seeing that lectures were attended and fees paid, keeping women at bay—but also some of the university's pedagogical functions as well.[23] By the early fifteenth century, all Oxbridge scholars were required to reside in approved university residences. A major reason was to root out licentious "chamberdeacons" who rented cheap rooms from local landlords, "sleeping by day and haunting taverns and brothels by night, intent on robbery and homicide."[24]

21 Matriculants in later universities, particularly in Central Europe, also took an oath to the sponsoring prince, king, or realm. Schwinges, "Admission," *HUE* 1:180–87; Robert Francis Seybolt, ed. and trans., *The Manuale Scholarium: An Original Account of Life in the Mediaeval University* (Cambridge, Mass.: Harvard University Press, 1921), ch. 1, at 20n4.

22 Some of the early Oxbridge and Paris colleges admitted a few poor grammar students or choristers. Cobban, *Medieval English Universities*, 182–83, 368–69; Astrik L. Gabriel, "Preparatory Teaching in the Parisian Colleges during the Fourteenth Century," in Gabriel, *Garlandia*, ch. 4.

23 Rainer Christoph Schwinges, "Student Education, Student Life," *HUE* 1:213–22; Cobban, *Medieval English Universities*, ch. 4, 174–80.

24 W. A. Pantin, *Oxford Life in Oxford Archives* (Oxford: Clarendon Press, 1972), 10 (from a 1410 statute). Thirteenth-century Paris confronted similar challenges from student crime. University officials sought to outlaw not only "unstudious . . . gamesters or haunters of whores and taverns," but also roving bands of armed students who "rape women, break into inns, oppress virgins" and rob, "wound or kill . . . many persons . . . by day and night." Thorndike, *University Records*, 77, 79 (statutes of 1269 and 1280).

In the major universities of England and France, the search for order began in the late thirteenth century with the construction and endowment of residential colleges, largely for advanced students in the professional faculties.[25] These facilities were often enclosed quadrangles that were accessed by defensible gated entrances to protect their scholars and faculty fellows from aggrieved townsmen. They also featured amenities such as chapels, libraries, dining halls, and classrooms in addition to living quarters.[26] Numerous though scattered, they gave universities more recognizable shapes and faces until the universities began in the next century to raise a variety of distinctive buildings for communal purposes. In 1320 Oxford completed the stone Congregation House to house its embryonic library and to host faculty meetings.[27] Later, the, two-story, Divinity School and contiguous quarters for other faculties were erected, which eventually morphed into the Bodleian Library. In Bologna, the Collegio di Spagna (1365–67) surrounded an arcaded courtyard, establishing a model for enlarged palazzos in other Italian universities.[28] By 1500 most universities could be recognized by their

25 Colleges remained scarce in provincial France and in Spanish and Italian universities, and even those in the northern universities housed only 10–20 percent of the student population. The first college in Paris—the Collège des Dix-huit (1180)—accommodated only 18 poor scholars in theology; the more famous college known as La Sorbonne (1257) began with 16 and expanded to 36. Cobban, *Medieval Universities*, 150; Verger, "Patterns," *HUE* 1:62; Gieysztor, "Management," *HUE* 1:116, 118; Schwinges, "Student Education," *HUE* 1:218 and 218n17.

26 Cobban, *Medieval Universities*, ch. 6; Pedersen, *First Universities*, 226–28; Verger, "Patterns," *HUE* 1:60–62; Gieysztor, "Management," *HUE* 1:116–19; Schwinges, "Student Education," *HUE* 1:213–22; Astrik L. Gabriel, "The College System in the Fourteenth-Century Universities," in Francis Lee Utley, ed., *The Forward Movement of the Fourteenth Century* (Columbus: Ohio State University Press, 1961), 79–124; Astrik L. Gabriel, *Student Life in Ave Maria College, Mediaeval Paris: History and Chartulary of the College*, Publications in Mediaeval Studies 14 (Notre Dame, Ind.: University of Notre Dame Press, 1955).

27 The University of Orléans's early fifteenth-century *Salles des Thèses* served the same functions.

28 For a photograph of the collegio's courtyard and arcade, see Berthe M. Marti, ed. and trans., *The Spanish College at Bologna in the Fourteenth Century* (Philadelphia: University of Pennsylvania Press, 1966), opp. p. 128.

specialized buildings and distinctive architecture.[29] In becoming so heavily "embodied," however, they lost their early bargaining power in which both students and faculty could simply threaten to move to a rival city, as Oxford scholars did to Cambridge and many of Bologna's lawyers did to Vicenza and Padua. For all their advantages, endowed lectureships for faculty in the colleges later had the same result.[30]

❁ ❁ ❁

The prospective students who came looking for a higher education, if not always a degree, were a socially mixed lot and changed composition over the university's formative three centuries. Initially, many were mature or novice priests, friars, and monks sent by their superiors to upgrade their skills and usefulness to the Church. Like most medieval students, they had pronounced vocational goals, only more so.[31] Their careers had begun in the Church, and they wanted them to end there, on higher rungs of the preferment ladder, of course. Yet the majority of students were middling-class urbanites, possessed of the scholastic backgrounds to take advantage of university offerings and the resources, familial or sponsored, to stay and pay for the relatively expensive course: room and board; matriculation, lecture, disputation, and commencement fees; fees for membership in student "nations;" socially and academically appropriate clothing; books, parchment, and entertainment.[32] Earlier, the sons

29 Gieysztor, "Management," *HUE* 1:136–39.

30 Ibid., 1:139; Cobban, *Medieval Universities*, 155–56.

31 Cobban, *Medieval Universities*, 8, 12, 18–19, 218–19, 237; F. M. Powicke, *Ways of Medieval Life and Thought: Essays and Addresses* (Boston: Beacon Press, 1951), ch. 10.

32 As universities proliferated, they tended to recruit from local regions rather than the whole continent, in turn reducing the students' need for protective and socializing nations. On the cost of university education, see Schwinges, "Student Education," *HUE* 1:235–41; Cobban, *Medieval English Universities*, 311–13; Cobban, *English University Life*, 36–42. The growth of international credit arrangements—loans, credit notes, and currency exchange—enabled students to study all over Europe. C. H. Lawrence, *The Medieval Idea of a University: An Inaugural Lecture* (London: Bedford College, University of London, June 1972), 3.

of noblemen and upper gentry had been conspicuous by their paucity except in Italy, but gradually they were attracted to the universities at least for cultural polish and social connections and younger sons for training for careers in the church or the law.[33]

Matriculants from the poorer classes, *pauperes* often without surnames or connections, made up between 15 and 25 percent of the best-documented universities, most in northern Europe, especially Germany. In the absence of a concerted social commitment to improve the lot of poor students, most universities simply allowed them to forgo matriculation fees and to pay discounted lecture fees, but often only "until the onset of better fortune," when they were expected to pay their debts.[34] Several Paris and a few Oxbridge colleges were endowed with provisions for poor students, particularly in the arts and theology. True paupers were given the license to beg (in the spirit of mendicant friars). Many students, not only the poor, worked their way through college by serving faculty and rich classmates, toiling in dining halls and kitchens, singing in local church choirs, tutoring younger students, gardening, laboring in college construction, and copying manuscript books for stationers.[35]

The growing popularity of higher education throughout Europe led to the proliferation of universities but only fluctuating growth in student enrollments because of epidemics, wars, drought, grain prices, and competitors. Paris was initially the largest university, with perhaps 5,000 students, but by 1464 its population—masters, students, and staff—numbered half that. At their height, Bologna, Toulouse, Avignon, and Orléans matriculated at least 400–500 students annually. Oxford seldom exceeded 2,000 students in all but equally seldom fell to fewer than 1,500. Cambridge settled for several

33 Schwinges, "Student Education," *HUE* 1:202–211; Cobban, *Medieval Universities*, 196–202; Cobban, *Medieval English Universities*, 300–303, 313–18.

34 Schwinges, "Admission," *HUE* 1:187; Schwinges, "Student Education," *HUE* 1:209; Jacques Paquet, "L'universitaire 'pauvre' au Moyen Age: problèmes, documentation, questions de méthode," in Josef Ijsewijn and Jacques Paquet, eds., *The Universities in the Late Middle Ages* (Louvain: Leuven University Press, 1978), 399–425.

35 *HUE* 1:209–11; Cobban, *Medieval Universities*, 148–50, 196–201; Cobban, *Medieval English Universities*, 303–10.

hundred, never more than 1,300, before 1500. German enrollments likewise numbered only a few hundred.[36]

❊ ❊ ❊

No matter how small they were by modern standards, medieval universities faced disciplinary challenges from their variegated and rambunctious student populations. The first line of defense against student—primarily undergraduate—disorder was the university statutes, which were written early and applied often. In 1209 Pope Innocent III, a former student in Paris, urged the nascent university there to turn its "decent customs" into "written statutes."[37] Statutes were crucial bulwarks because every matriculant swore to obey them, even if he did not know what they enjoined or how numerous they were. They accumulated as quickly as did boisterous student escapades. The earliest statutes invariably assigned the primary oversight of students' conduct to their faculty masters. At Paris, for example, orders in 1215 from the papal legate made it clear that "no one shall be a scholar at Paris who has no definite master" and "each master shall have jurisdiction over his scholar." Sixteen years later, Pope Gregory IX not only forbade the Parisians to "go about town armed" but also reiterated that "those who pretend to be scholars but do not attend classes or have any master shall by no means enjoy the privileges of scholars."[38]

With hard-won experience, the assembled faculties drew up further statutes to deal with a wide variety of offences. In 1314 the University of Toulouse worried that "superfluity of clothing" was both contrary to "an approved mediocrity" befitting clerics (as all university scholars were regarded) and the financial cause of many dropouts. So the faculty set price limits on "cloths and garments" and regulated what kinds of outfits various degrees of scholars could

36 Schwinges, "Admission," *HUE* 1:189–93; Cobban, *Medieval English Universities*, 121–22; J. I. Catto, "Citizens, Scholars and Masters," *HUO* 1:156; Leader, *University to 1546*, *HUC* 1:35–36.

37 Wieruszowski, *Medieval University*, 137–38.

38 Thorndike, *University Records*, 29, 30, 38, 118.

wear.[39] In the late fourteenth and early fifteenth century, the rector of Heidelberg had his hands full warning his scholars not to catch the burghers' pigeons, attend fencing schools or brothels, parade around in masks, play at dice, scale the city walls, attack its gates or bridges, or blaspheme the Holy Family or saints by swearing oaths upon their "head, hair, viscera, blood" or in "any other farfetched . . . or enormous manner." It's a wonder that he had any time to remind them to "attend each week at least some lectures." His counterpart at Angers felt obliged to rule against the students' "bringing or keeping women in the library" because it was what he deftly called "occasion for sin."[40]

Universities also had a hard time enforcing two statutes pertaining to inter-student behavior. One was a widespread admonition to speak Latin, the language of instruction, even out of class in university residences. But those who persisted in speaking the "vulgar" vernacular could only be fingered by fellow students who heard them lapse. Despite official expectations, most students were loath to report their classmates for such a petty offence. So systems of fines and paid spies were instituted, especially in German universities. "According to ancient custom," rectors and proctors (their enforcers) secretly appointed undergraduate "wolves" (*lupi*) to spy on offending *vulgarisantes*, whose names were reported, entered in a register, and read publicly every Friday.[41] In a colloquial Latin dialogue between students published first in Heidelberg in 1481, one victim (who had

39 Thorndike, *University Records*, 150–54. In the late fifteenth century, Heidelberg students were fined for wearing fancy dress, such as silk sleeves, pointed shoes, stomachers, and truncated tunics. Seybolt, *Manuale Scholarium*, 78, 117–18. For the most part, medieval students dressed little differently from their lay age-mates. A few Oxford, Cambridge, and Paris colleges put their fellows in colored livery; uniform black gowns were an invention of the sixteenth century. Dress regulations were aimed chiefly at the masters, whose garb was borrowed from the secular clergy but occasionally took a fashionable turn. Cobban, *English University Life*, 48–49; Gieysztor, "Management," *HUE* 1:139–41; Rashdall, *Universities of Europe*, 3:385–93; W. N. Hargreaves-Mawdsley, *A History of Academic Dress in Europe until the End of the Eighteenth Century* (Oxford: Clarendon Press, 1963).

40 Thorndike, *University Records*, 150–54, 260–61, 320, 332; Wieruszowski, *Medieval University*, 195–96.

41 Rashdall, *Universities of Europe*, 3: ch. 13; Thorndike, *University Records*, 78 (Paris college statute, 1280).

been reported a dozen times) swore revenge upon his anonymous accuser, but his interlocutor told him that he could have been indicted a *hundred* times: "To tell the truth, I haven't heard a single word from you in Latin for a whole week." If we don't speak Latin, his friend continued, "our speech would be as barren, as absurd, as nothing on earth" like the laity's or "*beani*'s."[42]

A second, virtually unenforceable, statute sought to prevent first-year students, or freshmen—*beani*, or *bejauni* in the student argot, from *bec-jaune*, "yellow-beak"—from being unduly hazed, hurt, or "mulcted" (fined or assessed) by their seniors. Such impositions were ancient rites of initiation that all-male student bodies devised to welcome newcomers to their privileged, misogynist, and cultured company. Most of these exercises in male bonding took the form of removing or "purifying" the freshman's offensive goatlike features: his stench and his ugly buck teeth, horns, and beard. Although the novice was occasionally compared to an ass, a worthless toad, a dumb ox, or a wild boar, the bestial goat was the favorite analogue because of its medieval associations with physical filth, sexual lasciviousness, uncontrolled libido, peasant rusticity, and diabolically horned Jews.[43] The "cure" that would make such a creature fit for polite academic society involved symbolically sawing off his horns and extracting his teeth (with pliers) and actually shaving his beard (in sewer water), and applying ointments and administering pills (made from horse or goat excrement). For good measure, he might be forced to "confess" a host of sins, ranging from theft and rape to heresy and perjury, and

42 Seybolt, *Manuale Scholarium*, 66n4, ch. 11, esp. 72–73. See Ruth Mazo Karras, "Separating the Men from the Beasts: Medieval Universities and Masculine Formation," in *From Boys to Men: Formations of Masculinity in Late Medieval Europe* (Philadelphia: University of Pennsylvania Press, 2003), 66–108, 181–94 at 78 and 185n49, for a close Leipzig predecessor, *Conversational Latin for New Students*, by Paul Schneevogel (Paulus Niavis).

43 Modern American fraternity rituals are still known to cast initiates as goats, "the dumbest species on earth." Ruth Mazo Karras, "Separating the Men from the Goats: Masculinity, Civilization and Identity Formation in the Medieval University," in Jacqueline Murray, ed., *Conflicted Identities and Multiple Masculinities: Men in the Medieval West* (New York: Garland Publishing, 1999), 189–213, at 212n67, citing Larry Colton, *Goat Brothers* (New York: Doubleday, 1993).

to purchase "penance," sometimes from a costumed "abbot," with a nice dinner and good wine for his new brethren.[44]

The time-honored force of such clandestine social customs, as modern university administrators keep discovering, drew from their medieval counterparts' numerous but largely futile attempts to eradicate—or even moderate—them. In 1340 Parisian officials outlawed the taking of "any money from a Freshman because of his class or anything else, except from roommates . . . or as a voluntary gift." Any landlords or students who knew that "any corporal violence or threats" had been made to a freshman were to report the offenders with dispatch. Orléans and Angers ruled that students' books were not to be seized to pay the initiation fee (*bejaunium*). In the fifteenth century, the university in Valence tried to prohibit the mulcts upon freshmen, particularly the poor, because several had dropped out due to the expense of the required banquets or "the improper and insulting things . . . said and done to them, when they could not pay so much money." At Avignon, protesting scholars formed a new charitable fraternity to supplant the "nefarious and incredible actions at the advent of each novice or what is vulgarly called the purgation of the Freshmen." They believed that those customs had something to do with God's bringing down on the university epidemics which "in times past" had scattered the student population.[45]

As persistent as student customs and adolescent behavior could be, university officials did not lack the disciplinary tools to deal with both. Proctors and bedels were rough and ready to apprehend offenders, by the scruff of the neck if need be. Yet despite the youth of many undergraduates, corporal punishment was seldom resorted to until the fifteenth century, when residential colleges received more and younger laymen and upper-class scions who were less focused on professional careers, taking a degree, or spending their evenings bent over a candlelit book. Before then, misbehavior was effectively dealt with by fines (which hurt *pauperes* the most), denial of college "commons" (food and drink), mulcts of candle wax or "sconces"

44 Rashdall, *Universities of Europe*, 3:376–85; Schwinges, "Student Education," *HUE* 1:230–31; Karras, "Separating the Men from the Beasts."

45 Karras, "Separating the Men from the Beasts," 101; Thorndike, *University Records*, 192–93, 322, 353, 365–66.

of wine, incarceration in university jails, postponement of degrees, suspension or expulsion from the college or university, banishment from town, or, as a last resort, excommunication from the Church.[46]

❁ ❁ ❁

As most students quickly discovered, the seriousness of a university's discipline was a faithful reflection of the seriousness of its intellectual goals and curriculum. Even the most carefree (or careless) freshmen soon realized that the length, cost, rigor, and competitive character of a university education demanded from them attention, effort, and resources if they wanted to remain in *statu pupillari* (student status) and to enjoy its considerable privileges and opportunities. In generalizing from his own student days at early Paris, Jacques de Vitry, a prolific preacher, crusading bishop, and cardinal, captured the range of motivations that matriculants brought to medieval universities. "Almost all the students . . . , foreigners and natives, did absolutely nothing except learn or hear something new. Some studied merely to acquire knowledge . . . ; others to acquire fame . . . ; others still for the sake of gain." His disappointment that "very few studied for their own [religious] edification, or that of others" says more about the prelate's zeal for converts than it does about the mixed and largely secular motives of thousands of young men going off to the university,[47] for although the universities were associated with the Church, they were not directly part of it, as a mendicant friary or a cathedral school was.[48]

46 Rashdall, *Universities of Europe*, 3:358–75; *HUE* 1:227, 229; Pedersen, *The First Universities*, 236–41; Cobban, *English University Life*, 43–47; Thorndike, *University Records*, 261, 349 (mulcts of wax).

47 Munro, *Medieval Student*, 18–19, at 18. Vitry likely borrowed St. Bernard's indictment of his monastic brothers to impugn the newer generation of university students. Lawrence, *Medieval Idea of a University*, 11.

48 Toulouse was the first and a rare example of a university founded directly by the Church, but it soon resembled other universities in its self-government and faculty control. It was established in 1229 by Pope Gregory IX specifically to combat the Albigensian heretics in the French Midi. Its initial faculty was recruited from Paris during the latter's dispersion during a town-gown quarrel. For a short time, Dominicans, the shock troops of the anti-heresy crusade, dominated all four faculties, particularly theology. Rashdall, *Universities of Europe*, 2:160–73.

The universities' primary goal, the reason for their creation, was not to produce edified Christians or zealous clergymen, but to prepare professionals to maintain and lead the established social order, secular as well as religious. They pursued that goal through faculty teaching, student study, and the collective pursuit of accepted and acceptable learning. Unlike their modern counterparts, medieval universities were not in the business of "research" or the pursuit of new knowledge and innovation for its own sake. The capital-*t* Truth was already largely known, certainly from the Bible and the teachings of the Mother Church and also from a relatively small number of authoritative authors and texts, some that needed to be *re*discovered from classical antiquity, but all of which needed to be properly interpreted, understood, and, if possible, reconciled. This was the task that university curricula—all of which were cut from the same cloth—sought to perform, and their students were well aware and in large measure willing, if not always eager, to cooperate.

Not unlike today, the higher professional faculties (law, medicine, and theology) depended on the preliminary preparation of undergraduates in the liberal arts and sciences and, to a lesser extent, in the three philosophies (natural, moral, and metaphysical). This was largely a six- or seven-year process that led to the B.A., the lower degree, and the M.A., the upper degree, in the arts faculty. Most students were content or forced by circumstance to stop at the B.A.[49] Only those who sought to teach at the upper secondary or university level or to pursue a degree in the other learned professions continued for two or three more years for the M.A., six or eight in medicine and law, and as many as fifteen in theology, thirty-five being the minimum age for Th.D.s (Doctors of Theology).[50]

49 Drop-out estimates range from 50 to 80 percent; in the fifteenth-century German universities, only 3 or 4 in 10 students received a B.A., 1 in 10 the M.A. Verger, "Teachers," *HUE* 1:147; Schwinges, "Student Education," *HUE* 1:196; Peter Moraw, "Careers of Graduates," *HUE* 1:254; Karras, "Separating the Men from the Beasts," 69; Cobban, *Medieval English Universities*, 354–57. I use the familiar modern American initials for Bachelor and Master of Arts (B.A., M.A.) instead of the invented contemporary abbreviations for *Baccalarius* and *Magister in Artibus* (A.B., A.M.).

50 Schwinges, "Student Education," *HUE* 1:235.

The degree sequence of the higher faculties resembled that of the arts. In each, the doctorate was less a separate degree than a title of mastery conferred after a rigorous private examination by several senior masters and an easier public inaugural disputation, with the award of the *licentia docendi* (the universal license to teach) by the university chancellor and induction (*inceptio*) of the candidate into the masters' guild. The former gave the candidate permission "to teach, to ascend the master's chair [*cathedra*], to comment, to interpret, to defend [in disputations] and to practice all activities of a doctor here and everywhere, in all countries and places."[51] The latter ceremony often occurred in a church and involved orations by the candidate's new peers and the bestowal upon him of a biretta or cap (to crown his achievement), a ring (to connote his betrothal to learning), an open book (to mark his dedication to teaching), and perhaps the kiss of peace. He was now prepared to assume the full range of professorial duties in a university. At Paris, Oxford, and Cambridge, he was indeed obligated to teach for one or two years of "necessary regency."[52]

The liberal arts curriculum through which most masters had passed was devoted to the *trivium*, the three verbal disciplines of grammar, rhetoric, and logic (or dialectic), and the *quadrivium*, the four mathematical subjects of arithmetic, geometry, music, and astronomy. Obviously missing from this rigid curriculum fashioned from classical and early medieval precedents were modern subjects

51 Wieruszowski, *Medieval University*, 172 (a fourteenth-century Bologna citation); see also Thorndike, *University Records*, 309. The papal or imperial privilege of teaching at "all" other *studia generalia* was not recognized even among the oldest and largest universities. Oxford and Paris refused to admit each other's doctors without administering their own examinations and licenses. Provincial universities were certainly denied parity. In founding Salamanca, Pope Alexander IV expressly exempted Paris and Bologna. Rashdall, *Universities of Europe*, 1:13–14; Cobban, *Medieval Universities*, 30–31. For Paris's complaint that "England" (Oxford and Cambridge) and Montpellier were not automatically accepting her "licentiates" (masters), "no matter how great [their] reputation[s]," see Thorndike, *University Records*, 123.

52 Schwinges, "Student Education," *HUE* 1:234–35; Gordon Leff, "The *Trivium* and the Three Philosophies," *HUE* 1:325; Rashdall, *Universities of Europe*, 1:224–31; Pedersen, *First Universities*, 262–70; Leff, *Paris and Oxford*, 147–60; Cobban, *Medieval English Universities*, 171–72.

such as history, poetry (regarded as pagan or profane), the social sciences, and the applied (or disreputably "mechanical") sciences.[53] The natural sciences came into view—in books, not labs—through the extensive study of Aristotle's natural philosophy and through glosses and updates by professors such as Oxford's Roger Bacon and Robert Grosseteste and Paris's Jean Buridan. More philosophical training came from exposure to Aristotle's other works and to the writings of Boethius (d. 525), Duns Scotus, William of Ockham, and the Arab commentators Averroës and Avicenna.[54]

The liberal arts were regarded hierarchically, but the order shifted with the rise of universities in the early thirteenth century. A century earlier, the trivium had outranked the quadrivium, and grammar and rhetoric outshone logic. But the appearance of the main body of Aristotle's works in Latin translation by 1200 rearranged the university syllabus. In the law-dominated faculties of Italy, rhetoric retained its dominance, but in the northern universities, the quadrivium increased its appeal, and logic assumed the top position overall, beneath only theology, the "queen of the sciences."[55] By the third quarter of the thirteenth century, the shift in Paris had so

53 The Goliardic tradition of songs was the students' response to the curricular lack of even classical poetry. See John Addington Symonds, ed. and trans., *Wine, Women, and Song: Students' Songs of the Middle Ages* (London: Chatto & Windus [1884] 1907).

54 Verger, "Patterns," *HUE* 1:41–42, ch. 10; Huff, *Rise of Early Modern Science*, 180–89; Edward Grant, "Science and the Medieval University," in James M. Kittelson and Pamela J. Transue, eds., *Rebirth, Reform, and Resilience: Universities in Transition, 1300–1700* (Columbus: Ohio State University Press, 1984), 68–102; David L. Wagner, ed., *The Seven Liberal Arts in the Middle Ages* (Bloomington: Indiana University Press, 1984; Leff, *Paris and Oxford*, 138–46; J. M. Fletcher, "The Faculty of Arts," *HUO* 1: ch. 9; P. Osmond Lewry, "Grammar, Logic and Rhetoric, 1220–1320," *HUO* 1:ch. 10; J. A. Weisheipl, "Science in the Thirteenth Century," *HUO* 1: ch. 11; Leader, *University to 1546*, *HUC* 1:chs. 4–6. For the development of medieval philosophy and its role in the university curriculum, see John Marenbon, *Medieval Philosophy: An Historical and Philosophical Introduction* (London: Routledge, 2007); Marenbon, *Medieval Philosophy*, Routledge History of Philosophy, vol. 3 (London: Routledge, 1998); David Knowles, *The Evolution of Medieval Thought* (Baltimore: Helicon Press, 1962).

55 Leff, "*Trivium*," *HUE* 1:307–8. As Robert de Sorbon reminded the fellows of his Paris college, "The sword of God's word is forged by grammar, sharpened by logic, and burnished by rhetoric, but only theology can use it." Charles Homer Haskins, *Studies in Mediaeval Culture* (Oxford: Clarendon Press, 1929), 46.

alarmed Henri d'Andeli that he penned a satirical poem, "The Battle of the Seven Arts," which he staged just outside Orléans, where Grammar fought to survive against Paris's Logic. Although Grammar recruited Homer and the set-book grammarians Donatus and Priscian, it was no match for the cavalry of Paris, where "the arts students . . . care for naught except to read the [Aristotelian] books of nature" and "children" of fifteen learn to "prattle" logic instead of discourse in elegant Latin. The higher faculties "did not care a fig about their dispute": Theology returned to Paris and "left the arts to fight it out together." The timorous Orléans medical faculty "all would turn to money making / If they saw in it no danger."[56]

❁ ❁ ❁

The contemporaneous advent of the Aristotelian corpus and the major universities of Paris, Oxford, and Bologna also gave rise to a signature spirit of inquiry and a pedagogical style that has come to be known, especially after Renaissance humanists assailed it, as "scholasticism," or the work and methods of the "schoolmen" (*scholastici*). Aristotle endowed the universities not only with "a common theoretical framework in a common vocabulary" but also with "the substantive knowledge to go with that framework for each of the recognized branches of knowledge." The universities adopted a pedagogy that fit the new logic-heavy curriculum precisely while building on some of the techniques of the great teachers and cathedral schools that preceded them.[57]

The main vehicles of instruction—always in distinctly scholastic, highly abbreviated Latin—were the lecture (*lectio*) and the disputation (*disputatio*). Lectures were of two kinds: "ordinary," given only by regent masters at "the doctoral hour" (beginning as early as 5 a.m.

56 Louis John Paetow, ed. and trans., *Two Medieval Satires on the University of Paris: La Bataille des VII Ars of Henri D'Andeli and the Morale Scholarium of John of Garland* (Berkeley: University of California Press, 1927), 39, 43, 44, 47, 58, 59.

57 Verger, "Patterns," *HUE* 1:43–44; Leff, "Trivium," *HUE* 1:319 (quotation); John W. Baldwin, *The Scholastic Culture of the Middle Ages, 1000–1300* (Lexington, Mass.: D. C. Heath, 1971); William Turner, "Scholasticism," in *The Catholic Encyclopedia*, 16 vols. (New York: Robert Appleton Co., 1907–14), 13:548–52 (also http://www.newadvent.org/cathen/13548a.htm).

and as late as 7 a.m., depending on the season), and "extraordinary," or "cursory," given in the afternoon by younger masters but more often by new "bachelors" (*baccalarii*) in their early twenties who were working toward their M.A.s, kin to modern American T.A.s (graduate teaching assistants). At least once a week, in the afternoon or evening, mostly within the master's *familia* of advisees in the hall or college, the same teachers would offer a review session (*repetitio*) on the master's lectures to ensure that the main points were memorized and lacunae filled. Ordinary lectures were devoted to systematically reading out, but mostly explaining and commenting on problems in, the canonical texts assigned. This offered the faculty their best chance to say something original and up to date, as long as it was not perceived as heretical.[58] Yet as masters and former masters such as William of Ockham, John Wycliffe, and Jan Hus sometimes discovered, their freewheeling arguments and conclusions *could* lead to trouble with external authorities for themselves and for the reflected reputation of their alma maters. In that, universities and their professors have remained true to form.

Since arts students were not expected to purchase their own books because of the expense, they relied largely on aural memory or, more rarely, took abbreviated notes on wax or cheap parchment tablets on their laps. The wax tablets gave rise to a distinctive script consisting of straight lines and downward strokes to avoid plowing an uphill furrow in the wax with the metal stylus.[59] Those who were inattentive or not blessed with sharp recall were known to make a ruckus or throw stones to slow the delivery of lecturers who, with university approval, "utter[ed] their words rapidly so that the mind of the hearer can take them in but the hand cannot keep up with

58 Schwinges, "Student Education," *HUE* 1:232; Cobban, *English University Life*, 170–74; Pedersen, *First Universities*, 250–54; Mary Martin McLaughlin, *Intellectual Freedom and Its Limitations in the University of Paris in the Thirteenth and Fourteenth Centuries* (New York: Arno Press, 1977 [1952]); J.M.M.H. Thijssen, *Censure and Heresy at the University of Paris, 1200–1400* (Philadelphia: University of Pennsylvania Press, 1998).

59 Richard H. Rouse and Mary A. Rouse, "Wax Tablets," *Language and Communication* 9:2–3 (1989), 175–91. See also Charles Burnett, "Give him the White Cow: Notes and Note-Taking in the Universities in the Twelfth and Thirteenth Centuries," *History of Universities* 14 (1995–96), 1–30, at 17.

FIGURE 1. Laurentius de Voltolina painted Bologna professor Henricus de Alemania speaking *ex cathedra* (from his raised chair) in the 1350s. Alemania's 23 male students ranged from young undergraduates to greybeards. At least one takes notes, ten follow (and perhaps gloss) the lecture in their own texts, and others chat or doze.

them," as in model sermons and lectures in the higher faculties.[60] Scholars in the higher faculties had an easier time of it because they were obliged to buy their textbooks and bring them to class to follow the lecture by making interlinear glosses or marginal notes (including cartoon portraits of the lecturer). They were also favored by having slanted desks provided, whereas the younger arts students had

60 Thorndike, *University Records*, 237; Jan Zolkowski, "Latin Learning and Latin Literature," in Nigel Morgan and Rodney M. Thomson, eds., *1100–1400*, vol. 2 of *The Cambridge History of the Book in Britain* [*CHBB*] (Cambridge: Cambridge University Press, 2008), 238; Charles Burnett, "The Introduction of Scientific Texts into Britain, c. 1100–1250," *CHBB* 2:453; M. B. Parkes, "The Provision of Books," in J. I. Catto and R. Evans, eds., *Late Medieval Oxford*, vol. 2 of *HUO* (1992), 470.

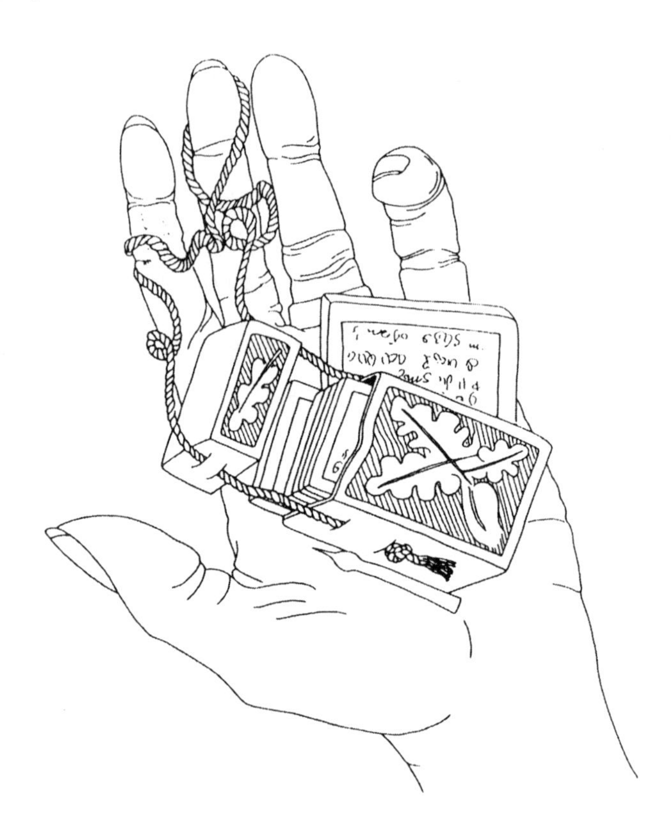

FIGURE 2. Medieval students often took class notes on wax tablets with a pointed stylus. This reconstructed set of eight small tablets, kept in a leather pouch and attached by a cord to a belt, was used in fourteenth-century York, England, in lieu of scraps of parchment.

only benches and were sometimes forced to sit on the straw-covered floor to suppress their pride.[61]

One of the signal innovations of the medieval university was the firm linkage of examinations with teaching as a way to evaluate the student's comprehension and application of what he had been

61 Thorndike, *University Records*, 246; Gieysztor, "Management," *HUE* 1:138; Parkes, "Provision of Books," *HUO* 2:407. In all faculties, the sons of nobles and prelates were seated in the front row, but well-to-do students of bourgeois origins were sometimes allowed to buy themselves an honorary seat on the "noble bench." Schwinges, "Student Education," *HUE* 1:206.

taught. The main instrument for doing that was the oral disputation, which was conducted ordinarily between two scholars according to Aristotle's well-defined syllogistic rules of engagement.[62] The conduct of disputations reflected the master's "ordinary" lectures, which established a textual authority's thesis and argument, presented counter-theses and objections from other authorities, offered his own commentary in an effort to clarify or resolve the question, and then often applied his results to contemporary problems in religion, politics, and law. The popular model for this dialectical approach was Peter Abelard's *Sic et Non* (*Yes and No*), an attempt to reconcile the contradictions in biblical and patristic sources. But the method developed fully in the mid-twelfth century with the arrival of the "new learning" grounded in Aristotle and spread into French cathedral schools and Italian law schools just as the new universities were being established. Gratian's *Decretum* (c. 1140), the basis of canon law, and Peter Lombard's *Book of Sentences* (c. 1160), the dominant theology text, set the standard for dialectical procedure. Both, like most lectures and disputations, revolved around questions (*quaestiones*).[63]

Disputations were conducted in three forms. Younger arts students learned and practiced the art in private sessions in their master's classroom or quarters. But they learned the fine points of verbal fencing—where logic counted more than rhetoric—by observing regular public disputations between older students, particularly bachelors or masters. In these a presiding master (*praeses*) posed a question germane to the subject and an appointed "respondent" attempted to reply and answer objections made by the master and other classmate "opponents." The next day the *praeses* would "determine," or sum up the debate, without necessarily resolving all of the points *pro* and *contra*.[64]

62 The six books comprising Aristotle's *logica nova* (new logic), especially *The Topics*, were foundational in setting the dialectical/disputational agenda. For a list of debating rules laid down for the Collège de Sorbonne in 1344, see Thorndike, *University Records*, 198–201.

63 Monika Asztalos, "The Faculty of Theology," *HUE* 1:410–11; Leff, *Paris and Oxford*, 120–21.

64 Nancy Siraisi, "The Faculty of Medicine," *HUE* 1:326–28; Leff, *Paris and Oxford*, 167–73; Pedersen, *First Universities*, 258–64, 267; Ku-ming (Kevin) Chang, "From

The third form of disputation was the *quodlibeta*, which began and continued with written or oral questions "on whatever" from any members of the large public audience, consisting of students of all ages, masters, prelates, and other urban eminences.[65] These disputations occurred largely in churches or cathedrals in conjunction with baccalaureate examinations during Advent and Lent. In thirteenth-century Paris, they might also feature as many as four respondents, one from each "nation." Because of their somewhat freer form, they could also become occasions for "piling on" the candidate or, if the respondent was a licentiate or master, for settling old intellectual or personal scores. The unpredictable choice of topics held the possibility of introducing and airing "hot" topics in current events.

Some subjects proved a little too hot for officials' taste, namely sex and religion. By the early sixteenth century, and probably much earlier, German masters and bachelors had to be warned not to pose quodlibetal questions "of little importance which are also commonly called *facetiae* or 'salts,' shameful, lascivious and impudent, which by their allurements may attract or provoke the religious or innocent youth ignorant of sexual matters, or any others, to unseemly or illicit lust." Much earlier, thirteenth-century Paris's hot arts topics included any "purely theological question," such as "the Trinity and incarnation." Any master who posed a question having to do with "the faith and philosophy" was expected to "settle it in favor of the faith" in his concluding "determination."[66]

Oral Disputation to Written Text: The Transformation of the Dissertation in Early Modern Europe," *History of Universities* 19:2 (2004), 129–87, esp. 131–45; *The Cambridge History of Later Medieval Philosophy from the Rediscovery of Aristotle to the Disintegration of Scholasticism, 1100–1600*, ed. Norman Kretzmann, Anthony Kenny, and Jan Pinborg (Cambridge: Cambridge University Press, 1982), ch. 1, esp. 21–29; Alex J. Novikoff, "Toward a Cultural History of Scholastic Disputation," *American Historical Review* 117:2 (April 2012), 330–64; Alex J. Novikoff, *The Medieval Culture of Disputation: Pedagogy, Practice, and Performance* (Philadelphia: University of Pennsylvania Press, 2013).

65 For a dozen topics thrown at an Italian bachelor of divinity in 1429, see Thorndike, *University Records*, 307–8.

66 Cobban, *English University Life*, 174–76; Thorndike, *University Records*, 104 (Paris, c. 1240), 372 (Heidelberg, 1518). On the general question of academic freedom,

Disputations served several purposes beyond the curricular. In a pre-Gutenberg age, they served masters as oral publications, complete with "footnotes" in the form of references to authoritative texts. The large and important public audiences that heard the masters' inaugural and quodlibetal disputations and the somewhat smaller assemblies that attended their weekly encounters could easily size up their intellectual trajectory and thrust over time, as we might by reading a scholar's works chronologically. Their opponents' renderings—sometimes rendings—of their positions lent critical perspective. In addition, the oral cast of the disputation influenced the textual form of many medieval books. Like Lombard's *Sentences* and many other scholastic texts, Thomas Aquinas's various *summae* were mounted on questions and ridden to conclusion on the dialectical procedures of disputation. The proliferation of written dialogues, debate poems, recorded disputations, visual images of debate, and even antiphonal music suggests that by the thirteenth century "a culture of disputation" had taken root in Europe, particularly in the north.[67]

Medieval students—graduate and undergraduate—found other important uses for the disputation. In their masculine microcosmos, where marriage and fatherhood were postponed, aristocratic jousts and swordfights were prohibited, and team sports were a phenomenon of the future, the ritual combat of disputing was a nonlethal alternative to warfare and a fair field upon which to establish one's masculinity and social status.[68] Although his father had been a Breton warrior-knight, Abelard confessed that he, the first-born son, "totally abdicated the court of Mars to be received into the

---

see William J. Courtenay, "Inquiry and Inquisition: Academic Freedom in Medieval Universities," *Church History* 58:2 (June 1989), 168–81.

67 Chang, "From Oral Disputation to Written Text," 133–34, 143–45; Novikoff, "Toward a Cultural History," 332, 364; Jody Enders, "The Theatres of Scholastic Erudition," *Comparative Drama* 27:3 (Fall 1993), 341–63.

68 William J. Courtenay, *Schools & Scholars in Fourteenth-Century England* (Princeton, N.J.: Princeton University Press, 1987), 29–30; Karras, "Separating the Men from the Beasts," 67–68, 88–95; Walter J. Ong, "Agonistic Structures in Academia: Past to Present," *Daedalus* 103:4 (Fall 1974), 229–38. Ong argues that learning Latin in all-male, corporally disciplined schools and wielding the language in a special fashion in a university setting was the equivalent of a tribal male "puberty rite" (231–32).

bosom of Minerva" well before he met Heloise. "Since I preferred the panoply of dialectical arguments to all the documents of philosophy," he wrote, "I exchanged other arms for these and esteemed the conflict of disputation more than the trophies of war."[69] The well-regulated practice of verbal fencing, with its sharp logical thrusts and deft parries, provided frequent occasions for the public display of skill, style, and endurance and of measured pride accruing from worthy performance as well as decisive victory.

As the early agonistic training against one's masters gave way to more consequential matches against one's peers, the temptation to rely on rhetorical tricks rather than logical precision, to lose one's composure, and to let conceit show its brazen face drew warnings from magisterial mentors. In *Metalogicon* (1149), a spirited defense of the trivium, Paris-educated John of Salisbury warned, first, that "we should not dispute everywhere, and always, on all sorts of topics." The verbal combat of disputation should remain in the academy, where two evenly matched opponents resort only to "proper weapons" and follow the established rules of the game. In disputations, as opposed to inductive arguments, rhetoric, whose goal is to persuade, should give way to logic, which seeks to convince. Ill-temper, verbosity, quibbling over definitions, ignoring syllogistic form, showing off, and feigning confusion were all signs of "perversity" and an unworthy opponent. A century later, John of Garland with less sportsmanship coached disputants, especially bachelors about to "determine," to "listen attentively, replying briefly to objections; conceal your own ignorance but exhibit the ignorance of your opponent by trimming him down as if you were hazing a yellow-bill [*bec-jaune*] student."[70] The competitive, even combative, spirit that animated academic jousting went a long way to help university students not only establish their superiority to women and the uneducated but also define themselves as men and intellectuals in a Latin West increasingly attuned to their value and eager for their services in church and state.

69 Thorndike, *University Records*, 3.

70 *The Metalogicon of John of Salisbury: A Twelfth-Century Defense of the Verbal and Logical Arts of the Trivium*, ed. and trans. Daniel D. McGarry (Berkeley: University of California Press, 1955), 189–202; John of Garland, *Morale Scholarium*, 160.

❁ ❁ ❁

From the twelfth century to our own, universities have always been bibliocentric, although the role of books has changed over time. The earliest university seals and coats of arms feature a book and often a hand in the act of donation or of pledging an oath on the Bible or a volume of the university's privileges or statutes.[71] As much as medieval teaching and learning depended on mouth and ear, early students depended heavily on books and eyes for their educations.[72] Having studied, indeed mastered, them to earn their positions, professors read out and commented on a number of standard books in the syllabus. Students argued about what they heard publicly and read privately and used their notes to create minibooks for their own purposes, even sale. Curious, inventive, and ambitious faculty wrote new books and tracts to resolve problems in old ones, to better explain the texts' lessons for new generations, and to apply those lessons to pressing current issues.[73] To assist all of their members, residential halls, colleges, and universities slowly began to collect books for reference, study, and lending. To provide adequate supplies of vital reading material, universities encouraged a host of bookmakers (including scribes, parchmenters, binders, and illuminators) and dealers to locate in their midst and then often regulated many of them to ensure the academic quality of their products.

Scholars in search of books, primarily but not exclusively in the higher faculties, could obtain them in four ways (in addition to theft,

71 Astrik L. Gabriel, "The Significance of the Book in Mediaeval University Coats of Arms," in Gabriel, *Garlandia*, ch. 3.

72 The use by Italians of a twelfth-century translation of an eleventh-century Arabic book on optics to invent eyeglasses in the late thirteenth century did much to help nearsighted scholars, particularly those over forty, by promoting the corrective properties of convex lenses. By the fourteenth century, saints and scholars reading books with handheld spectacles made frequent appearances in portraits. Edward Rosen, "The Invention of Eyeglasses," *Journal of the History of Medicine and Allied Sciences* 11:1–2 (Jan. and April 1956), 13–46, 183–218; Vincent Ilardi, *Renaissance Vision from Spectacles to Telescopes* (Philadelphia: American Philosophical Society, 2007), 13–18.

73 Daniel Hobbins, "The Schoolman as Public Intellectual: Jean Gerson and the Late Medieval Tract," *American Historical Review* 108:5 (Dec. 2003), 1308–37.

which then as now was not unheard of because books were so valuable). They could *buy* them, if they could afford the relatively high prices of handwritten (*manus-scriptus*) parchment codices, which all university books were for the first 250 years until paper became common and then mechanized movable-type printing was invented. They could *borrow* them from willing friends, masters, or libraries. They could laboriously *copy* the desired volume or hire someone—a fellow student in need of cash, a professional scribe—to do so. Or they could essentially *write their own* pocket-sized books from lecture, sermon, reading, and disputation notes by adding their own glosses, commentaries, and synopses.[74]

In the professional faculties, students were normally required to bring to class the texts on which their masters were lecturing. Especially during their first few years, theology students needed their own Bibles and copies of Lombard's *Sentences* and were admonished to carry them to class in order to make glosses between lines and in the margins. Future lawyers were obliged to bring their Justinians and Gratians for the same reason. Even in the Heidelberg arts faculty, every student was urged to have his own texts of Aristotle "which he should gloss, if he knows how to write [a surprising clause in a university statute]. If he does not know how to write, he shall

74 Kristian Jensen, "Textbooks in the University: The Evidence from the Books," in L. Hellinga and J. B. Trapp, eds., *1400–1557*, vol. 3 of *CHBB* (2002), ch. 16, at 355, 357; Parkes, "Provision of Books," *HUO* 2:424–26. Masters also produced full-sized books consisting of their "ordinary" lectures and learned commentaries, often recorded by a student and corrected by the master. These *glosses* on canonical texts were so popular and useful that manuscripts were formally laid out and often ruled to accommodate both text and commentary. The text was scripted in larger letters in one or two columns in the middle of the sheet; the glosses were written in a smaller hand between the textual lines and in all four margins to produce a kind of hypertext. Mary A. Rouse and Richard H. Rouse, *Authentic Witnesses: Approaches to Medieval Texts and Manuscripts* (Notre Dame, Ind.: University of Notre Dame Press, 1991), ch. 7; M. B. Parkes, "Layout and Presentation of the Text," *CHBB* 2:60–62; Rodney M. Thompson, "Parchment and Paper, Ruling and Ink," *CHBB* 2:154: Jeremy Catto, "Biblical Exegesis, Theology, and Philosophy," *CHBB* 2:219–21, 223–24; Zolkowski, "Latin Learning," *CHBB* 2:236; Nigel Ramsay, "Law," *CHBB* 2:253; Peter Murray Jones, "University Books and the Sciences, c. 1250–1400," *CHBB* 2:453–55.

pay careful attention . . . lest he annoy or impede the master" or other scholars "by clamor or insolence."[75]

To purchase these volumes, students resorted to stationers (*stationarii*) or booksellers (*librarii*), many of whom were under university supervision. In 1323 the University of Paris was served by twenty-eight booksellers in the Latin Quarter besides numerous keepers of open-air bookstalls on the Left Bank of the Seine. At the end of the thirteenth century, Bologna tried to limit its licensed stationers to five, although many other dealers were subject to municipal authorities. In 1346 Oxford had only four on its approved list.[76] If stationers wanted to do business with the university's bookish population, they had to swear an oath and give security that they would adhere to university rules and price limits. New book prices tended to follow the market, but the large secondhand trade was subject to university controls on mark-ups, sales, and condition.

Authorized texts had to be "good and legible and faithful" versions of exemplary originals, which, being hand produced rather than mechanically reproduced, were always difficult to verify.[77] In the larger universities, it was the duty of university-appointed boards of masters and bookdealers to see that exemplars were as accurate as possible and were never sold to persons outside the university's precincts without prior approval. At Bologna, the weekly tasks of the board were so onerous that its faculty members were excused from all other administrative offices and service duties for the year. To prevent artificial shortages from driving up demand and prices, stationers were obliged to put any secondhand book up for immediate sale and to write on the inside cover the name of the seller and the price he was paid for it. In Paris, the bookseller's commission

75 Thorndike, *University Records*, 194 (Paris, canon law, 1340), 244–45 (Paris, theology, 1366), 353 (Heidelberg, arts, 1466).

76 Rashdall, *Universities of Europe*, 1:423; Gieysztor, "Management," *HUE* 1:128; Elisabeth Leedham-Green, "University Libraries and Book-Sellers," *CHBB* 3:329.

77 Alfonso X el Sabio, *Siete Partidas* (1256–65), quoted in George D. Greenia, "University Book Production and Courtly Patronage in Thirteenth-Century France and Spain," in Donald J. Kagay and Joseph T. Snow, eds., *Medieval Iberia: Essays in the Literature and History of Medieval Spain* (New York: Peter Lang, 1997), 103–28, at 110.

was capped at 1.5 percent. If he tried to charge more, he could be blacklisted from all university business.[78]

Stationers dealt not only in whole codices but also in constituent quires, or *peciae*, of various lengths. Following ancient Roman and monastic techniques, some standard university texts were "mass"-produced by teams of scriveners or copyists writing to dictation, quire by quire. These, in turn, were delivered unbound to stationers or booksellers, who could then have them bound (in vellum, leather, or boards) or lend individual peciae out to students or hired scribes for further copying. (Thus the constant need for inspection of all texts to ensure their faithfulness to the best available exemplars.) The *regulated* pecia system, complete with university price lists, seems to have originated in Bologna and other Italian universities early in the thirteenth century. It spread to at least eleven universities, mostly in southern Europe, and also to Oxford, Paris, and Toulouse. In less- or unregulated iterations, it undoubtedly found its way to many other university towns before petering out in the mid-fifteenth century as printing made texts much cheaper and more readily available.[79]

Stationers also sold the "paper" of the day—parchment (*membrana*), made from young sheep, calf, or goat skins. Like books, this academic necessity was closely regulated for price and quality by the major universities. Paris's rules in 1291 underlined the importance of parchment for book-making and note-taking. Although most arts students took class notes and scholars incised first drafts with a

78 Rashdall, *Universities of Europe*, 1:189–90 (Bologna), 421–23 (Paris); Thorndike, *University Records*, 100–102 (Paris), 166–68 (Bologna); Gieysztor, "Management," *HUE* 1:128; Pedersen, *The First Universities*, 232–35. See also Richard H. Rouse and Mary A. Rouse, "The Book Trade at the University of Paris, ca. 1250-ca. 1350," in Louis J. Bataillon, Bertrand J. Guyot, and Richard H. Rouse, eds., *La Production du livre universitaires au moyen âge: exemplar et pecia. Actes du symposium tenu au Collegio San Bonaventura de Grottaferrata en mais 1983* (Paris: Éditions du Centre Nationale de la Recherche Scientifique, 1988), 41–114; also in Rouse and Rouse, *Authentic Witnesses*, ch. 8.

79 Pedersen, *First Universities*, 234–35; Graham Pollard, "The *Pecia* System in the Medieval Universities," in M. B. Parkes and Andrew G. Watson, eds., *Medieval Scribes, Manuscripts & Libraries: Essays Presented to N. R. Ker* (London: Scolar Press, 1978), 145–61; Thorndike, *University Records*, 112–17 (Paris price list, 1286), 166–68 (Bologna, 14th c.), 259 (Montpellier law faculty, 1396).

pointed stylus on wax tablets, their revised compositions were ultimately transferred, in a more fluid cursive hand, to more expensive parchment sheets with reed or quill pen and ink.[80] In order to hold down the price of parchment, Paris officials sought to restrict sales to the courtyard of St. Mathurin's Church, which was patrolled by university bedels and a quartet of sworn parchment-dealers. The university's dealers were given a 24-hour head start before foreign or other dealers were allowed to sell. Despite oaths, fraud was inevitable in such a competitive and lucrative market. Accordingly, the university ruled that sellers could not "hide good parchment, if they have it with them," in order to drive up the price. Scholarly customers were to "buy nothing by candlelight in secret" and forbidden to buy for resale. Sellers were to profit no more than 2.5 percent. So vital was parchment to academic life that the university regulations were to be read every year "in sermons and in classes."[81]

❋ ❋ ❋

In the end, if a scholar could not beg, buy, or build his own books, he might, if he had enough seniority, borrow them from his collegiate residence or a university library. But if England is any guide, residential halls and hostels had few books and fewer libraries, although they largely housed graduate students who had most need of them.[82] Moreover, until the fifteenth century, universities saw little reason to build expensive libraries for collective use. Oxford did so as early as 1320 only because of a large donation from a bishop, but the library did not open for general use until 1412. Large donations from Humfrey, Duke of Gloucester, beginning in 1435 led to the construction of a larger library in 1478 on the second floor of the new Divinity School. Cambridge took the first three-quarters of the century to

80 Rouse and Rouse, "Wax Tablets," 175, 177, 183; Burnett, "Give him the White Cow," 9, 12–15.

81 Thorndike, *University Records*, 119–23.

82 Among Oxford's numerous halls and Cambridge's hostels, only four (two at each university) appear to have had small libraries for their residents. Cobban, *Medieval English Universities*, 153, 381–82.

complete its Schools Quad with separate libraries for three of the faculties, but the divinity library was functional by 1416. Salamanca and Cracow were not far behind in launching libraries for their own advanced scholars.[83]

Until the sixteenth century, few undergraduates were allowed to borrow books from or even to study in university *or* college libraries. The official reason given for excluding them from Oxford's Congregation House library was that "an importunate multitude of students would prejudice in various ways the books of the university" and inconvenience serious scholars by the "excessive tumult of popular concourse."[84] Oxford dons seem to have been less worried than their Angers counterparts that undergraduate study dates might be "occasions for sin," though it may have crossed their minds. A more pragmatic reason for excluding undergraduates was that university libraries housed very few titles in the arts faculty syllabus. The books in academic libraries were largely hefty folios devoted to the classics in law, theology, and philosophy (and occasionally medicine), which were chained to the shelves to prevent theft or removal. When opened on the small lecterns or desks provided, they encroached on the access of two or three potential readers.[85]

Beginning in the thirteenth century, graduate students and masters had a better chance of finding the books they needed or wanted in their own colleges, if they were fortunate enough to be members. Both the "Sorbonne" (est. 1257) and the College of the Treasurer (est. 1268) allowed their initial fellows to "receive books from the common store" but forbade them "on no condition [to] remove or lend them

83 Parkes, "Provision of Books," *HUO* 2:470–83; Cobban, *Medieval English Universities*, 86, 381; Leedham-Green, "University Libraries and Book-sellers," *CHBB* 3:316–18; Gieysztor, "Management," *HUE* 1:138.

84 By 1453 Oxford's worries had been realized: an "importunate throng of [graduate] students . . . crowded each other" at the small and too-few desks and "got in each other's way." Parkes, "Provision of Books," *HUO* 2:477–78.

85 When Oxford established a new arts course in 1439, the books appropriate to it were housed separately in a new chest in the Congregation House, overseen by the chaplain-librarian. Regent masters and hall principals could borrow books from it after registering, in case of loss, a price of each greater than its replacement cost. Parkes, "Provision of Books," *HUO* 2:478, 479–80.

FIGURE 3. The most valuable books in medieval college libraries, usually large folios, were often chained and could be read only on a narrow desk below. This half-press in the library of Merton College, Oxford, retained a number of chained volumes well into the twentieth century.

out of the house" to be "copied or even studied, because thus they might be lost or mutilated or soiled."[86] Like most medieval colleges, Bologna's Spanish College, opened in 1370, kept books for its fellows in two places: a book cupboard and a larger library, where the books were chained. None of the books were to be "loaned to anyone, either within or without the college, under any pretext whatsoever." If a book was lost, the miscreant would "forfeit food and clothes and all emoluments owed [him] by the college" until he had replaced it with his own funds. If a fellow stole so much as "one sheet" of parchment from the library, he was "expelled irrevocably from the house."[87]

Oxford's earliest colleges operated much the same way. Merton College (est. 1264) was the first to add a substantial library to its fabric (1373–78) and New College (est. 1379) the earliest to include a library in its original design. Following the precedent of neighboring friaries and monasteries, their collections and other Oxford holdings were divided into a chained, or reference, component (about 20 percent) and a larger lending, or circulating, section. The fellows normally had keys to the *libraria*, but they could not remove the books, even when they were unchained. From the lending portion, which was stored in multiply locked chests in the college's treasury, the fellows, according to seniority, received annual allocations (*electiones*) of books for preparing and delivering their lectures. Absentminded professors frequently lent these smaller volumes to colleagues or lost them before the due date, which hastened the demise of the system in the early sixteenth century, as did the availability of affordable printed books.[88]

86 Thorndike, *University Records*, 77, 90.

87 Marti, *Spanish College at Bologna*, 283–87.

88 Cobban, *Medieval English Universities*, 382, 385–86; Parkes, "Provision of Books," *HUO* 2:431–32, 455–61, 481; Neil R. Ker, "Oxford College Libraries before 1500," in Ijsewijn and Paquet, *Universities in the Late Middle Ages*, 293–311, at 294–95; H. W. Garrod, "The Library Regulations of a Medieval College," *The Library* n.s. 8:3 (Sept. 1927), 312–35; Roger Lovatt, "College and University Book Collections and Libraries," in Elisabeth Leedham-Green and Teresa Webber, eds., *To 1640*, vol. 1 of *The Cambridge History of Libraries in Britain and Ireland* (Cambridge: Cambridge University Press, 2006); Leedham-Green, "University Libraries and Book-sellers," *CHBB* 3: ch. 15.

Part of the reason for the strict regulations was the small size and relative rarity of most college collections. All of their books were parchment manuscripts, which were difficult to produce and expensive to acquire and replace. Unlike a modern university library's vast and heterogeneous holdings, most medieval collections—largely the gifts of founders and other wealthy or pious donors—were indispensable to the concentrated scholastic curriculum. Before 1500, the largest Oxford college libraries numbered between 400 and 800 volumes. Cambridge's seldom topped 200.[89] Despite their size, they were not easy to use once entrance was gained. Even inflexible codex catalogues, lists on the face ends of book presses, and short titles and shelf marks written on the fore edges of the books (which faced out to accommodate the chain clasps) presented difficulties because the books might be organized by subject, date of acquisition, or size. Finding a book was only half the battle. Finding a place to read it was the other. In the early libraries, a patron opened the volume on a lectern or desk below tall or above short shelves and stood to read. Later, by popular demand, narrow seats were added. Later still came polished, finely constructed presses, which can still be seen in many Oxford and Cambridge libraries. Most libraries, open only a few hours during the day, were oriented east to west and the shelves and presses were situated perpendicular to the walls between the windows to take advantage of the light.[90]

❁ ❁ ❁

As they do today, universities in medieval Europe played a number of roles in their respective societies. But they spent much less

89 N. R. Ker, "Oxford College Libraries before 1500," in Ijsewijn and Paquet, *Universities in the Late Middle Ages*, 293–311. In contrast, the Sorbonne's catalogue in 1338 listed 1,722 books, 330 (19 percent) of which were chained. Cobban, *Medieval English Universities*, 383–84, 385n151; Richard H. Rouse, "The Early Library of the Sorbonne," *Scriptorium* 21 (1967), 42–71, 227–51; also in Rouse and Rouse, *Authentic Witnesses*, ch. 9.

90 Burnett Hillman Streeter, *The Chained Library: A Survey of Four Centuries in the Evolution of the English Library* (London: Macmillan, 1931), frontispiece, 57–58, 62, ch. 3.

time and effort than ours do defending the efficacy and utility of their faculties, curricula, and graduates. For they—the collective *Studia*—quickly became key institutions in the maintenance and direction of society, along with the *Imperium* or *Regnum* (empire or kingdom) and the *Sacerdotium* (church). They became repositories of knowledge, ancient and modern, and special workshops of judgment and opinion, "intellectual smith[ies], to which metal of every kind could be brought" by emperors and kings, princes, popes, and parliaments. "Almost anything might be referred to the judgment of the masters," whose learned commentaries often tackled sensitive issues of the day.[91] Admittedly, they were not incubators of startling new discoveries or practical inventions, as modern research universities are expected to be. They had nothing to do with the birth of the hourglass or the mechanical clock (both of which were welcomed to calibrate the academic day), three-field crop rotation or the blast furnace, cannons or the water-driven paper mill, spurs or spectacles, much less rat traps or the movable-type printing press. As economic engines they were of modest horsepower and reach. At best, their localities and regions benefitted from their steady, innumerable purchases from landlords, tavern keepers, grocers, parchment makers, book-makers and stationers, tailors, builders, glaziers, prostitutes, and many other purveyors of the mundane and the entertaining.

What they contributed most to a society increasingly dependent on written documents and devoted to the rule of law was trained personnel for the administration of the church and state. To European culture they contributed a substantial increase in literacy and a theoretical elevation and methodological refinement of thought in many disciplines, which in turn improved the efficacy of several practical arts, from surgery to the teaching of introductory Latin

91 Powicke, *Ways of Medieval Life*, 185. Paris theology masters, for example, played key intellectual and personal roles in persuading Pope Innocent III (the former Paris student Lothario di Segni) and the Lateran Council of 1215 to discredit and outlaw customary ordeals by fire, water, cold, and combat from ecclesiastical law, which example eventually led to their disappearance in secular law. The masters' learned glosses on the Bible, patristic decretals, and canon law undermined age-old arguments and assumptions that sustained the use of ordeals. John W. Baldwin, "The Intellectual Preparation for the Canon of 1215 against Ordeals," *Speculum* 36:4 (Oct. 1961), 613–36; Baldwin, *Paris, 1200*, 204–10.

grammar. Although we know little about most university alumni, especially those who took no degrees, it is certain that the Church at all levels was the principal employer of graduates throughout Catholic Europe. At the lowest level, parish priests who took leave for two or three years to attend university classes in the arts, canon law, or theology learned at a minimum a better grade of Latin with which to conduct their services and heard many model sermons by university preachers, some of whom also wrote manuals on the art of preaching. In England, Cambridge sent a third of its alumni whose careers are known into parish work, while Oxford men consistently won places in the upper echelons of the Church. In the thirteenth century, Oxford claimed a third of the bishoprics in England and Wales, Cambridge only 2 percent. Two centuries later, Cambridge had worked its way up to 21 percent, but Oxford commanded 70 percent of the seats; 46 percent of the occupants had previously taught at Oxford. Deanships of cathedrals and leadership positions in friaries and monasteries followed the same Oxford-dominant pattern.

By 1320 more than a third of Paris's theology masters had become bishops, abbots, or cardinals in the French hierarchy. More than another third held offices in cathedral chapters, and many students followed their masters' paths into church work. In Germany's new, small, and poor universities (fifteen founded before 1506), the arts faculties enrolled 75–80 percent of all students, creating an oversupply by 1480. Since only 3 percent earned higher degrees, it is not surprising that the majority of German alumni, with or without degrees, gravitated to minor church careers at the parochial level.[92]

92 C. H. Lawrence, "The University in State and Church," *HUO* 1: ch. 3; Jean Dunbabin, "Careers and Vocations," *HUO* 1:568; T.A.R. Evans, "The Numbers, Origins and Careers of Scholars," *HUO* 2:521–28; Leader, *University to 1546*, *HUC* 1:44; Verger, "Teachers," *HUE* 1:150; Moraw, "Careers," *HUE* 1:261, 270–73, 275; Stephen C. Ferruolo, "'*Quid dant artes nisi luctum*?' Learning, Ambition, and Careers in the Medieval University," *History of Education Quarterly* 28:1 (Spring 1988), 2–22; John W. Baldwin, "Masters at Paris from 1179 to 1215: A Social Perspective," in Benson and Constable, *Renaissance and Renewal*, 158; John W. Baldwin, "*Studium* and *Regnum*: The Penetration of University Personnel in French and English Administration at the Turn of the Twelfth and Thirteenth Centuries," *Revue des études Islamiques* 46 (1976), 199–215; Jacques Verger, *Men of Learning in Europe at the End of the Middle Ages*, trans. Lisa Neal and Steven Rendall (Notre Dame, Ind.: University of Notre Dame

As Europe's increasingly complex and litigious urban population grew, the Papal Schism (1378–1417) created dueling courts and curias in Rome and Avignon. Individual states and emperors sought to expand their authority in the gaps created by the decline of the "Universal Church." Sensibly, career-minded university students moved from theology to legal studies and sought employment upon graduation in imperial, royal, and noble service as well as ecclesiastical administration, which required similar sets of skills. Although the Church sought its share of canon lawyers, most regional episcopates and dioceses preferred those trained in civil law, as did the newly emerging urban and state bureaucracies. Toward the end of the thirteenth century, the philosopher-scientist Roger Bacon, former master at Oxford and Paris, lamented that "the civil lawyers have so bewitched prelates and princes that they receive nearly all the rewards and benefices; so all the best people, even those with the most aptitude for theology and philosophy, dash off to study civil law, because they see the jurists enriched." An increase in the number and seriousness of aristocratic matriculants in the fourteenth and fifteenth centuries also bumped up legal enrollments.[93]

University training in law, logic, rhetoric, and disputation served alumni well who entered ecclesiastical or lay administration.[94] England's King Edward III certainly thought so when he endowed King's Hall in Cambridge in 1337. His intention, he said, was that "youths of conspicuous ability may be instructed and made more apt for public counsels . . . and may be able to enrich the Catholic

Press, 2000 [1997], chs. 4–5. Between 1216 and 1499, 57 percent of the English bishops had attended Oxford; only 10 percent were Cantabrigians. Cobban, *Medieval English Universities*, 394–96.

93 Dunbabin, "Careers," *HUO* 1:574 (quotation); Cobban, *Medieval English Universities*, 394–96; Courtenay, *Schools & Scholars*, 365–66.

94 In undergraduate rhetoric classes, students were taught the *ars dictandi*, the art of official letter writing, and in the South the *ars notaria*, the craft of the notary public. Training in the creation and handling of legal and business documents was invaluable for administrative careers. Cobban, *Medieval Universities*, 221–23; Charles Homer Haskins, *Studies in Mediaeval Culture* (Oxford: Clarendon Press, 1929), chs. 1, 6, 9.

religion and strengthen the royal throne and the commonwealth with far-sighted advice."[95] In societies of "competing rights and privileges, conferred by a hierarchy of authorities and jealously guarded," skills honed in universities were given wide scope.[96] Careers could be made in diplomacy, propaganda, registries, courts, accounting, estate administration, and parliaments. The ability gained from disputation to "see two sides of a problem, to apply authority flexibly in solving it, and to defend [their] action[s] articulately" gave many university graduates an advantage in the competition, other things—such as birth, wealth, patronage, and seniority—being equal.[97]

Beyond their contributions to government, religion, the economy, and the personal careers of their masters and alumni, universities enhanced European culture by focusing powerfully and steadily on the life of the mind. Although under their aegis and nurture the pursuit of knowledge, secular and sacred, became an end in itself, the "incessant exercise of human reason" that went on in its precincts did much to remind Europeans that culture meant more than planting and reaping food for the body. By promoting intellectual seriousness and excellence, universities also altered the nature of what constituted intellectual achievement and redefined it in academic terms. Universities institutionalized knowledge through early forms of disciplinary specialization, group effort and inspiration, dissemination of new and challenging ideas, and the professionalization of the scholar through rigorous

95 Alan B. Cobban, *The King's Hall within the University of Cambridge in the Later Middle Ages* (Cambridge: Cambridge University Press, 1969), 13n4.

96 Cobban, *Medieval Universities*, ch. 9, at 219.

97 Dunbabin, "Careers," *HUO* 1:573 (quotation), 576, 583–93; Moraw, "Careers," *HUE* 1:246, 277; Verger, *Men of Learning in Europe*, 30–33; Courtenay, *Schools & Scholars*, 146:

> Although a brilliant university career did not ensure a distinguished ecclesiastical career, no one viewed it as a handicap. . . . The most useful royal servant (and the one most likely to receive a significant ecclesiastical appointment and income) was one who was of good family and bearing, sufficiently good at accounts, skilled in negotiation and diplomacy, and willing always to obey royal commands; one, perhaps, whose love of king and country . . . exceeded his love of books and ideas.

training, academic degrees, teaching licenses, and self-imposed guild restrictions.[98]

To the rigor of the scholastic education they sought to give their students, universities also subtly and persistently inculcated—by example more than precept—many of the virtues that suffuse all serious intellectual work and give it its ultimate value and meaning.[99] That they accomplished all of these things in challenging times and straitened circumstances, yet managed to preserve the university's "fundamental patterns and its basic social role and function over the course of history," is cause for recognition and celebration, even if we have some difficulty choosing the proper dates.[100]

98 Rashdall, *Universities of Europe*, 3:442; Powicke, *Ways of Medieval Life*, 191, 211; Vern L. Bullough, "Achievement, Professionalization, and the University," in Ijsewijn and Paquet, *Universities in the Late Middle Ages*, 497–510; Verger, *Men of Learning in Europe*, 165–66; Cobban, *Medieval Universities*, ch. 9.

99 The list of intellectual virtues is long, but it includes a zeal for truth, courage to follow it where it leads, accuracy, honesty, patience, persistence, disinterestedness, tolerance of complexity and uncertainty, respect for differing opinions, and humility in the face of all that is unknown. See Barry Schwartz, "Intellectual Virtues," *Chronicle of Higher Education* (June 26, 2015), B6–B9.

100 See above, p. 2 and n. 3

CHAPTER TWO

Oxbridge

The suns, eyes, and minds of the kingdom

SIR JOHN COKE

THE GENESIS OF America's great modern universities lies not in the continental experience of all European universities, but in the provincial antecedents of England's Oxford and Cambridge. Both were quintessential medieval universities, not unlike Bologna, Paris, and Salamanca. But because of England's tumultuous changes in government and religion in the sixteenth and early seventeenth centuries, they evolved in ways different from their European peers but similar to each other. To one keen observer, they seemed "one well-ordered commonwealth, only divided by distance of place and not in friendly consent and orders."[1] Although most European countries faced the challenges of the Protestant Reformation, state formation, nationalism, and socio-economic change, England's responses fostered the fullest and most direct transplantation of its culture and key academic institutions to what European explorers called the New World. To see clearly the nearly 400-year development of American higher education, we must first understand what preceded it in Tudor and early Stuart Oxbridge.[2]

1 William Harrison, *The Description of England* [London, 1587], ed. George Edelen (Ithaca, N.Y.: Cornell University Press for the Folger Shakespeare Library, 1968), 70.

2 The portmanteau noun "Oxbridge" was first coined in 1849 by William Makepeace Thackeray in his novel *Pendennis* to designate a fictional stand-in for either Oxford or Cambridge, not as a collective term for the two seats of learning. In the same novel he refers to Oxbridge's rival university, "Camford," a term that did not catch on. I tend to use "Oxbridge" as a collective because the two universities were so similar in the Tudor and early Stuart period. William Ham Bevan, "Oxbridge (and Camford): An Etymological History," *CAM: Cambridge Alumni Magazine*, no. 68 (Lent Term 2013), 18–21.

All universities are shaped by and must respond to the ambient conditions and life of their times, otherwise they wither and die. The eighty-some universities of medieval Europe were no exception. A significant number of them—about 20 percent—were starved for resources, students, or political support.[3] Despite their location in relatively small towns, Oxford and Cambridge were close enough to London and supple enough not only to hold their own and coexist but also to monopolize the higher education of England for several centuries.[4] They did so by adapting—or being forced to adapt to—a host of changing circumstances that threatened not only their vitality and national relevance but also, at least once, their very existence.

In a fast-moving century, England's universities confronted half a dozen game-changers. Of prime importance was the growth and legacy of oligarchic government under King Henry VIII. In seeking to annul his marriage to Catherine of Aragon, he also pulled his nation out of the spiritual and political orbit of the Roman Catholic Church and set it on a course that soon drifted into Protestantism. Together these actions ensured, through often deft but always forceful legislative and political maneuvering, that he became the supreme head of both state and church.

Academically, the universities rose more easily to four other challenges. One was the replacement of manuscript texts with smaller, less expensive books made possible by movable-type printing. Another was the coming to England of Renaissance humanism with its fascination with Greek and Latin classical literature and rhetoric and its newfound instances therein, the Greek Testament, and

3 Hilde Ridder-Symoens, ed. *Universities in the Middle Ages*, vol. 1 of *A History of the University in Europe* [*HUE*], gen. ed. Walter Rüegg, 4 vols. (Cambridge: Cambridge University Press, 1992), 62–65. Some of those that disappeared were reestablished later, and a few moved to other sites and were renamed. At least fifteen more were established only on paper or parchment. Hastings Rashdall, *The Universities of Europe in the Middle Ages*, rev. and ed. F. M. Powicke and A. B. Emden (Oxford: Oxford University Press, 1936), 2:325–31.

4 North of the border, Scotland's three small urban universities—St. Andrews (c. 1410), Glasgow (1451), and Aberdeen (1495)—were not founded until the fifteenth century and never rivaled Oxbridge in numbers, European prestige, or (even after the addition of Edinburgh in 1583) quality until the second half of the eighteenth century.

even the Hebrew scriptures. The third challenge was provided by the slow rise of a new natural science of observation and experiment, which sought to replace the less mathematical, less accurate, and less predictive texts of Aristotle, the astronomer Ptolemy, and the geographer Strabo. And, finally, the social composition of the universities changed as monks and friars were replaced by the sons of the gentry and aristocracy, who sought more formal preparation for leadership in country and nation. Together, these force fields moved the English universities in new directions without dismantling their essential structures or extinguishing their central animating spirit as centers of advanced teaching and learning.

England's two universities had depended on the state throughout the Middle Ages, largely because their original recognition as *studia generale* had come initially not from the pope but from the crown. Royal edicts conferred legal standing, guaranteed their corporate rights and privileges, and continued to protect them from the threats and aggrandizements of their respective towns. But under Henry VIII (r. 1509–47), their dependence on the state grew as they sought more protection from municipal assertiveness and aristocratic greed and more economic support for their physical and academic enhancement. The liberally though not university-educated king recognized their value to the nation, state, and church beyond the training of personnel and did his best to shelter them from their enemies and promote their well-being. But in return, he—and his successors—firmly reminded the universities that they owed the crown active and unqualified support for state policies, especially those based on royal desires.[5] The bear hug in which he embraced the universities made it difficult for them to distinguish affection from coercion.

Henry's embrace began to tighten after 1525 as he sought ways to annul his long marriage to Catherine, who had given him only a politically risky female heir, so that he could marry his new young

5 Claire Cross, "Oxford and the Tudor State from the Accession of Henry VIII to the Death of Mary," in James McConica, ed., *The Collegiate University*, vol. 3 of *The History of the University of Oxford* [*HUO*], gen. ed. T. H. Aston, 8 vols. (Oxford: Clarendon Press, 1986), 117.

mistress, Anne Boleyn. To do so he had to convince the Church that Catherine's early five-month marriage to his older brother, Arthur, had been valid by the standards of canon law because it had been sexually consummated (which she adamantly denied to her dying day). With Rome then invested by the troops of Catherine's nephew, Charles V, two successive popes remained immune to Henry's reasoning and affirmed their opposition to the divorce. Realizing that he could never win in Rome, Henry concluded that he would have to conduct his case at home. After an ecclesiastical court there, presided over by the papal legate, failed to return the desired verdict, Henry turned to the learned faculties of his two and several other European universities after Pope Clement VII moved the proceedings to Rome. In 1530 the scholars were asked to decide "whether it is prohibited by divine and natural law to marry the childless widow of one's brother."[6] In their collective wisdom, after suitable historical research and not-so-subtle pressure, Oxford and Cambridge at least ruled that it was not lawful—and therefore had not been lawful—to do so.

That decision helped to embolden Henry to divorce Rome itself. In quick succession, he persuaded Parliament to stop all payments and appeals to the Holy See (1532, 1533), to declare the king "Supreme Head of the English Church and clergy" (1534), and ultimately to confiscate the properties and revenues of all Catholic monasteries and other religious houses, some 800 in all (1536, 1539). In 1536 the English state formally renounced the pope's authority in all matters, a position whose reasonableness the faculties of Oxford and Cambridge had affirmed, not wholeheartedly, two years earlier.[7] When the Cambridge chancellor, John Fisher, publicly demurred, as he had done in the "Great Matter" of the king's divorce, he was beheaded, the first of four Tudor university chancellors to die on the

6 Damian Riehl Leader, *The University to 1546*, vol. 1 of *A History of the University of Cambridge* [*HUC*], gen. ed. Christopher Brooke, 4 vols. (Cambridge: Cambridge University Press, 1988), 327–28. In addition to Oxbridge, 160 European scholars and 23 Western European universities were consulted. Diarmaid MacCulloch, *Thomas Cranmer: A Life* (New Haven, Conn.: Yale University Press, 1996), 41.

7 G. R. Elton, ed., *The Tudor Constitution: Documents and Commentary*, 2nd ed. (Cambridge: Cambridge University Press), 350–58, 364–67, 383–89; Leader, *University to 1546*, *HUC* 1:329.

scaffold in the sixteenth century.[8] From then on, precious few university scholars or students dared to question the political supremacy of the sovereign or to refuse to swear the oath to that effect that was soon required for matriculation and graduation.

England's move away from the Catholic Church under Henry was confirmed and accelerated during the royal minority of his underaged heir, Edward VI (r. 1547–53). Liberally educated in reform humanism by Cambridge-educated tutors, particularly the Regius Professor of Greek Sir John Cheke, and religiously guided by his father's archbishop of Canterbury, Thomas Cranmer, the boy king and his advisors fully protestantized the Church of England. Clerical celibacy and the Mass were abolished, mandatory Sunday services were conducted in English rather than Latin, and all "superstitious" images and relics of saints were removed from churches, sometimes violently by mob action. Congregations were taught the predestination of the "elect," salvation "by faith alone," and the irrelevance of good works to salvation. Christ's "real presence" in the bread and wine of communion was denied, and the laity as well as the clergy was allowed to partake of both. *The Book of Common Prayer* regulated services and the Forty-Two [later Thirty-Nine] Articles laid out doctrine after passage of the Act of Uniformity in 1549.[9]

Another early Edwardian reform had the potential to cripple as well as rattle the universities. When chantries—endowments to support priests to sing masses, usually for the souls of the founders—were abolished in 1547, their landed incomes were confiscated by the crown. A number of schools, colleges, halls, and hostels would have been at risk had they not been specifically exempted by Parliament. The act reflected Henry's firm response to the greedy aristocratic "dingthrifts" (as he called them) who, having already gotten the

8 Leader, *University to 1546*, *HUC* 1:324–31. Another Cambridge chancellor, Stephen Gardiner, kept his head but, thanks to Edward VI, cooled his heels in the Tower for five years before Mary released him and reinstalled him as chancellor in 1553.

9 Jennifer Loach, *Edward VI*, ed. George Bernard and Penry Williams (New Haven, Conn.: Yale University Press, 1999); Diarmaid MacCulloch, *Tudor Church Militant: King Edward VI and the Protestant Reformation* (London: Allen Lane, 1999); Dale Hoak, "Edward VI (1537–1553)," *Oxford Dictionary of National Biography* (2004; rev. ed., 2008, www.oxforddnb.com).

lion's share of abbey lands earlier set their sights on college estates: "Whereas we had a regard only to pull down sin by defacing the monasteries, you have a desire also to overthrow all goodness by subversion of the colleges. . . . I judge no land in England better bestowed than that which is given to our universities, for by their maintenance our realm shall be well governed when we be dead and rotten." Parliament wisely reserved the chantry proceeds for the erection or maintenance of grammar schools, poor relief, and "the furthering of the Universities."[10]

The five-year reign (1553–58) of Edward's Catholic half-sister, Mary I, " Bloody Mary," threw England into new turmoil as she undid her father's and brother's Protestant reforms and re-romanized the national church. The universities were crucial to her campaign because of their proven importance as forges of opinion and molders of young elites for the church and state. Protestant chancellors and college heads were replaced with good Catholics. Three prominent Protestant reformers, including Archbishop Cranmer, were forced to debate eight conservative Cambridge dons at Oxford on the meaning of the Eucharist. When they were adjudged to have lost, they were declared heretics and publicly burned at the stake near Balliol College. These grisly deaths made it abundantly clear that Oxbridge was no longer safe for acknowledged Protestants.[11]

In the next few years, 137 graduates and dons, including several European scholars who had been attracted to the Edwardian universities, became so-called Marian Exiles on the continent. The majority were Cantabrigians, 60 were Oxonians. In 1556 Reginald Pole, the English-born papal legate and new chancellor of both Oxford and Cambridge, sent Visitors—mostly conservative bishops—to the universities and their colleges to restore ancient statutes, ferret out "heretical" books, and ensure the proper conduct of academic exercises. Lecturers in all subjects were ordered to teach nothing contrary to the Catholic faith, and disputations were expected to come to similar conclusions. Actions such as these signified that the

10 Harrison, *Description of England*, 80–81; Elton, *Tudor Constitution*, 391–94; D. W. Sylvester, ed., *Educational Documents, 800–1816* (London: Methuen, 1970), 83–85.

11 Cross, "Oxford and the Tudor State," *HUO* 3:140–49, at 142–44.

universities were highly susceptible to state coercion and henceforth "at the mercy of the monarch and successive royal governments."[12]

Yet even before Elizabeth I (r. 1558–1603) ascended the throne, some 340 Oxbridge academics had converted or reconverted to some form of Protestantism in hopes of seeing the restoration of the Henrician and Edwardian reforms. They were not disappointed and had not long to wait. In 1559 Parliament restored the crown's "ancient jurisdiction over the state ecclesiastical and spiritual," including the universities, where an oath to crown supremacy was required of "anyone taking holy orders or degrees at the Universities."[13] The great uncertainty created by the whipsaw changes of the previous thirty years slowly faded as the highly intelligent and politically adroit Virgin Queen re-settled the English church and oversaw the universities' vital growth from their Edwardian nadir.[14]

Marian exiles returned from the continent and coverts of the country. To make room for them, both faculties were purged of recusants and crypto-Catholics. Within two years, only one Marian college head remained in Oxford and another in Cambridge. Books re-defined as "heretical" were hunted down. Elizabeth herself

12 Ibid., 3: at 148, 149. For a list of the Cambridge exiles, see H. C. Porter, *Reformation and Reaction in Tudor Cambridge* (Cambridge: Cambridge University Press, 1958), ch. 4, at 91–98. On the credit side, Mary's gift to Oxford in 1554 of three rectories, worth £132 annually, tripled the university's paltry endowment and enabled it to repair and resurrect the Faculty of Arts Schools building, among other improvements. In her will she also bestowed £500 on both Oxford and Cambridge for poor scholars and funds to help build Trinity College, Cambridge. I. G. Philip, "Queen Mary Tudor's Benefaction to the University," *Bodleian Library Record* 5:1 (April 1954), 217–37. Elisabeth Leedham-Green, *A Concise History of the University of Cambridge* (Cambridge: Cambridge University Press, 1996), 56.

13 Elton, *Tudor Constitution*, 372–77.

14 Between 1542 and 1548, Oxford produced only 173 B.A.s, Cambridge, 191. For the rest of the century, Cambridge continued to outstrip Oxford. In 1583 Cambridge turned out 277 B.A.s, Oxford only 157. By 1600 Cambridge had a resident student population of almost 2,000, Oxford considerably less. Cross, "Oxford and the Tudor State," *HUO* 3:140; Craig R. Thompson, "Universities in Tudor England," in *Life and Letters in Tudor and Stuart England*, ed. Louis B. Wright and Virginia A. LaMar (Ithaca, N.Y.: Cornell University Press for the Folger Shakespeare Library, 1962), 337–82, at 363–64.

became the official Visitor to Christ Church College, Oxford (once Lord Chancellor Thomas Wolsey's big dream and partial benefaction, Cardinal College). But most college Visitors remained bishops or archbishops, although of a new persuasion and deferential to royal pleasure. In 1571 Parliament established both universities as self-governing corporations, replacing ten-year-old royal decrees, without any great diminution of royal intrusion. Royal commissions ordered new statutes for each university and their colleges (Oxford in 1565, Cambridge in 1570) and quietly elevated the authority of college heads at the expense of their fellows. That university chancellors were long-serving nobles or great officers of state close to the queen and assumed more say in the (short-term) appointment of vice-chancellors—who were always experienced college heads—reflected the close patterning of university governance upon the oligarchic state.[15]

The tight confluence of state policy, religion, and the universities achieved by Elizabeth was bequeathed to her Stuart successors, James I (r. 1603–25) and Charles I (r. 1625–49). By the time civil war erupted in 1642, the return of Catholicism as the state religion was perhaps feared but largely removed as a real possibility, yet Protestant factions still wrestled for control of the established church, Parliament, and the universities. These contests made the universities visible arenas in which national politics played out, as would remain true for centuries. When Parliament in 1604 granted each university two seats in Parliament, in part to enable them to explain and defend their interests directly, it signaled their conspicuous role in the high-stakes game of power and patronage. Recognized as "the nurseries & fountains of our Church and common wealth," the universities could not be ignored.[16] From the government's point of view, it was crucial that they set a sterling example of religious uniformity, ideological control, moral probity, and social order. As Sir Robert Cecil, Elizabeth's former secretary of state, reminded newly enfranchised Cambridge, "There can be noe greater Enemye, to all good

15 Penry Williams, "Elizabethan Oxford: State, Church and University," *HUO* 3: ch. 6; Victor Morgan, *1546–1750*, *HUC* 2:71, 75, 77, 90–91, 93, 107.

16 Morgan, *1546–1750*, *HUC* 2:109.

order, then Libertye in the education of all yonge gentlemen and scholers."[17] With sentiments like that, the Tudor bear hug was not about to loosen its hold upon Oxbridge under the new monarchs.

❁ ❁ ❁

The point men in the state's inroads upon the universities were their chancellors. Originally, they were clerical representatives of the bishops of Lincoln (in whose diocese Oxford lay) and of Ely (Cambridge's diocese) but elected by the respective guilds of masters. By the mid-fifteenth century, the masters' choices no longer needed ecclesiastical approval, and the chancellors' terms grew from two years to life. Increasingly they became nonresident dignitaries with political clout to mediate royal and academic agendas. Several were lords chancellor to the crown, many were bishops or archbishops. By the sixteenth century, they were all appointed by the crown. But as four of them learned the hard way, the crown could literally cut their tenure (and lives) short if they strayed too far from royal agendas or the law.[18]

While in office, the chancellors acquired considerable authority over their institutions. They had their own courts to enforce discipline, prisons to restrain offenders, and jurisdiction over townsmen who clashed with scholars, probate of scholars who died at university, school-teaching licenses, and assizes of food, drink, and trade at local fairs and markets. After 1604, the chancellors regularly chose the university's senior members of Parliament, who were, much like themselves, alumni, nonresidents, and lawyers or courtiers with experience in the House of Commons. Although the regent (teaching) masters elected the vice-chancellors, proctors, bedels, registrars, and other university officials, the chancellors pushed their own and the crown's favorites with signal success.[19]

17 Ibid., 2:112.

18 Alan B. Cobban, *The Medieval English Universities: Oxford and Cambridge to c. 1500* (Berkeley: University of California Press, 1990 [1988]), 64–76

19 Williams, "Elizabethan Oxford," *HUO* 3:401–402; Kenneth Fincham, "Oxford and the Early Stuart Polity," in Nicholas Tyacke, ed., *Seventeenth-Century Oxford*, vol. 4 of *HUO* (1997), 196–98; Morgan, *1546–1750*, *HUC* 2:93.

The chancellors also played a strong hand in choosing Visitors to their various colleges, who in the end were also crown appointments. Frequently they assumed the office themselves. Within seven years, William Laud, Oxford's chancellor from 1630, was a Visitor of nine Oxford colleges, and close allies oversaw all but one of the rest.[20] More often the job fell to their vice-chancellors, high clergy, statesmen, and London lawyers. Given the integration of church and state, bishops were the most popular choices, especially former heads of colleges, even those from the other university.[21] Visitors were instrumental in persuading colleges to revise their statutes, to appoint fellows likely to obey the dictates of the crown and the prevailing doctrines of the church, to reform their academic exercises, and to discipline the potentially unruly and even politically dangerous student bodies. Knowing that the weight of the state lay behind the Visitors, colleges normally—if reluctantly—honored their recommendations.[22]

Of greater symbolic force, royal visitations to the universities also occurred sporadically throughout the period. Before Elizabeth, the visits were conducted largely by royal surrogates and commissioners. Her father had visited Oxford briefly in 1522, but in 1535, Thomas Cromwell, Henry's chief counselor, sent orders there with two lay commissioners. Fourteen years later, the new king, Edward VI, dispatched two bishops to the universities in turn. Queen Mary sent Reginald Pole, the papal legate, in 1556 to reverse all of her relatives' Protestant reforms. Only in 1564 (at Cambridge) and 1566 (at Oxford) did Elizabeth see fit to impress her resettled universities with her personal presence, skills, and resolve, as she did again at Oxford in 1592 to help bring both Protestant factions and residual recusants into line with official church doctrine and practice. Her successor,

20 Upon becoming archbishop of Canterbury in 1635, Laud was keen to reform Cambridge as well, but he never made a metropolitan visit to put its house in order. Leedham-Green, *Concise History of Cambridge*, 70–71.

21 After 1581, all but three Oxford colleges were visited by bishops or archbishops. Williams, "Elizabethan Oxford," *HUO* 3:404–405.

22 Morgan, *1546–1750*, *HUC* 2:96–97; Williams, "Elizabethan Oxford," *HUO* 3:404–405; Fincham, "Oxford and the Early Stuart Polity," *HUO* 4:194, 205 (Laud).

James I, lent his royal weight to Oxford, his favorite university, on two major occasions, as did Charles I twice more. By then, more diverse and contentious Cambridge was no doubt grateful for the crown's relatively benign neglect.[23]

The monarchs' personal visits were invested with plenty of pomp, ceremony, and obsequiousness, but they also enabled the sovereigns to observe and participate in the quotidian workings of the universities they considered instruments—if not agencies—of the state. Elizabeth devoted five days to Cambridge in 1564, six days to Oxford in 1566 and a full week in 1592, when she visited the colleges for the first time; James engaged Oxford for four days in 1605. Each visit included often long speeches in English, Latin, and Greek from students, officials, and university orators. Students performed classical and newly composed comedies and dramas in college dining halls, often in Latin, not always winningly, and sometimes scandalously. Many plays were chosen to counsel the queen—not always subtly—on the reform of the church, the desirability of (her) marriage, and the settlement of the royal succession.[24] The students also engaged in full-throated Latin disputations on potentially hot topics such as "whether monarchy is the best condition of the body politic"

23 Cross, "Oxford and the Tudor State," *HUO* 3:125–28, 135–38, 145–48; Williams, "Elizabethan Oxford," 397–400; Fincham, "Oxford and the Early Stuart Polity," *HUO* 4:182n11; Morgan, *1546–1750*, *HUC* 2:451–53. James I visited Cambridge in the winter of 1614 only to see four plays. Ten years later he briefly attended a ceremony for the granting of honorary degrees to a number of foreign and domestic dignitaries. Yet he had "freely" confirmed the university's charter and privileges for a delegation of college heads in April 1603 while en route from Scotland to claim the English throne. Morgan, *1546–1750*, *HUC* 2:40, 322, 420; G. B. Harrison, ed., *Jacobean Journal* (London: George Routledge and Sons, 1941), 19.

24 In one excessively long pastoral comedy entitled *Alba*, five or six men made their appearance "almost naked," which, one male spokesperson opined, was "misliked by the Queen and Ladies." Harrison, *Jacobean Journal*, 225. For the playbills at both Oxford and Cambridge, see Frederick S. Boas, *University Drama in the Tudor Age* (Oxford: Oxford University Press, 1914; New York: Benjamin Blom, 1966), chs. 5, 11; Siobhan Keenan, "Spectator and Spectacle: Royal Entertainments in the Universities in the 1560s," in Jayne Elisabeth Archer, Elizabeth Goldring, and Sarah Knight, eds., *The Progresses, Pageants, and Entertainments of Queen Elizabeth I* (Oxford: Oxford University Press, 2007), ch. 5.

and "whether the authority of scripture is greater than that of the church." In all three visits, Elizabeth attentively followed many hours of Latin debates in several faculties. James, a well-known critic of the newly imported American "weed," listened with keen interest to a medical debate on "whether the frequent fumigation of *nicotiana exotica* be wholesome for the health." After another disputation in philosophy, he prevented one respondent from being cut off by the faculty moderator and later remarked to his noble retinue, "God keep this fellow in a right course, he would prove a dangerous heretic; he is the best disputer that ever I heard."[25]

The royal visits also allowed the universities to discover, if they had no foreknowledge, that the monarchs had full measures of solid learning by which to judge them. At both thirty-one and fifty-nine, Elizabeth understood every speech sent her way and needed no tele- or human prompters to respond in kind. In 1592 she surprised the Greek orator by thanking him "in the same tongue" and left Oxford, the vice-chancellor, and college heads with a graceful impromptu speech of thanks in Latin. In 1605 James was welcomed to Oxford in Latin and Greek while his queen and son were condescended to in English. The gift of a handsome "Greek Testament in folio" from the university meant much more to him than a pair of fancy gold-fringed gloves.[26] The next day he was awarded a doctorate, an honor that was not undeserved as he soon proved. While listening to disputations in theology, medicine, and law, he did not hesitate to comment—in Latin—on the arguments and performances. In natural philosophy, this most donnish of kings "determined" one of the

25 Williams, "Elizabethan Oxford," *HUO* 3:397–400; G. B. Harrison, ed., *An Elizabethan Journal . . . 1591–1594* (London: Constable, 1928), 170–74; Harrison, *Jacobean Journal*, 222–30, at 227–28. Before Elizabeth in 1564, one Cambridge scholar argued so well on behalf of Catholicism, noted the Spanish ambassador in attendance, that he was "attacked by those who presided, in order to avoid having to give him the prize." Keenan, "Spectator and Spectacle," 92, 93.

26 In 1566 Elizabeth was presented with a book of original Latin verses that flattered both her and her host (and suitor), Chancellor Robert Dudley, Earl of Leicester, and included a picture portfolio of the Oxford colleges skillfully drawn by a fellow of Exeter College. Louise Durning, ed., *Queen Elizabeth's Book of Oxford*, trans. Sarah Knight and Helen Spurling (Oxford: Bodleian Library, 2006).

questions himself. At the end of a long day of verbal swordplay, he stood up, removed his hat respectfully, and "spake very graciously in Latin, approving all their exercises, and exhorting them to worship God, His word, and His pure doctrine, fleeing from Romish superstitions, schisms and novel opinions."[27] The eighteen Oxford scholars he had chosen the year before to help prepare a new translation of the Bible—the enduring King James version—were no doubt gratified doubly by his confidence and favor.[28]

The next morning James solidified his reputation for learning during a lengthy visit to the newly endowed university library, the Bodleian. There he was presented with a printed copy of the formidable new catalogue of the library, perused several religious manuscripts and books (upon which he "gave his learned censure"), and promised founder Thomas Bodley his pick of manuscripts from the royal collection. Upon leaving he famously said, "If I were not a king, I would wish to be a University man; and if it were so that I might be a prisoner, if I might have my wish, I would desire to have no other prison than this library, and to be chained together with so many good authors, *et mortuis magister* [and die a master]."[29]

James's first visit and subsequent dealings with Oxford left unmistakable signs of the deepening state impress upon the university. Before his arrival in 1605, advance men oversaw "great preparations" and issued "divers ordinances for the proper behavior of the scholars," as they had done for Elizabeth's visits. The town and college "rails, posts and pumps" were freshly painted and "all coats-of-arms newly tricked out." More important, the students were ordered to "diligently frequent the ordinary [morning] lectures during the

27 Harrison, *Elizabethan Journal*, 170–74; Harrison, *Jacobean Journal*, 220–30.

28 Fifteen scholars were also chosen to work on the two Cambridge teams, or "companies." One of the Oxford translators was a Cambridge man and former college head. Nearly all of the remaining seventeen were Oxbridge products. Adam Nicolson, *Power and Glory: Jacobean England and the Making of the King James Bible* (London: HarperCollins, 2003), 251–59.

29 I. G. Philip and Paul Morgan, "Libraries, Books, and Printing," *HUO* 4: ch. 13, 661; Harrison, *Jacobean Journal*, 229; Sir Isaac Wake, *Rex Platonicus* (Oxford: Joseph Barnes, 1607), 116–23; William Dunn Macray, *Annals of the Bodleian Library, Oxford, A.D. 1598–A.D. 1867* (London: Rivingtons, 1868), 26–27.

King's abode," not to protest "upon pain of present imprisonment and other punishment" if they could not obtain admission to the plays, and to have any verses in honor of the royal family intended for public posting "first corrected [censored and perhaps copyedited] by the Deans of colleges."[30] Despite these precautions, "the boys" would be boys and rudely pulled down their verses from the college walls when the king failed to regard or read any of them in his academic circuit around town.[31] Even the day before he arrived, 140 students sat in a sermon beside the vice-chancellor with their hats on and were sent off to the university (and town) prison, the Bocardo, on their own honor. They nearly compounded their crimes when the king commented upon the disputations and they "applauded him by clapping their hands and humming, which though strange to him, yet when he understood upon enquiry what the noise meant"—a compliment—"he was well contented."[32]

Displeasing the monarch was never in the universities' best interest. The crown's enhanced power of ecclesiastical preferment was one excellent reason to toe the royal line. Of the 27 Oxford vice-chancellors who served during Elizabeth's reign, 9 became bishops and 5 deans of cathedrals, as did other accommodating heads of colleges. By 1640, 14 Cambridge college heads had been elevated to bishoprics directly, 3 more eventually.[33] Royal philanthropy was another reason. Kings, queens, and even their mothers (such as Henry VII's) built colleges and chapels—commodious Trinity College and the magnificent King's College Chapel, Cambridge, and

30 The Oxford students received a similar set of instructions before Elizabeth's visit in 1592. In 1564, in contrast, the Cambridge undergraduates were ordered, after welcoming the queen on her arrival, "quietly & orderlye to departe Home to their Colledges & in no Wyse to come to the Courte, the Disputacoñs, or to the Playes." Boas, *University Drama*, 92, 253.

31 In 1592 Elizabeth had had the courtesy to "cast her eyes on the walls of St. Mary's Church, All Souls, University, and Magdalen Colleges, which were mostly hung with verses and emblematical expressions of Poetry." Boas, *University Drama*, 267.

32 Harrison, *Jacobean Journal*, 222–23, 229–30.

33 Williams, "Elizabethan Oxford," *HUO* 3:430; Morgan, *1546–1750*, *HUC* 2:105. When heads were so promoted, the crown had the right to name replacements, thus reducing fellows' traditional authority of election.

Christ Church, Oxford, among others—and endowed lectureships and professorships, including five regius chairs in theology, Greek, Hebrew, civil law, and medicine at both Oxford (1540) and Cambridge (1546).[34] Even other people's largesse sought the king's blessing. When widow Dorothy Wadham in 1610 offered £7,000 for a college quadrangle and £800 more a year for 16 fellows and 40 scholars, James approved the deal but "wished his statue to be set over the gate," which it still guards with suitable regal bearing, above statues of the Wadhams.[35]

The previous year the king had thrown his royal weight around even more roughly. When James, also the king of Scotland (as James VI), learned that most Oxford college statutes prohibited the awarding of fellowships to "Scottishmen," he threatened to send the Cambridge chancellor (his own lord treasurer) and the archbishop of Canterbury to visit both universities to remove those disabling "ancient statutes." They were, he made known, "an indignity which [he] will not endure, especially as he hath been so good and gracious a patron: but if they persist he will make them see he can be otherwise than he hath been."[36]

College elections and statutes were persistent points of state annoyance, pressure, and occasionally reform. As the colleges and their fellows assumed more importance in university teaching throughout the sixteenth century, the selection of fellows became more vital to

34 Leader, *University to 1546*, *HUC* 1:344–48; 2:16; Cross, "Oxford and the Tudor State," *HUO* 3:132; G. D. Duncan, "Public Lectures and Professorial Chairs," *HUO* 3:344–45; John Newman, "The Physical Setting: New Building and Adaptation," *HUO* 3: ch. 9.

35 A life-size statue and the royal arms of founder Henry VIII similarly greet visitors at the Great Gate of Trinity College, Cambridge. Douglas Ferguson, Nick Segal, and Dona Haycraft, *Cambridge*, 2nd rev. ed. (Cambridge: Covent Garden Press, 1995 [1987]), 46 (photo).

36 G. B. Harrison, ed., *A Second Jacobean Journal . . . 1607–1610* (London: Routledge and Kegan Paul, 1958), 165, 191. When six fellowships opened in St. John's College, Cambridge, in 1620, undergraduate Simonds D'Ewes noted that a Scotsman got one thanks to a royal mandate. J. H. Marsden, *College Life in the Time of James the First, as Illustrated by an Unpublished Diary of Sir Symonds D'Ewes* (London: John W. Parker and Son, 1856), 94.

FIGURE 4. Despite the great generosity of college founders Nicholas and Dorothy Wadham, King James I asserted his royal rank over them even in the Main Quad's statuary.

the corporate autonomy and quality of the faculties. Most college statutes closely regulated the election of fellows and scholars. Some restricted tenure to relatively brief periods to encourage newly qualified M.A.s and D.D.s (Doctors of Divinity) to take up benefices and lectureships in the church, particularly in the "dark [ungospelized] corners" of the country. Others allotted fellowships to men from select counties, often favoring the homelands of founders and aristocratic patrons or the neighborhoods of college estates. The statutes of large colleges obliged them to distribute places to fellows in most or all of the major subjects in the university curriculum. And, according to the long-standing traditions of the academic guild, each college sought the freedom to choose its members—from "fresher" to fellow—according to its own criteria of merit. The accelerating assimilation of the universities by the Tudor and early Stuart state rendered all of these statutes and procedures subject to stress and compromise.

In attempting to clean up the universities' allegedly declining acts, King Henry's injunctions of 1535, aimed initially at Cambridge, underlined two deficiencies in the governance of the colleges. Through his surrogate, Thomas Cromwell, whom he appointed Visitor to both universities, he ordered that college fellowships were not to be sold by their incumbents and that geographical and collegiate factionalism should cease so that all elections could be made solely on merit.[37] But the problems would not be solved by royal resolutions. With the quick changes in religion forced by the Tudors upon the nation and universities, religious (and therefore political) factionalism was rampant in the colleges. Another problem was poverty, as Henry's chantry-act commissioners discovered in 1544 when they inventoried the revenues and enrollments of each Oxbridge college. Nearly all colleges reported deficits, only in part because they poorly managed their landed endowments. The king immediately scuttled the idea of confiscating their chantries, saying that "he had not in his realm so many persons so honestly maintained in living by so little land and

37 Leader, *University to 1546*, *HUC* 1:332–33.

rent." Instead he founded and handsomely endowed two colleges: Trinity in Cambridge and Christ Church in Oxford.[38]

Criticism of college elections did not subside. In 1549 the future Protestant martyr, Bishop Hugh Latimer, complained to King Edward in a sermon that university decay was still underway, largely because wealthy graduates were taking—buying—the fellowships initially intended for the poor and the godly.[39] Election malfeasance only accelerated under Elizabeth. In 1577 William Harrison, who had failed twenty years earlier to obtain a place on the endowed foundation of Christ Church, Oxford, criticized both universities for allowing the rich to usurp poor men's places and censured those with friends in high places or among past benefactors for "packing" fellowship elections, though the winners were often "the worst scholar[s]." Once ensconced, he lamented, too many fellows "live like drone bees on the fat of colleges, withholding better wits from the possession of their places and yet doing little good in their own vocation and calling." "Long continuance in those places is either a sign of lack of [powerful] friends or of learning or of good and upright life," otherwise they would have been elevated to useful and better-paid positions in church or state.[40]

Even more stinging was a pamphlet published in 1592 by Father Robert Parsons, an Oxford M.A. and former fellow and brilliant tutor of Balliol College. Previously a Calvinist, Parsons had turned Catholic and fled Elizabeth's England for Louvain, where he joined

38 Ibid., 1:344–45. Many college estates grew rapidly during Elizabeth's stable reign from the gifts of elite alumni and well-wishers, as did wiser forms of management. G. E. Aylmer, "The Economics and Finances of the Colleges and University c. 1530–1640," *HUO* 3: ch. 8; Morgan, *1546–1750*, *HUC* 2: ch. 6.

39 Leader, *University to 1546*, *HUC* 1:343. In truth, more fellowships were being taken at this juncture, and would continue to be, by the sons of modest clergymen than by younger sons of the gentry or aristocracy. Rosemary O'Day, *Education and Society, 1500–1800: The Social Foundations of Education in Early Modern Britain* (London: Longman, 1982), 86, 92, 100–105.

40 Harrison, *Description of England*, 71, 74. See also Frederick S. Boas, ed., *The Diary of Thomas Crosfield, M.A., B.D., Fellow of Queen's College, Oxford* (London: Oxford University Press, 1935), 6. On Nov. 5, 1626, Crosfield felt obliged to "justify the long residence of seniors in the university against the censure of laziness."

the Jesuit order. Among his indictments was that the lay chancellors of Oxford and Cambridge had "overthrown" all good order, whereby "headships [are] given to light and wanton companions," "statutes of founders condemned and broken," and "the places of fellows and scholars publicly sold." That he went on to declare the Jesuit seminaries of Europe the equals of Oxford and Cambridge added bite to his turncoat attack.[41]

Since academically inclined graduates were always more numerous than college fellowships, candidates and their friends resorted to several tactics to overcome career roadblocks. Standing in their way were opponents determined to thwart them, either for personal or party profit. Gaining the favor of the college head was the first choice, but he was often hamstrung by the fierce factionalism in his fellowship. Passions could get so aroused that candidates—or incumbents—were ejected from their rooms, expelled from the university on trumped-up charges, physically attacked (even in chapel), made drunk and jailed on election eve, or had their fully earned degrees held up by procedural foot-dragging. More frustrating perhaps was the *pre*-election of candidates, often months or years in advance, to fellowships that had not yet been vacated. The reluctant election—or rather imposition by powerful outside parties—of "supernumerary" fellows whose stipends were not budgeted by the college worked the same effect of frustrating ambition and postponing opportunity.[42]

If fellowships did remain open, candidates often felt compelled to call for assistance from influential patrons in and outside the university. Serious factional fights in colleges, clearly beyond the control of the heads, were in the first instance refereed by the university or college Visitor, chancellor, or vice-chancellor. Invariably, both sides went beyond their own officers to recruit "famous men," often alumni, from their home counties or those holding important offices in the court, state bureaucracy, or, less frequently, the church.[43]

41 Williams, "Elizabethan Oxford," *HUO* 3: 412; Harrison, *Elizabethan Journal*, 154–55.

42 Morgan, *1546–1750*, *HUC* 2: 358–62, 393, 394–95.

43 Boas, *Diary of Thomas Crosfield*, 6.

When Gabriel Harvey was frustrated in his quest for a mere "grace" (permission) to proceed to his M.A. in 1573 and then for a place in the fellowship of Pembroke Hall, Cambridge, his sympathetic head advised him to seek the help of Sir Thomas Smith, an influential patron from his home town in Essex. It worked, fortunately, because the impecunious Harvey was not prepared to buy a place for any amount, much less the £100 that one fellow had paid recently.[44]

If a candidate's mid-level patrons could not obtain the desired results, the ultimate power broker to approach was the monarch. It might take a few "gratuities" to his secretaries and several punishing fifty-mile rides to London, but if a candidate could obtain a letter of mandate, sealed with the royal signet, his chances of success improved exponentially. Of course, the monarchs and their various ministers and courtiers had their own reasons to favor some candidates over others, so all supplicants had to navigate carefully the shoals and mysterious depths of patronage. As more blatant methods of securing fellowships—and headships as well—fell out of favor, increasingly in the face of parliamentary disapproval, the resort to royal mandates grew. In the 1580s and 1590s, at least 5 nominations to Oxbridge fellowships issued yearly from the queen's office. Under James, the annual totals climbed to between 13 and 17. Charles, his successor, was more diffident in issuing mandates for fellowships, but he did see fit in 1632 to order Cambridge to grant 60 honorary D.D.s to chaplains and other friends of his courtiers.[45] When it was rumored that the recipients had each paid a "large rate for their doctorships," the use of signet letters to affect academic decisions was again called into serious question, but without making the practice disappear.[46]

Not without some risk, the colleges and universities pushed back against these intrusions into their internal affairs. They used two main arguments: the force of long-standing college statutes and the

44 Edward John Long Scott, ed., *Letter-Book of Gabriel Harvey, A.D. 1573–1580*, n.s., vol. 33 (London: Publications of the Camden Society, 1884), 8, 32, 40–43, 162.

45 In the 1560s, Elizabeth had secured only M.A.s for a number of her noble companions. Keenan, "Spectator and Spectacle," 94, 101.

46 Morgan, *1546–1750*, *HUC* 2:159–64, 380, 413–15, 421, 423, 427.

principle of intellectual merit. The growing use of mandates in the early years of James's reign drew from Cambridge's vice-chancellor and college heads in 1607 a complaint to their chancellor about "the hindrance of our free elections of Fellowships and Scholarships in our several Colleges by the procurement of his Majesty's letters." These forced elections were "against statutes of foundations, oaths and free choice of the fittest." Too many requests to the king, they argued, were made "partly by the boldness of unfit youths moving suit by their parents and partly by the partial affections of their tutors, when they cannot have their pupils preferred as they would, whence also grows faction in houses [colleges]." Those who succeeded by greasing the palms of royal secretaries and other intermediaries also excluded plebeians from places originally designed for them.[47] Ten years later, Samuel Ward, the master of Sidney Sussex, Cambridge, was still complaining to a high official—probably the chancellor—of the mandate for a less worthy candidate at the expense of "the most eminent Bach[elor] which ever stood [for election] in College." This action contradicted the official's original charge to Ward: *Detur Dignissimo*, "choose the most eminent scholers." A reversal of the mandate, Ward suggested, would "encourage all good Scholers and discourage all Dunces [from] hoping for preferment with us."[48]

Calling upon influential friends to help overturn mandated elections was only one way to block them. Another was stonewalling, the best form of which was pre-electing someone, or several persons in order, to the fellowship. A third tactic, used by St. John's College, Cambridge, in 1625, was to inform the king that "all the places are appropriated to particular countreyes [counties]" and the college fellows "cannot without Breach of theyr oaths, obey any direction contrarye to theyr Statutes." The bishop of Lincoln, the advocate for St. John's and a former fellow, added a note from the "Clergie" that they, too, sought the curtailment of mandates from "his majestie and his great ministres" in order to promote the "encouragement

47 Ibid., 2:416–17.

48 *Two Elizabethan Puritan Diaries by Richard Rogers and Samuel Ward*, ed. M. M. Knappen (Chicago: American Society of Church History, 1933), 131–32.

of the better schollers, and consequentlye the weale of both the universityes."[49]

Ironically, simony in the church compounded the unfortunate effects of manipulated college elections. The buying and selling of benefices made it exceedingly difficult for godly scholars, especially those from modest circumstances who may have expended £500 on their necessary degrees (and perhaps more for a vendible college fellowship), to afford to purchase from a lay patron a lifelong lease for a "poor parsonage or vicarage" that paid only £40 or £50 a year. A well-publicized sermon in 1597 at Paul's Cross in London had predicted that such "sinful" practices would cause "the Universities to be decayed" and "the Church supplied with ignorant pastors."[50] By this time, the selling and buying of college fellowships was simply the logical extension of the commerce in public offices throughout the land. But it did nothing to secure the principles of academic autonomy and merit and everything to blur the distinction between state and university.

❁ ❁ ❁

The Tudor interventionist state not only sought to manipulate the composition and politico-religious beliefs of the Oxbridge faculties, it also sought to rewrite the universities' statutes, which regulated—at least in theory—such aspects as college and university governance, academic exercises, student discipline, and the curriculum. The audacious young Edward VI set the tone when he told the universities that "your statutes being antiquated, semi-barbarous, and obscure, and for the most part unintelligible on account of their age, you may henceforth obey royal laws framed under our auspices."[51]

49 Morgan, *1546–1750*, *HUC* 2:398, 421. Lack of reliable and accessible information about the candidates' qualifications continued to hamper the process. German academics had not yet invented the dossier, or *curriculum vitae*. William Clark, *Academic Charisma and the Origins of the Research University* (Chicago: University of Chicago Press, 2006), ch. 7.

50 G. B. Harrison, ed. *A Second Elizabethan Journal . . . 1595–1598* (London: Routledge & Kegan Paul, 1931), 240–41.

51 Morgan, *1546–1750*, *HUC* 2:63, 76.

The quick changes in monarchs and state religions that ensued postponed any major revisions of university statutes until the advent of the relative stability of the "Elizabethan Settlement." By the 1560s and 1570s, a number of changes in the universities and the outside world convinced many in the faculties that some statutory changes were needed and to heed the calls for reform coming from their crown-appointed chancellors and Visitors, elected vice-chancellors, and influential college heads.

At the personal urging of Elizabeth, Oxford's long-term chancellor, Robert Dudley, Earl of Leicester (1564–88), and Cambridge's even longer-term leader, William Cecil, Lord Burghley (1559–98), did the most to put their institutions on a more "orderly" footing. Now that the universities were very much in the national gaze, the crown sought to prevent these populous institutions from contributing to social unrest and to encourage them to live up to their enhanced responsibilities as opinion makers, religious models, and producers of trained alumni for church and state. The answer to collegiate "disorder" was thought to be better governance and firmer discipline. Both could be gained, the crown and reformers decided, if governance was concentrated in fewer hands, on the Tudor oligarchic model.

This was accomplished by statutory reform and also by subtle changes in practice. As the lay chancellors acquired more control over the appointment of vice-chancellors and other officers, they also elevated the authority of college heads above the traditional powers of the various faculties, the fractious regent (teaching) and nonregent masters, and the fellows of their colleges. By the 1570s, the colleges themselves—six of which had been added since 1500 to the ten already belonging to each university—had supplanted most of the medieval halls and hostels and had assumed the lion's share of the universities' oversight of student teaching, discipline, finances, morals, and manners.[52]

In 1565 Leicester made a start in reforming Oxford by giving the university a set of *Nova statuta* (New Statutes), most of which had

52 Thompson, "Universities in Tudor England," 338–39; *HUO* 3:esp. chs. 1 and 10 (James McConica, "The Rise of the Undergraduate College" and "Elizabethan Oxford: The Collegiate Society"); Morgan, *1546–1750*, *HUC* 2:chs. 2–4, 6.

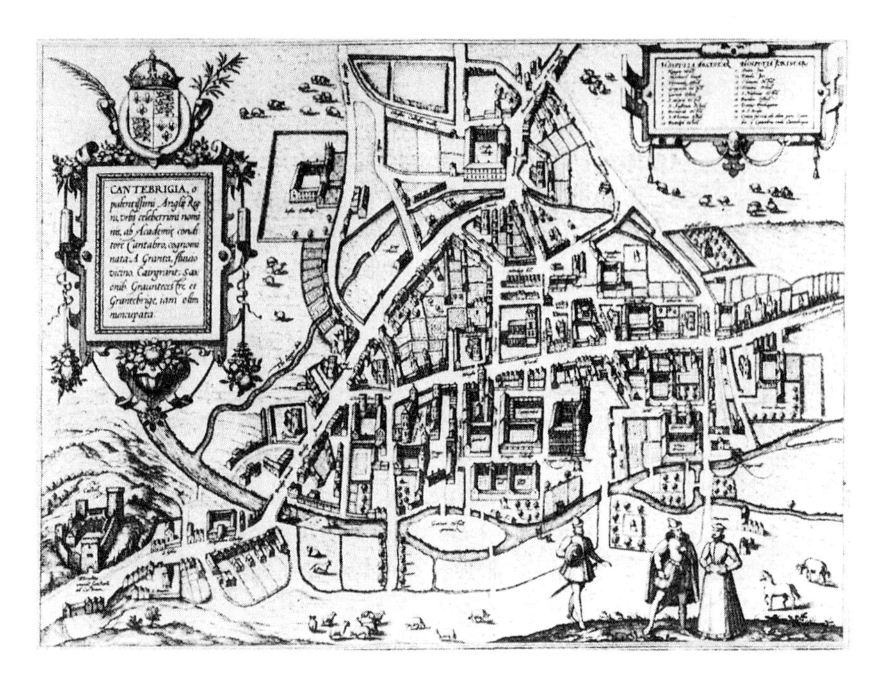

FIGURE 5. In 1575 Georg Braun and Frans Hogenberg depicted the predominantly collegiate character of Elizabethan Cambridge in their multivolume *Civitas orbis terrarum* (Cologne).

been suggested by its own doctors and proctors. In order to better manage its potentially obstreperous young population, the university was enjoined to keep a detailed matriculation register of all entering students sixteen or older, charging fees according to social rank (12 shillings for sons of aristocrats, only 4 pence for plebeians). The ordinance was only loosely enforced and had to be reinforced several times.[53] In 1579 and again a year later, all students living with townsmen—some poor chamberdeacons, wealthier "commoners" who were not on any collegiate foundation—were required to move into a supervised college or hall. Moreover, all who sought degrees or graces (dispensations) from various degree requirements had to

53 Cambridge had begun a matriculation register in 1544, but it, too, enjoyed only spotty success in capturing the university's numbers until Chancellor Burghley began to attack the problem in the 1560s. Morgan, *1546–1750*, *HUC* 2:119.

be matriculated and therefore members of a college or hall, whose faculty and heads could personally vouch for their attainments. In 1581 a statute published in English—to preclude any excuses from ignorance—required each matriculant to subscribe to both the royal supremacy and the Thirty-Nine Articles of the Anglican faith. Henceforth, only two major groups of students escaped capture by the new matriculation regime: well-to-do commoners, who intended to take only occasional notice of the official curriculum, and diehard Catholics or Puritans, who hoped to avoid subscribing to the established church's articles.[54]

The rest of Leicester's new statutes tackled a host of perceived academic shortcomings. They called for more frequent disputations, a sermon in English at the beginning of every term and each Sunday thereafter, and the abolition of some antiquated statutes relating to Catholic masses. They emphasized the intellectual importance of academic exercises and recommended the study of a number of books by title (most of which were already being assigned). But Leicester, even before he made the first of six visits to the university, was and remained fixated on the inappropriate dress of the Oxonians. At a time when crown and Parliament sought to halt the blurring of lines between social classes, the universities were expected to model the sartorial manifestations of hierarchy in their classrooms, quadrangles, and streets.[55]

In 1576 an act of Convocation, Oxford's reformed legislative body, clearly reflected Leicester's serious interest in sumptuary discipline. The statute mandated—under threat of steep graduated fines—the wearing of black gowns, hoods, and square caps (the floppy

54 McConica, "Rise of the Undergraduate College," *HUO* 3:49–51; J. A. Venn, *Oxford and Cambridge Matriculations, 1544–1906* (Cambridge: W. Heffer & Sons, 1908). Between 1560 and 1640, 20–30 percent of Oxbridge students failed to matriculate. Lawrence Stone, "The Educational Revolution in England, 1560–1640," *Past and Present*, no. 28 (July 1964), 41–80, at 47–51. Many rock-ribbed Catholics went instead to English colleges on the Continent, or to Jesuit colleges in France, and Presbyterians to Scottish universities.

55 James McConica, "Studies and Faculties, Introduction," *HUO* 3:152; J. M. Fletcher, "The Faculty of Arts," *HUO* 3:159; Williams, "Elizabethan Oxford," *HUO* 3:424–25.

predecessors of modern mortarboards) at all ceremonies. It outlawed the wearing of fancy colored velvet or silk ruffs, breeches, or hose imported from France or Italy, and any "D[o]ublet or Jerkin of Blew, greene, Redd, white, or other lite colour or layd with lacegard, welt or Cutt or Pinched except he weare a cote with the sleeves on." When out of the university, every graduate or college scholar was obliged to wear a black hat, no matter how stylish. Exempt from all of these strictures were "Lords and knights Sones and the Heires of Esquires not being Graduats."[56] These young scions constituted some of the increase in upper-class students whose fathers sought to prepare them for leadership in an age of changing roles and heightened expectations.[57] While the gentry increasingly recognized a measure of academical learning and the ease of making lasting connections with social peers as good reasons to attend a university, if not to proceed to a degree, the universities did nothing to impair the English class system or to erase the sartorial signage that sustained it.

Elizabeth's chancellors found other signs of "disorder" in their respective universities. In 1584 Leicester initiated a statute to remedy a number of sins of commission and omission "as lat[e]ly have bin

56 Strickland Gibson, ed., *Statuta Antiqua Universitatis Oxoniensis* (Oxford: Clarendon Press, 1931), 403–405; also Sylvester, *Educational Documents*, 150–51. Two years later, a Cambridge decree, showing the hand of Chancellor Burghley, complained that the college heads allowed "sundry . . . children of gentlemen and men of wealth . . . to use very costly and disguised [i.e., nonacademic] manner of apparel . . . unseemly for students in any kind of human[e] learning," which set a poor example for other students less well funded and entitled. Yet there, too, the young aristocrats were allowed to dress more stylishly and colorfully "so the same be not excessive." In 1602 Cambridge's new chancellor (Burghley's son, Robert) complained that scholars still affected "silks and velvets, liker to courtiers than scholars," a sure sign of disorder "tending to the decay of learning, and other dissolute behavior." Charles Henry Cooper, *Annals of Cambridge*, 4 vols. (Cambridge: Warwick, 1842–53), 2: 360–61, 616.

57 O'Day, *Education and Society*, 88–97; Felicity Heal and Clive Holmes, *The Gentry in England and Wales, 1500–1700* (Stanford, Calif.: Stanford University Press, 1994), 261–70; Patrick Wallis and Cliff Webb, "The Education and Training of Gentry Sons in Early Modern England," *Social History* 36:1 (Feb. 2011), 36–53; Mark H. Curtis, *Oxford and Cambridge in Transition, 1558–1642* (Oxford: Clarendon Press, 1959), chs. 3–4. See McConica, "Elizabethan Oxford," *HUO* 3: 666n1 for the historiography of this trend.

complained of by her Majestie." The worst fault was excessive use of graces to shorten the path to degrees, such as skipping certain obligatory lecture courses and "cursory" (afternoon) lectures by candidates for higher degrees. As usual, the letter of the law did not apply to the sons of kings, earls, knights, and members of the House of Lords. But even ministers and deacons were not exempt from the prohibition on "pla[y]inge at football," quarreling, or brandishing a weapon.[58] Offending clergymen were to be banished and any scholars over eighteen fined and jailed in the Bocardo. Athletes or scrappers under eighteen risked "open punishment" (whipping) in St. Mary's Church. Stage plays in the town were also discouraged to reduce the danger of crowds during the plague, unnecessary expense, and the "many lewde and evil sportes as in them are practiced." But Leicester added a personal note to approve the "learned" study and performance of comedies and tragedies as part of the undergraduate curriculum.[59]

Another form of student "sport" earned censure at both Oxford and Cambridge. In a burlesque of academic exercises, freshmen were hazed in their college halls by seniors who conducted various "exams." A poor performance earned the newcomer a draught of salted beer and perhaps a "tuck," a thumbnail cut or abrasion from chin to upper lip. A solemn end of the ceremony might have the initiate kissing an old shoe after taking an oath of loyalty to it. In 1618 Simonds D'Ewes, an upper-crust freshman at St. John's College, Cambridge, paid 3 s. and 4 p. for either the dubious privilege of being "salted" or exemption from it.[60]

58 Football was frowned upon at Cambridge as well. In the spring of 1620, the St. John's College student Simonds D'Ewes broke his shin in a rough game with Trinity on Trinity Green (now Trinity's Neville Court). On a field behind Queens' he observed "some hot foot-ball playing," though it was prohibited by authorities as hurtful and unbecoming gentlemen-scholars. Marsden, *College Life* , 94–95.

59 Gibson, *Statuta Antiqua Universitatis Oxoniensis*, 431–34; also Sylvester, *Educational Documents*, 151–53. On discipline in the colleges, see Lawrence Stone, "Social Control and Intellectual Excellence: Oxbridge and Edinburgh, 1560–1983," in Nicholas Phillipson, ed., *Universities, Society, and the Future: A Conference Held on the 400th Anniversary of the University of Edinburgh, 1983* (Edinburgh: University of Edinburgh Press, 1983), 3–30, at 6–13.

60 Marsden, *College Life*, 14–15; Rashdall, *Universities of Europe*, 3:385n1.

The most consequential reforms were inscribed in the Cambridge statutes of 1570 and applied by Parliament to both universities the following year. The statutes' main thrust was to concentrate power and responsibility in the hands of "a small group of identifiable men who could be held answerable" to Elizabeth's top-down government.[61] Abetted by gradual changes in practice, the new rules augmented the authority of the college heads within the university and the heads within their individual colleges. Until the government reforms of the mid-nineteenth century, Oxford and Cambridge continued to be governed by cliques of college heads and vice-chancellors chosen invariably from the college heads. The cliques assumed the power of nomination to most university and college offices, dominated the judicial processes, and set the agendas for the weakened faculty senates, which were now required to vote in open, not secret, ballots. Given the enhanced power of college heads to approve higher degrees, profitable offices, and future preferments, the young dons understandably protested—without success—that "this opening of voices enforces men, agaynste their o[a]thes and mynde, to give their voices according to their master's request or commandment, for feare of his heavie indignation." In their crown-inspired campaign to reduce the "ruling of inordinate youth," the greyer college heads had clearly won.[62]

Disenfranchised were the regent and nonregent fellows, the dons who were proliferating in response to the advent of new and enlarged colleges and the noticeable growth in undergraduate enrollments. Most of these new professors were recent M.A.s, whose degree obligated them to serve as college tutors for specified periods: one or two years at Oxford, five at Cambridge, which experienced the more robust growth before 1600.[63] The colleges and their tutors

61 Morgan, *1546–1750*, *HUC* 2:76, 78.

62 Ibid., *HUC* 2: ch. 3, at 66, 82–83. Oxford college heads were variously titled *master*, *provost*, *president*, *principal*, *rector*, *warden*, or *dean*, but the great majority of Cambridge heads were known as *master*; one *president* and one *provost* made up the roster. No one has satisfactorily explained why Oxford was so profligate with titles.

63 Cambridge counted 1,630 collegians in 1569, nearly 2,000 in 1597. In 1583 Cambridge produced 277 B.A.s compared to Oxford's 157. Between 1564 and 1573, Cambridge college fellows grew by one-third, to 320. Thompson, "Universities in Tudor England," 341, 361, 363–64. See also Lawrence Stone, "The Size and Composition

assumed ever-greater responsibility for undergraduate discipline: for ensuring attendance at lectures and exercises, religious uniformity, and personal behavior.

Every college had tutors who supplemented (and sometimes supplanted) university lecturers with in-house lectures in "the tongues" and "liberal [arts and] sciences." Tutors adjusted the statutory curriculum to each student's social class and likely future calling by including more up-to-date subjects and personalized reading lists. They conducted classes and exercises in the college hall or chapel and review and practice sessions in their own rooms. Both formats, testified Archbishop Matthew Parker, a former head of Corpus Christi, Cambridge, "trained up youth privately" for the public battles of disputation in the university "schools" (classrooms and performance halls). In addition, tutors often prayed daily with their students and accompanied them to Sunday chapel. They controlled their finances—allowances having been put in their hands by prudent parents—by seeing that college and university fees and tradesmen's bills were paid and entertainments kept to modest proportions. Some of the most conscientious tutors accompanied their tutees to and from their homes and pled their causes with stern or clueless paterfamiliae. And, as best they could, they guarded their young charges' virtue by enforcing college curfews and firm rules against "night walking," inebriation, fornication, and especially bringing young women into the college.[64]

❁ ❁ ❁

Although the changing demography of Oxbridge students expanded the duties of college fellows, it largely confirmed the universities' place

of the Oxford Student Body, 1580–1909," in Stone, ed., *Oxford and Cambridge from the 14th to the Early 19th Century*, vol. 1 of *The University in Society*, ed. Stone, 2 vols. (Princeton, N.J.: Princeton University Press, 1974), 91 (table 1A) for the most recent figures.

64 Kenneth Charlton, *Education in Renaissance England* (London: Routledge & Kegan Paul, 1965), ch. 5; O'Day, *Education and Society*, ch. 6; Morgan, *1546–1750*, *HUC* 2: ch. 9; Curtis, *Oxford and Cambridge in Transition*, chs. 4–5, at 104.

in English society. The lack of consistent matriculation registers (only semi-complete after 1580) makes generalizations about student populations and especially their social origins difficult. But the registers that do exist, combined with detailed studies of select college registers at both universities, have established several trends. Overall, after 1560, both universities grew appreciably, almost in lockstep, before slowing late in the century and accelerating again in the first three decades of the next.[65] Contrary to earlier studies that overemphasized the influx of sons of gentlemen and aristocrats at the *expense* of the "plebeian" class, the social make-up of the universities remained much the same as they grew in numbers, reflecting the sturdy class hierarchy of the nation and patterns of preparatory schooling. Part of the Tudor and early Stuart emphasis on academic "order" did less to promote social mobility than to maintain familiar social ranks, though each with more learning. After Queen Elizabeth allowed the clergy to marry, many of their male offspring sought university degrees for what they hoped would be ascendant church careers. At the same time, gentlemen and aristocrats were increasingly persuaded, partly by humanist educators such as Roger Ascham and Richard Mulcaster, that some university book learning would better prepare their sons for either common-law studies at the Inns of Court in London or leadership positions in their home counties as lords lieutenant, deputy lords, justices of the peace, and members of Parliament.[66]

Despite the numerical increase in clerical and elite sons, their proportions remained largely the same and behind the growing numbers and steady proportion of plebeian students, who came from families of modest wealth and needed either college scholarships or the sponsorship of wealthier patrons to attend. Between 1560 and 1640, 500 new scholarships for the deserving poor were endowed at Oxbridge colleges.[67] These enabled plebeian students to continue to

65 Stone, "Educational Revolution in England," 51 (table 2); Stone, "Oxford Student Body," 6, 16–17, 91 (table 1A), 92 (table 1B).

66 Curtis, *Oxford and Cambridge in Transition*, ch. 3; O'Day, *Education and Society*, 88–97; Charlton, *Education in Renaissance England*, ch. 3; Joan Simon, *Education and Society in Tudor England* (Cambridge: Cambridge University Press, 1966), ch. 14; Wallis and Webb, "Education and Training of Gentry Sons."

67 W. K. Jordan, *Philanthropy in England, 1480–1660: A Study of the Changing Pattern of English Social Aspirations* (New York: Russell Sage Foundation, 1959), 294.

constitute about half of the undergraduate bodies and to equal if not exceed the ranks of elite sons.[68] In fact, the increase in elite sons, particularly those titled "fellow-commoners," augmented the opportunities for plebeian attendance because they—like college fellows—hired needy students to perform personal services in termtime.

Fellow-commoners had been admitted to a few Oxbridge colleges since the fourteenth century, but their numbers, never large, increased steadily throughout the Tudor and early Stuart periods. Early on, fellow-commoners were graduate theologians or lawyers who paid for a college room and dining privileges while pursuing higher degrees. They were not fellows on the foundation nor did they teach; they were paying guests who helped the colleges meet their narrow budgets. By the sixteenth century, however, they were largely the sons of aristocrats in pursuit of a year or two of undergraduate study. They earned their name by taking their meals and associating with the college masters and senior fellows at "high table," which featured high-backed chairs, stood at the head of the dining hall, and was raised a step or two so as to look down upon the long tables and benches of the undergraduates. Sons of the highest rank roomed either in the master's lodge or in the best (i.e., driest) upper-story rooms in the first quadrangle, thereby moving the less exalted, foundation scholars into jerry-rigged outbuildings or newly dormered cocklofts in former attic spaces. When the fellow-commoners left the university, they were expected to tip the college staff handsomely and to donate a pricey piece of silver plate or a silver tankard to the college collection, much of which is still in service.[69]

From the moment they arrived, fellow-commoners were set apart from their social inferiors. They wore costly and richly decorated gowns to meals, class, and exercises. They paid the highest matriculation, tuition, room, board, and (if they persisted, which they seldom did) graduation fees. If they were not accompanied by a personal servant from home, they quickly acquired the services

68 Stone, "Oxford Student Body," 93 (table 2); James McConica, "Scholars and Commoners in Renaissance Oxford," in Stone, *University in Society*, 1: ch. 3, at 168 (table 8) and 170 (table 10).

69 Morgan, *1546–1750*, *HUC* 2:27, 120, 214, 309–10, 316–20; Aylmer, "Economics and Finances," *HUO* 3:548–49, 630, 632.

of a fellow student in need of financial aid, sometimes a young lad known from their own parish or neighborhood.[70] "Sizars" at Cambridge and "battelers" at Oxford did a variety of personal services for their commoners. Thomas Manning, Simonds D'Ewes's "subsizar" in St. John's, Cambridge, at a minimum called him to chapel, kept him on time for classes and other obligations, and carried messages between colleges and letters into town. Although the clergyman's son suffered little more degradation than any work-study student does today, he apparently was not befriended, even though his quick thinking may have saved D'Ewes's life after he sustained an early morning head injury while ringing the college bell. As D'Ewes reminded his younger brother at St. Catherine's College across town, "You are maintained with the best of your rank, dishonorate not your self by your unseemly associating with pensioners [paying students of lesser wealth] and subsizars though of other colleges."[71]

Colleges and tutors created a brisk demand for fellow-commoners as the sixteenth century proceeded and especially under the early Stuarts. Tutors were paid handsomely for their instruction and oversight to augment meager fellowship stipends. They also sought the sheer prestige of having high-status students; some dons—and college heads—were notorious collectors of such. John Preston, a fellow of Queen's College, Oxford, and later master of Emmanuel, Cambridge, was known as "the greatest pupil-monger in England" for his aggressive recruitment of fellow-commoners. In one year alone, he added sixteen to his elite stable and table.[72] Later, in 1627 and 1631, Queen's was proud of having snagged Henry Coventry, the second of the royal lord keeper's sons, while Christ Church and Trinity got

70 In 1602 Cambridge decreed that sizars had to be matriculated students and not imports from home. Morgan, *1546–1750*, *HUC* 2:141, 229–30, 329–30.

71 O'Day, *Education and Society*, 90–91; Marsden, *College Life*, 56–58. D'Ewes's counsel was consonant with Henry Peachem's advice to the "complete gentleman" who attended university: "For the companions of your recreation, consort yourself with gentlemen of your own rank and quality. . . . To be over-free and familiar with inferiors argues a baseness of spirit, and begetteth contempt." Henry Peachem, *The Complete Gentleman* [1622], ed. Virgil B. Heltzel (Ithaca, N.Y.: Cornell University Press for the Folger Shakespeare Library, 1962), 51.

72 Morgan, *1546–1750*, *HUC* 2:261n15, 325, 329, 331; O'Day, *Education and Society*, 91–94, at 92.

scions of only a mere knight and a judge respectively. Yet in 1612, Queen's already had 184 commoners of various ranks.[73]

Perhaps the tutors' biggest reason for recruiting high-born students was anticipated patronage from their fathers, which they hoped would elevate them from the spare rigors of college teaching to cushier preferments in the church, court, or government. Supervising aristocratic youths was no easy task. Since they usually came for only a year or two, they frequently failed to matriculate and, much more often, to graduate. It was therefore necessary to adjust the statutory curriculum to accommodate their less scholastic interests and brief tenure. Because most were "to the manor born," high-spirited, on average two years younger than their plebeian classmates, used to ordering servants around, and their fathers were paying plenty to their latest pedagogues, discipline was a frequent problem. Commoners in general and fellow-commoners in particular had reputations among university officials and observers for "ruffling and roistering," excessive imported dress, immodestly long hair (sometimes compared to that of American "savages" and "wild Irish"), and keeping "riotous company" in taverns and other "bawdy" houses. In 1577 William Harrison jibed that "most of them study little other than histories [tales, romances], tables, dice, and trifles." Ten years later, the Cambridge chancellor, Burghley, complained that the rich heirs, "corrupt with liberty and remissness," were poorly governed because the tutor, beneficiary of a handsome stipend, was "more afraid to displease his pupil through the desire of great gain . . . than the pupil is of his tutor." Exempt by rank from corporal punishment or deprivation of "commons" (food and drink), aristocratic malefactors were equally unmoved by fines. Locked gates and high walls were no match for determined fun seekers, particularly those with female company on their minds. Officials were especially alarmed by elite students who became engaged to or secretly married lower-class town girls.[74]

73 Boas, *Diary of Thomas Crosfield*, 13, 52–53; Charlton, *Education in Renaissance England*, 136.

74 Harrison, *Description of England*, 71; Boas, *Diary of Thomas Crosfield*, 52, 61, 64 (long hair); Morgan, *1546–1750*, *HUC* 2:318–20. Cash-strapped St. John's College, Oxford (1557), much indebted to commoners for revenue and endowment, found to its dismay in the 1580s that they would not "abide chastisement." Unfortunately, the

❁ ❁ ❁

The studies pursued by all of these young elite and plebeian scholars were still scholastic legacies from the late Middle Ages, which in turn were the offspring of the Seven Liberal Arts—the trivium and quadrivium—of the late Roman empire. But several shifts in scheduling and emphasis were made by the two universities, largely in lockstep, during the sixteenth century. The first shift was to make the universities predominantly undergraduate institutions of the arts and sciences. Beginning with the abolition of canon law in 1535 and the loss of the older student population of monks and friars, advanced (or what we would call graduate) studies were allowed to atrophy as undergraduate numbers climbed during Elizabeth's reign.

Degrees in medicine and civil law, never numerous, declined noticeably. Despite the addition of a regius chair of medicine at each university in the 1540s, the medical curriculum was so conservative and out of date that many students chose, or were advised, to study abroad, at Padua, Leiden, Bologna, Paris, and later Montpellier. Future lawyers also sought training on the continent or, more frequently, at the Inns of Court in London, which specialized in common law. The advent of regius professorships in civil law produced only a handful of graduates annually. After the M.A., the B.D. (Bachelor of Divinity) remained the most popular advanced degree, partly because the great majority of college fellowships were reserved for divinity students. Divinity held its own also by shifting its emphasis from scholastic speculation and theological "wrangling" to Protestant attention to scripture, preaching, and practical piety.[75]

---

college still had at least 30, down from 57 a decade earlier. McConica, "Rise of the Undergraduate College," *HUO* 3:47; McConica, "Elizabethan Oxford," *HUO* 3:663–65.

75 Curtis, *Oxford and Cambridge in Transition*, chs. 6–7, esp. 150; Gilliam Lewis, "The Faculty of Medicine," *HUO* 3: ch. 4.2; John Barton, "The Faculty of Law," *HUO* 3: ch. 4.3; S. L. Greenslade, "The Faculty of Theology," *HUO* 3: ch. 4.4; Robert G. Frank, Jr., "Medicine," *HUO* 4: ch. 8, esp. 514 (table 8.1); Brian P. Levack, "Law," *HUO* 4: ch. 9; Simon, *Education and Society in Tudor England*, chs. 7, 10, at 206, 245, 250–51 (monks), 207n3 (foreign study). The Chantries Act of 1546 also freed many college fellows from praying for founders' and donors' souls, which time they could now devote to secularized undergraduate teaching.

As Oxbridge became increasingly focused on undergraduates, the nonvocational B.A. became an end in itself for the majority of students. But to accommodate a broader range of student seriousness and future careers, the universities made several adjustments in their curricula, less through statutory decree than in pedagogical practice. University statutes rarely mandated specific authors or books, although it was assumed, and occasionally stated, that Aristotle would remain the foundation of the academic edifice. At Tudor Oxbridge, college tutors, lecturers, and catechists assumed larger roles in the choice of readings and teaching styles. Students were still expected to attend the statutory university lectures, but attendance at even these fell off as more familiar college lecturers covered the same ground closer to home. University lecturers who ended up giving "wall lectures" to few or no auditors were only too happy to pay a few shillings for permission to forgo their duties.[76]

As the B.A. became the universities' focus, they sought to ensure that the curriculum continued to provide a conspectus of the seven liberal arts and to direct their pedagogical attention toward the undergraduates. These emphases were particularly important because early in the Tudor period the four-year B.A. curriculum could too easily be truncated to a little over three years through the granting of "graces" for partial residence in the summer and Easter terms. By the same token, the M.A., the degree required for university teaching, became largely a product of advanced self-study in the subjects introduced in the undergraduate years. However divided, the B.A. (which returned to a four-year degree under Elizabeth) and the M.A. required a total of seven years and entailed a thorough immersion in the traditional arts and sciences.[77]

The ascendancy of humanist approaches to the arts curriculum, particularly the all-important trivium (grammar, logic, and rhetoric),

76 Curtis, *Oxford and Cambridge in Transition*, 92n30 (wall lectures); Damien Riehl Leader, "Teaching in Tudor Cambridge," *History of Education* 13:2 (June 1984), 105–19, at 112–19; Leader, *University to 1546*, *HUC* 1:242–63; Morgan, *1546–1750*, *HUC* 2: ch. 9, 185–96.

77 Curtis, *Oxford and Cambridge in Transition*, 124–25; Fletcher, "Faculty of Arts," *HUO* 3:165; Mordechai Feingold, "The Humanities," *HUO* 4:258.

led to several key shifts in the student experience. These approaches were northern adaptations of Renaissance goals and skills pursued largely in Italian schools, universities, and ducal and papal chanceries in the fourteenth and fifteenth centuries. One priority was to locate and concentrate on the best available texts of classical authors, Latin and Greek, rather than medieval commentators and glosses: the battle cry was "*ad fontes*" (back "to the sources"). Another goal was to broaden classical studies by establishing the texts' cultural and historical contexts so as to better plumb their full meaning and moral import. A third aim was to seek out the best—the clearest and most eloquent—classical stylists for close study and emulation. These authors were to be presented in critical editions printed in the new roman and italic type fonts that mimicked the cursive economy and fluidity of the best chancery scripts.[78]

In the second decade of the sixteenth century, humanists pushed hard to include the study of Greek in the Oxbridge curricula. Erasmus led the charge from Queens' College, Cambridge, where he taught Greek and divinity and wrote a number of best-selling pedagogical guides between 1511 and 1514.[79] The humanists' major argument for Greek was that the New Testament, as well as the most reliable, often newly recovered, texts of the Attic classics (including Aristotle), were written in Greek. In order to reconcile the "pagan" and Christian features of the university curriculum, they argued, a mastery of Greek was required. Well before regius chairs in the subject were funded in the 1540s, lectureships and tutors were installed

78 Paul O. Kristeller, "Humanism and Scholasticism in Renaissance Italy," in *Studies in Renaissance Thought and Letters* (Rome: Edizioni di Storia e Letteratura, 1956), 553–83; Anthony Grafton, Glenn W. Most, and Salvatore Settis, eds., *The Classical Tradition* (Cambridge, Mass.: Belknap Press of Harvard University Press, 2010), 462–67; Antonia McLean, *Humanism and the Rise of Science in Tudor England* (New York: Neale Watson Academic Publishers, 1972), ch. 2; James Kelsey McConica, *English Humanists and Reformation Politics under Henry VIII and Edward VI* (Oxford: Clarendon Press, 1965), esp. ch. 4; Simon, *Education and Society in Tudor England*, 60, 70 (*ad fontes*).

79 Erika Rummel, "Erasmus and the Greek Classics," in Elaine Fantham and Erika Rummel, eds., *Literary and Educational Writings*, vol. 29 of *Collected Works of Erasmus* (Toronto: University of Toronto Press, 1989), xxi-xxxiii.

in a number of colleges.[80] The first lectureship may have been launched in Corpus Christi, Oxford, in 1517. But thanks to Erasmus and several crusading successors, Cambridge became better known for promoting the study of the language and its literature. When Cuthbert Tunstall, the bishop of London, gave his alma mater an important collection of classical and neoclassical Greek texts in 1529, the university replied that it was "as though he had transported Athens itself to Cambridge." In mid-Tudor Cambridge, the second-most frequently owned books on student shelves were Greek grammars, accompanied often by Greek dictionaries.[81]

Although Oxford had as many champions of Greek as did Cambridge, Oxford's "Trojans" got in hot water with Thomas More, its chief legal officer, and with King Henry for denigrating Cambridge's and their own "Grecians." From his new outpost on the continent, Erasmus reported to a friend in 1518 that although Greek literature was taught well in both English universities, at Cambridge it was taught "tranquilly" because at Oxford "a barbarous preacher in a public [Lenten] sermon began to rage against Greek [and eventually all liberal] learning in great and violent abuse. But the King, who was in the neighborhood," having heard about the incident from More, "gave orders that those wishing and approving it should embrace Greek letters." More followed up with a long scolding letter to the Oxford community, aimed particularly at a coterie of teaching faculty who took Trojan names to "pour ridicule on those devoted to the study of Greek." To those like the hidebound preacher who argued that only theology should be studied,

80 Henry's injunctions of 1535 enjoined all Oxbridge colleges to provide daily lectures, one in Latin, the other in Greek. Leedham-Green, *Concise History of Cambridge*, 37.

81 *Erasmus and Cambridge*, ed. H. C. Porter, trans. D.F.S. Thomson (Toronto: University of Toronto Press, 1963), 200–201; Leader, *University to 1546*, *HUC* 1:291–301, at 300 (quotation); J.C.T. Oates, *Cambridge University Library: A History, From the Beginnings to the Copyright Act of Queen Anne* (Cambridge: Cambridge University Press, 1986), 60–67 (Tunstall's benefactions); Lisa Jardine, "Humanism and the Sixteenth Century Cambridge Arts Course," *History of Education* 4:1 (1975), 17; Jefferson Looney, "Undergraduate Education at Early Stuart Cambridge," *History of Education* 10:1 (March 1981), 9–19, at 12 (table 1), 14 (table 3).

he retorted that the humanistic disciplines and ancient languages were the best paths to divinity and to "train the soul in virtue," citing the writings of the Church Fathers, the majority of Roman philosophers, and the authors and best scholars of the New Testament. To call students and teachers of Greek "heretics" and "devils" was only to substantiate Erasmus's famous indictment of academic Folly. "The study of Greek is tried and true," More concluded his reprimand in no uncertain terms.[82]

Humanism infiltrated the Oxbridge curricula in other ways as well. In reaction to what many humanist educators regarded as the dry, impractical, technical, and sophistical hairsplitting of medieval scholasticism, they urged the English universities to subordinate the study of formal syllogistic logic, or "dialectic," which had dominated the medieval curriculum, to newer brands of grammar and especially rhetoric. Humanistic grammar was speculative and more descriptive of how languages, including vernaculars, actually worked in common (literate) thought and speech.[83] And instead of being geared to producing verbal warriors for university disputations, humanistic rhetoric sought to use "natural" language, eloquent speech, and diverse arts of persuasion to improve "discourses" of every kind. But rhetoric could not be separated from logic because the content and reasonableness of propositions were as important as their form and style. Nor could logic do without rhetoric, because logic lacked its own matter or content. But to gain acceptance, logic had to change from a prescriptive and deductive "science" to a more discourse-friendly art. This major change was effected in the dialectic handbooks of early sixteenth-century humanists such as Rudolph

82 Leader, *University to 1546*, *HUC* 1:299–300; *St. Thomas More: Selected Letters*, ed. Elizabeth Frances Rogers (New Haven, Conn.: Yale University Press, 1961), 94–103 (March 29, 1518). More referred to Erasmus's *In Praise of Folly*, written in 1509 at More's country estate with his witty assistance. The Latin title was *Moriae encomium*, a play on his friend's name.

83 Grammar (typically Latin) was largely dropped from Tudor university curricula in the 1530s because it was increasingly taught in schools and knowledge of it was effectively the basic requirement for university admission. Jardine, "Sixteenth Century Cambridge Arts Course," 18–19; Feingold, "Humanities," *HUO* 4:243–44.

Agricola (1515), Philip Melanchthon (1527), Peter Ramus (1543), and the Cambridge don John Seton (1545).[84]

Despite the salutary shift toward rhetoric, logic in new incarnations retained its powerful hold on the Oxbridge curricula. Symptomatically, five of the first nine lectureships established in the humanist stronghold of Trinity College, Cambridge (est. 1546), were in dialectic. None was in rhetoric per se because dialectic was assumed by this time to include rhetoric. Two of the remaining four were in Greek and Latin literature, which addressed the rhetorical qualities of such humanist favorites as Cicero, Ovid, Virgil, and Terence. Between 1535 and 1590 (and well beyond), the "most studied" books at Oxbridge were dialectic manuals, many of them written by contemporary authors of rhetoric manuals. College tutors invariably assigned the challenging Latin texts of Bartholomew Keckermann, Franco Burgersdijk, and Robert Sanderson, to which they personally added more familiar explanations and illustrations. They often gave their charges their own manuscript compendia to copy for easier digestion.[85] No matter how brief or accessible the manuals became, logic remained an object of student animosity and satire. One "Jovial Philosopher" at early seventeenth-century Cambridge urged his fellow sufferers to

> Hang Brirewood and Carter, in Crakenthorps garter,
> Let Keckerman too bemoan us,
> I'll be no more beaten for greasy Jack Seaton
> Or conning of Sandersonus.[86]

84 The Elizabethan statutes of 1570, which otherwise removed the Marian statutes and replaced them with Edward's, allowed Cambridge to replace mathematics with rhetoric as the major first-year subject. The only texts mentioned (not mandated) were Cicero and Quintilian, which left the choice of texts in the hands of college tutors. James Bass Mullinger, *The University of Cambridge: From the Royal Injunctions of 1535 to the Accession of Charles the First*, 2 vols. (Cambridge: Cambridge University Press, 1884), 2:403.

85 Jardine, "The Place of Dialectic Teaching in Sixteenth-Century Cambridge," *Studies in the Renaissance* 21 (1974), 31–62, at 44–45, 46–49; Jardine, "Sixteenth Century Cambridge Arts Course"; Feingold, "Humanities," *HUO* 4:295–97.

86 Thomas Randolph, *Aristippus, or the Jovial Philosopher* (London, 1631), 21, quoted in Curtis, *Oxford and Cambridge in Transition*, 100 and explained 284 (note F). See also Feingold, "Humanities," *HUO* 4:287–89.

The look-alike Oxbridge curricula constituted an "eclectic culture" compounded of old and new, scholasticism and humanism, but was still encyclopedic in its ambitions.[87] Aristotle remained the bedrock because he was comprehensive and convincing. He covered so many vital subjects systematically, with such earned authority as "The Philosopher," that no one until Descartes, Newton, and their fellow avatars of the New Science could rival his cultural hegemony. Humanist scholars weeded out spurious Aristotelian titles, re-edited and re-translated the rest after collating the oldest and most reliable texts, and by the seventeenth century focused their teaching on the Greek texts with suitable commentaries for new times. They downgraded the study of metaphysics in general, including Aristotle's, and elevated his moral and political philosophy in their search for pagan virtue and justice to complement Christian values. They also dropped his physics and astronomy from the curriculum because these had been superseded by the recent discoveries of Tycho Brahe, Copernicus, Kepler, and Galileo.[88] Aristotle continued to be read in college tutorials and explicated in university lectures, but faculty were no longer afraid to disagree with him. Students also ensured his relevance by openly exploring his propositions in disputations, pro and con, in light of the latest discoveries and theories. Despite its flaws in certain areas, the Aristotelian system endured throughout much of the seventeenth century to challenge all comers and new student generations.[89]

87 James McConica, "Humanism and Aristotle in Tudor Oxford," *English Historical Review* 94:371 (April 1979), 291–317, at 296, 310.

88 This did not prevent his general framework from dominating seventeenth-century textbooks in natural philosophy. These theoretical, teleological, nonmathematical, nonpractical texts, which valued "reason" over "experience," did little to promote the new observational and experimental sciences that would prove revolutionary later in the century. Patricia Reif, "The Textbook Tradition in Natural Philosophy, 1600–1650," *Journal of the History of Ideas* 30:1 (Jan.–Mar. 1969), 17–32.

89 Charles B. Schmitt, "Philosophy and Science in Sixteenth-Century Universities: Some Preliminary Comments," in *The Cultural Context of Medieval Learning*, ed. J. E. Murdoch and E. D. Sylla (Dordrecht and London: D. Reidel, 1975), 485–530, at 489–91; Mordechai Feingold, "The Mathematical Sciences and New Philosophies," *HUO* 4:389–404.

❋ ❋ ❋

If Aristotle represented curricular traditionalism, the tutorial fashioning of courses to serve the influx of nongraduating elite students and the establishment of numerous professorships and lectureships in new academic fields spoke for the universities' ability to change. In the 1540s Henry created a regius chair at each university in Hebrew as well as Greek. Chancellor Laud gave Oxford a chair in Arabic in 1636, four years after Cambridge got one. Sir Henry Savile endowed Oxford chairs in geometry and astronomy in 1619. Three years later the renowned historian William Camden established a chair in his specialty at Oxford, with an emphasis on ancient civil rather than medieval ecclesiastical history. When Lord Brooke founded a chair of history at Cambridge in 1628, he sought a man who not only knew but had published in Greek and Latin cosmography and chronology, preferably knew some modern languages through travel abroad, and had some experience in public affairs.[90] Unhappily, the Duke of Buckingham, Cambridge's unpopular chancellor, managed with support from Oxford's Laud to suppress Brooke's lectureship to prevent the drawing of analogies from classical history that might be unfavorable to the political status quo. Although history was widely regarded as "philosophy teaching by example," critics sought to restrict its study to older students out of concern for the "wrong" lessons that immature students might draw from readings on tyranny, resistance, and regicide.[91]

Unfortunately, the founding of most of these chairs coincided with the decline in attendance at the large university lectures, which had been losing audience share for some time to college lecturers and tutors, most of whom provided better lessons and syllabi tailored to their various students. In the sixteenth as well as the seventeenth century, Oxbridge students, particularly those not aiming at clerical careers, were avid consumers of ancient and modern histories and

90 Mordechai Feingold, "Oriental Studies," *HUO* 4:488 and n122; Curtis, *Oxford and Cambridge in Transition*, 101–102; Mullinger, *University of Cambridge*, 2:420–21n5.

91 Leedham-Green, *Concise History of Cambridge*, 70; Feingold, "Humanities," *HUO* 4:331, 334–35.

books in political theory, affairs of state, geography, and travel. In addition to Caesar's *Commentaries* and Plutarch's *Lives*, Tudor students gravitated to such books as Guicciardini's *History of Italy*, Camden's *Britannia*, Bodin's *De republica*, Machiavelli's *The Prince*, and More's *Utopia*. *A Mirror for Magistrates*, English legal statutes, and handbooks for justices of the peace were also popular with future country squires and city jurists. Between 1613 and 1638, 13 percent of the nearly 1,000 titles bought by nonclerical students at Christ's College, Cambridge, were historical in nature. Another 5 percent were books on geography, cosmography, and travel.[92] In concert with the student desire to travel and perhaps to be employed on diplomatic missions for the crown, French and Italian (rarely Spanish or German) grammars, dictionaries, and literature—in the vernacular and translation—found room on undergraduate shelves. Private tutors more frequently than college tutors gave lessons to the young gentlemen who also sought instruction in fencing, dancing, and horsemanship.[93]

The final shift in the Oxbridge curriculum was a concerted effort to revamp an old subject—mathematics—in order to improve students' receptivity to and readiness for the emerging world of physical science. Surprisingly, early Tudor humanists such as Erasmus and Thomas More were among the strongest supporters of the quadrivium (arithmetic, geometry, astronomy, and music) and sought to raise it from the curricular shadows, particularly for the M.A. In 1500 Cambridge added a university lecture in mathematics to those already available in humanities, logic, and philosophy. In an effort to reduce the excessive amounts of Aristotle being imposed on the bachelors, the lecturer was required to treat arithmetic and music (harmonics being mathematically based) in the first master's year, geometry and perspective in the second, and astronomy in the third. Student fees paid the lecturer, but an endowment from the late Sir Robert Rede in 1524 improved the professor's social and economic position.[94]

92 Curtis, *Oxford and Cambridge in Transition*, 102–105; Jardine, "Sixteenth Century Cambridge Arts Course," 16–17; Mark H. Curtis, "Library Catalogues and Tudor Oxford and Cambridge," *Studies in the Renaissance* 5 (1958), 111–20, at 113–14; Looney, "Undergraduate Education," 12 (table 1).

93 Feingold, "Humanities," *HUO* 4:269–76.

94 Paul Lawrence Rose, "Erasmians and Mathematicians at Cambridge in the Early Sixteenth Century," *Sixteenth Century Journal* 8 Supplement (July 1977), 47–59.

The Edwardian statutes of 1549 moved the whole quadrivium to the first undergraduate year. The M.A. curriculum still featured perspective and astronomy. Most of the texts remained medieval standbys—Pliny, Strabo, Euclid, Ptolemy—but new texts in arithmetic by Cuthbert Tunstall—the first arithmetical book printed in England (1522)—and others reflected the influence of leading mid-century humanists, such as Sir John Cheke, regius professor of Greek, and Sir Thomas Smith, professor of civil law and vice-chancellor. The leading humanist colleges, St. John's and Queens', early supported plural lecturers in mathematics: Queens' had two, St. John's, four. Other colleges caught the math fever. When the Edwardian statutes were passed in 1549, freshmen were required to spend their first six or seven months on arithmetic and geometry. The requirement was not superfluous, because grammar schools seldom taught even arithmetic, and when they did, the numerals used were clumsy Roman ones. The first challenge of college arithmetic teachers, therefore, was to introduce their classes to the "new" Arabic numbers (with the indispensable zero) in order to proceed to calculations as simple as addition and subtraction. The second was to move them forward enough in geometry—beyond Euclid and Johannes de Sacrobosco—to appreciate and calculate the newly discovered elliptical, rather than spherical, orbits the planets made around the fixed Copernican sun.[95]

These were the tasks initially of the university lecturers who chose to teach mathematics as part of their post–M.A. regent duties. During Elizabeth's reign, Henry Savile at Oxford and Henry Briggs at Cambridge, both accomplished humanists who regarded math as *one* of the humanities, forged a path for numerous college lecturers. When Savile endowed his chair in geometry in 1619, it was Briggs who was persuaded to return from his professorship at Gresham College in London to take it.[96]

95 Ibid.

96 Gresham College was established in 1597 to teach practical math and science—in English—to sailors, workingmen, and others for whom the universities' esoteric "quibbling" in an ancient tongue was suspect. It also fostered and popularized research. Like Briggs, its professors regularly accepted calls to university chairs and fellowships. McLean, *Humanism and the Rise of Science*, 165–67; Robert Goulding, "Humanism and Science in the Elizabethan Universities," in *Reassessing Tudor*

At both universities, mathematics was taught largely at an introductory level, whether to undergraduates or bachelors, but it was taught. Oxford's new statutes of 1564 mandated three terms of arithmetic, without specifying just when they should be offered. From 1570, Cambridge required applicants to possess an aptitude for math (as well as logic) and would not graduate a B.A. without some math study. Math and new discoveries in the sciences were frequent topics for disputations in the colleges and public exercises. Chancellor Laud, a devotee of the traditional humanities, erected a math library in St. John's College, Oxford, to make a point about the subject's importance. In other colleges, math books and instruments were donated to their libraries. When students could not advance as fast or as far as they desired, private tutors and accommodating tutors in other colleges were available and eager to help.[97]

One of the ways university math teachers won over students, especially gentlemen's sons, was to emphasize the subject's practical applications. University lecturers often took their classes into the physical or figurative field to apply classroom and textbook lessons to surveying, navigation, optics, astronomy, and geography. Both faculty and students purchased appropriate instruments: scales, compasses, dials, slide rules, maps, quadrants, and globes. Few owned telescopes powerful enough to go beyond Galileo's discoveries, but several colleges in the seventeenth century installed them in makeshift observatories in college gate towers or the tallest rooms in the public "schools."[98]

❁ ❁ ❁

No matter how many additions, deletions, and shifts of emphasis the Oxbridge curricula experienced, both universities remained

---

Humanism, ed. Jonathan Woolfson (Basingstoke, UK: Palgrave Macmillan, 2002), ch. 11 (223–42); Mordechai Feingold, *The Mathematicians' Apprenticeship: Science, Universities, and Society in England, 1560–1640* (Cambridge: Cambridge University Press, 1984), ch. 5.

97 Feingold, *Mathematicians' Apprenticeship*, chs. 1–3; Feingold, "Mathematical Sciences," *HUO* 4: ch. 6, esp. 359–404.

98 Feingold, *Mathematicians' Apprenticeship*, 25, 108, 115–19; Feingold, "Mathematical Sciences," *HUO* 4:372–77.

dependent on books. All of their academic exercises, oral and written, were based on and revolved around the content and meaning of books, as they had been since their foundings. However, with Johann Gutenberg's invention of printing from movable metal type in the early 1450s, book-making entered a revolutionary new phase. Manuscript codices were not discarded or forgotten; scholars and the occasional student owned and used them well into the sixteenth century. Some wealthy collectors even had manuscripts copied from the texts of printed books.[99] Many early type fonts were made to resemble the Gothic, Carolingian, and Roman scripts used to create handwritten books for medieval consumption. Colors could now be added in press as well as by hand to elaborate printed initials, borders, and woodcut illustrations to imitate their hand-drawn predecessors.

Printing on paper had three major advantages. First, paper, which was initially manufactured in Spain and Italy and then throughout Europe, was much cheaper than animal-skin parchment or vellum, which might require the pelts of a whole herd of calves or sheep to produce one manuscript Bible.[100] Second, printed books could be produced in hundreds or even thousands of copies in a relatively short time. Both of these features served to greatly increase the supply of books and reduce their price. Third, the texts of printed books could be replicated uniformly rather than individually and often idiosyncratically by scribes working from imperfect exemplars. Uniform replication contributed to clearer understandings of, and therefore more substantive conversations about, academic texts across time and space. In addition, because paper could easily be cut to any size, printed pages, and therefore books, could now be produced in sizes much smaller than the manuscript folios (the size

99 M. D. Reeve, "Manuscripts Copied from Printed Books," *Manuscripts in the Fifty Years after the Invention of Printing* (London: Warburg Institute, 1983), 12–20.

100 The earliest surviving manuscript of the whole Bible in Latin required the skins of 500 calves and weighed 90 pounds. In thirteenth-century Spain, paper was known as "cloth parchment." James J. O'Donnell, *Avatars of the Word: From Papyrus to Cyberspace* (Cambridge, Mass.: Harvard University Press, 1998), 202; Steven Roger Fischer, *A History of Writing* (London: Reaktion Books, 2001), 264; Lothar Müller, *White Magic: The Age of Paper* (Cambridge: Polity Press, 2015).

of modern coffee-table books) essentially dictated by the rectangular dimensions of the skins used for parchment.[101] All of these innovations changed the face, use, sale, and storage of academic textbooks at Tudor and early Stuart Oxbridge.

The faculty's and senior scholars' book source of first resort was their own college libraries. By Henry VIII's coronation, all of Oxbridge's colleges had library rooms or separate library buildings to house their books, as did the numerous colleges built during the rest of the century. The books in the main room were largely chained to short stalls equipped with two-sided lecterns or small reading desks because the volumes were bulky manuscript folios, expensive to produce, easy to damage, and tempting to steal. The fellows, who had keys to the library, could also borrow from locked chests smaller, less valuable, volumes—*electiones*—for as long as a year to prepare lectures. The college collections were not large—having fewer, often many fewer, than 500 titles—and they were difficult to navigate in the absence of catalogues and cogent shelving principles. At the beginning of the century, the collections grew slowly through donations and bequests from fellows or alumni, seldom from purchases. This changed after the humanistic "new learning" made itself felt in England, Henry made his visitations in 1535, and printed books began to proliferate throughout Europe.[102]

101 Paul Needham and Michael Joseph, *Adventure and Art: The First One Hundred Years of Printing* (New Brunswick, N.J.: Rutgers University Libraries, 1999); S. H. Steinberg, *Five Hundred Years of Printing* (London: Faber and Faber, 1959 [1955]); Lotte Hellinga and J. B. Trapp, eds., *1400–1557*, vol. 3 of *The Cambridge History of the Book in Britain* [*CHBB*] (Cambridge: Cambridge University Press, 1999). esp. ch. 3; Eugene F. Rice, Jr., and Anthony Grafton, *The Foundations of Early Modern Europe, 1460–1559*, 2nd ed. (New York: W. W. Norton, 1994 [1970]), 1–10; Richard Abel, *The Gutenberg Revolution: A History of Print Culture* (New Brunswick, N.J.: Transaction Publishers, 2011).

102 N. R. Ker, "The Provision of Books," *HUO* 3: ch. 7; [Ker], *Oxford College Libraries in 1556* (Oxford: Bodleian Library, 1956), 6–9; N. R. Ker, "Oxford College Libraries in the Sixteenth Century," in Ker, *Books, Collectors and Libraries: Studies in the Medieval Heritage*, ed. Andrew G. Watson (London: Hambledon Press, 1985 [1959], ch. 25; J.C.T. Oates, "Books at Cambridge in the Sixteenth Century and After," in Oates, *Studies in English Printing and Libraries* (London: Pindar Press, 1991 [1971]), 74–88; J.C.T. Oates, "The Libraries of Cambridge, 1570–1700," in Francis Wormald and

Since most college budgets were constrained, new books to complement, augment, or replace existing holdings had to come less from decedents and older donors, whose books were often dated in content or format, than from alumni and aristocratic prospects who were approached for cash or specific titles. Additional book funds were raised from student fines, levies on fellows, graduation fees, and the sale of college valuables. In the 1540s, several Oxford colleges added to their collections with proceeds from the sale of silver chapel plate; in a fair trade, Oriel's £30 bought mostly then-acceptable theology. In 1570 King's College, Cambridge, sold off a "greate heape of Popish pelfe"—copes, vestments, mass books, candlesticks—that a former provost had squirreled away against the day that Catholicism returned. The fellows purchased a goodly number of books, "specially of divinitye, both of ould and new wryters," to stock a new library in three side rooms of the impressive chapel. The former library in the Old Court had been "utterly spoiled" and depleted by events of the previous thirty-five years.[103]

Many college collections, and both university libraries, were the target of various Protestant and Catholic commissions, iconoclasts, and thieves between 1535 and 1557. One of Henry's commissioners in Oxford reported that "we have set Duns [Scotus] in Bocardo, and have utterly banished him [from] Oxford for ever with all his blind glosses [on Aristotle]."[104] "The second time we came to New College . . . we found all the great Quadrant Court full of the

---

C. E. Wright, eds., *The English Library before 1700* (London: University of London, Athlone Press, 1958), ch. 10.

103 [Ker], *Oxford College Libraries in 1556*, 6–7; W.D.J. Cargill Thompson, "Notes on King's College Library, 1500–1700, in Particular for the Period of the Reformation," *Transactions of the Cambridge Bibliographical Society* 2 (1954), 38–54, at 38, 50.

104 Although Duns was allegedly drummed out of the official curriculum in 1535, his books made numerous appearances in Oxbridge scholars' libraries to 1590. E. S. Leedham-Green, *Books in Cambridge Inventories: Book-Lists from Vice-Chancellor's Court Probate Inventories in the Tudor and Stuart Periods*, 2 vols. (Cambridge: Cambridge University Press, 1986), 2:288–89; Robert J. Fehrenbach and Elisabeth S. Leedham-Green, *Private Libraries in Renaissance England: A Collection and Catalogue of Tudor and Early Stuart Book-Lists* (Binghamton, N.Y.: Medieval and Renaissance Texts and Studies, 1992–), online version and extension at http://PLRE.folger.edu.

[parchment] leaves of Duns, the wind blowing them into every corner." A country gentleman was retrieving them to make scarecrows "to keep the deer within his wood" for better hunting. Others put Scotus and fellow glossators to even baser uses: pages from their works were nailed on posts "in all common howses of easement" as toilet paper. Whenever and wherever medieval manuscripts, even precious pre-Catholic Anglo-Saxon documents, were found, they often received ill treatment from zealous or ignorant parties. Many were sold as waste to grocers, soap sellers, apothecaries, and bookbinders. The latter used the leaves as binding strips, flyleaves, or endpapers in newly printed books, where they may be found today. Many manuscripts were sold to book dealers in the Low Countries and beyond, only a few ever to return.[105]

The damage to medieval books continued during and after Edward's visitations to the universities in 1549–50. At Oxford, the commissioners and the colleges that feared to be found wanting in Protestant zeal disposed of cartloads of library volumes. Books that "treated of controversial or scholastical Divinity were let loose from their chains, and given away or sold to Mechanicks [tradesmen] for servile uses." Crowds paraded plundered books on biers through the streets and then burned them. The depleted and under-used university library was dispersed and its desks and stalls sold to Christ Church. Books became "dog cheap" on local markets. In both Cambridge and Oxford, medieval codices were liberated or defaced by having their illuminations and decorated initials cut out. Even astronomical diagrams and mathematical books, "accounted Popish or diabolical or both," were targeted for oblivion. If an Oxford professor of Greek had not accidentally come along, "the Greeke Testament had been thrown in the fire for a conjuring booke too."[106] By 1556 Cambridge's

105 C. E. Wright, "The Dispersal of the Libraries in the Sixteenth Century," in Wormald and Wright, *English Library before 1700*, ch. 8, at 153–54, 156, 165; James P. Carley, "Monastic Collections and Their Dispersal," in *1557–1695*, ed. John Barnard and D. F. McKenzie, vol. 4 of *CHBB* (2002), 340.

106 Charles Edward Mallet, *The Sixteenth and Seventeenth Centuries*, vol. 2 of *A History of the University of Oxford*, 3 vols. (New York: Longmans, Green, 1924), 91; Ian Philip, *The Bodleian Library in the Seventeenth and Eighteenth Centuries* (Oxford: Clarendon Press, 1983), 6 ("Divinity"); Wright, "Dispersal of the Libraries," 168–70;

FIGURE 6. In the tumultuous sixteenth century, "heretical" books as well as humans (or their disinterred remains) were burned in public in English university towns, as in this Cambridge scene from John Foxe's Protestant-leaning *Actes and Monuments of the Christian Church* . . . , known popularly as *Foxe's Book of Martyrs* (London, 1563).

university library had been reduced from 500–600 volumes to just 175. Fortunately, not all of the losses were permanent. Many books had been rescued by bibliophiles, such as the longtime master of Peterhouse Andrew Perne, for later reinstallation.[107]

The accession of Mary in 1553 allowed Catholic partisans and commissioners to take their own swipes at—and from—Oxbridge's

---

Ker, "Provision of Books," *HUO* 3: 466 ("Christ Church"); Cargill Thompson, "King's College Library," 44–45. As the library was being resurrected after 1574, the first set of rules (1582) mandated that all manuscripts, "all other books of Imagerie with colors," and "all other books mathematicall or historicall" were to be kept locked up. Oates, *Cambridge University Library*, 121–22.

107 J.C.T. Oates, "The Cambridge University Library: 1400–1600," in *Studies in English Printing*, ch. 15, at 68–70; Cargill Thompson, "King's College Library," 47–48.

learned treasuries. Cardinal Pole's commission to Cambridge in early 1557 had little to pick on in the shrunken university library, but the colleges and all of their fellows were required to present lists of their books on suspicion of (Protestant) heresy. A cartload of condemned books was burned in the market square along with chained coffins containing the mortal remains of two Swiss theologians who had taught at Cambridge in Edward's reign. In the days to follow, "greate baskettes full of books" were immolated in public, including many belonging to the fellows of King's, Clare, and Trinity. Oxford, Chancellor Pole's alma mater, received similar scrutiny if marginally gentler treatment.[108]

Both university libraries ceased to be used by mid-century, and college collections suffered some diminishment at the hands of various reformers. Yet most colleges added many new printed titles and renovated their libraries to accommodate them. College faculty and student book purchases accelerated between 1530 and 1570 and continued thereafter in an effort to acquire the most reliable printed texts of older authorities who remained ensconced in the statutory curricula and those of newer authors making their way onto the more flexible tutorial syllabi.[109] Most of these purchases were of less-expensive printed books in increasingly smaller formats.[110] These new formats enabled scholars and students to accumulate their own libraries for teaching or study. If Chaucer's Clerk of Oxenford had only "twenty bookes, clad in blak or reed," Tudor college fellows more likely had

108 Cargill Thompson, "King's College Library," 46–47; Cross, "Oxford and the Tudor State," *HUO* 3:145–48.

109 Kristian Jensen, "Universities and Colleges," in *To 1640*, ed. Elisabeth Leedham-Green and Teresa Webber, vol. 1 of *The Cambridge History of Libraries in Britain and Ireland* [*CHLBI*] (Cambridge: Cambridge University Press, 2006), 348–49; Ker, "Oxford College Libraries," 400–405.

110 Between 1456 and 1465, about 45 percent of all printed books were folios. By 1551–1560, the percentage of folios now in the Bodleian Library, Oxford, had fallen to 15. Jensen, "Universities and Colleges," *CHLBI* 1:353–54. The probate inventory of an Oxford M.A. and fellow of Brasenose who died in 1588 also illustrates the change in book formats. He left 250 titles, including 32 folios, 37 quartos, 165 octavos, and 16 smaller books. Mark H. Curtis, "Library Catalogues and Tudor Oxford and Cambridge," *Studies in the Renaissance* 5 (1958), 111–20, at 116–20.

seventy; some had double or triple that number. "By the 1570s and 1580s, junior scholars could easily have more books in their private libraries than even senior scholars had in the first half of the century."[111]

Another benefit of personal collections for both students and faculty was improved teaching and learning. The students' possession of the required texts allowed lecturers to forgo the time-consuming and tedious dictation of the course materials and to devote more time to their elucidation, appreciation, and criticism, often by comparison with other authorities, new and old. The need for "cursory" lectures, taught by junior faculty in the afternoon, also waned. Such a change also emphasized the more personal role of the college tutors, who could guide their students through close readings, daily study sessions, and oral quizzes to maximize comprehension.[112]

Several of the college purchases were expertly edited multivolume sets of the collected works of major figures. These made it possible for colleges to discard older, especially manuscript, versions of individual works and to make room on their shelves for the pronounced growth of printing's products. Because of their reduced cost, the smaller leather- or vellum-covered volumes also no longer warranted chaining to lecterns. This forced libraries to build taller stalls with more shelves to accommodate them, to provide more reading desks and benches, to appoint librarians who were no longer double-duty chaplains, and to improve finding aids.[113]

❁ ❁ ❁

The Elizabethan Settlement ushered in much-needed growth and stability for the universities and dispelled most of the politico-religious uncertainty that had prevented potential donors from

111 Sears Jane, *Library Catalogues of the English Renaissance* (Berkeley: University of California Press, 1956); http://PLRE.folger.edu; Jensen, "Universities and Colleges," *CHLBI* 1:351–52 (quotation); Ker, "Provision of Books," *HUO* 3:472–77.

112 Morgan, *1546–1750*, *HUC* 2: ch. 9; McConica, "Elizabethan Oxford," *HUO* 3:693–701; Leedham-Green, *University of Cambridge*, 30; Curtis, *Oxford and Cambridge in Transition*, 78–81, 107–14.

113 Jensen, "Universities and Colleges," *CHLBI* 1:361–62; Ker, "Oxford College Libraries," 409–13.

giving their books and manuscripts to academic libraries. Cambridge began a push to restore its university library in 1574. By 1600, through the generosity of several large donors, including the Archbishop of Canterbury, Matthew Parker, the two spacious second-story rooms in the Old Schools quadrangle housed more than 950 volumes handsomely and safely. No longer was the library what the university's public orator once described as "a cavern in the middle of the Schools . . . without desks or shelves, like some gloomy prison." It now had a lay (if not yet professional) librarian, regular hours (at least four a day), and a set of rules that restricted entry to ten graduate students and senior scholars at a time. Undergraduates had worn out their welcome by 1472 (unless accompanied the entire time by a graduate in proper academic dress), as they had in Oxford's library much earlier.[114]

Although Cambridge got a head start, it soon had reason to envy Oxford's sumptuous new library, planned and funded by Sir Thomas Bodley (1545–1613), an Oxford alumnus, former fellow of Merton, and one of Elizabeth's chief diplomats. His wealth came chiefly from marrying—and outliving—a wealthy widow. Beginning in 1598, Bodley and his scholar-librarians transformed a "greate desolate roome" over the Divinity School into one of the premier libraries of Europe. The space was once the home of the richly endowed humanist library donated by Humfrey, Duke of Gloucester and the youngest son of King Henry IV.[115] Through generous gifts, timely bequests (including Bodley's own), and targeted purchases, the Bodleian had to add large rooms in 1612 and 1640 to accommodate the influx of printed books and manuscripts that resulted. Books were purchased at the then-biannual Frankfurt book fair and from dealers throughout France, Italy, and the Netherlands. In 1610 the

114 Oates, *Cambridge University Library*, 35–36, 171 (quotation) and chs. 4–5; M. B. Parkes, "The Provision of Books," in J. I. Catto and R. Evans, eds., *Late Medieval Oxford*, *HUO* 2:472, 477–78. Unfortunately, Cambridge's progress was subdued after 1600 by the lack of accessions and the need for a new building, which was unmet due to the assassination of the university's unpopular but wealthy chancellor, the Duke of Buckingham. Oates, *Cambridge University Library*, ch. 6.

115 Stanley Gillam, *The Divinity School and Duke Humfrey's Library at Oxford* (Oxford: Clarendon Press and the Bodleian Library, 1988).

monopolistic Stationers' Company in London was persuaded to treat the Bodleian as a national deposit library for receiving gratis copies of its members' publications.[116]

By 1620 Oxford could boast of 16,000 books and manuscripts, a collection so rich that it drew scholars from all over Europe. Their errands were made easier because the library published complete catalogues of its holdings—a shelf list in 1605 and an alphabetized author list in 1620—and several subject catalogues by faculty (theology, medicine, law, and arts) before 1623. Local readers included senior graduates, the "Sonnes of lords of the parliament," and undergraduates of at least two years' standing. The last were required to wear cap and gown, to defer to their seniors at bench or bookshelf, and to "abstain from reading books ill-adapted to their studies," perhaps some of the lighter English-language fare that trickled in from the Stationers. In its first year alone, 248 readers used the library, including 10 foreigners and almost 40 percent of Oxford's graduate population.[117]

Although undergraduates were gradually admitted to a number of Oxbridge college libraries in the seventeenth century, younger students in general had little need for their contents. Undergraduate studies were largely confined to statutory curricula in the first two years. The few required texts could be bought inexpensively in print editions, new or secondhand, or borrowed from one's tutor or upperclassmen. Books purchased for them by their college tutors were chosen with care for price as well as quality because the tutors usually controlled their students' allowances and answered to their parents. During his fellowship at Christ's College, Cambridge, between 1613 and 1638, Joseph Mede purchased 3,294 books—some 1,647 different titles—for his 103 students. Since undergraduates were not allowed to enter, much less to borrow from, either Christ's or the university

116 Even though the company never fully lived up to its obligation, Cambridge failed to receive equal privileges—and treatment—until the Copyright Act of 1710. Oates, *Cambridge University Library*, 489–90.

117 J.N.L. Myres, *The Bodleian Library in the Seventeenth Century* (Oxford: Bodleian Library, 1951), 7–21; Philip, *Bodleian Library*, chs. 1–2; Philip and Morgan, "Libraries," *HUO* 4: ch. 13, at 659–72; Mary Clapinson, "The Bodleian Library and Its Readers, 1602–1652," *Bodleian Library Record* 19:1 (2006), 30–46.

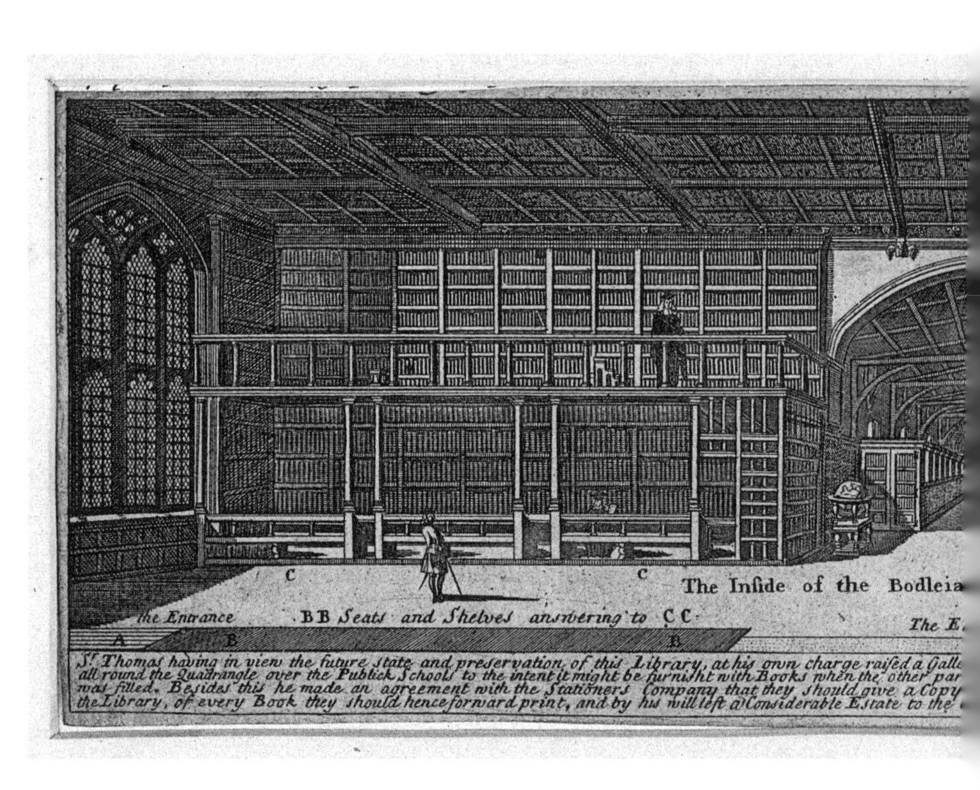

FIGURE 7. The impressive size of the Bodleian Library at Oxford is suggested

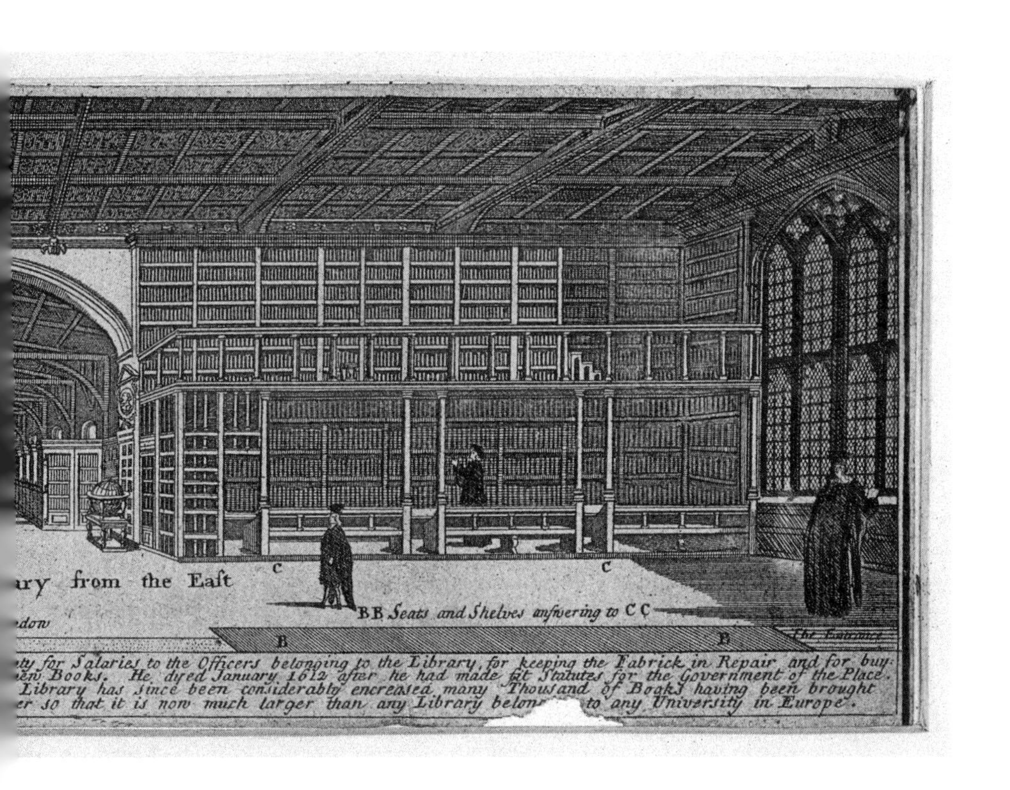

in this eighteenth-century German engraving. Wellcome Library, London.

library, they obtained virtually all of their reading matter through Mede. On average, each student during his academic stay bought 16 books through Mede. Poorer but ambitious sizars stayed the longest, pensioners for somewhat shorter and fellow-commoners for considerably shorter periods; accordingly, Mede spent on average only 1s. 9d. for each of the sizar's books, but 2s. 3d. on each book for the rest of his students.[118] Although undergraduate studies did not require library use, the one exception may have been preparation of declamations, oral or written, and formal epistles. Yet even these drew rhetorical principles and examples almost exclusively from standard rhetoric texts, published compendia of classical Latin and Greek quotations and anecdotes, and personal commonplace books.[119]

Graduate students, faculty members, and undergraduates without conscientious tutors obtained their books mostly from local booksellers or "stationers," who operated under university oversight and regulations. After posting a £40 bond, the stationers promised to provide "sufficient store of all manner of books"—save seditious and unlawful titles—"for the furnishing of all students" at "reasonable prices." In 1534 Cambridge had three stationers, adding another by 1556. On the eve of the English civil war, the town of 8,000 had 15 dealers in printed matter. Larger Oxford was able to sustain a few more. Early in the sixteenth century, an occasional stationer operated his own press, but their activities never lasted long for lack of a sufficient market. Not until the demographical growth of town and gown in the early 1580s did Cambridge and Oxford get their first bona-fide printers, both of whom operated privately but under the aegis and with the approval of the university.[120]

118 Looney, "Undergraduate Education," 17–18.

119 Fletcher, "Faculty of Arts," *HUO* 3:193–94; McConica, "Elizabethan Oxford," *HUO* 3:698, 709–10; Jardine, "Sixteenth Century Cambridge Arts Course," 18.

120 David McKitterick, *Four Hundred Years of University Printing and Publishing in Cambridge, 1584–1984: Catalogue of the Exhibition in the University Library Cambridge* (Cambridge: Cambridge University Press, 1984), 4–7, 12 (quotation); Thompson, "King's College Library," 45; McKitterick, *Cambridge University Press*, 18, 20, 228; Carl I. Hammer, Jr., "Oxford Town and Oxford University," *HUO* 3:77; Ker, "Provision of Books," *HUO* 3:443–44.

Cambridge was merely acting upon the permission King Henry granted to three "stationers and printers" in 1534 to publish books for sale locally and elsewhere. Lacking such a charter, Oxford sent a plea to Queen Elizabeth through Chancellor Leicester appealing to English pride: "Seeing that no university, however small, in Germany and France is without its press, foreigners find it as good as a marvel that in this whole realm of England printers are to be met with only in one city [London], and that, having no university, prints in virtually nothing but English." Surely, officials argued, Oxford, which "surpasses all the universities of Europe in the grandeur of its colleges and the amount of their yearly incomes," deserved a press of its own.[121] By an order of the Star Chamber in 1586, the Stationers' Company allowed a single printer with one apprentice to operate in each of the university towns, both fifty miles away from their members' 23 printing houses and 53 presses. By the late 1620s, the company was complaining that Cambridge alone was harboring four or five presses, which ate into its members' profits by publishing almanacs, school texts, the occasional Bible, and other steady sellers. In 1637 the company seemingly solved its problem by agreeing to pay Oxford's printers £200 a year *not* to compete in those categories.[122]

They worried needlessly. University-press books were rarely big sellers, at home or abroad. The great majority of books in the academic market, including the dialectic or logic mainstays of the curricula, were imported either from London or from the Rhine and the Low Countries via Frankfurt or England's less specialized Stourbridge fair. Imports continued to dominate scholarly book purchases even after the university presses acquired high-quality Greek, Hebrew, Arabic, and Oriental type fonts in the second quarter of the seventeenth century. The Cambridge tutor Joseph Mede's book

121 Harry Carter, *A History of the Oxford University Press*, vol. 1: *To the Year 1780* (Oxford: Clarendon Press, 1975), 19 (quotation). See Aylmer, "Economics and Finances," *HUO* 3: ch. 8, for a more nuanced assessment of college wealth.

122 McKitterick, *Cambridge University Press*, ch. 11, at 217–29; David McKitterick, "University Printing at Oxford and Cambridge," *CHBB* 4: ch. 8, at 196, 204–205; Carter, *History of Oxford University Press*, 1: ch. 2, at 21–22.

selections for his students included very few titles from his own university press.[123]

All students and scholars benefitted from changes in printing styles introduced first in Renaissance Italy and soon in Northern Europe. The most salutary change was in legibility. Heavy blackletter **gothic** was gradually replaced by cleaner, cursive, better spaced, and more economical **roman** and *italic* fonts, like those favored by humanist scholar-printers such as Aldus Manutius of Venice and Robert Estienne in Paris. Scholarly aids such as colophons, title pages, running heads, woodcut and engraved illustrations, pagination, and indexes were added. These and several technological changes, from improved oil-based inks to the metal screw plate, contributed greatly to intelligibility and quicker, more productive reading. Spelling, both Latin and English, became more standardized in print, replacing the erratic phonetic spelling of manuscripts. Scholar authors, correctors, and proofreaders worked with printers to establish the most accurate texts possible, *editiones principes* or critical editions, which could be published in large or small formats and in single or collected volumes. Censorship of the new intellectual medium, particularly in the Catholic Index of Prohibited Books and ecumenical book burnings, did its share to stimulate sales of the offending texts.[124]

Two other bookish trends in Tudor Oxbridge were carryovers from the pre-print world. The first was that the great majority of academic texts continued to come from Europe. English scholars still produced only a small part of the intellectual content of their own assignments. University booksellers stocked more imports than domestic titles

123 McKitterick, *Cambridge University Press*, 15, 217, 221–22, 224; McKitterick, "University Printing," *CHBB* 4:198.

124 McKitterick, *Cambridge University Press*, 12–13; Carter, *Oxford University Press*, 21; Lotte Hellinga, "Printing," *CHBB* 3: ch. 3, at 72–79; Steinberg, *Five Hundred Years of Printing*, 24–27, 34, 52, 57–60, 64–67, 92, 105–17, 127, 185–91; Anthony Grafton, *The Culture of Correction in Renaissance Europe* (London: British Library, 2011). See the master craftsman Warren Chappell's *A Short History of the Printed Word* (New York: Alfred A. Knopf, 1970), chs. 4–5, for a richly illustrated discussion of fifteenth- and sixteenth-century calligraphy and printing.

because university and tutorial syllabi required or recommended them and European publishers pushed their products in personal visits or through English agents in London. The embryonic university presses also reprinted popular European texts in number. When Oxbridge professors and libraries sought to keep up with the latest or best scholarship, they instinctively turned to continental sources, to scholastic authorities with Latinized pen or press names, such as Agricola, Burgersdicius, Erasmus, Lipsius, Lombardus, Oecolampadius, Paracelsus, Ramus, and, not least, Scotus. One strong measure of that preference is the huge presence in Cambridge libraries today of sixteenth-century books printed in Europe, well over 30,000 titles. Obviously, some titles were duplicated in various libraries and not a few were purchased or donated after 1600. But an impressive number were acquired, particularly by college libraries, contemporaneously from printers and publishers all over Western Europe. Suppliers who did the briskest business were in Paris, Venice, Rome, Antwerp, Basle, and Cologne.[125]

The second continuation was a function of the first. The *lingua franca* of European academic life was and remained Latin well beyond the close of the sixteenth century. As late as 1636, William Laud, Oxford's reforming chancellor, attempted to require the adequate use of colloquial Latin from all new B.A.s and fluency from all M.A.s.[126] In order to sell to readers beyond their own linguistic borders, publishers throughout Europe had to trade in Latin because it remained the common tongue of Europe's learned classes. Nearly

125 H. M. Adams, *Catalogue of Books Printed on the Continent of Europe, 1501–1600, in Cambridge Libraries*, 2 vols. (Cambridge: Cambridge University Press, 1967); McKitterick, *Cambridge University Press*, 1: ch. 11, at 217–21; Leedham-Green, *Books in Cambridge Inventories*, 1:xviii; 2:820–27. Fellows' inventories demonstrate that printed books kept company in college rooms with few manuscripts, even in the 1530s, but with assorted maps, pictures, musical instruments, gaming tables, reading glasses, compasses, globes, and the occasional skull (one in gold), doubtless a *memento mori* for the scholar worried about publishing before he perished.

126 Leedham-Green, *University of Cambridge*, 71; Mallet, *History of Oxford University*, 2:328, 334, 341; Kevin Sharpe, "Archbishop Laud and the University of Oxford," in Hugh Lloyd-Jones, Valerie Pearl, and Blair Worden, eds., *History & Imagination: Essays in Honour of H. R. Trevor-Roper* (London: Duckworth, 1981), ch. 12, at 153, 158.

90 percent of the books in the libraries of Oxford college fellows and students who died in the sixteenth century were in Latin, of those who died before 1551, 95 percent. About 13 percent of the Latin books contained some Greek; only a minority, typically grammars and dictionaries, were largely Greek texts. Most classical Greek authors were read in Latin translations. Only a few books were in Hebrew or French. Most of the rest were in English, some chosen by their owners for diversion, others chosen by college tutors as more fitting for the future careers of their fellow-commoners and other elite charges. The stock of university stationers was also Latin-heavy, though to make a living in a relatively small town they had to stock some English titles for local and area customers. The situation in Cambridge was no different.[127]

❁ ❁ ❁

The effects of printing, as many historians have suggested, spread widely throughout European culture.[128] In the particularly bookish precincts of academic culture, its effects were even more keenly felt and earlier, despite durable features of the universities' oral heritage.

127 In the sixteenth century, two-thirds of the books belonging to deceased Oxford scholars had been published on the continent. http://PLRE.folger.edu; Leedham-Green, *Books in Cambridge Inventories*; McKitterick, *Cambridge University Press*, 1: ch. 11, at 224–25; Andrew Pettegree, *The Book in the Renaissance* (New Haven, Conn.: Yale University Press, 2010), 124–25, 326.

128 Steinberg, *Five Hundred Years of Printing*; Marshall McLuhan, *The Gutenberg Galaxy: The Making of Typographic Man* (Toronto: University of Toronto Press, 1962); Walter J. Ong, *The Presence of the Word* (New Haven, Conn.: Yale University Press, 1967); Walter J. Ong, *Orality and Literacy: The Technologizing of the World* (London: Methuen, 1982); Lucian Febvre and Henri-Jean Martin, *The Coming of the Book: The Impact of Printing, 1458–1800* (London: Verso, 1976); Elizabeth L. Eisenstein, *The Printing Press as an Agent of Change: Communications and Cultural Transformations in Early-Modern Europe*, 2 vols. (New York: Cambridge University Press, 1979); Eisenstein, *The Printing Revolution in Early Modern Europe* (New York: Cambridge University Press, 1983), a revised and condensed version of her earlier book; O'Donnell, *Avatars of the Word*; Pettegree, *Book in the Renaissance*; Ian F. McNeely with Lisa Wolverton, *Reinventing Knowledge: From Alexandria to the Internet* (New York: W. W. Norton, 2008).

From reading aloud to oneself or a group, book reading became silent and private.[129] As a function of sight rather than hearing, reading tended to invest authority or "truth" in the text, the printed page, rather than in a speaker's reputation, social rank, or accent. This shift enabled students to question their lecturers more often than had been usual and to search for their own solutions to intellectual problems, a process that sharpened the exchanges in the still-frequent disputations. Owning one's own book and having access to larger and improved libraries also lightened the heavy scholastic burden of memory, allowing for more creative uses of mind.

The expansion of print and the proliferation of primary and secondary "grammar" schools extended literacy in general among the European population, but it also expanded the size, reach, and cooperation of the learned class. This gave rise to the pan-European Republic of Letters, rendered self-conscious by Erasmus at the beginning of the sixteenth century, notable during the Scientific Revolution of the seventeenth century, and famous during the Enlightenment of the eighteenth century, when its lingua franca completed a transition from Latin to French. Scholars in and beyond universities crossed all kinds of borders to create "a new kind of virtual community," because the uniformity of mass-reproduced texts invited feedback and often pushback from other smart readers focused on the same texts or sets of questions. Such interchanges quickly gave birth to errata sheets and corrected editions. They also spawned international networks of correspondence, literary and scientific societies (local and national), and an irenic ethic of "high Stoicism" and friendly cooperation as well as competition in a world rent by war, religious intolerance, and dynastic rivalry.[130]

129 Paul Saenger, "Silent Reading: Its Impact on Late Medieval Script and Society," *Viator: Medieval and Renaissance Studies* 13 (1982), 367–414, modifies the conclusions of McLuhan (*The Gutenberg Galaxy*) and others on the dating and contexts of silent reading.

130 Anthony Grafton, *Worlds Made by Words: Scholarship and Community in the Modern West* (Cambridge, Mass.: Harvard University Press, 2009), esp. ch. 1 (quotations at 16 and 23). See also Grafton, *Bring Out Your Dead: The Past as Revelation* (Cambridge, Mass.: Harvard University Press, 2001).

When words "metastasized" in print, undergraduates were not particularly alarmed because their reading assignments remained relatively stable in length, if not in content.[131] But faculty scholars and graduate students who sought to follow an academic career found to their dismay that the print revolution produced "too much to know." If they wanted to master their own civilization, as so many of their polymathic predecessors had theirs, they had to devise ways to cope with the flood of publications that produced greater volumes of older, often rediscovered, knowledge as well as freshets of new information begging to be refined into knowledge. One response of stubborn conservatives was to bear down and read harder and longer. To assist in this task, they allowed themselves the liberty of underlining or marking key passages in a text (even with different colored inks) and marginal abbreviations and notations as *aide-mémoires*. They might even add their own citations to alphabetical indices or resort to bibliographies to ensure that they did not miss anything important.

The diehards no doubt frowned on the shortcuts of their less industrious (if more realistic) colleagues who leaned on new, often polyglot, dictionaries and concordances, encyclopedias and other works of reference, book-review journals, ready-made *florilegia* of excerpts and quotations on given subjects (in place of personalized commonplace books), short lists of essential reading, and varieties of note-taking, by hired hands or even by cutting and pasting book pages into one's own notebooks.[132] Before 1650, few scholars chose either of two responses to biblio-inundation that would become increasingly familiar in the future. One was specialization, a simple concession made by focusing on more manageable fields or garden plots. The other was dilettantism, a more grievous evasion that usually failed to gain one admission to the Republic of Letters, though perhaps not to a long-term college fellowship and academic career. All of these responses gave early-modern scholars an anticipatory modern look.

131 O'Donnell, *Avatars of the Word*, 148 (quotation).

132 Ann Blair, "Reading Strategies for Coping with Information Overload ca. 1550–1700," *Journal of the History of Ideas* 64:1 (Jan. 2003), 11–28; Ann M. Blair, *Too Much to Know: Managing Scholarly Information before the Modern Age* (New Haven, Conn.: Yale University Press, 2010).

❋ ❋ ❋

However successfully Oxford and Cambridge responded to the vicissitudes and challenges of their times, they could always find comfort in a medieval myth that located them solidly in a great tradition. The pedigree they fashioned for themselves was more aspirational than strictly historical because it placed them in a direct line of leading centers of learning that ran from Athens to Rome, Rome to Byzantium, and hence to Paris and the grassy banks of the Isis and the Cam. But it helped them and the other nascent European universities of the twelfth and thirteenth centuries to argue successfully for a place (as the *Studium*) in the triadic structure of Christian society beside the older Church (*Sacerdotium*) and State (*Regnum*). When conditions in early Stuart England, exacerbated by the High-Church policies of Archbishop Laud and the absolutist tendencies of Charles I, drove many Puritan reformers to North America, the myth of *translatio studii* went with them as a kind of educational compass. Christianity, like the pre-Copernican sun, was seen taking an inexorable westward path from Jerusalem to Rome and Canterbury en route to circling the globe, but so, too, was higher learning on its way to a new Cambridge in the raw wilderness its unschooled natives called Massachusetts.[133] As George Herbert, Cambridge M.A., fellow of Trinity College, and the university's public orator, put it in "The Church Militant" in 1633, "Religion stands on tip-toe in our land / Readie to passe to the *American* strand." That Herbert's college classmate Charles Chauncy was to become the second president of the future Harvard College endowed his poem with particular prescience.[134]

133 A. B. Cobban, *The Medieval Universities: Their Development and Organization* (London: Methuen, 1975), 22; George Huntston Williams, "Translatio Studii: The Puritans' Conception of Their First University in New England, 1636," *Archiv fuer Reformationsgeschichte* 57 (1966), 152–81; Jurgen Herbst, "*Translatio Studii*: The Transfer of Learning from the Old World to the New," *History of Higher Education Annual* 12 (1992), 85–99.

134 *The Works of George Herbert*, ed. F. E. Hutchinson (Oxford: Clarendon Press, 1941), xxv, 196.

CHAPTER THREE

The Collegiate Way Abroad

If we norish not Larning
both church & common wealth will sinke.

REV. JOHN ELIOT

IN THE HECTIC century after King Henry VIII declared and secured England's independence from Rome and the Catholic Church, the new Church of England sought religious unity under one banner. But persistent Catholic loyalties and insistent Protestant calls for more reforms overlay shifting socio-economic ambitions and political tensions and kept the kingdom in turmoil. When Puritan reformers and Catholic recusants could not see a future for themselves at home, thousands left for more hospitable sites in Europe, the Caribbean, and North America.

Understandably, the emigrants sought to replicate the best and most familiar of their former ways of living. In *New* England, where some 21,000 religious and economic seekers settled between 1630 and 1642 alone, English laws, family structure, and communal patterns were part of their cultural baggage.[1] So were educational institutions, for these Protestants believed that that "old deluder Satan" sought to "keep men from the knowledge of the Scriptures" and that

1 Nicholas Canny, ed., *Europeans on the Move: Studies in European Migration, 1500–1800* (Oxford: Clarendon Press, 1994), ch. 4; Bernard Bailyn, *The Peopling of North America: An Introduction* (New York: Alfred A. Knopf, 1986), ch. 1; David Grayson Allen, *In English Ways: The Movement of Societies and the Transferal of English Local Law and Custom to Massachusetts Bay in the Seventeenth Century* (Chapel Hill: University of North Carolina Press, 1981); Virginia DeJohn Anderson, *New England's Generation: The Great Migration and the Formation of Society and Culture in the Seventeenth Century* (Cambridge: Cambridge University Press, 1991).

his pastoral foes needed to be highly educated to be able to grasp and convey the Gospel's subtle truths.[2]

Their spiritual and spatial distance from the mother country soon posed another problem for the New English. Although seventy-two university-educated men, mostly ministers, immigrated to New England by 1636, the colonists worried that the supply of qualified pastors would not be sufficient for the growing population, especially "when our present Ministers shall lie in the Dust."[3] In late October 1636, therefore, the General Court of Massachusetts, the colony's legislature meeting in Boston, passed a bill giving £400 "toward a schoale or colledge" in a town and form to be determined in the next session. The public commitment was impressive: almost one-quarter of the colony's tax levy for the year, more than half of the previous year's. A year later, in November, the court fixed the location of the new institution in "Newtowne"—soon renamed Cambridge—and determined that it would be a "colledg" rather than a mere school.[4]

In two weeks, a twelve-man board of Overseers—six ministers and six magistrates—was appointed to guide the building and work of the new college. These men in turn proceeded to appoint 27-year-old Nathaniel Eaton, a recent immigrant with university experience but no degree, as head, or Professor, to handle the design and erection of a suitable collegiate edifice, to fashion a curriculum, and to pursue additional funding. He did so, in a fashion, and classes began sometime in the late summer of 1638, even before the three-story, E-shaped "University house" (as one correspondent called it) was fully "reared." Within a fortnight, the Rev. John Harvard

2 James Axtell, *The School upon a Hill: Education and Society in Colonial New England* (New Haven, Conn.: Yale University Press, 1974), ch. 1; John Morgan, *Godly Learning: Puritan Attitudes towards Reason, Learning, and Education, 1560–1640* (Cambridge: Cambridge University Press, 1986); Lawrence A. Cremin, *American Education: The Colonial Experience, 1607–1783* (New York: Harper & Row, 1970), chs. 1–3.

3 *New Englands First Fruits* (London, 1643), 12, reprinted in Samuel Eliot Morison, *The Founding of Harvard College* (Cambridge, Mass.: Harvard University Press, 1935), 432. This 26-page pamphlet was a plea to English Puritans to support the colony's missions to the Indians and its struggling college.

4 Morison, *Founding of Harvard*, 168, 169, 179.

FIGURE 8. A scholarly reconstruction of Harvard's first, all-purpose, building by Harold R. Shurtleff.

died at the age of thirty, leaving to the "infant seminary" half of his considerable estate, reported to be as much as £1,700, and all of his 400-volume library. The following spring the General Court signaled their gratitude by naming Anglo-America's first institution of higher education "Harvard Colledge."[5]

Master Eaton proved to be an embarrassing failure and within a year was removed from office. His crimes against students and tutors were so serious that he was also excommunicated from the Cambridge church by the Rev. Thomas Shepard, an Overseer and next-door neighbor.[6] For almost a year the college remained closed, until Henry Dunster, an equally young but more credentialed and experienced pedagogue, was chosen in 1640 to reopen its doors. To give him ballast for the task ahead, the Overseers named him President,

5 Ibid., 193, 208, 220–21, 264.

6 Ibid., 228–40; Susan Drinker Moran, "Thomas Shepard and the Professor: Two Documents from the Early History of Harvard," *Early American Literature* 17:1 (Spring 1982), 24–42.

a title rare in English colleges but one that became nearly universal in American academe thereafter.[7] To the Overseers' great relief, President Dunster celebrated his and Harvard's first commencement in September 1642, when nine "senior sophisters" demonstrated their "proficiency in the [ancient] tongues and arts" before an august assembly and "proceeded B.A."[8] New England's "School of the Prophets" was finally in business.

❁ ❁ ❁

Where did the idea of Harvard come from? Or was it *sui generis Americani*? The prevailing answer is that Harvard was closely modeled after Emmanuel College, Cambridge, a famous producer of Puritan preachers after it was founded in 1584 by Sir Walter Mildmay, Queen Elizabeth's chancellor of the exchequer. In 1935 Samuel Eliot Morison, Harvard's official tercentenary historian, carefully described the college's precedents in Oxford, Cambridge, Dublin, Scotland, and the Netherlands. But he concluded that when Puritans from Cambridge and other parts of East Anglia decided to migrate to North America, they believed that "New England must include a new Emmanuel." Four years later, the religious historian Winthrop Hudson challenged "the Morison myth concerning the founding of Harvard," but he accepted and even magnified Emmanuel's importance. "Harvard," he argued, "was the step-child of that hot-bed of English Puritanism, Emmanuel College at Cambridge. . . . It was this institution that the founders sought to reproduce . . . in the Massachusetts Bay Colony." Thereafter most historians of higher education have followed Hudson's, and what he said was Morison's, lead in tracing Harvard's paternity back to Emmanuel's monastic

7 Dunster's alma mater, Magdalene College, Cambridge, had a President, but he was subordinate to the Master. Richard G. Durnin, "The Role of the Presidents in the American Colleges of the Colonial Period," *History of Education Quarterly* 1:2 (June 1961), 23–31, at 24.

8 Morison, *Founding of Harvard*, 246, 257–62.

quads.[9] Unfortunately, virtually no one has bothered to specify just who the college's effective "founders" were.[10]

The *official* founders were the forty-three members of the General Court who authorized the building of a college and underwrote its initial costs. The court's presiding officer was Henry Vane, the recently arrived (and soon departed) 23-year-old governor of the Massachusetts Bay Colony. He had attended but, for religious reasons, not matriculated at Magdalen Hall, *Oxford*. The other 42 members included only seven university men: six from various colleges at Cambridge (two *without* degrees from Emmanuel) and one from Protestant Trinity College, Dublin. Their vague plans for a "colledge or schoale," however, and their noninvolvement in its planning suggest that their academic experiences had little influence on the eventual shape of Harvard.[11]

9 Ibid., 107; Winthrop S. Hudson, "The Morison Myth Concerning the Founding of Harvard College," *Church History* 8:2 (June 1939), 148–59, at 150–51; John S. Brubacher and Willis Rudy, *Higher Education in Transition: A History of American Colleges and Universities* (New York: Harper & Row, 1958; New Brunswick, N.J.: Transaction Publishers, 1997), 3; Frederick Rudolph, *The American College and University: A History* (New York: Alfred A. Knopf, 1962), 24; Lawrence A. Cremin, *American Education: The Colonial Experience, 1607–1783* (New York: Harper & Row, 1970), 211, 216; Jurgen Herbst, "The First Three American Colleges: Schools of the Reformation," *Perspectives in American* History 8 (1974), 7–52; Christopher J. Lucas, *American Higher Education: A History* (New York: St. Martin's Griffin, 1994), 104. Orthodox Harvard opinion was reconfirmed as the university's 350th anniversary approached in 1986. See Bernard Bailyn, "Foundations," in *Glimpses of the Harvard Past* (Cambridge, Mass.: Harvard University Press, 1986), 9, and Alan Heimert, "Let Us Now Praise Famous Men," *The Cambridge Review* 106:2289 (Nov. 1985), 177–82. In large part for his advocacy of the Emmanuel-Harvard connection, Heimert was made a fellow of Emmanuel the following year. The editor of *The Cambridge Review* in 1985 was Derek Brewer, fellow and former master (1977–80) of Emmanuel. In 1998 he in turn largely retold the Heimert tale in "Emmanuel and Harvard," *Emmanuel College Magazine* 80 (1997–98), 54–69.

10 J. David Hoeveler cites the alumni of the various Cambridge (and Oxford) colleges involved in Harvard's founding, but he does not distinguish the *effective* founders from the rest. In a rare slip, he also attributes Nathaniel Eaton's education to Emmanuel rather than Trinity, though he is accurate in a previous reference. *Creating the American Mind: Intellect and Politics in the Colonial Colleges* (Lanham, Md.: Rowman & Littlefield, 2002), chs. 1–2, at 7, 29.

11 Morison, *Founding of Harvard*, 164–68.

Undoubtedly more influential (though we lack specifics) were the twelve Overseers appointed by the General Court in the fall of 1637. Nine of them were university men, if not always graduates: one attended Oxford and much later graduated with a Bachelor of Divinity. The other eight were Cambridge men: four were products of *Trinity*, one each of *King's* and *Christ's*, and only *two* were Emmanuelites (one of whom had taken a B.A. at Trinity before transferring; the other was Thomas Shepard, who catechized and preached to the Harvard students weekly until his death in 1649). One of the earliest proponents of a college and later a longtime Overseer was the Rev. John Eliot of nearby Roxbury, a graduate of *Jesus* College, Cambridge. In 1633 Eliot tried to persuade Sir Simonds D'Ewes, the wealthy English Puritan whom we have met at *St. John's*, Cambridge, to endow "a schoole of larning, a colledg among us." Eliot had in mind a small dormitory to begin, a "little" library, and a place for "disputations, & lectures, not only in divinity: but in other arts & sciences, & in law also." He did not have to tell D'Ewes twice that "if we norish not Larning both church & common wealth will sinke."[12]

The historians who favor Emmanuel as Harvard's progenitor seem to rely heavily on two numbers rather than more direct evidence of influence. One is the dominant number of Emmanuel men among the 100 Cambridge-educated emigrants to New England before 1646: 35, more than the 32 Oxford sent altogether. Trinity (with 13) and St. John's (with 10), both havens of Puritans before the crackdown by Archbishop Laud in the 1630s, had the next most. But gross numbers do not pinpoint the individuals who had the *most* significant experience, authority, or suasiveness to shape the college, foremost among them the Harvard heads. Master Eaton was a nongraduated product of *Trinity* College, Cambridge, and the University of Franeker in the Netherlands;

12 Ibid., 193–99, app. B; Franklin M. Wright, "A College First Proposed, 1633: Unpublished Letters of Apostle Eliot and William Hammond to Sir Simonds D'Ewes," *Harvard Library Bulletin* 8:3 (Autumn 1954), 255–82, at 273–74, 276, excerpted in Richard Hofstadter and Wilson Smith, eds., *American Higher Education: A Documentary History*, 2 vols. (Chicago: University of Chicago Press, 1961), 1:5–6.

Henry Dunster, whose impact cannot be overestimated, was a *Magdalene* man.[13]

The other number is the single figure of John Harvard, who graduated with a B.A. from Emmanuel in 1632 and an M.A. three years later. But since he did not emigrate until after the college was authorized, did not live in Cambridge, never served as an Overseer, and died prematurely in September 1638, he had no opportunity and probably no desire to affect the design of the college that was already underway and would soon honor his name posthumously.[14] Indeed, it appears certain that Harvard borrowed most of its essential features from the *university* at Cambridge, but not from any single college among several with notable tendencies to turn out ministers and magistrates of a Puritan persuasion.

Even if Emmanuel's protagonists happened to be correct, the college had several features that made it considerably less than a single-minded seminary for puritanical protesters. Indeed, according to the college and religion historian Patrick Collinson, Emmanuel "never was, least of all in [its formative decades], simply, or even predominantly, a seminary, still less a puritan seminary."[15] It did work hard to produce a reformist elite of ministers and lay leaders, but it still had to operate within the national Anglican framework and under social and demographic constraints imposed by its relative youth and endowed poverty.

First of all, Emmanuel did not do a very thorough job of sending out "godly and learned" preachers to leaven the Anglican loaf because it took in too many unlikely prospects. In the five decades before 1645, when all of early New England's university men were educated, Emmanuel admitted nearly twice as many aristocrats' and gentlemen's sons—as fellow-commoners (who paid double fees) and pensioners (who paid full freight)—as it did sizars, boys of humble origin who needed to be subsidized as they prepared largely for

13 Morison, *Founding of Harvard*, 359–63. Harvard's second president, Charles Chauncy, was also a graduate of Trinity before teaching Greek there. Ibid., 371.

14 Ibid., 210–23.

15 Sarah Bendall, Christopher Brooke, and Patrick Collinson, *A History of Emmanuel College, Cambridge* (Woodbridge, UK: Boydell Press, 1999), 48.

clerical or teaching careers. The college had far more privileged sons than Jesus, King's, or St. John's. Of these scions, 72 percent failed to graduate, 27 percent even to matriculate, and 14 percent went on (usually without graduating) to the Inns of Court in London for legal training. Only 38 percent of Emmanuel's students entered the ordained ministry, worse marks than the other three elite colleges earned.[16]

A second unstereotypical feature was Emmanuel's size: by 1621 it had the fourth-largest population in Cambridge, some 260.[17] Yet by statute it had only 12 teaching fellows, making the student-faculty ratio a heavy 15–22:1 throughout the 1620s. Against these odds, the tutors could not guide and monitor the students' learning, conduct, spending, and faith as closely as the college statutes and most parents desired. The numbers also meant that many students, particularly freedom-and-fun-loving fellow-commoners, had to live out of college in town, which made their supervision even more challenging. The hefty Admonition Book makes it apparent that "the real Emmanuel was never simply the pious hothouse of legend."[18]

No more was Emmanuel a "landlocked Calvinist seminary" intellectually. Its first three masters and most of its fellows, all advanced divinity students, were Calvinist *moderates* who chose to tread nimbly between "simple conformity" to the English Church's canons and ceremonies and "outright nonconformity." They did this so well that pre–Civil War Emmanuel became a "nursery of college heads" and parish priests "of every religious and political complexion, . . . from high church to puritan." Symptomatically, it bred most of the irenical Cambridge Platonists, who not only denied the doctrine of predestination but questioned whether Hell had any occupants at

16 Bendall, Brooke, and Collinson, *Emmanuel College*, 47–48. See also Morgan, *Godly Learning*, 253–54.

17 In the 1620s, the town population was under 8,000; the university comprised c. 2,900 of them. Victor Morgan, *A History of the University of Cambridge* [*HUC*], vol. 2: *1546–1750* (Cambridge: Cambridge University Press, 2004), 120n107, 247, 464.

18 Bendall, Brooke, and Collinson, *Emmanuel College*, 48–50, 53. Emmanuel was also notable for having several "unpuritan" amenities, such as an outdoor bathing pool, a tennis court, and its own brewhouse. Morison, *Founding of Harvard*, 98.

all.[19] Many Emmanuelites, perhaps a majority, therefore, would not have been welcome in New England's Genevan "City upon a Hill," much less invited into Harvard's planning and oversight.

Furthermore, Harvard derived few of its distinctive features specifically from Emmanuel, as distinguished from the generality of Cambridge colleges. Without a national church to contend with, for example, Harvard had no need to impose a formal religious test or oath upon its students, as Oxford and Cambridge did upon all those who wished to take a degree or to teach.[20] Emmanuel's statutes (largely borrowed from Trinity and neighboring Christ's) also bore little resemblance to Harvard's earliest "law, liberties, and orders," drafted between 1642 and 1650 by President Dunster, that loyal *Magdalene* man. Founder Mildmay's statutes focused on the Emmanuel *fellows* and how to move them into parish ministry as quickly as possible after they earned their doctorates of divinity.[21] Harvard's rules mostly sought to regulate the lives and learning of its *undergraduates*. Instead of mirroring Emmanuel's marching orders, Harvard's echoed the 1570 Cambridge statutes, a copy of which Dunster owned. These established an unspecific university curriculum around rhetoric, logic, and philosophy while leaving to the now-elevated colleges and their tutors the devising of more flexible studies for their particular and changing student populations.[22]

19 Ibid., 183, 204; *HUC* 2:471, 475–76, 526.

20 Bendall, Brooke, and Collinson, *Emmanuel College*, 238, 333.

21 Ibid., 23–30; *HUC* 2:315n6; Stanford E. Lehmberg, *Sir Walter Mildmay and Tudor Government* (Austin: University of Texas Press, 1964), ch. 14, at 226–27. The 1585 statutes and 1588 additions in Latin and translation are found in Frank Stubbings, *The Statutes of Sir Walter Mildmay Kt Chancellor of the Exchequer and One of Her Majesty's Privy Councillors; Authorized by Him for the Government of Emmanuel College Founded by Him* (Cambridge: Cambridge University Press, 1983).

22 Harvard University, *Harvard College Records*, vol. 1, in vol. 15 of *Publications of the Colonial Society of Massachusetts* (Boston: Colonial Society of Massachusetts, 1925), 24–38; Bendall, Brooke, and Collinson, *Emmanuel College*, 238; Morison, *Founding of Harvard*, 337. The first code of Harvard statutes (c. 1646) is reprinted in Morison, *Founding of Harvard*, 333–37, and in Hofstadter and Wilson, *American Higher Education*, 1:8–10.

❁ ❁ ❁

This collegiate freedom is particularly pertinent to Harvard because the new institution was only a single, small, residential college without a sustaining university. Until the College of William & Mary was royally chartered in Virginia in 1693, Harvard was the only source of higher education in the British colonies; until 1701, when Yale made its frail appearance, Harvard had New England all to itself. This meant that Harvard could not confine its undergraduate clientele to future ministers. The fledgling colonies needed advanced education for future leaders of all kinds—for lawyers and physicians who would go on to apprenticeships with practitioners, for public servants and teachers, and for planters, gentlemen, and merchants who sought to earn or confirm status in the more fluid social hierarchy of a new country. Harvard *College*, in other words, had to serve as a kind of "mini-versity" for all of British North America until it could be joined by similar kinds of undergraduate schools in the other Atlantic colonies. That it attracted precious few students from beyond New England owed to its homogeneous religious complexion as much as to its distance from the other colonies and its expense.

Yet Harvard did produce a large number of Puritan ministers for New England and beyond, including a number who returned to England during the Interregnum (1640–60), when Puritans were in control.[23] Morison found that just over 40 percent of its matriculants and over half of its graduates in the seventeenth century became ministers.[24] What we must remember, however, is that reformist

23 William L. Sachse, "The Migration of New Englanders to England, 1640–1660," *American Historical Review* 53: 2 (Jan. 1948), 251–78; Harry S. Stout, "The Morphology of Remigration: New England University Men and Their Return to England, 1640–1660," *Journal of American Studies* 10:2 (Aug. 1976), 151–72.

24 Morison, *Founding of Harvard*, 247n5; Samuel Eliot Morison, *Harvard College in the Seventeenth Century*, 2 vols. (Cambridge, Mass.: Harvard University Press, 1935), 2:562; Samuel Eliot Morison, *Three Centuries of Harvard College, 1636–1936* (Cambridge, Mass.: Belknap Press of Harvard University Press, 1936), 241. Morison's figures were accepted by Cremin, *American Education: Colonial Experience*, 221. A more recent estimate—based only on an unexplained counting of the students before 1660—puts the total as high as 80 percent. Michael Sletcher, "Historians and

ministers in New England, as in England, were not regarded as fully qualified to lead a church until they had added an M.A. to their B.A. But unlike Oxford and Cambridge, Harvard had no graduate courses or faculty besides the president. So Harvard graduates who wished to enter the ministry had to study largely on their own for the M.A. exams, which could not be taken for at least three years. The most conscientious sought the guidance of a learned minister in the country or the college president, often while serving as a schoolmaster or college tutor to make ends meet. The two degree citations emphasized this vocational preparation. President Dunster said (in Latin) to the new bachelors: "I admit you to the first degree in Arts . . . with the privilege of reading in public [preparing], in such profession as you shall select," made easier by "liberty of studying in the [College] Library." Successful M.A.s, on the other hand, received "the privilege of practicing a profession," largely clerical or educational.[25]

The undergraduate curriculum, therefore, was designed, like most of the Cambridge colleges' courses of study, including Emmanuel's, to prepare a diverse cross-section of *future* leaders and professionals, not to turn them out directly or immediately. This is reflected in Dunster's initial (1642) plan of studies for a three-year curriculum.[26] It was dominated by the study of Latin and Greek and the familiar scholastic classics in rhetoric, logic, and philosophy. Ancient history and elementary math and science (physics in the first year, astronomy in the second, and botany every summer) were included in the requirements. In the morning the president lectured on the subject

---

Anachronisms: Samuel E. Morison and Seventeenth-Century Harvard College," *History of Universities* 19:2 (2004), 188–220, at 189, 209.

25 Cotton Mather, *Magnalia Christi Americana*, 2 vols. (Hartford, Conn., 1820 [London, 1702]), 2:6–10, reprinted in Hofstadter and Wilson, *American Higher Education*, 1:18–19.

26 Morison, *Harvard College*, 2:301. In 1652 Harvard shifted to the then-standard four-year course of the English universities, and all of its American successors followed, even after Oxford and Cambridge by the eighteenth century gradually reduced their undergraduate programs to three years, where they remain. The difference is minimal because English secondary schools have an additional year, grade thirteen, to prepare for university.

of the day, often to all three classes at once (as in rhetoric, history, and botany). Lectures were followed by study hours to prepare for afternoon recitations on the morning lesson, declamations to analyze or practice the subject, or disputations with classmates to argue formal propositions. To that extent, Harvard's academic offerings differed little from those of old Cambridge.

One difference, however, was Harvard's inclusion of required work in all three biblical languages: Hebrew, Chaldee (Aramaic), and Syriac (Christian Aramaic written in a different alphabet).[27] The goal was to enable every graduate of America's school of the prophets to translate "the Originalls of the *Old* and *New Testament* into the Latine tongue, and to resolve them *Logically*." It went without saying, though it constantly was said, that graduates also needed to be "of godly life and conversation." To ensure that outcome, tutors met their charges twice a day for Scripture and prayer. Saturday mornings were given over to an exposition of Scripture by the president, the memorization of a Puritan catechism, and in the third year, the hearing of "commonplaces," short practice sermons by M.A. candidates. The Sabbath was devoted literally to Thomas Shepard's First Church sermons, one repeated in the college hall at noon.[28]

This was a curriculum of "godly learning," not exclusively for future ministers, although it was aptly designed for them, but for any well-educated Puritan layman or leader. It was less vocational than spiritual preparation for strenuous (male) lives in a Bible commonwealth. It was also, as Morison argued, a multipurpose *liberal arts* curriculum for contemporary undergraduates. He had sound evidence for saying so. As early as 1642, *New England's First Fruits* told potential English supporters that President Dunster had taught his "Pupils" so well in "the tongues and Arts" and so "seasoned them with the principles of Divinity and Christianity" that they had duly impressed monthly audiences of "Magistrates, Ministers, and other Schollars" with their academic skills and comportment. Thomas Shepard, the college's pastor, declared the infant college "a nursery of

27 Individual college tutors at Cambridge offered work in Hebrew and, more rarely, "Chaldee." Morgan, *Godly Learning*, 195, 226, 227, 254, 255, 282, 288.

28 Morison, *Founding of Harvard*, 141, 267–68, 271–72, 434, 436.

knowledge in these deserts" as well as "a supply [of ministers] for posterity." Seven years into his presidential term, Dunster petitioned the New England Confederation for funds to buy books, "especially in law, phisicke [medicine], Philosophy and Mathematicks" for the use of scholars (most likely postgraduates) "whose various inclinations to *all* professions might thereby be incouraged and furthered." But most convincing of all was the college's first charter in 1650. Without once mentioning theology or preparation for ministry, Harvard said—twice—that its official purpose was "the advancement & education of youth in all manner of good literature[,] Artes and Sciences."[29]

Harvard did not become a university even in name until the alumnus and future U.S. president John Adams included the chapter "University at Cambridge" in the new state constitution of 1780.[30] But only a dozen years after Massachusetts had been planted as a colony, Harvard had begun to act, if not yet look, something like a fully fledged English university. First, it required its matriculants, much as Oxford and Cambridge did, to be able to read and speak classical Latin, "in verse and prose," and to decline Greek nouns and verbs "perfectly." This was necessary because the whole academic program—lectures, reading, and exercises—was conducted in Latin and included three years of Greek grammar, dialects, and style.[31] These high expectations, in turn, required Latin grammar schools, like those found in England. Cambridge had one (next to the college) by 1642, as had Boston and several other towns. More were added after 1647 when the Bay Colony passed the "Old Deluder Satan Act" requiring towns of 100 or more families to provide a "Grammar-School . . . to instruct youth so far as they may be fitted for the Universitie."[32]

29 Ibid., 247–49 (my emphasis), 433. The charter is reprinted in Morison, *Harvard College*, 1:5–8, and Hofstadter and Smith, *American Higher Education*, 1:10–12.

30 Morison, *Three Centuries of Harvard*, 160.

31 Morison, *Harvard College*, 1:84–85, 169; Arthur Orlo Norton, "Harvard Text-Books and Reference Books of the Seventeenth Century," in *Transactions, 1930–1933*, vol. 28 of *Publications of the Colonial Society of Massachusetts* (Boston: Colonial Society of Massachusetts, 1935), 361–438. Even out-of-class conversations were expected to be in Latin, though few probably were. Morison, *Founding of Harvard*, 336.

32 Morison, *Founding of Harvard*, 157–58; Morison, *Harvard College*, 1:333–34; Axtell, *School upon a Hill*, ch. 5, esp. 169–70, 176, 181.

Second, and perhaps most presumptuous of all in the absence of the royal and papal approval that sanctioned Oxford and Cambridge, upstart Harvard simply *assumed* the customary and perhaps legal right to award degrees to its graduates.[33] Even the charter of 1650 was silent on this delicate subject. With even more temerity, the college also expected its degrees to be accepted in England as the equal of Oxford's and Cambridge's, which, surprisingly, they were after 1648. When the president intoned the degree citations, both B.A. and M.A. recipients were admitted to the company of learned men "*pro more Academiarum in* Angliâ" ("according to the custom of the English Universities"), which also included the traditional gift of a book (minus the medieval cap, ring, and kiss).[34]

❋ ❋ ❋

The fledgling college would never have grown into the best-known and perhaps greatest (not to mention wealthiest) university in the world had its founders and their successors not found a way to keep the school afloat. Politics in the mother country—civil war, Puritan ascendance, restoration of the monarchy, and a "glorious" replacement of crowned heads—also affected Harvard's fortunes. The Puritan interregnum, for example, drew many first-generation ministers and lay friends of Harvard back to England. It also siphoned off 20 percent of the second, American-born, generation of New

33 The English universities did not award diplomas until the twentieth century. Yale began to offer them at least by 1738; in 1701 the legally wary "Collegiate School" was content to grant only "degrees or Licences" rather than legal diplomas. Harvard did not offer them routinely until 1813. Before that they were available for a fee, mostly to those going abroad. Brooks Mather Kelley, *Yale: A History* (New Haven, Conn.: Yale University Press, 1974), 10, 21; Richard Warch, *School of the Prophets: Yale College, 1701–1740* (New Haven, Conn.: Yale University Press, 1973), 31, 249; Franklin Bowditch Dexter, ed., *Documentary History of Yale University, 1701–1745* (New Haven, Conn.: Yale University Press, 1916; New York: Arno Press and the New York Times, 1969), 23; Morison, *Harvard College*, 1:299n1; Morison, "Harvard Degree Diplomas," *Harvard Alumni Bulletin* 35 (May 12, 1933): 804–13.

34 Morison, *Harvard College*, 1:70–71, 298–300; Hofstadter and Wilson, eds., *American Higher Education*, 1:18–19.

Englanders, many of whom completed their educations at Oxford, Cambridge, or the Inns of Court, married, and remained.[35]

That Harvard was neither fully public nor private in its origins and governance complicated its struggle for funding. Although the colonial legislature called it into being and confirmed its legal existence in a series of charters beginning in 1650, the college was a private corporation like the English colleges. Half of the Overseers were lay magistrates, the other half ministers (who by colony law were barred from secular public office), but the college needed its own corporate leadership closer to its daily operations. This the charter of 1650 provided in the form of a self-perpetuating, seven-person Corporation: the president, five fellows (often tutors), and the treasurer or bursar. Of considerable economic influence, following a long line of medieval privileges, it also exempted Harvard from taxes on its property and revenues, and its faculty, students, and servants from customs, tolls, and all military and civil obligations.[36] Reluctant to turn its creation out into the New World cold, the colony made several payments toward college buildings, the president's house, and repairs to both. It also underwrote most of the president's and fellows' salaries. Together, government support composed 27 percent of the college's gifts and bequests before 1712. Without long-term public support, "private" Harvard would not have survived.[37]

Public support took numerous other forms. One of the earliest was the government's donation of the leasing fees from the indispensable ferry connecting Charlestown and Boston. Another was the direct levy of one peck of corn (or twelve pence in specie or kind) on every family in three of the four United Colonies of New England. Both ventures, along with numerous student payments in kind, involved the college treasurer in elaborate transactions of

35 Stout, "Morphology of Remigration," 164–67.

36 Morison, *Harvard College*, 1: ch. 1, at 5–8. See above, ch. 1, p. 000–00.

37 Morison, *Founding of Harvard*, ch. 21; Morison, *Harvard College*, 2: ch. 18; Margery Somers Foster, *"Out of Smalle Beginings . . ." : An Economic History of Harvard College in the Puritan Period* (Cambridge, Mass.: Belknap Press of Harvard University Press, 1962), ch. 5 and p. 122, fig. 2B.

FIGURE 9. William Burgis's "Prospect" of Harvard College's three "Colledges" in 1726. Left: the second college building (1672–82); Middle: Stoughton College (1697–99); Right: Massachusetts Hall (1718–20), which replaced the President's House (1680).

resale when the remissions could not be consumed in the dining hall or used to repair the "Old [wooden] College." Similarly, gifts of land from towns and the colony entailed recruitment of, and timely collections from, lessees.[38] In early America, a college bursar's lot was not an happy one.

38 Morison, *Founding of Harvard*, 300–301, 322–24; Morison, *Harvard College*, 2:373–76; Foster, *"Out of Smalle Beginings"*, 88–96, 101–103. Between 1669 and 1677, the treasurer became a major timber merchant when some wealthy Piscataqua River friends donated cuttings worth £60 a year from their rich forests. By the same token, he had to resell often substandard Indian wampum beads (early used as currency) from the ferry lease to fur traders.

Easier to spend, though not always easy to collect, were public subscriptions (often government sponsored), individual gifts, and bequests. Before 1712, Harvard reaped some £10,000 from such sources. Some as early as 1650 took the form of annuities, establishing historical precedent for the modern alumni enterprise of "annual giving." An impressive 31 percent of these funds came from England: farm-estate rentals in Norfolk and Yorkshire, bequests from Puritan relatives and well-wishers, leather books and silver plate. The namesake of Harvard's late-nineteenth-century "sister" college, Lady Ann *Radcliffe* (Mowlson), succumbed in 1641 to the blandishments of Harvard's first fundraisers by giving £100 to endow a scholarship fund—for men, of course.[39]

All of this effort and treasure went to support the annual work of the president, two or three young tutors, and an average of eight B.A. graduates throughout the seventeenth century.[40] The largest classes matriculated 22, but the college housed no more than 75 students, which was on the small side for an English Cambridge college. Without a stable of endowed fellows, Harvard had to make do with a polymathic president, who taught the whole curriculum, and an ever-changing brace of recent B.A.s en route to more promising careers in churches. The education and degrees their 446 undergraduates earned in the seventeenth century not only were respected by Oxford and Cambridge but also fitted them for leadership and public service in New England and occasionally beyond. At least half became ministers; 67, "magistrates" and public officials above the local level; 38, merchants, planters, and gents; 35, physicians; 17, career teachers; and 10, soldiers and sailors. One playwright, a printer, an Indian teacher, an unpopular lawyer, and an alchemist rounded out the alumni rolls.[41] Harvard was certainly no university yet, but its graduates and the education they received were scarcely distinguishable from those of its larger, more illustrious English progenitor.

39 Morison, *Harvard College*, 2:378–87, 437–38, 485–86; Foster, *"Out of Smalle Beginings"*, 107, 110, 115–16.

40 Eighteen percent of Harvard's matriculants died, dropped out, or were expelled before graduation. Morison, *Harvard College*, 2:557.

41 Ibid., 2:562–63.

❁ ❁ ❁

Harvard would not remain the sole source of educated men in New England or in Anglo-America. Swelling immigrant populations in the southern and Middle Atlantic colonies and further additions to fecund New England created needs and demands for higher education up and down the Atlantic seaboard. By 1750 the colonies hosted a black and white population of well over one million, with many more, mostly non-English, emigrants on the way: Palatine Germans, French Huguenots, Swiss, Ulster Scots-Irish, Lowland Scots, and African slaves. Substantial towns and cities—New York and Philadelphia—were natural sites for colleges, with the requisite populations, wealth, preparatory schools, postgraduate professions, and civic pride. But so were smaller towns and villages—Williamsburg, Princeton, Hanover—whose boosters believed that geographical proximity, low costs, religious uniformity, a "collegiate way of living," and distance from urban disease and immorality would attract students.[42] Serving a variety of Protestant religious preferences, eight new colleges were able to secure charters—one directly from the crown, the rest from colonial governors and legislatures—before the Americans rebelled in 1776. By the time the class of 1780 graduated, America's colleges had matriculated about 6,517 and graduated about 5,271 candidates for leadership in church and state. At least another 321 had chosen to study abroad—Anglicans in England, Catholics on the Continent, and future physicians in Scotland.[43]

42 Beverly McAnear, "College Founding in the American Colonies, 1745–1775," *Mississippi Valley Historical Review* 42:1 (June 1955), 24–44; Beverly McAnear, "The Selection of an Alma Mater by Pre-Revolutionary Students," *Pennsylvania Magazine of History and Biography* 73:4 (Oct. 1949), 429–40.

43 Email (Jan. 25, 2011) from James McLachlan, who had compiled a complete record of pre-1780 American college students. Much of it is incorporated in the Massachusetts Historical Society–New England Historical and Genealogical Society CD-ROM, *Colonial Collegians: Biographies of Those Who Attended American Colleges before the War for Independence* (2005); James McLachlan, "Education," in *Scotland and the Americas, 1600 to 1800* (Providence, R.I.: John Carter Brown Library, 1995), 65–72. I am grateful for Jim's continued generosity in sharing his data and insights.

Harvard gambled when (during the English Interregnum) it obtained and operated with a corporate charter issued by the Massachusetts Bay Colony, another chartered corporation, in violation of a basic principle of English law. But the new colleges were more careful to secure charters either directly from the crown, as William & Mary did, or from crown-appointed governors or proprietors.[44] In the charter colony of Connecticut, the ten ministers who sought authorization in 1701 for what became Yale—nine of them graduates of Harvard—were the most cautious after Massachusetts had its original charter withdrawn in 1684 and replaced by royal control. "Not daring to incorporate it," they sought to give "the Academie as low a Name as we could," by "calling it a collegiate school" and its head a mere "Rector." From the very first year of operation, however, it did, like its Harvard model, assume and exercise the right to award degrees. When the "school" was finally incorporated in 1745, its *rector* became a *president*, and the name given to its first major building in New Haven, Yale College, was transferred to the whole institution.[45] Neither the crown nor the Board of Trade and Plantations ever contested Yale's or any of the other new colleges' charters.[46] In hindsight, Virginia's royal governor, Sir Francis Nicholson, was too cautious when he declined to charter William & Mary himself and sent the newly appointed Anglican commissary James Blair to obtain a charter directly from the sovereigns.[47] Princeton's founders were also too skittish about the charter they secured in 1746 from

44 Princeton, King's College, Dartmouth, and later Harvard also tried to obtain royal charters but failed. Joseph Stancliffe Davis, *Essays in the Earlier History of American Corporations. Numbers I–III*, 2 vols. (Cambridge, Mass.: Harvard University Press, 1917), 1:105; David C. Humphrey, *From King's College to Columbia, 1746–1800* (New York: Columbia University Press, 1976), 146–47.

45 Ibid., 1:22; Warch, *School of the Prophets*, 6, 21, 31, 46, 88n41, 95.

46 Davis, *Earlier American Corporations*, 1:10, 22, 25. In 1691 the Board of Trade allowed the newly authorized Massachusetts General Court to re-"incorporate their College, and to make it an University, with as ample privileges as they should think necessary." The General Court was content to retain Harvard's collegiate identity. Ibid., 1:18.

47 Ibid., 1:12; Thad W. Tate, "The Colonial College, 1693–1782," in Susan H. Godson et al., *The College of William & Mary: A History*, 2 vols. (Williamsburg, Va.: King and Queen Press, Society of the Alumni, College of William & Mary, 1993), vol. 1, pt. 1, 7–15.

acting-governor John Hamilton. To hedge their bets, they obtained another two years later from the new royal governor, Jonathan Belcher.[48]

❁ ❁ ❁

As with Harvard, the funding and therefore governance of the eight new colleges was largely a private-public coalition. Provincial legislatures provided initial grants to erect college buildings and occasionally to subsidize faculty salaries and operating expenses. Localities competed with land, wood, tax exemptions, and cash subscriptions to woo and retain the colleges and their economy-boosting (if mischievous) student populations. Churches and congregations, at home and abroad, passed the plate for colleges with trustees, presidents, and faculties of similar faiths.[49] In return for public support, most boards of trustees included numerous lay members (to balance the ubiquitous ministers) and public officials, at least *ex officio*.[50] These mixed boards prevented the growth of, and

48 Fortunately, in 1756, he modestly declined their offer to name the handsome new college building after himself. It was dubbed Nassau Hall instead and still stands as the foundation of Princeton's identity. Thomas Jefferson Wertenbaker, *Princeton, 1746–1896* (Princeton, N.J.: Princeton University Press, 1946), 21, 26–27, 39.

49 Beverly McAnear, "The Raising of Funds by the Colonial Colleges," *Mississippi Valley Historical Review* 38:4 (March 1952), 591–612. King William III and Queen Mary II endowed their college in Virginia more handsomely than most colleges were. Besides £1,985 for a building, they gave a portion of the duty on tobacco exports and fees from the colony surveyor, and 20,000 acres of land. The colonial assembly later granted the college a duty on skins and furs worth £100 a year and a duty on imported liquor worth twice that. In return, the college paid only a symbolic annual quitrent of two copies of Latin verses on Guy Fawkes Day, November 5, to commemorate the saving of the Parliament building from a political bomber. Tate, "Colonial College," 1:12, 51, 63; Kristin A. Zech, "'So Well Endowed': Economic Support of the College of William and Mary during the Colonial Period" (senior honors thesis, Dept. of History, College of William & Mary, 2001); copies in the college archives and the Dept. of History library.

50 Yale was a prominent exception: its ten trustees were all ministers. Connecticut had no legal jurisdiction over the college until 1792, when eight public officials, including the governor and lieutenant-governor, joined the board. Brown, too, had no civil officials on its board initially. Warch, *School of the Prophets*, 30; Elliott and

were a necessary substitute for, the kind of self-government ideally enjoyed by the faculties of Oxford and Cambridge while ensuring that private colleges remained somewhat responsive to the will and needs of the public.[51]

Although all but one of the 36 colonial-era presidents were ministers, and many faculty were or planned to be, no college was overtly sectarian. Even Queen's College (later Rutgers), founded in 1766 by members of the Dutch Reformed Church, sought to accommodate the dominant Presbyterians of New Jersey and the Anglicans of New York. All had charters that opened their classrooms to adherents of any Protestant Trinitarian faith.[52] America's ethnic, political, and religious pluralism, exacerbated by the Great Awakening of religious ardor and factionalism in the mid-eighteenth century, required colleges to reach beyond their own sectarian origins and propensities if they wished to attract all varieties of Protestant and survive.

Growth was necessary because all of the colleges began small and most boosted their student numbers very slowly. More than a few began as "academies" or grammar schools and proceeded tardily to full college status. What became the University of Pennsylvania in 1791 began in 1740 as a charitable school before being chartered

---

Chambers, *Charters and Basic Laws*, 589n3; Walter C. Bronson, *The History of Brown University, 1764–1914* (Providence, R.I.: Brown University, 1914), 32.

51 Jurgen Herbst, *From Crisis to Crisis: American College Governance, 1636–1819* (Cambridge, Mass.: Harvard University Press, 1982), chs. 3–10; *Universities in Early Modern Europe (1500–1800)*, ed. Hilde de Ridder-Symoens, vol. 2 of *A History of the University in Europe* [*HUE*], gen. ed. Walter Rüegg, 4 vols. (Cambridge: Cambridge University Press, 1996), ch. 6 at 261, 272; Sheldon Rothblatt and Martin Trow, "Government Policies and Higher Education: A Comparison of Britain and the United States, 1630–1860," in Colin Crouch and Anthony Heath, eds., *Social Research and Social Reform: Essays in Honour of A. H. Halsey* (Oxford: Clarendon Press, 1992), 174–79.

52 Baptist Rhode Island College and Anglican King's College were the exceptions in allowing Jews to attend, though few did. McAnear, "College Founding," 24, 27; Durnin, "Role of Colonial College Presidents," 23, 24, 27; Jurgen Herbst, "The Eighteenth Century Origins of the Split Between Private and Public Higher Education in the United States," *History of Education Quarterly* 15:3 (Fall 1975), 273–80, at 274–75, 277; *HUE*, 2:273–74; Bronson, *History of Brown University*, 15–17, 22–23, 29; Humphrey, *From King's College to Columbia*, 98; William H. S. Demarest, *A History of Rutgers College, 1766–1924* (New Brunswick, N.J.: Rutgers College, 1924), 76, 82, 86.

in 1755 as the nonsectarian College and Academy of Philadelphia.[53] After receiving a royal charter in 1693, William & Mary remained a grammar school until it acquired its full statutory complement of six (mostly Oxford-educated) professors thirty-six years later. While all of the other colleges had grammar schools available or nearby to prep their students for admission, William & Mary's usually had more students than the college proper, whose undergraduates topped out around sixty. Given the shortage of Tidewater towns, most of the students were planters' sons, who stayed only two or three years divided between the school and the college. By 1780 only 24 had taken B.A.s, almost all of whom were headed for ordination in England as Anglican clergy.[54] In the South, a smattering of learning was sufficient until the Revolution brought changes to the political economy and ambitions of the region.

In the northern colonies, colleges multiplied to accommodate new populations, settlement patterns, urbanization, and social needs. After Yale was founded, Harvard no longer provided the major blueprint for college-building. The College of New Jersey (1746; later known as Princeton) and Dartmouth College (1769) were founded by Yale men and followed Yale patterns. Rhode Island College (1764; later Brown University) and Queen's (1766; the second New Jersey college) were Princeton offshoots. After the Revolution and well into the nineteenth century, Congregational Yale and Presbyterian

53 Despite its nonsectarian origins, the Philadelphia college soon became dominated by aggressive Anglicans and feisty Presbyterians. Hoeveler, *Creating the American Mind*, ch. 7; Edward C. Elliott and M. M. Chambers, eds., *Charters and Basic Laws of Selected American Universities and Colleges* (New York: Carnegie Foundation for the Advancement of Teaching, 1934; Westport, Conn.: Greenwood Press, 1970), 411, 415; Edward Potts Cheyney, *History of the University of Pennsylvania, 1740–1940* (Philadelphia: University of Pennsylvania Press, 1940), ch. 2.

54 Tate, "Colonial College," 1:19, 49, 77, 103, 110. Tate ("Colonial College," 1:113) and J. E. Morpurgo (*Their Majesties' Royall Colledge: William and Mary in the Seventeenth and Eighteenth Centuries* [Williamsburg, Va.: The Endowment Association of The College of William and Mary of Virginia, 1976], 149, 155) err in stating that William & Mary awarded its first B.A.s in 1772. The correct number of graduates is in James McLachlan, "MS Directory of Students at William and Mary through 1780" (copy in my possession).

Princeton were the predominant inspirations, models, and providers of presidents for the colleges that proliferated throughout the American Midwest and South.[55]

Not all colleges secured permanent homes immediately by accepting alluring offers from towns bidding for their presence. Since every founding president was a minister, the location of the college sometimes depended on proximity to his congregation or church. Starting small, the infant institution could be, and often was, housed and taught in the minister's own home. If the president died or was otherwise unable to continue in office, the college—in the form of students, a few books, and maybe a tutor or "usher"—simply moved to a new location, not unlike early medieval universities. For its first eighteen years, Yale was a veritable college on wheels. Classes were conducted in five different Connecticut towns and villages before the college finally found a permanent home in New Haven in 1719. The College of New Jersey also wandered for a decade between presidential manses in Elizabethtown and Newark before Princeton outbid New Brunswick, and commodious Nassau Hall, then the largest building in British North America, was erected in 1756 to house the peripatetic scholars. That Princeton stood on a healthy rise, halfway between New York and Philadelphia, and at the demographic center of the colonial north-south axis clinched the trustees' decision.[56]

55 McAnear, "College Founding," 25; Donald Robert Come, "The Influence of Princeton on Higher Education in the South before 1825," *William & Mary Quarterly* (3rd ser.) 2:4 (Oct. 1945), 359–96; Donald G. Tewksbury, *The Founding of Colleges and Universities before the Civil War* (New York: Teachers College, Columbia University, 1932), 91–103, at 100, 119–29, at 120; Frederick Rudolph, *The American College and University: A History* (New York: Alfred A. Knopf, 1962), 52–53, 54–55, 57–58.

56 Warch, *School of the Prophets*, 95; Wertenbaker, *Princeton*, ch. 1, at 36, 40; James McLachlan, *Princetonians, 1748–1768: A Biographical Dictionary* (Princeton, N.J.: Princeton University Press, 1976), xx. For Nassau Hall, see Henry Lyttleton Savage, ed., *Nassau Hall, 1756–1956* (Princeton, N.J.: Princeton University Press, 1956); William K. Selden, *Nassau Hall: Princeton University's National Historic Landmark* (Princeton, N.J.: Office of Mailing and Printing, Princeton University, 1995); Karl Kusserow, ed., *Inner Sanctum: Memory and Meaning in Princeton's Faculty Room at Nassau Hall* (Princeton, N.J.: Princeton University Art Museum, 2010).

FIGURE 10. Princeton's Nassau Hall (1755–57) and the President's House (1756), both designed and built by Robert Smith, a carpenter-architect from Philadelphia. In this 1764 engraving, the fancy fence in front of Nassau Hall, enclosing what came to be called the campus for the first time in American history, is probably the artist's invention. The president may have needed one.

The geographical spread of new colleges had a discernible effect on student demography. Before Yale opened for business in 1703, Harvard had graduated 69 young men from Connecticut, about one a year. But in Yale's first forty years, only a dozen locals made the trek to Cambridge for their education. In contrast, 42 Massachusetts lads, mostly from the western interior, graduated from Yale.[57] In Princeton's first twenty years, even during its peripatetic phase, the college managed to draw three-quarters of its students from *outside* New Jersey, just the opposite pattern of its more parochial predecessors and successors. Princeton's low costs (the lowest in the colonies) and its willingness to admit qualified students with advanced standing as sophomores and juniors (further reducing costs)

57 In 1702 four Harvard graduates took their M.A.s at Yale's tiny first commencement, presumably after demonstrating their intellectual skills acquired on the banks of the Charles. Warch, *School of the Prophets*, 8, 46, 251, 252–53.

made the college a magnet for matriculants from eleven mainland colonies and the Caribbean as well. College rivals in Massachusetts, Connecticut, New York, and Pennsylvania each lost an average of two scholars a year to the upstart in New Jersey. Once enrolled, Princeton students enjoyed the added advantage of completing the course and graduating with their class. Even its few dropouts tended to finish elsewhere. Philadelphia and King's (1754; later Columbia)—both city colleges—were much less retentive, losing between a third and a half of their matriculants to remunerative work that did not require a college education.[58]

❁ ❁ ❁

The nearly 6,000 boys and men who got past the colleges' none-too-strenuous admissions process and matriculated before 1776 were an even more diverse lot than those who entered Harvard in the previous century. They had prepared their "small Latin and less Greek" (Ben Jonson's phrase) and, belatedly, arithmetic at a greater variety of schools and academies and with more private tutors (largely in the South) and ministers. Although precocious boys as young as twelve or thirteen and men in their late twenties made the generous cut, most freshmen were sixteen or seventeen (as they were at Tudor and early Stuart Oxbridge), except at King's and Philadelphia, where they were only fourteen on average.[59] Many were eldest or only sons, dedicated by their families to higher callings. As the century wore on, more had fathers who had attended college, often at the same institution (thus creating the first American "legacies"). The city colleges, King's and Philadelphia, served mostly the local commercial and upper-middle classes. More countrified Yale and Princeton, and

58 Harvard and Yale rivaled Princeton in graduating most of those they admitted. McLachlan, *Princetonians, 1748–1768*, xx–xxi. See also Richard A. Harrison, *Princetonians, 1769–1775: A Biographical Dictionary* (Princeton, N.J.: Princeton University Press, 1980), xxi.

59 Warch, *School of the Prophets*, 254; McLachlan, *Princetonians, 1748–1768*, xxi; Harrison, *Princetonians, 1769–1775*, xx; Humphrey, *From King's to Columbia*, 194; Ann D. Gordon, *The College of Philadelphia, 1749–1779: The Impact of an Institution* (New York: Garland Publishing, 1989), 111–12.

even suburban Harvard, took in large numbers of sons of farmers, merchants, ministers, and artisans.[60]

At the beginning of most colleges, students were forced to live where they could, with parents, relatives, guardians, teachers, or in local boarding houses. But the English and American ideal of a collegiate way of living soon asserted itself with trustees, who sought help from legislators and donors to build commodious three-story structures for living, study, and discipline. As American universities today are engaged in athletic "arms races" to see who can build the biggest stadiums and best gymnasiums, their colonial counterparts seemed to be competing to erect the largest and most impressive "colleges" or "halls."[61]

With a handsome gift in 1718 from East India trader Elihu Yale, Connecticut's mobile college was able to seat itself in New Haven in the unpainted "Wooden College," measuring 170 feet by 22 feet, with "Chambers and Studies as well as a hall and Library" distributed off three staircases.[62] Not to be outdone by its northern rival, Princeton employed a leading Philadelphia craftsman to design and build an imposing stone edifice at least 7 feet longer and 32 feet wider than Yale's, capable of housing 147 students and their tutors. Although it had three staircases, it did pose disciplinary challenges

60 Conrad Edick Wright, *Revolutionary Generation: Harvard Men and the Consequences of Independence* (Amherst: University of Massachusetts Press in association with Massachusetts Historical Society, 2005), 228 (table 3); *Sibley's Harvard Graduates: Biographical Sketches of Those Who Attended Harvard College*, 18 (1772–1774), xx, xxv; McLachlan, *Princetonians, 1748–1768*, xxii; Harrison, *Princetonians, 1769–1775*, xxv (table C); William Bailey, "A Statistical Study of the Yale Graduates, 1701–92," *Yale Review* 16 (1908): 400–426, at 406 (table 2); Gordon, *College of Philadelphia*, 116–27; Humphrey, *From King's to Columbia*, 97–98, 191, 199.

61 For illustrations of eight colleges' buildings, see Hoeveler, *Creating the American Mind*, 58, 97, 138, 174, 182, 210, 234, 308.

62 Unfortunately, its 25 "Chambers" were soon outgrown. When enrollment exploded after 1745, leaving more than half of the students to fend for themselves in the small town, Yale took inspiration from Harvard's Massachusetts Hall and built Connecticut Hall (1750) in Georgian brick, only 100 feet by 40, but with seven more double rooms. Kelley, *Yale*, 40–41, 59–60; Warch, *School of the Prophets*, 71, 88; Louis Leonard Tucker, *Puritan Protagonist: President Thomas Clap of Yale College* (Chapel Hill: University of North Carolina Press, 1962), frontispiece, 74–75.

for the faculty. The halls ran the length of the building, affording rebellious students too much opportunity to cabal and supplying a noisy bowling alley for cannonballs.[63]

When the College of Philadelphia decided to move out of a remodeled auditorium that poorly housed a mixed population of schoolboys and girls and all-male college students, the trustees sent two professors to examine Nassau Hall for inspiration. The 100-by-70-foot College Hall they constructed in 1765 ended up as "no more than a supervised boarding house" for some 50 academy and college boys, some as young as ten or twelve; the rest roomed in town. King's, the richest colonial college, had done much better in 1760, when it opened a grand grey-stone "college," 180 feet long and 30 wide, with 20 student apartments, a large hall, and a library above it.[64] Although its functionality followed Oxbridge lines, its design resembled more closely Yale's old Wooden College. That King's president Samuel Johnson had been a tutor at Yale in 1718 undoubtedly affected the outcome.[65]

❁ ❁ ❁

Once the students were enrolled and ensconced in the college barracks, the faculty went to work. Standing *in loco parentis* over young, energetic, male "pupils," college authorities sought to create a "carefully regulated male hierarchy," free from maternal authority.[66] Rules were stringent and extensive. As students were expected to obey and defer to their faculty elders, so underclassmen were taught by their peers to defer to those above them in class rank. The small world of the college was made in the (often idealized) image of the larger social order beyond the campus. For many years, until class sizes

63 Savage, *Nassau Hall*, 7, 13; Selden, *Nassau Hall*, 5.

64 As at early modern Oxford and Cambridge, colonial libraries were invariably located on the second floor, away from the damp of the roof and the foundation.

65 Cheyney, *University of Pennsylvania*, 55–56; Humphrey, *From King's to Columbia*, 111–15.

66 Gordon, *College of Philadelphia*, 184 (quotations); Phyllis Vine, "The Social Function of Eighteenth-Century Higher Education," *History of Education Quarterly* 16:4 (Winter 1976), 409–24; Walter J. Ong, "Latin Language Study as a Renaissance Puberty Rite," *Studies in Philology* 56:2 (April 1959), 103–24.

grew too large, Harvard and Yale assigned their matriculants places in their classes according to a presidential calculus of parental status, individual merit, and future usefulness. In that assigned position a student would recite in class, seat and serve himself at meals, sit in chapel, march in academic processions, and appear in the social registers of the day, the printed college catalogues. If he offended the authorities, he could be "degraded" one or more places until reformation and penitence were manifest. Similarly, obstreperous collegians in New York and Philadelphia felt the sting of having their status-laden gowns, like epaulets, "stripped off" before the student body.[67]

College faculties, then as now, did not prize discipline as the chief joy of their job. They wanted and were hired primarily to teach. Their preparation for that task was hit or miss. Postgraduate education, mostly in the form of an M.A. after self-directed study, included little to no practice teaching and certainly no coursework in pedagogy or adolescent psychology. Some master's students remained at their alma mater to receive reading suggestions from the president and to use his or the college library. Most of those resident graduates, aiming at eventual careers in the ministry, were sometimes hired as tutors to put the underclassmen through their academic paces. Often they lived in the dorm among their charges, like a cross between today's R.A. (resident advisor) and T.A. (teaching assistant).[68]

It was not an easy cross to bear and tutor turnover was high.[69] Aroused students who chafed under a tutor's sarcasm, gimlet eye, or

67 Axtell, *School upon a Hill*, ch. 6, esp. 219–34; Humphrey, *From King's to Columbia*, 129, 185, 187, 206; Gordon, *College of Philadelphia*, 193.

68 Wilson Smith, "The Teacher in Puritan Culture," *Harvard Educational Review* 36: 4 (Fall 1966), 394–411; Morison, *Three Centuries of Harvard*, 108–109, 179; Wright, *Revolutionary Generation*, 39–41, 50, 249n43; Warch, *School of the Prophets*, 245–46; Tucker, *Puritan Protagonist*, 71–72, 91–92; Wertenbaker, *Princeton*, 99–100.

69 In the eighteenth century, Yale tutors stayed an average of 2½–3 years; Rhode Island College and Dartmouth were also revolving doors for tutors. Before 1685, Harvard's 41 tutors lasted about the same; only 6 stayed more than 3 years. But between 1685 and 1701, they stayed an average of 6½ years. Between 1745 and 1771, the average grew to 9 years, although the contract remained a renewable 3 years. Warch, *School of the Prophets*, 245; Kathryn McDaniel Moore, "The War with the Tutors: Student-Faculty Conflict at Harvard and Yale, 1745–1771," *History of Education Quarterly* 18:2 (Summer 1978), 115–27, at117; Wright, *Revolutionary Generation*, 40; Smith "Teacher in Puritan Culture," 400, 401; Martin Finkelstein, "From Tutor to Specialized Scholar:

heavy hand frequently struck back with japes, gibes, libels, pranks, threats, sabotage, or even weapons. Those colonial forms of "student evaluation" also could get a tutor fired or otherwise persuade him to quit. In the years leading up to the American Revolution, the students imbibed a heady draught of "the spirit of Liberty" with which to protest the "arbitrary government" of college presidents and the pettifoggery of tutors. At all of the northern colleges, even loyalist King's, the enlarged "Spirit of Contumacy" was seriously, if sporadically, disturbing.[70]

Less endangered by student pique were the more senior professors, who enjoyed a modicum of tenure to compensate for salaries seldom equal to their social status. In 1750 only ten professors were active in the four existing colleges, the great majority at Harvard and William & Mary. Most teaching was still being done by the president, who tended the upperclasses, and two or three tutors, who ran recitations and rode herd on the younger boys. Twenty-five years later, the nine colleges employed 33 professors, most of them occupying privately endowed chairs. But college teaching was not yet a profession. Tutors rarely rose to professorships, and most professors taught only part of their working lives; many combined teaching with other careers. Most were ministers or physicians before teaching, and many were after. Perhaps 40 percent began their teaching stints before they turned thirty. Those who were older were often mature, published clergymen enticed by a college presidency,

---

Academic Professionalization in Eighteenth and Nineteenth Century America," *History of Higher Education Annual* 3 (1983), 99–121, at 101; John D. Burton, "The Harvard Tutors: The Beginning of an Academic Profession, 1690–1825," *History of Higher Education Annual* 16 (1996), 5–20.

70 Sheldon S. Cohen, "Harvard College on the Eve of the American Revolution," in Frederick S. Allis, ed., *Sibley's Heir: A Volume in Memory of Clifford Kenyon Shipton*, vol. 59 of *Publications of the Colonial Society of Massachusetts* (Boston: Colonial Society of Massachusetts, 1982), 173–90, at 184, 188; Axtell, *School upon a Hill*, ch. 6, esp. 237–44; Moore, "War with the Tutors," 115–27; Louis Leonard Tucker, "Centers of Sedition: Colonial Colleges and the American Revolution," *Proceedings of the Massachusetts Historical Society* 91 (1979), 16–34; David W. Robson, *Educating Republicans: The College in the Era of the American Revolution, 1750–1800* (Westport, Conn.: Greenwood Press, 1985), ch. 3.

another form of ministry. With the exception of the faculty at Anglican William & Mary, King's, and Philadelphia, which preferred English or Scottish graduates when they could get them, almost all professors taught at their own alma maters and, unlike modern academics, never made career moves to other schools. Although few taught college exclusively, at least half gave up the lectern and the ghost in the same year.[71]

Professors differed from tutors not only in age, experience, and job satisfaction but also in the degree to which they specialized in particular subjects. Until the 1760s or later, tutors taught most of the traditional required subjects, largely in recitations, to a single academic class throughout the three- or four-year B.A. course. Professors, in contrast, taught their specialties, which were often quite broad before disciplinary fission, in year-long lecture courses.[72] Given the denominational origins and governance of the colleges, it is no surprise that the first endowed chairs tended to be in divinity.[73] But with the seismic shifts in the intellectual geography after Bacon, Boyle, Locke, and Newton, American curricula were slowly rearranged to depose Aristotle, to reflect the New Learning, and to appeal to other preferences of students and their fee-paying parents. In the process, sundry old subjects and teaching methods were discarded, but few voices of regret were heard as political revolution and nation building approached.

71 William D. Carrell, "American College Professors: 1750–1800," *History of Education Quarterly* 8:3 (Fall 1968), 289–305; William D. Carrell, "Biographical List of American College Professors to 1800," ibid., 358–74; Finkelstein, "From Tutor to Specialized Scholar," 99–121.

72 Joe W. Kraus, "The Development of a Curriculum in Early American Colleges," *History of Education Quarterly* 1:2 (June 1961), 64–76, at 69; Frederick Rudolph, *Curriculum: A History of the American Undergraduate Course of Study Since 1636* (San Francisco: Jossey-Bass, 1977), 25–53, esp. 42–44.

73 Congregational Harvard's first chair was endowed, ecumenically, in 1721 by Thomas Hollis, a wealthy London merchant and Baptist. William & Mary filled its two long-planned chairs of divinity (the second putatively in "Oriental languages") with local clergymen in 1729. Yale had to wait until 1746 for its first chair, also in divinity, but it was not filled for nearly ten years. Morison, *Three Centuries of Harvard*, 66–67; Tate, *William & Mary*, 1:69; Finkelstein, "From Tutor to Specialized Scholar," 102.

❁ ❁ ❁

The first noticeable change in the traditional curriculum was the gradual decline of Latin for in-class discussion and out-of-class conversation. This shift began at Harvard by 1692, when the new college laws released the boys from the necessity of speaking like Roman senators after class. More English-language textbooks and lectures in class hastened the change. Yale held out until 1774 before dropping its rule, but by then enforcement had long since ceased. For the same loss of relevance, Hebrew fell out of Harvard's list of required subjects for freshmen in 1723 and for the upper three classes in 1755, when it was made elective. Within five years, the college's discouragingly tedious instructor of Hebrew retired. Yale's devotion to the language of the Old Testament was much more superficial. Although it was, with Greek, part of the first-year course of study and Yale's third rector, Timothy Cutler (1719–22), was known as "a great Hebrician," graduating seniors had long forgotten what little they knew. The first president, Thomas Clap (1745–66), offered Hebrew only to ministerial candidates. In 1751 Princeton freshmen too were reluctantly introduced to Hebrew grammar, but twenty years later it was gone, along with ontology. All of President John Witherspoon's lectures were in English, inflected by his strong Scottish burr.[74]

A second change that reinforced the first was the replacement of Latin syllogistic disputations, a medieval and Tudor-Stuart staple, with more freewheeling and intelligible forensic debates in English. These better prepared the increasing numbers of eighteenth-century seniors who chose careers in law and public life rather than the ministry.[75] The formal constraints of the scholastic syllogism,

74 Kraus, "Development of a Curriculum," 66–68, 71–72; Rudolph, *Curriculum*, 36–37, 38; Morison, *Three Centuries of Harvard*, 30–31, 57–58; Kenneth P. Minkema, "Reforming Harvard: Cotton Mather on Education at Cambridge," *New England Quarterly* 87:2 (June 2014), 319–40, at 322, 332, 335; Warch, *School of the Prophets*, 198–200; Tucker, *Puritan Protagonist*, 77–78, 79n. 55; Wertenbaker, *Princeton*, 98–99.

75 Over half of Yale's graduates before 1744 became ministers; from 1778 to 1791, fewer than a quarter did. In the same periods, law increased its share from 9 percent to nearly a third. More than half of Harvard alumni before 1721 became "settled" ministers. In the next eight decades only 27 percent did. Even Princeton's still-healthy

whose major source of subject matter was the prescribed curriculum, cramped the students' sense of style and range of evidence. It also proved a weak tool for discovering new knowledge. Debates offered freer range for ethical and emotional, as well as logical, proof and for rhetorical display.[76] In contrast, Latin disputations, no matter how initially impressive they might be, were not engaging spectacles for guests at commencement, when public relations were paramount. Partly to prevent audience ennui, colleges shifted from debates altogether to student orations on more contemporary topics. The approach, advent, and aftermath of the Revolution suggested many themes—just war, patriotism, federalism, taxation, slavery, Indian policy, and science—as well as more frolicsome questions about literature and the female sex. These gave the speakers not only "a greater Scope to their Genius," as President Clap argued, but a way to apply their scholastic acquirements to adult-world concerns.[77]

The New Learning of the English, French, and Scottish enlightenments produced the third, most notable, change in the eighteenth-century curriculum. By 1740—at least a century after Oxbridge—"the mathematical sciences had established themselves firmly" in American classrooms. The major vehicle was endowed professorships of mathematics and "natural philosophy" (largely physics and astronomy); by 1776, six of the nine colleges had them.[78] The earliest

---

production of clerical alumni slipped from 47 percent (1748–1768) to 40 percent (1769–1775). Bailey, "Statistical Study of Yale Graduates," 407; Morison, *Three Centuries of Harvard*, 241; Harrison, *Princetonians, 1769–1775*, xxvii-xxviii.

76 By the 1760s, Yale and Princeton had added teaching in rhetoric, oratory, and belles lettres, all in English. During and after the American Revolution, French entered the formal curricula of King's, William & Mary, and Harvard, having been a favorite student choice for private tutoring earlier. Rudolph, *Curriculum*, 38–39, 51–52.

77 Kraus, "Development of a Curriculum," 70–71; Rudolph, *Curriculum*, 45–47; David Potter, *Debating in the Colonial Chartered Colleges: An Historical Survey, 1642 to 1900* (New York: Bureau of Publications, Teachers College, Columbia University, 1944), chs. 1–2 and pp. 120–21.

78 Although Yale did not get a chair until 1770, two tutors had introduced the new science and math after 1716, and Rector/President Thomas Clap (1739–1766) made Yale the first college to require arithmetic for admission, reduced the number of courses in logic to make room for math, and appointed several tutors with math and science skills. Rudolph, *Curriculum*, 34–35; Tucker, *Puritan Protagonist*, 80–91.

was established in 1711 at William & Mary. Unfortunately, the incumbent taught only grammar-school boys and was fired within a year for "intemperance" and living with an "idle hussy he brought over with him" from London.[79] Not to be outdone, Harvard persuaded its great benefactor, Thomas Hollis, to endow a similar chair in 1727. It was filled for a decade with conspicuous success by the Harvard alumnus and English-trained Isaac Greenwood. He promoted mathematics education in the colonies by writing two textbooks before he, too, was let go for drunkenness. His successor, John Winthrop (Harvard class of 1732), quickly earned a sober reputation as America's best mathematician and scientist. He did the most to introduce the study of fluxions and to promote Newtonian physics in America, for which, and for valuable observations in geology and astronomy, he was made a fellow of the Royal Society of London. It was a sign of the times that when the College of Philadelphia was established in the mid-1750s, 40 percent of its curriculum was devoted to science and math. Small wonder that as early as 1744 a poetry-loving Harvard student complained that

> Now algebra, geometry,
> Arithmetick, astronomy,
> Opticks, chronology, and staticks,
> All tiresome parts of mathematicks,
> With twenty harder names than these
> Disturb my brains, and break my peace.[80]

For students whose minds did not run to higher math, the scientific apparatus used to demonstrate the operations and principles of science appealed more. In 1727 Thomas Hollis donated some of London's finest equipment to enliven Harvard's classes. By the 1750s,

79 Theodore Hornberger, *Scientific Thought in the American Colleges, 1638–1800* (Austin: University of Texas Press, 1946; New York, Octagon Press, 1968), 25, 26–27, 29, 47, 51.

80 Hornberger, *Scientific Thought*, 68. See also Brooke Hindle, *The Pursuit of Science in Revolutionary America, 1735–1789* (Chapel Hill: University of North Carolina Press, Williamsburg, Va., 1956), ch. 5, and Raymond Phineas Stearns, *Science in the British Colonies of America* (Urbana: University of Illinois Press, 1970).

most of the colleges were in competition, at home and abroad, to raise funds for, or donations of, the latest apparatus. Isaac Greenwood had been hired by Harvard largely on the strength of his popular Boston lecture series, *An Experimental Course of Mechanical Philosophy*, which employed "Various Instruments and Machines" to explain "the Principles of Nature, and the Wonderful Discoveries of the Incomparable Sir Isaac Newton." Textbook illustrations were of some help, but actual telescopes, pendulums, barometers, quadrants, and air pumps made more impression on students bored by daily doses of words in ancient tongues.[81]

Perhaps the most wonderful machine was the orrery (also known as a "copernicus"), an intricate mechanical model of the solar system. Harvard gained one in the Hollis donation and Thomas Clap made a simple one for Yale in 1743. But Philadelphia clockmaker David Rittenhouse built one in 1767 that was regarded as "the miracle of the age." This marvel Princeton managed to snatch from under the jealous nose of the local college in 1770. Graciously, the maker made the college another to restore local pride.[82]

Through such devices and teachings, the eighteenth-century colleges sought to "lead [their students] from the Study of Nature to the Knowledge of themselves, and of the God of Nature."[83] This new sequence of goals signaled a decline in the American Protestant belief in the efficacy of faith over works as a means of salvation, and entailed a turn away from the Bible as the sole guide to human conduct. Accordingly, the curriculum in the 1750s and '60s, paralleling the growth of science, sprouted new courses to recognize the rise of ethics at the expense of cold logic and speculative metaphysics. The main result in most colleges was a capstone course for seniors

81 Morison, *Three Centuries of Harvard*, 79; Hornberger, *Scientific Thought*, 45–47, 57–67; Tucker, *Puritan Protagonist*, 57–67, 89–91; I. Bernard Cohen, *Some Early Tools of American Science: An Account of the Early Scientific Instruments and Mineralogical and Biological Collections in Harvard University* (Cambridge, Mass.: Harvard University Press, 1950), esp. chs. 2–3.

82 Hornberger, *Scientific Thought*, 67; Howard C. Rice, Jr., *The Rittenhouse Orrery: Princeton's Eighteenth-Century Planetarium, 1767–1954* (Princeton, N.J.: Princeton University Library, 1954), chs. 1–3.

83 Quoted in Hornberger, *Scientific Thought*, 30.

FIGURE 11. A realistic likeness of the second Rittenhouse orrery on the seal of the newly chartered University of Pennsylvania (1782).

in moral philosophy. It grew out of older courses in divinity and started from theological premises but was influenced in a major way by thinkers of the Scottish Enlightenment. In addition to seeking moral laws in Scripture, students were led through a more familiar landscape to explore the ways and duties of man. From textbooks of Scottish philosophers (and Moderate churchmen) such as Francis Hutcheson and David Fordyce, American presidents taught their senior classes to trust in "common sense realism," which denied pure forms of both idealism and materialism and relied on reason and human nature (conscience, especially), to guide their conduct.

Scottish-educated leaders at Philadelphia and Princeton in particular introduced their students not only to the important social scientists of the Scottish Enlightenment—Adam Smith, Hutcheson, Adam Ferguson—but also to complementary texts by Hugo Grotius, Samuel Pufendorf, Algernon Sidney, James Harrington, and Locke. Like those of other peers, John Witherspoon's lectures at Princeton contained a semi-systematic blend of ethics, politics, history, economics, and jurisprudence.[84] They also played no small part in leading more than 98 percent of Princeton's alumni to choose the "rebel" side in the American Revolution.[85]

❊ ❊ ❊

In the fluid society of eighteenth-century America, colleges provided a tiny elite with more than a modicum of book learning and cultural polish. As they forged an educated class, however small, they also enabled many sons of ordinary colonists to do better than their fathers. Although the costs of college were substantial, college founders and

84 Kraus, "Development of a Curriculum," 74–75; Rudolph, *Curriculum*, 39–42, 53; Gladys Bryson, *Man and Society: The Scottish Inquiry of the Eighteenth Century* (Princeton, N.J.: Princeton University Press, 1945); Gordon, *College of Philadelphia*, 165–68; Douglas Sloan, *The Scottish Enlightenment and the American College Ideal* (New York: Teachers College Press, Columbia University, 1971), esp. chs. 3–4; Nicholas Phillipson, "The Pursuit of Virtue in Scottish University Education: Dugald Stewart and Scottish Moral Philosophy in the Enlightenment," in Phillipson, ed., *Universities, Society and the Future* (Edinburgh: Edinburgh University Press, 1983), 82–101; Richard B. Sher, *Church and University in the Scottish Enlightenment: The Moderate Literati of Edinburgh* (Princeton, N.J.: Princeton University Press, 1985); Sher and Jeffrey R. Smitten, eds., *Scotland and America in the Age of Enlightenment* (Princeton, N.J.: Princeton University Press, 1990), esp. pts. 1, 3; Sher, "Professors of Virtue: The Social History of the Edinburgh Moral Philosophy Chair in the Eighteenth Century," in M. A. Stewart, ed., *Studies in the Philosophy of the Scottish Enlightenment* (Oxford: Oxford University Press, 1990), 87–126; Hoeveler, *Creating the American Mind*, 122–26; Francis L. Broderick, "Pulpit, Physics, and Politics: The Curriculum of the College of New Jersey, 1746–1794," *William & Mary Quarterly* (3rd ser.) 6:1 (Jan. 1949), 42–68, esp. 62–68; Robson, *Educating Republicans*, 64–70, 81–82 (table 3–2), 85–87.

85 Harrison, *Princetonians, 1769–1775*, xxxi. Perhaps 16 percent of Harvard alumni were Loyalists, as were at least half of King's bluebloods. Morison, *Three Centuries of Harvard*, 147n.; Humphrey, *From King's to Columbia*, 140.

trustees used admissions, scholarships, and "work-study" opportunities to sponsor the social mobility of promising boys from farms, shops, and manses.[86] The great majority of elite sons did not need a college education to maintain their social or economic positions. But in fast-growing, expanding America, the upper classes were neither hereditary nor fixed, and ambitious sons of humbler origins were only too ready to move up, if given a chance. For most, horizontal movement to less populated frontiers and cheaper land was their ticket to improvement. But for some, college was that chance. By mingling with and befriending the sons of more prominent families, these promising candidates could work their way into alliances and careers traditionally reserved for the well-to-do.[87]

One traditional way to advance was through marriage. About a quarter of the students at Princeton, King's, and Philadelphia married sisters of classmates or daughters of trustees or presidents. Another route was through business connections with classmates' fathers or college trustees. In a very modern-sounding piece of advice to a friend, King's alumnus John Jay argued that "connections founded at School and College have much influence. . . . If judiciously formed, they will endure and be advantageous through life." The city colleges in particular touted such an advantage. Provost William Smith of Philadelphia was keen to give his students "a more general conversation with Gentlemen," experience in "practical Politeness," and exposure to the needs and opportunities of commerce. He favored regular student visits to "Coffee Houses, the Exchange, and all the Resorts of Business, except"—of course—"Taverns."[88]

But the primary route to social mobility for graduates not to the manor born was simply using their degrees and connections to enter professions socially and economically above those of their fathers. Although college degrees were not required, apprenticeships in law and medicine were easier to obtain through college-made connections.

86 Ralph Turner, "Sponsored and Contest Mobility in the School System," *American Sociological Review* 25:6 (Dec. 1960), 855–67; Axtell, *School upon a Hill*, 207–11.

87 Rudolph, *Curriculum*, 25–29; Vine, "Social Function," 415–16; Jackson Turner Main, *The Social Structure of Revolutionary America* (Princeton, N.J.: Princeton University Press, 1965).

88 Vine, "Social Function," 415; Gordon, *College of Philadelphia*, 200.

Scotland's advanced medical schools certainly welcomed the graduates of Princeton and Philadelphia, with their strong scientific and Presbyterian backgrounds. Careers in the church and teaching invariably required a degree.[89] The college that produced the least mobility was King's. Its strongly local, upper-class clientele largely followed their fathers', or parallel, careers to status, property, and public office. With a more diverse student population, the College of Philadelphia fostered greater movement up the social ladder. More of its graduates chose first careers in law than in the church, a trend that accelerated as the Revolution approached. Even merchants' sons became lawyers more often than they followed trade. The sons of urban professionals, like those at King's, followed their fathers into law and medicine. But rural professionals—mostly strong Presbyterians—sent more of their sons into the ministry. Farmers' sons also chose the ministry and teaching rather than returning home to inherit sometimes profitable domains.[90]

The strongest engine of social mobility was Princeton, the third largest college, where young men from eleven colonies and the West Indies could measure themselves against America's striking diversity and prepare for its opportunities. Like Harvard, the largest number of its students came from farms; only a third were sons of ministers or other professionals. But at Princeton, the farmers' sons invariably, and three-fourths of the sons of clergymen and professionals, outdid their fathers. Before the Revolution, it seems fair to say, one of Princeton's primary functions in American society was to "transform the sons of modest farmers into prospective clergymen, lawyers and medical men."[91] And, at least temporarily, teachers.

89 Vine, "Social Function," 414–15; McLachlan, "Education," 68–69.

90 Humphrey, *From King's to Columbia*, 224–28; Gordon, *College of Philadelphia*, ch. 8.

91 McLachlan, *Princetonians, 1748–1768*, xxii (quotation); Harrison, *Princetonians, 1769–1775*, xxiv-xxv; Morison, *Three Centuries of Harvard*, 102–103; *Sibley's Harvard Graduates*, 18:xxvi (table 4) and 19 (1775–1777), ms. intro. by Conrad Edick Wright, tables 3 and 6 (thanks to Conrad Wright for a preview copy); Jason Sharples, "When Farmers Became Lawyers: Colonial Harvard and Princeton as Vehicles of Social Mobility" (research paper, History 150w: "Higher Education in America," College of William & Mary, Fall 1999); copy in my possession. Some of the colonial colleges also attempted to "raise up"—culturally and religiously convert—American

After a rigorous education at the hands of two ministers, Philip Vickers Fithian, the son of a New Jersey grain farmer, entered Princeton at twenty-three and graduated in two years. Orphaned in his senior year, he pursued theological studies for a year and then became a tutor to a wealthy Virginia planter's family for another. In a letter to a college friend whom he had nominated as his successor, he described one of the major benefits of a Princeton education. In contrast to the social and economic equality of New Jersey, he told his friend, "if you should travel through this Colony, with a well-confirmed testimonial of your having finished with Credit a Course of studies at Nassau-Hall; you would be rated, without any more questions asked, either about your Family, your Estate, your business, or your intention, at 10,000£ . . . and you would be dispised & slighted if yo[u] rated yourself a farthing cheaper." Clearly, and maybe even more, in less ambitious William & Mary's backyard, a college "Reputation & learning" were worth a great deal in social status and credit, if something less than "a handful of Shillings in ready Cash."[92]

❁ ❁ ❁

In October 1770, after attending a Princeton commencement and the awarding of honorary D.D. degrees to three Scottish and two American ministers, the Rev. Ezra Stiles, a future president of Yale, noted with pride that "all the Learned Degrees are now conferred in the American Colleges as amply as in the European Colleges."[93] He might be forgiven his chauvinism but for the inconvenient fact that

---

Indian youth, most in preparatory schools, a few in college proper. Most attempts did not succeed or end well for the students. James Axtell, "The Little Red School," in *The Invasion Within: The Contest of Cultures in Colonial North America* (New York: Oxford University Press, 1985), ch. 8; Axtell, "Poison Ivy: Indian Education at the Best Colonial Colleges," *Colonial Williamsburg* 30:1 (Winter 2008), 58–63.

92 Hunter Dickinson Farish, ed., *Journal & Letters of Philip Vickers Fithian, 1773–1774: A Plantation Tutor of the Old Dominion* (Williamsburg, Va.: Colonial Williamsburg, 1943), 211–12.

93 Franklin Bowditch Dexter, ed., *The Literary Diary of Ezra Stiles, D.D., LL.D., President of Yale College*, 3 vols. (New York: Charles Scribner's Sons, 1901), 1:71–72.

none of the highest American degrees had been earned, except perhaps the M.D.s awarded by the new medical schools at King's and Philadelphia, for none of the colonial colleges was yet a university, even in name, offering advanced postgraduate work as part of the regular curriculum; the highest earned degree was the M.A. Nor can Stiles get off scot-free with downgrading the European universities to collegiate status, as if leveling the aspirational originals could elevate the unfinished facsimiles.

The declaration of independence from Great Britain and the revolutionary war to realize it brought forth many similar boasts and plans for educational parity or dominance. But as of 1770 or 1776, America's colleges were much too small and limited in their work to be considered universities. Their enrollments were minuscule by any standard. Most colleges enrolled only 40–50 students; none ever reached 200, the size of Emmanuel College, Cambridge in the 1620s. At their peak in 1775, Harvard and Yale, the largest colleges, enrolled only 180 and 170 students respectively.[94] Unlike Oxford, Cambridge, Glasgow, and Edinburgh, they taught only undergraduates. Their libraries were small, seldom up to date or open, bereft of efficient finding aids, and rarely used by undergraduates, who spent most of their time with assigned textbooks for a largely prescribed curriculum. None (except Harvard briefly in the seventeenth century) had a university press to publish the work of their largely unoriginal and often part-time faculties, who concentrated more on transmitting the wisdom of the past than on creating knowledge for the future.[95]

94 McAnear, "College Founding," 32–33n26; Harrison, *Princetonians, 1769–1775*, xx (table A).

95 Louis Shores, *Origins of the American College Library, 1638–1800* (New York: Barnes & Noble, 1935); Morison, *Harvard College*, 1:chs. 14, 17; W. H. Bond and Hugh Amory, ed., *The Printed Catalogues of the Harvard College Library, 1723–1790*, vol. 68 of Publications of the Colonial Society of Massachusetts (Boston: Colonial Society of Massachusetts, 1996), xi-xxiv; Warch, *School of the Prophets*, 240–43; William S. Dix, *The Princeton University Library in the Eighteenth Century* (Princeton, N.J.: Princeton University Library, 1978); John M. Jennings, *The Library of the College of William and Mary in Virginia, 1693–1793* (Charlottesville: University Press of Virginia, 1968); Joe W. Kraus, "The Book Collections of Early American College Libraries," *Library Quarterly* 43:2 (April 1973), 142–59.

Most of all, the American colleges stood alone, each (with two New Jersey exceptions) in its own province and not part of any larger institutional structure or plan. They had borrowed several bits and pieces from English and Scottish universities—leaders' titles (rector, provost, president), the listing of debate topics on (Scottish-inspired) commencement programs, degrees, academic term names, gowns, graduation ceremonies, nonresident chancellors and college representation in public legislatures (William & Mary), exemptions (from the draft, public works, and taxation) for students and faculty, academic exercises and curricula—but they had failed to replicate a whole university in its essence and character. Someday they would, but not until the United States was born and the individual states began to take the measure of their growing needs, resources, and ambitions.

CHAPTER FOUR

A Land of Colleges

Colleges rise like mushrooms in our luxuriant soil.

PHILIP LINDSLEY, 1827

SINCE HIGHER EDUCATION was not a major concern for the great majority of colonists in pre-revolutionary America, nine small colleges satisfied their felt needs. But independence from the British Empire, the creation of a constitutional republic, and the opening of vast tracts of land west of the original thirteen colonies created novel opportunities, challenges, and responsibilities for the new Americans. By 1783 once-imperial territory as far as the Mississippi River had been added. Twenty years later, President Thomas Jefferson nearly doubled the nation's width by purchasing from France—for three cents an acre—the middle third of the continent south of British Canada. By extending U.S. boundaries to the Rocky Mountains, space was claimed for fifteen future states. Human fecundity more than modest immigration made the U.S. population jump from 5.3 million to 7.2 million in the ten years after 1800.

But beginning in the 1830s, immigration from economically distressed and revolution-torn Europe force-fed the settlement and population of the new western lands. In 1840 the federal census captured more than 17 million white and black denizens, of whom 600,000 were recent immigrants. In the next decade, immigrant arrivals almost tripled. On the eve of the Civil War, the nation stretched from the Atlantic to the Pacific, encompassing 33 official states, several large "territories," and more than 31 million inhabitants. Inevitably, their educational needs were different from—and much greater than—those of the largely British colonists who disembarked throughout the previous two centuries.

Not unlike colonial America, antebellum America was predominantly a rural landscape of farms, villages, and small towns, only more so because of the frequent addition of extensive new lands available for settlement. The few cities grew only at the intersection of major transportation routes and commercial arteries. The economy was heavy with small-to-middling farmers, merchants, and craftsmen and only sprinkled with professionals—ministers, lawyers, and physicians—who might have sought or required some degree of higher education (though not always *a* degree). Unlike England and other European nations, the United States, collectively and individually, had no established religions. Separate, largely Protestant, denominations competed for members and funding in a climate of evangelical piety broadly tolerant of other Protestants (but not Catholics, Jews, or unbelievers). They differed as much on their perceived need for congregational literacy and ministerial learning as they did on scriptural interpretation. As they had in the colonial period, churches and missionary societies led the fight to prevent the spread of "popery" and frontier "barbarism"—the recidivism of "white savages," who lived too close to or mimicked America's aboriginal peoples and forsook Christian "civility."[1]

Moreover, post-revolutionary America inherited from the nation's founders a republican ideology that placed a premium on an informed and educated—at least literate—electorate. Although the franchise was restricted to adult white males, women played a key supporting role by rocking the republican cradle and nurturing virtuous citizens-to-be. Yet education was not a federal concern. The Constitution included no provision for education at any level, leaving that responsibility to the states and localities. Several early leaders, including the first six presidents, favored the creation of a national university. But widespread suspicion of centralization and jealous protection of states' rights nipped the idea in the bud.[2] The

1 James Axtell, *Natives and Newcomers: The Cultural Origins of North America* (New York: Oxford University Press, 2001), chs. 6, 8; Peter N. Carroll, *Puritanism and the Wilderness: The Intellectual Significance of the New England Frontier, 1629–1700* (New York: Columbia University Press, 1969); Francis Jennings, *The Invasion of America: Indians, Colonialism, and the Cant of Conquest* (Chapel Hill: University of North Carolina Press, 1975), Part 1.

2 David W. Robson, *Educating Republicans: The College in the Era of the American Revolution, 1750–1800* (Westport, Conn.: Greenwood Press, 1985), ch. 7, esp. 227–36; Frederick Rudolph, ed., *Essays on Education in the Early Republic* (Cambridge, Mass.:

federal government and various states donated public lands for the endowment of education, particularly in the upper Midwest and later in the South and Southwest. But the supply of frontier land was so great, even with a burgeoning population, that it outran settler demand, sold cheaply, and therefore failed to provide adequate fiscal foundations for schools and colleges.

The result was that the country, except in New England, a few emerging cities, and the old Northwest in the 1850s, lacked public *systems* of primary or secondary education, much less anything higher. It was left largely to private enterprise to provide lower and higher *schooling* for the cultivation of popular literacy, numeracy, and habits of obedience and virtue, as well as to prepare a small minority of students for college.[3] By 1800 sixteen colleges had been added to the colonial nine. Fourteen of them were planted in regions not long removed from the frontier, such as western Massachusetts (Williams), southern coastal Maine (Bowdoin), upstate New York (Union), and northeastern Georgia (Franklin).[4] But together they admitted less than one percent of the relevant national age group and graduated many fewer.[5] Collegiate education was by definition and intent an elite enterprise at a time when more democratic needs begged to be met.

Yet America was notable at home and increasingly abroad as a land of opportunity, of social mobility and economic betterment. In such a young, laissez-faire social economy, a little learning was *not* a particularly dangerous thing and could well endow a person not only with useful knowledge but also with enough prestige to allow him—or her—to rise from one social station to a better.[6] Antebellum Americans had a touching faith in education. The results of that faith were not only a proliferation of "common schools" at

---

Belknap Press of Harvard University Press, 1965); David Madsen, *The National University: Enduring Dream of the USA* (Detroit: Wayne State University Press, 1966).

3 Lawrence A. Cremin, *American Education: The National Experience, 1783–1876* (New York: Harper and Row, 1980), ch. 4.

4 David W. Robson, "College Founding in the New Republic, 1776–1800," *History of Education Quarterly* [*HEQ*] 23:3 (Autumn 1983), 323–41.

5 Roger Geiger, "The Reformation of the Colleges in the Early Republic, 1800–1820," *History of Universities* 16:2 (2000), 129–82, at 139.

6 Theodore R. Sizer, ed., *The Age of the Academies*, Classics in Education, no. 22 (New York: Bureau of Publications, Teachers College, Columbia University, 1964), 104.

the primary level, but the wildfire spread of versatile academies and small denominational colleges, and even a few institutions dubbed universities.

The irregular structure of antebellum education stood on a broad base of local or district common schools. By 1830 primary schooling was available to most white Americans in the North, and soon in the upper Midwest; the more sparsely settled South lagged behind, partly because funding there depended more on student fees than on public subventions. By 1850 some 3.4 million students were enrolled, despite voluntary attendance and a paucity of state funding. Pupils, some under five and over fifteen, created major challenges for their underprepared teachers, who were outnumbered, nationally, 36 to 1. Schoolhouses were small (often one room), cold in winter, and stifling in summer. Most pupils sat on benches without desks. Textbooks were few and often family hand-me-downs. Pedagogical results were mixed because attendance was short-term and irregular: winter and summer terms of six to ten weeks sought to accommodate rural planting and harvest schedules. By the 1850s, reformers had made headway in ousting toddlers, improving attendance, and instituting graded classes, longer terms, and more professional teaching training.[7]

In addition to common schools, the antebellum ecology of education included an uncoordinated assortment of church schools, dame schools, grammar schools, and so-called venture schools, all legacies of the colonial period. Churches of many denominations catechized and taught the 3 Rs (reading, 'riting, and 'rithmetic). Some were all-week charity operations for poor whites and even blacks; some functioned only on Sunday for members' children. Women—"dames"—in their own homes taught handfuls of fee-paying children to read, do sums, sew, and sometimes write. Many towns,

7 Lawrence A. Cremin, *The American Common School: An Historic Conception* (New York: Bureau of Publications, Teachers College, Columbia University, 1951); Albert Fishlow, "The American Common School Revival: Fact or Fancy? " in Henry Rosovsky, ed., *Industrialism in Two Systems: Essays in Honor of Alexander Gerschenkron* (New York: Wiley, 1966), 40–67; Carl F. Kaestle, *The Pillars of the Republic: Common Schools and American Society, 1780–1860* (New York: Hill and Wang, 1982).

particularly in the Northeast and Middle Atlantic states, continued to support secondary grammar schools—English for most students, Latin for those preparing for college or seeking a boost in social prestige. Both male and female entrepreneurs placed newspaper advertisements to offer town or city dwellers instruction in "useful" or "decorative" subjects, such as surveying, navigation, calligraphy, music, painting, and French. Some were day schools; others met in the evening (from "early candle-light to half past nine") to accommodate those with jobs.[8] Many were coeducational, some boarded students, all of them for a fee. Like many small businesses, they came and went with demand and competition.[9]

While this variety of schools gave an educational start to many, if not most, white Americans, the dominant institution of *higher* schooling before the Civil War, and indeed throughout most of the nineteenth century, was the academy. Its heyday was between 1790 and 1860. According to a careful count in 1850, nearly 6,100 academies (sometimes called institutes or seminaries) enrolled some 263,000 students across the country (9½ times as many as the nation's 239 colleges enrolled and 5–6 percent of the relevant age group). New York led the way with 887 academies, followed by Pennsylvania with 524. New England boasted nearly 1,100 academies, including some of the country's oldest grammar schools. The eleven Southern states served more than 62,000 students in nearly 2,000 academies. Venerable Virginia was out front with 317 academies, but less-settled Georgia, with only 219, enrolled as many students (c. 9,000). The Midwestern states, populated by large numbers of education-conscious New Englanders and New Yorkers, had jumped from 184 to 550 academies in just the previous decade. Five-year-old Texas was in a hurry to catch up. With a white population of only 213,000, the vast Lone Star state provided 97 academies. The prize for academic ambition must

8 Edgar W. Knight, ed., *A Documentary History of Education in the South Before 1860* [*DHES*], 5 vols. (Chapel Hill: University of North Carolina Press, 1949–53), 4:36 (quotation from an 1829 advertisement for a night school in Martinsburg, Virginia).

9 Kim Tolley, "Mapping the Landscape of Higher Schooling, 1727–1850," in Nancy Beadie and Kim Tolley, eds., *Chartered Schools: Two Hundred Years of Independent Academies in the United States, 1727–1925* (New York: RoutledgeFalmer, 2002), 19–43.

go to the little town of Marshall, Texas, population 1,411 in 1859. It attracted—in addition to a paper "university" (chartered in 1856 but not opened until 1862 at a secondary level) and a select boarding and day school—an "Academy," a "Republican Academy," a "Masonic Female Institute," and a "Collegiate Institute," all bearing the town's proud name.[10]

The proliferation of academies before the Civil War was a quintessentially American response to a rapidly growing and changing society. The egalitarian spirit of Andrew Jackson's presidency (1829–37) leached into the nation's educational subsoil. Local boosters, seeking post offices, newspapers, and hotels, also sought academies and colleges to crown their search for status. The commercial revolution reached down from cities to towns and even rural crossroads, demanding greater command of words, numbers, and practical knowledge through the book learning of higher schooling. And for both sons and daughters, the personal search for lives, careers, and social niches different from those assumed at birth and sanctioned by custom demanded more flexible and accessible paths. Academies provided those avenues as they were needed and wanted. Once initial funding and a board of trustees were secured, academies were relatively easy to establish, without or without a state charter. They offered flexible curricula at rates affordable to families of both the new, small-town, white-collar and the older, rural middle classes, whether the parents were enterprising businesspeople or hardworking proprietor-farmers.[11]

To keep tuition fees manageable for middle-class customers, academy trustees turned to a host of revenue sources besides their own subscriptions or joint-stock shares. They accepted payments in kind and skimped on teachers' salaries, that age-old route to

10 Henry Barnard, "Educational Statistics of the United States in 1850," *American Journal of Education* 1 (1855), 368; Tolley, "Mapping the Landscape," 23, 29; Colin B. Burke, *American Collegiate Populations: A Test of the Traditional View* (New York: New York University Press, 1982), 356.

11 Daniel J. Boorstin, *The Americans: The National Experience* (New York: Random House, 1965), 152–53; Nancy Beadie, "Academy Students in the Mid-Nineteenth Century: Social Geography, Demography, and the Culture of Academy Attendance," *HEQ* 41:2 (Summer 2001), 251–62, at 255–57.

economy. They curried the favor of religious denominations and fraternal orders (Masons, Odd Fellows, Sons of Temperance) and sought testamentary bequests and donations of all kinds for endowment or immediate use.[12] They also took advantage of sporadic state support in the form of land, lotteries, "literary funds," or proceeds from fines and forfeited property.[13] Because they performed a valuable public service (while enhancing local property values), school buildings were exempt from real estate taxes, as teachers were from militia and road-building duties.[14]

Many students also worked at their schools or for local families to make ends meet. In the South, "manual labor" schools enjoyed brief popularity with frugal parents and students intended for the ill-paid ministry. Seeking to make white labor respectable in a slave economy, the schools paid small wages—two to five cents an hour—to their student-farmers and apprentices. Although they managed to provide secondary education on the cheap, they soon folded when the students rebelled, broke or "lost" their axes and hoes, mistreated livestock, and sabotaged farm equipment, fences, and springs—tactics that slaves on their fathers' farms and plantations might have used to protest their own, more onerous, condition.[15]

Although academy trustees kept faculty salaries and student fees low, they sought to plant impressive buildings in the "republican geography" beside the local courthouse, post office, and perhaps

12 One Indiana academy's annual tally was "one day's work, one horse collar, one steel trap, five pounds of coffee, six pounds of sugar, fifty pounds of flour, and four bushels of wheat." Sizer, *Age of the Academies*, 26.

13 In 1825, 20 percent of the operating income of New York's academies came from the state; by 1850, it was still 15 percent. Bruce Leslie, "Where Have All the Academies Gone?" *HEQ* 41:2 (Summer 2001), 262–70, at 265.

14 Buford C. Utley, "The Early Academies of West Tennessee," *West Tennessee Historical Society Papers*, 8 (1954), 5–38, at 11ff.; Tolley, "Mapping the Landscape," 27–28; Sizer, *Age of the Academies*, 22–28; Edgar W. Knight, *The Academy Movement in the South* [Chapel Hill?, 1919?], 49–50.

15 Knight, *Academy Movement in the South*, 40–48; Knight, *DHES* 4: ch. 2; Gerald W. Mullin, *Flight and Rebellion: Slave Resistance in Eighteenth-Century Virginia* (New York: Oxford University Press, 1972, 1981); Michael Mullin, *Africa in America: Slave Acculturation and Resistance in the American South and the British Caribbean, 1736–1831* (Urbana: University of Illinois Press, 1992).

lyceum or library.[16] The earliest academies often began in rented or donated spaces. But as soon as possible, most raised the funds, sometimes with state help, to erect two- or even three-story wood, brick, or stone edifices, often with a bell in a cupola to regulate the academic day.[17] Students were given individual desks and chairs and provided with textbooks. Blackboards were standard, except in the South. Many academies owned up-to-date geographical and scientific apparatus for demonstrations. Initially, libraries were few and small, but they grew with the curriculum and endowment. In short, most antebellum academies were sufficiently designed and equipped to become public high schools, preparatory departments of colleges, or small colleges themselves after the war. If the postbellum academy largely disappeared or "died," it was, as historian Bruce Leslie has noted, "an organ donor."[18]

❁ ❁ ❁

The academy was well suited to satisfy pre-war America's needs because it was multipurpose. It served a wide age range of students (8–25+ years), it was flexible in its academic requirements (especially

16 J. M. Opal, "Exciting Emulation: Academies and the Transformation of the Rural North, 1780s–1820s," *Journal of American History* 91:2 (Sept. 2004), 445–70, at 450 (quotation).

17 In 1860 the nation's academies and grammar schools received an average of $120 from all government sources. Georgia normally granted $815 toward the construction of each of its academy buildings. In 1845 New York paid its academies $3.50 for every grammar student enrolled. Burke, *American Collegiate Populations*, 37; E. Merton Coulter, "The Ante-Bellum Academy Movement in Georgia," *Georgia Historical Quarterly* 5:4 (Dec. 1921), 11–42, at 20; Sizer, *Age of the Academies*, 23–26, 106, 110; Tolley, "Mapping the Landscape," 27.

18 Leslie, "Where Have All the Academies Gone?" 269; Opal, "Exciting Emulation," 450; Sizer, *Age of the Academies*, 22, 27, 33; Knight, *Academy Movement in the South*, 53–54; Tolley, "Mapping the Landscape," 30; Sevan G. Terzian and Nancy Beadie, "'Let the People Remember It': Academies and the Rise of Public High Schools, 1865–1890," in Beadie and Tolley, *Chartered Schools*, 251–83; Nancy Beadie, "From Academy to University in New York State: The Genesee Institutions and the Importance of Capital to the Success of an Idea, 1848–1871," *History of Higher Education Annual* 14 (1994), 13–38.

admissions), and its curriculum was eclectic and broad. In 1845 the Rev. Edward Hitchcock, the president of Amherst College (which itself had descended from an academy), described its two essential features. First, he said, "it affords an opportunity for youth of both sexes, from every class in the country, to enjoy an elevated course of instruction, on almost every elementary branch of science or literature, to which he may choose to attend, and for a longer or shorter period, as they shall wish." At the same time, he added, "it enables those youth, who aim at the liberal professions [primarily men], or a literary life [both men and women] to pursue a prescribed course of classical studies, preparatory to an admission to higher seminaries [colleges]."[19]

In order to survive, most academies were coeducational (thus doubling the potential enrollment) and terminal (offering diplomas but no uniform credentials or recognizable degrees). Throughout the nineteenth century, 90 percent of New York's academies taught males and females together, though often in separate "departments" or on opposite sides of the classroom; before the war, 75 percent of Alabama's did.[20] Unlike the few agricultural schools and mechanics' institutes, academies provided broadly liberal educations rather than narrow vocational training. Within the liberal curriculum, "parallel" courses were offered for different fees. The English track might cost $12, math and science, $15, the classics, $5 more.[21] Yet enough advanced courses could be taken in the better schools to earn advanced placement in the best colleges. Many academicians entered colleges such as Yale, Amherst, and Princeton in the sophomore or even junior class, a considerable saving.[22] In short, individual academies

19 Edward Hitchcock, *The American Academic System Defended* (Amherst, Mass.: J. S. & C. Adams, 1845), in Sizer, *Age of the Academies*, 92–126, at 98; W. S. Tyler, *History of Amherst College . . . 1821–1871* (Springfield, Mass.: Clark W. Bryan, 1873), ch. 3.

20 Beadie and Tolley, *Chartered Schools*, 332; Beadie, "Academy Students," 255.

21 Knight, *DHES* 4: 34, 47, 55.

22 In Princeton's class of 1853, only 19 of 89 matriculants entered in the first semester of freshman year (7 in the second semester), 43 as sophomores, and 19 as juniors. The great majority had attended academies or Latin grammar schools. James Buchanan Henry and Christian Henry Scharff, *College as It Is, or, The Collegian's Manual in 1853*, ed. J. Jefferson Looney (Princeton, N.J.: Princeton University Libraries, 1996), 106n5.

might offer studies from what we might regard as late elementary and junior high school through the first two years of college.

This challenging range of courses was typically taught by faculties of from one to four young college or female-seminary graduates, many, particularly in the South and West, from the Northeast.[23] Marriage or ministry often punched holes in their ranks, but many current or would-be ministers and "learned ladies" stayed at their schools over many years. One historian has called the average academy instructor "a poorly educated transient."[24] Given academy pay scales, the faculty may have been transient, but they were as educated as the average college tutor fresh from an undergraduate course of study.

Nor were the female teachers less qualified. Most female academies and colleges aimed to provide educations equal to those offered by the best men's institutions, and many succeeded. By 1860 female academies and seminaries outnumbered men's colleges three to two and equaled their enrollments. At a time when the average college enrollment was 116, Emma Willard's seminary in Troy, New York, averaged 240 girls a year in its first half-century. Many southern "institutes" taught between 100 and 200 students before the Civil War. Most female academies had a three-year curriculum, but their sister seminaries and colleges took four to finish. Beginning in the 1820s, the increasingly standard curricula of female schools—content and methods—began to mirror those of male colleges. Before the war broke out, the female schools introduced more Latin courses (with an emphasis on classical culture rather than language alone), while the men's colleges offered more of the sciences—natural philosophy, astronomy, chemistry, and botany—that their sisters had been exposed to for some time.[25]

23 The national average was only two teachers per academy. Barnard, "Educational Statistics," 368.

24 Sizer, *Age of the Academies*, 39.

25 Barnard, "Educational Statistics," 368; Mary Kelley, *Learning to Stand & Speak: Women, Education, and Public Life in America's Republic* (Chapel Hill: University of North Carolina Press, 2006), 83–92; Deborah Jean Warner, "Science Education for Women in Antebellum America," *Isis* 69 (March 1978), 58–67; Kim Tolley, *The Scientific Education of American Girls: An Historical Perspective* (New York: RoutledgeFalmer, 2003), ch. 2.

Academy curricula in general blended the traditional core subjects of Latin grammar schools with the broader offerings of private venture schools. Some academies offered twenty or more subjects in both male and female departments. They ranged from the 3 Rs, geography, history, and grammar to introductory versions of college courses in rhetoric, logic, moral philosophy, algebra, geometry, astronomy, chemistry, Christianity, and, of course, Latin and sometimes Greek. Extra tuition in bookkeeping, navigation, music, French, needlework, optics, or conchology might be obtained for an additional charge. While there were plenty of courses to choose from, they usually lasted only six weeks. Because it was difficult to find or afford specialized teachers in each of the newer subjects, the faculty had to be jacks and jills of many trades. With a national student-faculty ratio of 21-to-1, a customer-oriented elective principle in place, and somewhat irregular attendance, academy curricula were necessarily unsystematic and often superficial, especially in the eclectic "English department." The more traditional Classical track, aimed at preparing students for college, was more confining and rigorous. In those subjects, college preparatory departments and academies were interchangeable in form and function, and many of each made the shift.[26]

In the classroom, academies in all departments were indistinguishable from the underclass years of most colleges. Memorization of a few textbooks and daily graded recitations (faculty questions, student responses) of the material were the dominant modes of learning and teaching. Weekly reports, periodic exams, honor rolls, prizes, and end-of-term public exhibitions (not unlike college commencements with student orations, debates, and other performances) sought to institute a new "economy of esteem," ambition, and elitism among the middle-class student body. Discipline was still strict, but in the North at least, corporal punishment ebbed in favor of "emulation." Since expulsion was a poor fiscal option, academy faculty hoped that healthy competition among one's peers

26 Tolley, *Science Education of American Girls*, 44–49; Kim Tolley, "The Rise of the Academies: Continuity or Change?" *HEQ* 41:2 (Summer 2001), 225–39, at 234–36; Sizer, *Age of the Academies*, 28–33; Knight, *Academy Movement in the South*, 50–53.

would keep students to the task and banish the rod.[27] In the South, appeals to the honor of young gentlemen (young ladies were presumed to be more docile) sought the same ends but enjoyed less success, to judge by the length of school rules, the ubiquity of Black Books of misdeeds, and the boys' early and sometimes sustained behavior in college.[28]

The geographical spread and popularity of academies brought many benefits to nineteenth-century America. First and foremost, they constituted an uncoordinated but effective and supple superstructure of secondary education across the country.[29] Like colleges, they increased community pride and aspirations. They raised the nation's intellectual capacity by stimulating a largely unthreatening brand of elitism. While educating future public leaders, professionals, and workers for the new market economy, they helped build support for lyceums, lectures, libraries, and bookstores. Through their coeducational openness and curricular equality, the academies enlarged the educational and career possibilities of thousands of young women for whom neither marriage nor returning home was a viable option. They trained the great majority of teachers, primarily women, for the nation's common schools. In their classrooms, dining halls, rooming houses, and literary societies, they fostered a cultural identity and social networks among their middle-class students and future alumni. And

27 Opal, "Exciting Emulation," 456–58. The 1834 advertisement for a proposed Episcopal academy near Raleigh, North Carolina, was somewhat of an outlier. The school's rector announced that "no honors or distinctions" would be conferred, "the spirit of emulation being considered only a temporary excitement." He promised to exercise "parental supervision" over his academic "family" and to eschew both "premiums and severity." Knight, *DHES* 4:37–38.

28 Robert F. Pace, *Halls of Honor: College Men in the Old South* (Baton Rouge: Louisiana State University Press, 2004); Christie Anne Farnham, *The Education of the Southern Belle: Higher Education and Student Socialization in the Antebellum South* (New York: New York University Press, 1994).

29 In 1850, America's 6,085 academies enrolled an average of 43 students, ranging from 27 in Arkansas to 170 in Ohio. Texas and Massachusetts academies averaged 35. New York's league-leading 887 academies served an average of 55 students. Barnard, "Educational Statistics," 368.

of major relevance to our theme, academies prepared hundreds of students for higher education in colleges and universities, emerging professional schools, and theological seminaries.[30]

❁ ❁ ❁

The founders of antebellum colleges responded to the same national growth, opportunities, and conditions that the underwriters of the myriad academies did, only in far smaller numbers. The demand for a college education also grew with the nation's geography, but it did not—could not—keep pace with the immigrant-fed population and its broad dispersion across the continent. The academies may have produced enough qualified students to justify the creation of many more colleges, but most academicians who bothered to finish their course of study had no need or desire for further book learning. College degrees did not yet carry the prestigious clout they would a century later. What we regard as the learned professions seldom required a college education for entry. Lawyers, physicians, and even most ministers depended largely on apprenticeships with practitioners for their training. The older northeastern and Middle Atlantic denominations—Congregational, Presbyterian, German and Dutch Reformed, and Episcopal—still expected their clergymen to be formally educated in college and theological seminary. But the newer evangelical clergy, particularly Baptist and Methodist, who flooded into the West and South from the 1830s put their faith more in spiritual experience than in books and recitations. Roman Catholic clergy, who tended largely immigrant flocks from Ireland, Germany, and southern Europe, were more concerned with primary and secondary schooling and with the training of their own members in

30 Beadie and Tolley, "Legacies of the Academy," in *Chartered Schools*, 331–51; David F. Allmendinger, Jr., "Mount Holyoke Students Encounter the Need for Life-Planning, 1837–1850," *HEQ* 19:1 (Spring 1979), 27–46; Kim Tolley and Margaret A. Nash, "Leaving Home to Teach: The Diary of Susan Nye Hutchinson, 1815–1841," in *Chartered Schools*, 161–85; Keith E. Melder, "Woman's High Calling: The Teaching Profession in America, 1830–1860," *American Studies* 13:2 (Fall 1972), 19–32.

orthodox Catholic settings.[31] But they also founded many colleges for lay students before the Civil War, from Massachusetts to California.

Much uncertainty surrounds the numbers of antebellum colleges and even what "college" meant. The best estimates put the maximum number between 200 and 250.[32] Most bona fide colleges taught the liberal arts and sciences (as conceived in that period in shifting iterations and combinations) and were given state charters to conduct business and award degrees. This is what Noah Webster had in mind when he defined "college" in his first dictionary of American English (1828) as "the society of persons engaged in the pursuit of literature, including the officers and students, . . . incorporated and endowed with revenues." A college might also be called a *seminary*, but a *university* was different. According to Webster, a university was "properly a universal school, in which are taught all branches of learning, or the four faculties of theology, medicine, law, and the sciences and arts." According to that (imported) token, antebellum

31 Lutheran synods founded numerous seminaries and colleges in the Midwest. Sydney E. Ahlstrom, *A Religious History of the American People* (New Haven, Conn.: Yale University Press, 1972), chs. 27–28, 32–33; Jon Butler, *Awash in a Sea of Faith: Christianizing the American People* (Cambridge, Mass.: Harvard University Press, 1990), ch. 9; Edwin Scott Gaustad and Philip L. Barlow, *New Historical Atlas of Religion in America* (New York: Oxford University Press, 2001), 90 (fig. 2.30), 101 (fig. 2.40), 108 (fig. 2.46), 132 (fig. 2.67), 158 (fig. 2.89), 220 (fig. 2.138), 225 (fig. 2.142), 347 (fig. 4.14); Kathleen Mahoney, *Catholic Higher Education in Protestant America: The Jesuits and Harvard in the Age of the University* (Baltimore: Johns Hopkins University Press, 2003), ch. 1.

32 Barnard, in "Educational Statistics," 368, counted 239 colleges. Colin Burke, in *American Collegiate Populations*, 18 (table 1.3), counted 217 in operation at some point during the 1850s. In 1850 the U.S. Census Bureau captured only 119 colleges but also 96 professional schools of various sorts. Lawrence A. Cremin, *American Education: The National Experience, 1783–1876* (New York: Harper & Row, 1980), 44. As of November 1992, the U.S. Department of Education's National Center for Educational Statistics counted 343 permanent colleges and universities founded between 1800 and 1860, which seems greatly exaggerated. *120 Years of American Education: A Statistical Portrait*, ed. Thomas D. Snyder (Washington, D.C., 1993), 81 (table 27). In contrast, David B. Potts found only 50 colleges offering college-level classes in the fall of 1828; 17 more operated at some point during the 1820s, but not in 1828; 12 of those continued at a later date. *Liberal Education for a Land of Colleges: Yale's* Reports *of 1828* (New York: Palgrave Macmillan, 2010), 75–81.

universities were exceedingly rare.[33] "It is one of the glories of American colleges," boasted Theron Baldwin, a major supporter of western colleges, "that they are not concentrated into one vast University, but scattered far and wide among the people."[34] These people's colleges, claimed President Philip Lindsley of the University of Nashville, "are better adapted [than European-style universities] to the habits, wants, and circumstances of our widely dispersed and comparatively poor population."[35]

The democratic proliferation of colleges—which required much more expense and risk than academies—soon led to what President Lindsley deemed, as early as 1829, "the excessive multiplication and dwarfish dimensions of Western colleges." When he addressed the problem less than twenty years later, he spoke from hard experience. When he arrived in Nashville in 1825, he told his "university" audience that there were no colleges in Middle or Western Tennessee or in five neighboring southern and southwestern states. Now there were thirty within a radius of 200 miles of Nashville, nine within 50 miles. "These all claim to be our superiors, and to be equal at least to old Harvard and Yale."[36]

Others declared America's colleges guilty of titular inflation as well. In 1846 a snooty English visitor opined that "the numerous little boys' schools [perhaps academies] scattered over the country, where the dirty-nosed urchins are whipped, or ought to be, once a week, are all designated *colleges*. Thus there are more colleges and universities, so called, in America, than throughout Europe."[37] A more charitable

33 Noah Webster, *An American Dictionary of the English Language*, 2 vols. (New York: S. Converse, 1828).

34 Theron Baldwin, *Eleventh Report of the Society for the Promotion of Collegiate and Theological Education at the West* (New York, 1854), 43.

35 *The Works of Philip Lindsley*, ed. Le Roy J. Halsey, 3 vols. (Philadelphia: J. B. Lippincott, 1866), 1:404–05 (1837).

36 *Works of Philip Lindsley*, 1:254 (1829); John Pomfret, "Philip Lindsley," in *The Lives of Eighteen from Princeton*, ed. Willard Thorp (Princeton, N.J.: Princeton University Press, 1946), 158–77, at 170 (quotation, 1848).

37 T. Horton James, *Rambles in the United States and Canada during the Year 1845* (London: J. Olivier, 1846), 66–67. Horton added that the United States also lacked worthy professors, "very few" of whom were "eminent or learned men" because there was "not

interpretation came from a Wisconsin college president: "We call our institutions colleges on the same principle upon which we call Christians saints; not for what they are but for what we expect they will be." Thus, although many antebellum colleges were launched on paper, as the historian Jurgen Herbst observed, their charters "can best be seen as promissory notes than as certificates of character."[38] That many colleges quickly folded or never opened or failed to offer college-level instruction, and when they did, enrolled more students in their preparatory departments than in their collegiate courses, suggests that many notes as well as bills went unpaid.[39]

❋ ❋ ❋

Most college failures were due to lack of students—often caused by keen or "excessive" competition—and of revenues. These causes were not unrelated. Small new colleges were not able to build secure endowments as fiscal foundations and therefore depended heavily on student tuition fees, which could not be set beyond a certain amount without risking the loss of potential students to the nearest competitors. To supplement inadequate revenues from tuition and fees, colleges turned to a host of other sources. Trustees were the first line of defense against financial failure, as they tend to be today. Initially they fronted the start-up funds required to obtain a state charter. One famous group of founder-trustees was the so-called Yale Band, not musicians but seven students in Yale's Theological Department. In 1829 they pledged their own ministerial and academic service and $10,000 in subscriptions primarily to establish a college in the tiny

---

much encouragement for them" and no "learned leisure, except in divinity." Nor would they ever increase, he predicted, "while [the United States] continues a democracy."

38 Jurgen Herbst, "American Higher Education in the Age of the College," *History of Universities* 7 (1988), 37–59, at 48 (both quotations).

39 Burke puts the 1800–1860 failure rate at 17 percent. He corrects Donald G. Tewksbury's exaggerated failure figure of 81 percent (*The Founding of American Colleges and Universities Before the Civil War* [New York: Teachers College, Columbia University, 1932; Hamden, Conn.: Archon Books, 1965], 28 [table 2]), as does Natalie A. Naylor, in "The Antebellum College Movement: A Reappraisal of Tewksbury's *Founding of American Colleges and Universities*," *HEQ* 13 (Fall 1973), 261–74.

two-year-old prairie town of Jacksonville, Illinois. The seven became Illinois College's first trustees along with three elected by local boosters, who had already raised $2,000–$3,000. The funds were enough to erect a small two-story brick building and to engage the first faculty.[40] Many similar stories were told elsewhere.

Trustees were also called upon to bail out colleges with too few students and too little cash, but since many trustees were local middle-class boosters rather than financial fat cats, their pockets were only so deep. The colleges then might go public with their needs by advertising in regional newspapers for both students and donations. When the University of Georgia was in its infancy, a committee of the governing board "gave notice in one of the public Newspapers of Savannah, one of Augusta, and one of Louisville, that they would receive lists of subscriptions for Money, to be advanced in aid" of its establishment.[41] Donors of cash, bonds, land, books, and apparatus were all welcome. The women of Raleigh and Newbern gave the fledgling University of North Carolina in Chapel Hill a pair of globes, a compass, and a quadrant to support the teaching of geography and science. Not to be outdone, a group of "munificent gentlemen" threw in several thousands of dollars and acres (much of it hornswoggled from Indian tribes) and many "valuable books" for the library. Even earlier, the university offered naming rights to the six persons who gave the largest gifts toward the building of the "public hall of the library and four of the colleges [academic halls]."[42] Private colleges, unfortunately, could sell their institutional name only once, though specific buildings remained—and still remain—targets of nominal opportunity for wealthy donors.

Gifts of another kind were long-term, or perpetual, scholarships. Substantial donors of endowment funds were entitled to send one person to the college tuition-free during a period limited by the amount given. Typical was North Carolina's Davidson College,

40 Known also as the Illinois Band, the Yalies were joined in 1842 by an Iowa Band, formed at the Andover Theological Seminary. Julian M. Sturtevant, *An Autobiography*, ed. J. M. Sturtevant (New York: Fleming H. Revell, 1896), 135–39.

41 Knight, *DHES* 3:41 (1800).

42 Knight, *DHES* 3:13 (1789), 17 (1791), 296–97 (1843).

which sought in 1851 to sell a thousand scholarships for $100 apiece. Each buyer was entitled to send "a son or nominee" to the college during the next twenty years. Donors of $500 could send a student at any time, well into the future if so desired. Since college costs were likely to rise unpredictably and the funds were (supposed to be) invested in order to draw interest for coping with future inflation, such scholarships were more often than not rendered disappointing by in-state and national financial crises and bank failures. In short, "the scholarship plan accomplished its object only when most of the holders of certificates regarded their purchase as a donation and refused to avail themselves of its privileges."[43]

Of similar uncertainty were the lotteries that states, like their colonial predecessors, were asked by needy colleges to allow them to run. When a state authorized a lottery, it invariably put a dollar limit on it so as not to drain the regional pool of liquid assets from which rival colleges also sought to draw. The more colleges there were in the vicinity or state, the less likely it was that those limits would ever be reached. Even gamblers have their limits.[44]

States also lent additional aid to their colleges, private as well as public. Land was the easiest provision, though bestowing too much at once drove down sale prices. Like academies, colleges received exemptions from real estate taxes and their faculties from military service and other public obligations. Some states furnished cash to their public colleges to erect impressive buildings or libraries; others underwrote faculty and presidential salaries, the purchase of library books and scientific apparatus, or the annual tuition of one or more orphans. Throughout the 1850s, the legislature of South Carolina funded most of those needs of its namesake college to the annual tune of $7,600, a hefty pre-war sum.[45]

43 Ibid., 4:375 (1851); George P. Schmidt, *The Old-Time College President* (New York: Columbia University Press, 1930), 68 (last quotation). Ohio's Denison College had 88 scholarships outstanding as late as 1907; in 1910 the college began to buy them back because tuition costs had risen dramatically in the interim. Frederick Rudolph, *The American College and University: A History* (New York: Alfred A. Knopf, 1962), 190–92.

44 Rudolph, *American College and University*, 185–87.

45 Knight, *DHES* 3:346–51.

The most crucial support—moral and financial—for antebellum colleges came from religious denominations and congregations. The opening of the West, Southwest, and new parts of the South created a fertile field for old and new denominations. One of the first community buildings settlers built was a church, in hopes of attracting a minister if one had not already led the local migration from the East. Religion was a growth industry, particularly in the middle third of the century. The 1850 census counted over 38,000 churches; within ten years, that number grew by 16,000, led by Methodists, Baptists, and Presbyterians.[46] Once a community raised a church, it often thought next of an academy or a small college with a preparatory department for those without enough Latin or English grammar to matriculate. As the Yale Band and other "home mission" societies believed, "evangelical religion and education must go hand in hand." Their fears were two: unless "churches and schools kept pace with the tide of migration . . . these coming millions would be given over to the superstitions of all-grasping Rome or to the horrors of a godless infidelity."[47] In 1847, four years after it was founded, the Society for the Promotion of Collegiate and Theological Education at the West (happily parsed as the Western College Society) was convinced that it was a "present and most urgent necessity to raise up institutions to do for the mighty West what Yale, and Dartmouth, and Williams, and Amherst have done for New England: to call forth from the bosom of the Western church a learned and pious ministry; to send life, and health, and vigor through the whole system of popular education, and to . . . found society on the lasting basis of religious freedom and evangelical truth."[48]

❋ ❋ ❋

This burst of Protestant evangelical fervor led to the founding of some 160 denominational colleges by 1860, well over 80 percent of

46 Cremin, *American Education*, 379 (table 6).

47 Sturtevant, *Autobiography*, 134, 138.

48 *Fourth Report of the SPCTEW* (New York, 1847), quoted in Edwin Scott Gaustad, *A Religious History of America* (New York: Harper & Row, 1966), 168.

the total.[49] Most were small like their peers, but they were hardy. Although 26 percent of state colleges, 30 percent of Catholic colleges, and 63 percent of *non*denominational institutions failed before the war, the Protestant colleges lost many fewer: Methodist and Presbyterian only 13 percent, Baptist 6 percent, and Congregational none. Thirty colleges suspended operations for various periods and reasons, but many were resuscitated and often enjoyed full, if seldom rich, lives well into the twentieth century.[50]

For the most part, denominational colleges were only loosely tied to their religious sponsors. They were interdenominational and nonsectarian of necessity because they were not governed and only minimally funded by a central church organization (most denominations had none), even their faculty did not always share the same faith, and their regional member churches could seldom furnish enough students to make the college fiscally viable. The college president and many of the trustees were ecclesiastically "safe," but the religion and morality taught in class and daily chapel tended toward a broadly acceptable Protestant Christianity. If it did not, political schism and parental disapproval reduced enrollments quickly and sent budgets into the red.

Since the average college enrollment in 1840 was 93, in 1850, 116, and on the eve of war still only 120, college presidents were hard-pressed to keep their frail craft afloat.[51] Uncannily like their modern successors, they were perpetually on the hunt for donations for endowment, new facilities, and operating expenses. Many colleges sent their presidents or paid agents East—for as long as a year—to solicit funds from member congregations and the big-city

49 See a representative list in Gaustad, *Religious History of America*, 168–69, and a detailed map of surviving denominational colleges founded before the Civil War in Gaustad and Barlow, *New Historical Atlas*, 347 (fig. 4.14). The latter should be used with *some* caution (see above n. 39) because it is based upon Tewksbury's sometimes flawed *The Founding of American Colleges and Universities* (1932).

50 Burke, *American Collegiate Populations*, ch. 1, esp. 22 (table 1.9), 25 (table 1.13), 26.

51 Arthur M. Cohen and Carrie B. Kisker, *The Shaping of American Higher Education: Emergence and Growth of the Contemporary System*, 2nd ed. (San Francisco: Jossey-Bass, 2010 [1998]), 69.

headquarters of the major home-mission societies. Rev. Edward Beecher, one of the Yale Band and the first president of little Illinois College, was gone so long that he finally moved back East to raise funds full-time, leaving his duties to Professor Julian Sturtevant, another band member. Sturtevant, in time, made at least three long trips for the same reasons, necessitated by the relative poverty of antislavery Illinois, the financial panic of 1837, and the nettlesome opposition of a Methodist minister who openly ridiculed "collegiate education." Illinois, like many colleges, more easily secured aid for their students headed for the ministry from the American Education Society (as Sturtevant had at Yale), the American Home Missionary Society (est. 1826), and particularly the Western College Society, which over the years deposited a total of $61,178.17 directly into the college's coffers.[52]

In its thirty-year history (1844–74), the Western College Society made direct grants totaling more than $600,000 to some twenty-six liberal arts colleges and theological seminaries. In 1874 it merged with the older American Education Society, which from its beginnings in 1815 made small but vital grants ($75–$100 a year) to academy, college, and seminary students who showed academic promise and aimed for the ministry. Overall, the AES aided some 5,000 students—c. 10 percent of all collegians, a quarter of all seminarians in the 1830–40s. Because of the high demand for its funds in the wake of religious revivals and western expansion, it shifted from grants to loans (often forgiven if the graduate became a missionary or a minister in a poor church) before moving to direct grants to institutions. Most members of the governing boards of the AES and the Western Society were Congregationalists or Presbyterians, but the boards supported all evangelical Christian colleges in a nonsectarian fashion. The AES, in particular, promoted a highly educated clergy—four years in a classical liberal arts college and three years in a theological seminary. It was also a major supporter of public education by encouraging its beneficiaries to teach in common schools and

52 Sturtevant, *Autobiography*, 160–62, 181, 209–13, 253, 262, 384.

academies in the summer; 10 percent of its ministerial beneficiaries later became college and seminary presidents and faculty.[53]

The presidents of all colleges, denominational or not, were saddled with budgetary challenges that could be met only by ceaseless searches for outside funds. One source that could never be relied upon was current students, the majority of whom came from families whose economic circumstances ranged from modest middle-class to plainly poor. Both the increasingly competitive college market and the colleges' own sense of public obligation and religious charity kept their fees as low as possible. But after sufficient numbers graduated and entered remunerative careers, former students—*alumni* in the familiar Latin parlance—were fair game for revenue-seeking presidents.

Beginning in the 1820s in the Northeast, alumni associations began to form.[54] When they held reunions on campus or in nearby cities, the key speaker was invariably the college's president, who lost no chance to remind them how much they owed alma mater and to plead for donations. At the University of Nashville, President Lindsley informed his alumni in 1834, "we count not on the State's treasury, nor upon legislative indemnification. We rely not upon ecclesiastical patronage, or sectarian zeal; or individual munificence; nor, indeed, upon any of the usual sources of pecuniary revenue which have reared and sustained so many flourishing institutions in other sections of our happy Republic." His audience did not have to

53 David F. Allmendinger, *Paupers and Scholars: The Transformation of Student Life in Nineteenth-Century New England* (New York: St. Martin's Press, 1975), ch. 5; Natalie A. Naylor, "'Holding High the Standard': The Influence of the American Education Society in Ante-Bellum Education," *HEQ* 24:4 (Winter 1984), 479–97; James Findlay, "The SPCTEW and Western Colleges: Religion and Higher Education in Mid-19th Century America," *HEQ* 17:1 (Spring 1977), 31–62; Daniel T. Johnson, "Financing the Western Colleges, 1844–1862," *Journal of the Illinois State Historical Society* 65:1 (Spring 1972), 43–53. See also Merle Curti and Roderick Nash, *Philanthropy in the Shaping of American Higher Education* (New Brunswick, N.J.: Rutgers University Press, 1965) and Rupert Wilkinson, *Aiding Students, Buying Students: Financial Aid in America* (Nashville: Vanderbilt University Press, 2005).

54 Williams formed an alumni group in 1821, Middlebury and Brown in 1824, Union in 1825, Princeton in 1826, Yale in 1827, the University of Georgia in 1834, Wesleyan in 1836, Amherst and Harvard in 1842, the University of North Carolina in 1843, Dartmouth and Bowdoin in 1855, and Columbia in 1856.

guess what would follow. After all, he readily dubbed himself King Beggar. When he retired in 1850, the endowment stood at $140,000 above indebtedness, no small feat for a nondenominational, urban institution surrounded by a growing and equally needy set of rural, denominational rivals.[55]

Unlike Nashville, more sectarian colleges found it easier to raise money for specific religious ends. Well before it was established as a liberal arts college, Howard, a Baptist institution in Marion, Alabama, raised $20,000 in a single year to endow a professorship of theology. The state Baptist convention had concurred with the trustees that "funds would be more cheerfully contributed for this object than for the literary branch of the proposed institution."[56] Thirteen years later, nine Episcopal bishops in the South were confident that "the well known and ample wealth belonging to our communion generally" could easily to be tapped to raise $500,000 to found a true university of the South, superior to the denominational colleges within their dioceses and equal to the best universities abroad and to the "institutions of the highest grade in the Northern States," such as "Presbyterian" Princeton, "Unitarian" Harvard, and "Congregational" Yale. That the money was fully pledged or in hand by 1860, in time to lay the cornerstone of an ambitious university on a Tennessee mountaintop, suggests that their estimate of donor capacity was on the mark.[57] Few antebellum colleges were as fortunate.

❁ ❁ ❁

College founding on the various frontiers of white settlement entailed not only nonstop fund-raising but also the construction of buildings to hold classes, religious services, resident students and

55 Pomfret, "Philip Lindsley," *Lives of Eighteen from Princeton*, 169–71, at 169 (quotations). Illinois College's president, Julian Sturtevant, called himself Beggar General.

56 Knight, *DHES* 4:395 (1843).

57 Ibid., 4:462, 468, 470 (1856); Samuel R. Williamson, Jr., *Sewanee Sesquicentennial History: The Making of the University of the South* (Sewanee, Tenn.: University of the South, 2008), 9, 16–17.

faculty, dining facilities, books, and scientific collections and equipment. Likewise, older colleges needed to grow with new student numbers and to upgrade or replace existing buildings when undergraduate wear-and-tear or fires took their toll. Like Abe Lincoln, several western colleges were born in a log cabin, but with luck the rustic accommodations were quickly outgrown and replaced.[58] The initial campus buildings were usually multi- if not omni-purpose, partly to save construction costs, partly to hedge the founders' bets that the colleges would outlast the paper on which their charters were printed. They were also small and undistinguished. In 1829 Princeton-educated Philip Lindsley drew attention not only to the "excessive multiplication" of western colleges, but to their "dwarfish dimensions."[59]

He could easily have noticed the plain design and poor quality of new college buildings everywhere. In 1805 and 1809, South Carolina College built its first two "colleges" in downtown Columbia. Brick had to be used in the absence of state stone of sufficient quality. The first three-story Federalist structure housed the chapel and a few classrooms in its stucco-fronted central portion, and rooms for about fifty students in its two wings. President James Thornwell (1851–55) later dubbed it an "awkward and ungainly pile" and considered it lacking in comfort as well as beauty. Before both suffered fires in the 1850s, they badly needed and received upgrading in 1835 because they were "originally built of bad materials and in a very unworkmanlike manner."[60]

58 For six years Maryville College in Tennessee made do with an itinerant Presbyterian preacher operating alone in a log cabin. Schmidt, *Old-Time College President*, 41. For an engraving of Franklin College's initial log home (1836) in Indiana, see Paul Venable Turner, *Campus: An American Planning Tradition* (Cambridge, Mass.: MIT Press, 1984), 19 (fig. 15).

59 Richard Hofstadter and Wilson Smith, eds., *American Higher Education: A Documentary History*, 2 vols. (Chicago: University of Chicago Press, 1961), 1:233.

60 Daniel Walker Hollis, *South Carolina College*, vol. 1 of *University of South Carolina*(Columbia: University of South Carolina Press, 1951), 29–30, 93, 131. For a photograph of Rutledge and DeSaussure Colleges' still-plain façades, see John Morrill Bryan, *An Architectural History of the South Carolina College, 1801–1855* (Columbia: University of South Carolina Press, 1976), 32–33 (figs. 18 and 19).

Three years earlier, Illinois College replaced its original "small two story brick building" (1830) with a more ambitious 104-by-40-foot, four-story, all-purpose structure, which included two wings to house the families of the president and his indispensable professor, Julian Sturtevant. Well before it burned in 1852, the now president Sturtevant declared it "poorly planned and imperfectly built. Good material at that time was very scarce" on the south-central Illinois prairie, he noted graciously, "and it would have been difficult for anyone to build well." Nonetheless, it was not regarded as "an ornament to the beautiful [hilltop] site, a fact that occasioned much sorrow in after years." Fortunately, in the fall of 1857, classes opened in "a really good building for instruction," fitted with "ample and pleasant rooms."[61]

Once enrollments and endowments rose to sustainable heights, frontier colleges in particular looked to eastern models for architectural inspiration as well as curricular standards and faculty. Since it was largely Yale and Princeton graduates who led the western-college charge from late in the eighteenth century, new and aspiring colleges understandably turned to the architectural signatures of those eastern pacesetters.[62] From Princeton, frontier architect-contractors borrowed much of Nassau Hall's length, stone façade, green front campus, and internal configuration. South Carolina College's first two "colleges," Union's 1805 Stone College, Transylvania's 1816 Main Building, Williams's 1828 Griffin Hall, and many late-eighteenth-century colleges took their cues from Princeton. Yale, the other Mother of Colleges, offered two models: the three-story, double-entry, brick-block Connecticut Hall (1752) and the Old Brick Row, an impressive set of dorms, chapel, and Lyceum classrooms lined up along College Street facing the large New Haven Green. Connecticut Hall was twice imitated at Miami University in Oxford, Ohio. The Brick Row concept was adopted at

61 Sturtevant, *Autobiography*, 166, 190–91, 270–71.

62 Tewksbury, *Founding of American Colleges*, 14; William Lathrop Kingsley, *Yale College: A Sketch of Its History*, 2 vols. (New York: Holt, 1879), 1:412–14; Donald Robert Come, "The Influence of Princeton on Higher Education in the South before 1825," *William & Mary Quarterly* (3rd ser.) 2:4 (Oct. 1945), 359–96.

FIGURE 12. The University of Georgia campus in the 1840s, an engraving from *Gleason's Drawing-Room Companion* (May 13, 1854). From left: Phi Kappa Hall (1833), one of the two literary societies; Philosophical Hall (1821) for science instruction; Old (originally Franklin) College (1801–6), the original all-purpose structure; New College (1823, burned and rebuilt 1832); Chapel (1832) with columns and belfry; Demosthenian Hall (1824), the first literary society; Ivy Building.

hilltop Amherst in the 1820s; Western Reserve before 1845 in Hudson, Ohio; the University of Vermont (1829); and, after a visit from Yale president Timothy Dwight in 1811, at Middlebury College in its Old Stone Row.[63]

Although most college architecture was adapted to local materials and building traditions, the classical curriculum and the search for academic pedigree led many colleges to adopt Greek Revival styling for key buildings. Some of the all-purpose main buildings received Greco-Roman treatment: temple-like profiles, colonnades or porticos, Doric or Corinthian columns, decorative friezes, and lots of white paint. Especially popular were Greek features in the student

63 Turner, *Campus*, 42–45, 47–50, 55 (fig. 49); Codman Hislop, *Eliphalet Nott* (Middletown, Conn.: Wesleyan University Press, 1971), opp. p. 146 (Union); Bryant F. Tolles, Jr., *Architecture & Academe: College Buildings in New England before 1860* (Hanover, N.H.: University Press of New England, 2011), 97–103 (figs. 4-3, 4-4, 4-7, 4-11).

FIGURE 13. The Yale College Library, a Gothic Revival confection of the 1840s, like Harvard's Gore Hall library (1838) was modeled loosely after King's College Chapel at Cambridge University. The former became a chapel (Dwight Hall) in 1931, when Yale built the huge new Collegiate Gothic library, Sterling Memorial.

literary societies, most of which took Attic-sounding names such as Cliosophic, Philolexian, and Demosthenian. Often their "halls" sat side by side or, more appositely, facing each other, as if they were engaged in friendly debate in the Athenian Academy or Lyceum.[64]

For similar reasons, several colleges dipped their toes in the first wave of the Gothic Revival, which began seriously in the 1830s. In 1834 Kenyon College, under Episcopal auspices, completed its first building, an H-shaped, all-purpose stone block. Its pointed Gothic windows and exaggerated roof pinnacles must have bemused the local residents of simpler Gambier, Ohio. Harvard's Unitarian neighbors may have been equally nonplussed by cathedral-like Gore Hall, erected in 1838 to house the college's library. Not to be left

64 Turner, *Campus*, 90–100.

behind, Yale's library moved into *über*-Gothic Dwight Hall four years later. Located well behind the Old Brick Row, the flamboyant confection was possibly, like Gore Hall, meant as a belated bow to Cambridge's famous King's College Chapel, begun in the fifteenth century by His Catholic Majesty Henry VI and completed in the sixteenth by once-Catholic Henry VIII. When the true craze for Collegiate Gothic began in the 1890s, these early pathbreakers were more highly prized.[65]

No matter what architectural style was in favor, antebellum colleges, particularly those in small frontier towns, were obliged to house their students in campus dormitories and feed them in refectories, or commons.[66] In the local absence of sufficient facilities for room and board, colleges had little choice if they were to attract enough students to stay solvent. Many students, particularly those in preparatory departments, were quite young and needed plenty of care and supervision. The older "academic" students—mostly adolescent boys—were thought to need more supervision than care.

Antebellum educators were of two minds about dormitories. The great majority, despite their idealized preference for the moral purity and salubrity of country life, believed that rambunctious young males, removed from parental oversight, needed close moral and academic policing by faculty. Acting *in loco parentis*, tutors (and occasionally bachelor professors) were assigned to live in the dorms among the students. Doing so enabled faculty to make twice- or thrice-daily room checks to ensure that the budding scholars were swotting their texts during prescribed study hours. But the tutors' egregious proximity also made them easy targets of student noise, pranks, and abuse (sometimes life-threatening). Accordingly, a strong minority view developed among faculty that dorms were both personally insupportable and fertile breeding grounds for student

65 Ibid., 110–20, ch. 6; Tolles, *Architecture & Academe*, 21–22, 37–39.

66 Refectories were commonly located in campus basements or in undistinguished separate quarters. The food was usually as bad as the setting, giving the students one more reason to complain and riot. On some larger campuses, two refectories operated, a less expensive one for poorer students and a more savory one for wealthier diners. Rudolph, *American College and University*, 101–102.

FIGURE 14. To help solve student disciplinary problems, Union College built two matching dormitories, North and South College, flanked by professors' quarters (1812–14). Both are still in use.

rebellions, which were widespread before the Civil War and brought numerous colleges to their knees.[67] In the eyes of religious faculty, presidents, and trustees, dorms were, in the words of Manassah Cutler, one of the founders of Ohio University, "too often . . . the nurseries of every vice and cages of unclean birds."[68] But the majority view prevailed and much expense and anxiety were expended in creating dorm life as the pale simulacrum of Oxbridge's collegiate way.

Some college officials, however, sought to enlist architecture to reduce the student opportunity for high jinks and rebellion. One expensive way was to house fewer students in more but smaller dorms. This was a road seldom taken, even when endowments and budgets were unusually flush. Another tactic, tried at Union College in 1814

67 Ibid., 97–99; Steven J. Novak, *The Rights of Youth: American Colleges and Student Revolts, 1798–1815* (Cambridge, Mass.: Harvard University Press, 1977); Pace, *Halls of Honor*, ch. 4.

68 Rudolph, *American College and University*, 96–101, at 99.

and elsewhere, was to tightly sandwich a student dorm between two contiguous professors' quarters.[69] More feasible—though it, too, required extra expense—was the internal alignment of entries, staircases, corridors, and rooms to minimize what officials regarded as student "combinations" or calculated "sprees" to disturb the peace and get the faculty's collective goat. Colleges that followed Princeton in building lengthy Nassau-Hall lookalikes were especially dismayed, as Princeton officials constantly were, to discover that corridors that ran the length of the building, with individual rooms lining both sides, made perfect bowling alleys for cannon balls and rendezvous for rebellious plotters. The material solution, as Oxbridge had long proved, was to build multiple entries in the façade with only two or four rooms on each level. Malefactors would then be obliged to exit in small enough numbers to be identified, if not apprehended, and subjected to the college's reticulate code of justice.[70]

❁ ❁ ❁

If it is possible to have a college without students (witness All Soul's College, Oxford) and without a built campus (witness any number of online "universities"), it is impossible to have one without a faculty, however small. Many antebellum colleges began with only a president, who taught the entire basic curriculum, perhaps with the help of a young tutor in the two younger classes. With growth, the colleges were able to add somewhat more specialized professors in Latin and Greek, mathematics, rhetoric and belles lettres, and natural philosophy and science. The president did the lion's share of hiring them. He alone taught Evidences of Christianity when it was offered and the senior capstone course in moral philosophy, the colonial legacy that included elements from ethics, religion, and natural law, as well as some of the nascent social sciences, such as politics, psychology, and

69 Turner, *Campus*, 72 (fig. 66).

70 Ibid., *Campus*, 89; Henry and Schaff, *College as It Is*, 126–43, 157–71, 203 and 203n14; Schmidt, *Old-Time College President*, 85. Rutledge Hall and other dorms at South Carolina College had such an arrangement. Hollis, *South Carolina College*, 26–27, 132; Bryan, *Architectural History*, 15, 73. See 175 (fig. 14).

economics.[71] Not unlike a modern college executive, his antebellum predecessor had a lengthy job description. Not only was he the head panhandler, he was also the custodian of the college's "interests and reputation," its chief disciplinarian, corresponding secretary, community liaison, overseer of examinations, convener of commencements, model of character and decorum, and resident pastor.[72]

The last role came naturally because over 90 percent of pre-war presidents were ordained ministers. Reflecting the spread of denominational colleges and their presidents' alma maters, 77 Presbyterian presidents (22 from Princeton) outnumbered 55 Congregationalists (36 from Yale), who in turn exceeded Episcopal (39), Baptist (30), Methodist (28), and Lutheran (4) leaders.[73] Even the few lay presidents believed that education was not bona fide unless it was informed by Protestant religion and Christian morality. Thus, in addition to the senior course in moral philosophy, the president was also in charge of the required chapel services first thing in the morning (before breakfast) and late in the afternoon (after the last classes), the longer service on Sunday morning, and often a catechetical recitation on Sunday afternoon or evening. His Sunday sermons in particular, or those of inspiring guest preachers, sometimes ignited major or minor revivals of student piety, professions of faith, and church joining. Beginning in 1831, a national day of prayer for colleges assisted the presidential efforts.[74]

71 Schmidt, *Old-Time College President*, ch. 4; Frederick Rudolph, *Curriculum: A History of the American Undergraduate Course of Study since 1636* (San Francisco: Jossey-Bass, 1977), 90–94; Daniel Walker Howe, *The Unitarian Conscience: Harvard Moral Philosophy, 1805–1861* (Cambridge, Mass.: Harvard University Press, 1970). The best-selling American textbook of moral philosophy, by Brown president Francis Wayland, was *The Elements of Moral Science* (1837), ed. Joseph L. Blau (Cambridge, Mass.: Belknap Press of the Harvard University Press, 1963).

72 Schmidt, *Old-Time College President*, ch. 2, at 54 (quotation). Some of the early frontier presidents also had to be handymen. Josiah Meigs, the Yale-educated founding president of the University of Georgia, made bricks for the first building when he wasn't teaching the first few students under an oak tree. Ibid., 63.

73 These figures come from a study of 71 colleges founded before 1840 that survived until at least 1860. Ibid., 96, ch. 7, at 184–87.

74 The following year, a census of 3,582 students in 59 colleges found that 683 (19 percent) were "hopefully pious." Ibid., 150–51.

A president's religious message often reached well beyond the college-chapel walls, particularly if he published his sermons or expounded his views in the burgeoning religious press. Many denominational presidents were feistily sectarian on occasion and got themselves into fierce controversies near and far with other believers. Some opponents were on their own boards of trustees (often suffused with ministers), others were in rival colleges or denominational conferences. Giving offence to trustees was the most dangerous course and often led to short tenures. But even controversialists who managed to avoid riling their bosses or getting themselves brought up on charges of heresy seldom proved great presidents. "A college executive whose chief interests remained theological," concluded historian George P. Schmidt, "was apt to fail or at any rate to achieve no more than mediocre success."[75]

For all their duties and troubles, college presidents seldom received fair compensation. A few, such as the president of the tiny college in Maryville, Tennessee, received no salary at all for the first several years, ten in his case. The lucky rest sometimes had a house provided to augment their salaries, which ranged from a few hundred dollars to as much as $3,000 at Harvard and Transylvania in later decades. Many earned extra money from diploma fees and part-time clerical stints. A few earned royalties from publishing textbooks in their specialties, such as moral philosophy, political economy, and chemistry. Needless to say, no college president got rich, save one. Eliphalet Nott of Union College made such a fortune on his New York land deals, steamboat inventions, and patents of a heating stove that he bequeathed $600,000 to the college at the end of his 62-year presidential tenure.[76]

75 Ibid., ch. 7, at 225 (quotation). Samuel W. Doak, the long-time president of Tusculum College in Tennessee, was eulogized as having "never allowed his college duties to interfere with his ministerial assignments." Not surprisingly, he was unpublished—not even a sermon—at his death. Francis X. Corgan, "Toward a History of Higher Education in Antebellum East Tennessee," *East Tennessee Historical Society Publications* no. 60 (1988), 39–66, at 49 (quotation), 50.

76 Schmidt, *Old-Time College President*, 69–73, 103. See Hislop, *Eliphalet Nott*, for the complex and often unsavory details of Nott's financial dealings.

❁ ❁ ❁

One of the earliest and most important presidential duties was the hiring of additional faculty. Initially, only a tutor or two might be needed to assist the all-purpose president. Before frontier colleges could produce their own graduates, tutors had to be found farther east or north. The likeliest prospects were top recent graduates of established colleges or theological seminaries who aimed at the ministry but could not immediately find church openings. Regarding college teaching idealistically as a form of pastoral practice and its paltry pay as a future cleric's introduction to genteel poverty, the young graduates signed on for short-term "home missions" in the West. They usually stayed no more than two or three years because tutorships rarely led to professorships, whose specializations required deeper learning in particular subjects as well as more pedagogical experience.[77]

In the first two or three decades of the century, most professors were hired with experience either in the pulpit or an academy classroom. Others had made livings as physicians, lawyers, or missionaries.[78] Given the late appearance of American graduate schools, medical practice was one of the few ways to acquire scientific training, as it was in Great Britain. Likewise, education in a theological seminary was the likeliest and best way to acquire advanced learning in Hebrew and classical Greek, but only few of the subjects that later became known as the humanities, without

77 Sister M. St. Mel Kennedy, "The Changing Academic Characteristics of the Nineteenth-Century American College Teacher," *Paedagogica historica* [Ghent] 5 (1965), 351–401; Martin Finkelstein, "From Tutor to Specialized Scholar: Academic Professionalization in the Eighteenth and Nineteenth Century America," *History of Higher Education Annual* 3 (1983), 79–121, at 104, 108.

78 At Princeton, Basil Gildersleeve (class of 1849) took a class in rhetoric and belles lettres from a former M.D. and missionary to China. "In those days," he recalled, "missionaries, returned in failing health or proved inefficiency, formed one of the reservoirs from which academic rills were replenished." "The College in the Forties," in Ward W. Briggs, Jr., ed., *Soldier and Scholar: Basil Lanneau Gildersleeve and the Civil War* (Charlottesville: University of Virginia Press, 1998), 60.

going to Germany.[79] By 1840 more than fifty seminaries had been established, some freestanding, some associated with colleges.

Andover Theological Seminary in Massachusetts (founded in 1808) was one of the best, partly because over 90 percent of its matriculants were college graduates and teaching could begin at a high level. When Amherst graduate William Tyler attended Andover in the early 1830s, the "high scholarship" of its classes and its national reputation had long since made it a major conduit to college teaching. Twenty-six of its graduates in the first decade became college or seminary professors. In nearly forty years of teaching sacred literature, Moses Stuart taught seventy future college presidents and professors. Similarly, 15 percent of the alumni of the Princeton Theological Seminary (founded in 1812) in its first decade became college professors. No less than Yale and Princeton, the major seminaries also deserved the title of "mothers of colleges." They were intellectually vibrant, and their publications were often the best scholarly journals covering a wide variety of subjects, including the sciences and social sciences. Antebellum presidents and trustees found nothing strange about hiring seminary graduates to teach college courses "without the special studies" that were, by the later nineteenth century, "deemed requisite as a preparation for the office."[80]

❁ ❁ ❁

At a time when colleges were proliferating and faculties being sought, hiring committees were often hard pressed to find qualified candidates other than seminarians and secondary pedagogues. Once

79 See below, ch. 5. Jon H. Roberts and James Turner, *The Sacred and the Secular University* (Princeton, N.J.: Princeton University Press, 2000), chs. 4–6; James Turner, *Philology: The Forgotten Origins of the Modern Humanities* (Princeton, N.J.: Princeton University Press, 2014).

80 During its first century, the Presbyterian seminary in Auburn, New York (founded in 1818) produced 34 college presidents and 78 college professors. Natalie A. Naylor, "The Theological Seminary in the Configuration of American Higher Education: The Ante-Bellum Years," *HEQ* 17:1 (Spring 1977), 17–30, at 17–18, 20, 22, 25; Elizabeth A. Clark, *Founding the Fathers: Early Church History and Protestant Professors in Nineteenth-Century America* (Philadelphia: University of Pennsylvania Press, 2011), 9–10; *Autobiography of William Seymour Tyler, D.D., LL.D* (n. p., 1912), 45 (quotation).

they were found, they seldom stayed long enough to make an exclusive career of college teaching or a disciplinary specialty.[81] Having come from a variety of backgrounds and experiences, they often left after a time to pursue similarly diverse paths. Among the early faculty hires made by Joseph Caldwell, the young Princeton-educated president of the University of North Carolina, were a French ex-Catholic monk and a deserter from the British navy who became a strolling player in the South. Thereafter Caldwell did his best to forgo European-born professors, partly because he distrusted their religious and political principles, but largely because he thought they couldn't enforce discipline for lack of understanding "the disposition of American youth," especially the southern variety.[82]

In Chapel Hill and elsewhere, early antebellum faculty frequently moved—or were moved—from one chair to another, with no apparent difficulty. Caldwell himself shifted to moral philosophy after twenty years in mathematics; eighteen years later he added astronomy to his portfolio. After leading a nearby female boarding school, Walker Anderson began as a professor of rhetoric and logic and resigned at the age of thirty-five to go into business and law in Florida. William Hooper, a professor of classical languages for five years before taking leave to become an Episcopal priest, soon returned to assume the rhetoric and logic duties for three years before being re-seated in his old chair of ancient languages. After he resigned from the University of North Carolina in 1837, his *curriculum vitae* exploded with occupational changes. Having become a Baptist in 1831, he taught theology at Furman Institute, Greek and Roman literature at South Carolina College, and classics at a boy's school and

81 Finkelstein, "From Tutor to Specialized Scholar," 103.

82 Kemp P. Battle, *History of the University of North Carolina . . . 1789–1868* (Raleigh: Edwards & Broughton, 1907), 154, 160–61, 419 (quotation). Other academic leaders were much more open to hiring European faculty. In planning his first faculty at the University of Virginia, cosmopolitan Thomas Jefferson chose four Englishmen and a German. In 1819 Jefferson had written to John Adams that "our wish is to procure natives, where they can be found . . . but preferring foreigners of the first order to natives of the second, we shall certainly have to go for several of our Professors, to countries more advanced in science than we are." Two Harvard professors, one who had studied in Germany, the other in Paris, had just turned him down. He later looked to Edinburgh. Knight, *DHES* 3:185, 211.

presided over a Baptist church, Wake Forest College, and three female seminaries in North and South Carolina. Elisha Mitchell, an accomplished Yale graduate with a short stint at Andover Seminary, was a striking contrast to the restlessness of many of his colleagues. At twenty-four, he assumed the mathematics chair at UNC, made a slight shift later to the professorship of chemistry, mineralogy, and geology, and resigned after thirty-nine years of polymathic teaching and learning.[83]

Two major reasons for the relatively short tenure of antebellum professors were their low pay and extracurricular policing duties. As late as the 1850s, faculty salaries ranged from $3,000 a year plus a house and firewood to $500 a year without free housing. The national average salary was $1,269, seven and a half times higher than the pay of unskilled urban workers (*not* the faculty's preferred reference group) but lower than that of comparable professionals such as lawyers and physicians. Understandably, the older, better endowed, and more prestigious colleges in New England and the Middle Atlantic states and a few elite state institutions in the South paid their professors much more than their peers in the Midwest or on the frontier did. Among denominational colleges, Lutheran and German Reformed colleges paid the least, Congregational and Episcopal institutions the most.[84] Since the average college in 1850 enrolled only 116 students, most of whom came from working- or middle-class families, officials could never raise tuition enough to compensate their faculties adequately.

Even at the Ancient Three (Harvard, Yale, and Princeton), professorial "poverty" was a standard, if relative, lament. In 1839 Francis Grund, a one-time unsuccessful candidate for the mathematics chair at the University of Pennsylvania, was told that the reason Harvard professors were being hired at a younger age was that they were "too poorly paid to induce first rate men to devote themselves to the business of lecturing." Those who did sign on may have been encouraged to learn, as a Bostonian informed Grund, that it was also "quite the fashion for our rich girls to buy themselves

83 Battle, *History of the University of North Carolina*, 436–38, 537–41.

84 Burke, *American Collegiate Populations*, 47–48 (table 1–22), 233 (table 5.9).

a professor."[85] In the 1840s Princeton salaries were so low that "it was said" that the wife of the renowned (and rotund) science professor Joseph Henry made his suits to economize on custom tailoring, even though they lived in a handsome two-story brick house built for him by the college on campus.[86] Senior Yale professors, meeting in the president's house in 1851, complained that they couldn't live (in suitable parts of town) on their salaries. The professor of Latin James Kingsley had, "during the forty years since his marriage, expended annually for living [costs] alone some 500 dollars more than his salary." The professor of mental and moral philosophy (and future president) Noah Porter had "with all economy . . . exceeded his by $200 or $300" and was "obliged to use nearly half his available strength in eking out the deficiency. Apart from this," he added for emphasis, he "would have been worth twice as much to the College." That James Hadley, an assistant professor, had just been promoted to full professor and his salary raised to all of $1,140, on the eve of his marriage at the age of thirty, must have rendered the discussion for him somewhat discomfiting.[87]

❁ ❁ ❁

Many faculty would have been more content with their pay and their lot had they been relieved of their disciplinary duties. But being the only wardens of their almost "total institutions," which closely regulated students' lives 24–7, they could hardly forgo their obligatory oversight of the restless male inmates.[88] One reason for

85 Robert A. McCaughey, "The Transformation of American Academic Life: Harvard University 1821–1892," *Perspectives in American History* 8 (1974), 239–332, at 257, 272.

86 Edward Wall, *Reminiscences of Princeton College, 1845–1848* (Princeton, N.J.: Princeton University Press, 1914), 3–33, at 10; Wheaton J. Lane, ed., *Pictorial History of Princeton* (Princeton, N.J.: Princeton University Press, 1947), 30.

87 *Diary (1843–1852) of James Hadley, Tutor and Professor of Greek in Yale College, 1845–1872*, ed. Laura Hadley Moseley (New Haven, Conn.: Yale University Press, 1951), 267, 274.

88 "Total institution" is a sociological concept popularized by Erving Goffman and Michel Foucault.

the collegiate "police state" was the youth of many students. Most frontier colleges could not afford to be too selective in their admissions policies, so they matriculated smooth-cheeked boys in their young teens as well as bearded men in their mid- to late twenties and even thirties. More established colleges tried to set the entry bar at fifteen or sixteen, though even Brown took fourteen-year-olds.[89] Away from home for the first time, unless they had been sent to residential grammar schools or academies, younger students tended to confuse freedom with license and to strain against the reins their new surrogate fathers placed upon them in their serious all-male settings. The strictures were voluminous and largely negative.[90] Every matriculant was obliged to read and sign a long list of the college laws, which he had to buy or copy by hand. Most compilations of thou-shalt-nots were dauntingly killjoy in and of spirit. Even those *not* written by Calvinist-Protestant presidents and trustees (as most were) assumed that adolescent males, particularly in groups, were unstable compounds of lust, rebellion, and devilish imagination, if not direct inheritors of Adamic sin. Both assumptions led to exaggerated forms of patriarchalism as well as genuine concern for the moral health and mental development of the young charges in the faculty's temporary care.

Institutional restraints on youthful spirits were manifested in several ways. First, until later in the pre-war decades, most college curricula were fully prescribed. The students marched through time-tested courses in Latin, Greek, mathematics, logic, rhetoric, natural philosophy, and moral philosophy in lockstep, without any choices of subject or timing. Only later in the period did the temporary advent of "irregular" students (who stayed only a year or two) "parallel courses" of study (often only three years) with different

89 New England's "hill colleges," which experienced considerable growth as farming declined, admitted more than a third of their students over the age of twenty-five between 1820 and 1860. Even 12–17 percent of Harvard and Yale classes in those years were over twenty-five. Allmendinger, *Paupers and Scholars*, 10 (table 1).

90 John DeWitt, a graduate of Princeton in 1861, regarded its laws as excessively detailed and "far too large a proportion of them . . . merely negative." "Personal Recollections of Princeton Undergraduate Life: III—From 1858 to the Civil War," *Princeton Alumni Weekly* (March 22, 1916), 550–54, at 553.

emphases and degrees, short-term "partial courses" of maximal electivity but leading to no degree, and upper class electives lessen the suppression of student differences and desires.[91] Changes in teaching techniques also made for more variety. Professorial lectures and demonstration science labs (every one of the latter was "doomed to success") spurred greater student interest in the two upper years after the forced marches of underclass recitations through a few set books had lost their charm.[92] The uniformity of written exams, although they demanded greater mastery of broader subjects than of narrow texts, also measured each student against the same standard. Oral exams, not unlike recitations, were hit-or-miss affairs, as the examiner went around the class two or three times asking different short questions.[93]

The second set of constraints on student life was the colleges' expressed and implied goals and associated means. Princeton's aptly described those of most antebellum colleges. In the circular it sent home with the student's first report card, the college affirmed that it "earnestly" sought to "avoid all harshness, severity or rigour" in the teaching and discipline of the students, and to "make all suitable allowance for the inconsiderateness of youth." Indeed, it was the faculty's constant goal to "make their pupils happy," and to send them home "manly, well-taught and virtuous." "But," the circular continued tellingly, "to the attainment of these ends, strict order, prompt obedience, unblemished morals, and constant industry" were considered "indispensable." Princeton's students in large part did not disagree with the college's main goals, though they would substitute "character" (the bellwether word of the circular) for "manliness" and "religious principles" for "morals." What they—and most antebellum students—objected to was the adjectival severity of the means the faculty used to achieve those goals: *strict*, *prompt*, *unblemished*, and

91 Rudolph, *Curriculum*, 84–86.

92 Herman Eschenbacher, "When Brown Was Less Than a University But Hope Was More Than a College," *Brown Alumni Bulletin* (Feb. 1980), 26–33, at 30 (quotation).

93 Kennedy, "Changing Academic Characteristics," 370–81; Rudolph, *Curriculum*, ch. 3; Cohen and Kisker, *Shaping of American Higher Education*, 73–83.

constant, a set of demands for perfection that few students thought possible or even desirable.[94]

❁ ❁ ❁

The college instruments of student control and "perfection" were so all encompassing as to justify the modifier in "total institution." Like natural parents with their endless responsibility for their children, faculty who stood over their students *in loco parentis* took their duties seriously, if seldom uncomplainingly. As America's faculties became more specialized, professionalized, and conscious of their intellectual and social status, they increased their complaints against their protoparental obligations. The more celebrated and mobile faculty demanded and sometimes received full exemptions.[95] And no wonder. Faculty were enmeshed in the adamantine daily schedules of the undergraduates, a regulatory form of preemptive exhaustion: chapel twice daily, three hour-long classes, two hours of required study for each class (requiring room checks), refectory or dining hall appearances, and nightly curfews, the abrogation of which frequently led to student high jinks, or "sprees," requiring nocturnal policing by faculty and other officials.[96] The whole schedule was faithfully marked by the ringing of the college bell, beginning at 5 or 6 a.m. (except on Sunday when it began at 9) and ending at 8:30 or 9:00 p.m.

94 Henry and Scharff, *College as It Is*, 74, 99–103.

95 The aspiring University of Georgia may have been the most liberal with its exemptions. One was for the first professor in the new department of agriculture. Others were for science stars and a teacher of modern languages. E. Merton Coulter, *College Life in the Old South* (Athens: University of Georgia Press, 1983 [1928]), 39, 64; Thomas G. Dyer, *The University of Georgia: A Bicentennial History, 1785–1985* (Athens: University of Georgia Press, 1985), 90–95.

96 Faculty members who enjoyed night patrols and the chase were rare. One of the most gleeful was Princeton's bachelor professor of Greek and vice-president, John Maclean, affectionately known to the students as "Johnny." This fleet-footed adversary took obvious pleasure in hiding behind buildings and trees to surprise and identify, by "dark lantern" light, spreers and other miscreants. Many students believed that he never undressed during the school year. In judicial proceedings, he often called for leniency for those whom he had outfoxed and outrun. Henry and Scharff, *College as It Is*, 35n50, 136, 139–40, 158n62; Wall, *Reminiscences of Princeton College*, 7–8.

Princeton's rang twelve times a day, East Tennessee University's, fifteen. This noisy fidelity made bells throughout academe the target of student abductors, arsonists, and saboteurs, which temporarily reduced hired bell ringers (often black slaves) to horns or handbells.[97]

Despite the long lists of laws (which the students had all sworn to obey) and the vigilance of the faculty, student bodies accumulated impressive "rap sheets" in most colleges, particularly the larger ones where the ratio of students to faculty was high. So many undergraduates were caught and charged that most faculties met weekly to deal with academic but mostly moral "crime" and punishment. Symptomatic of the trend was the University of Georgia, whose legal code listed at least 90 prohibitions. Between 1820 and 1861, the faculty there dealt with nearly 1,300 separate incidents requiring disciplinary action. Some 210 students were dismissed for short terms or expelled, though several were allowed to return after due contrition and exile from their friends and co-conspirators (128 had acted with others).[98]

The college codes were so extensive that scarcely a facet of student life was left unregulated. If the student imagination concocted new forms of disorder, new rules were quickly added. If it did not, the mere mention of novel prohibitions may have planted seeds in new freshmen for future cultivation. The offenses were impressive in number and variety, everything from youthful pranks and "waywardness" to full-blown "combinations," or plots, to resist authority "contumaciously." In 1838 the University of North Carolina's rules in

97 Henry and Scharff, *College as It Is*, 96–97; Stanley J. Folmsbee, "Campus Life at the University of Tennessee, 1794–1879," *East Tennessee Historical Society Publications*, no. 45 (1973), 25–50, at 30n16; Coulter, *College Life in the Old South*, 81; Battle, *History of the University of North Carolina*, 1:195, 275–76, 465, 562. Henry Martin, born a slave at Monticello the day Thomas Jefferson died, regulated the University of Virginia's student and faculty life by bell from 1847 (when he was freed) to 1909. Anne E. Bromley, "Plaque Honors Henry Martin . . . ," *UVA Today*, Oct. 5, 2012. After 1837, the University of Alabama hired a student to ring the bell. The bell rope terminated in the ringer's room on the second floor of the laboratory. He was paid $16 a month to move his schoolmates around campus on time. James B. Sellers, "Student Life at the University of Alabama before 1860," *Alabama Review* 2:4 (Oct. 1949), 269–93, at 278n22.

98 Dyer, *The University of Georgia*, 57–58.

"College Duties and Restrictions" ran to 19 paragraphs, "Moral and Religious Conduct" to 35, and "Miscellaneous Regulations" to another dozen before highlighting a catalogue of 10 "Punishments."[99]

Mature lists usually began by warning that any "adult" actions that broke state or federal laws would not be shielded from public prosecution. They then proscribed various forms of disorderly conduct (in dorms, chapel, classrooms, and town, even during vacations), disrespect to the faculty, academic neglect, property damage (burning outhouses and stoning tutors' windows were favorites), assaults on each other or townspeople (especially involving guns, swords, and knives, all of which were banned), dueling (to which honor-sensitive southern students were prone), intoxication (a universal sport), smoking, gambling, fornication (particularly in houses of ill repute or with "Negroes"), card-playing, mistreating servants and animals, profanity and other impieties (including the use of *dash* and *drat*), and "indecency." One of the stranger manifestations of the last offense, apparently, was the "wearing of women's apparel," which was especially frowned upon in all-male institutions.[100] Much more common, though it was never mentioned by name, was masturbation. Decorously disguised as the biblical "sin of Onan," it appeared in John Todd's popular *The Student's Manual* (1835)—in three pages of chaste Latin in an otherwise English chapter on reading.[101]

99 Saul Sack, "Student Life in the Nineteenth Century," *Pennsylvania Magazine of History and Biography* 85:3 (July 1961), 255–88, at 257, 260; Knight, *DHES* 3:277–86. The antebellum laws of the University of Georgia occupied 19 pages of close handwriting in a large ledger book. Coulter, *College Life in the Old South*, 62.

100 Coulter, *College Life in the Old South*, 88–89; Dyer, *University of Georgia*, 55–59; Sack, "Student Life in the Nineteenth Century," 257 (Dickinson College laws, 1830). This prohibition may have been aimed at theatrical productions or burlesques, but it certainly trapped a number of boys at the University of Alabama who donned girls' apparel (shoes, sunbonnets, and all) in order to accompany a girl's seminary class that had permission to attend a university professor's chemistry lectures. Sellers, "Student Life at the University of Alabama," 289n66.

101 Allmendinger, *Paupers and Scholars*, 105. Timothy J. Williams in "Confronting a 'Wilderness of Sin': Student Writings, Sex, and Manhood in the Antebellum South," *Perspectives on the History of Higher Education* 27 (2008), 1–30, documents both masturbation and sex with black and white prostitutes among University of North Carolina students in the 1840s, as do Rex Bowman and Carlos Santos in *Rot, Riot, and*

Given the insufficiency and marginal quality of most college dining halls, the rustling of neighbors' chickens and turkeys for midnight roasts in dorm fireplaces was a popular infraction. During a nocturnal chase in pursuit of one such raiding party, Francis Lieber, South Carolina College's popular professor of political economy, fell on a brick pile and barked his shins. Brushing off his clothes and Teutonic dignity, he was heard to exclaim, "Mein Gott! All dis for two tousand dollars!" thus coupling the faculty's two major complaints.[102]

When trustees refrained from pulling rank and watering down faculty judgments, student infractions earned a graduated set of punishments. Sincere confession usually got the sinner a pass, but written warnings to student and parents and temporary probation were the next-best results. Presidential admonition before the faculty and/or public shaming "in the presence of the students" at chapel were regarded as appropriate for moderate offenders. For worse actors, "rustication" for a few months to a nearby farm or manse was mandated. For the worst, those of a "vicious" character who corrupted others, outright expulsion was deemed best for all.[103] To prevent bad apples from spoiling other barrels, the colleges shared an extensive blacklist of expelled students and pledged not to accept them. A few colleges, including Union and the University of Pennsylvania, were notorious for breaking ranks and accepting scapegraces.[104]

Rebellion: Mr. Jefferson's Struggle to Save the University That Changed America (Charlottesville: University of Virginia Press, 2013) throughout the University of Virginia's early years.

102 Hollis, *South Carolina College*, 189. In the South, opossums were regarded as delicacies, even at coed party suppers. Sellers, "Student Life at the University of Alabama," 288; Williams, "Confronting a 'Wilderness of Sin,'" 12.

103 In an effort to treat students as "young gentlemen," college officials wisely did not resort to corporal punishment of any kind, except occasionally upon minors (under sixteen) in the associated grammar school or preparatory department. Folmsbee, "Campus Life at the University of Tennessee," 30–31; Knight, *DHES* 3:284–85.

104 Steven J. Novak, *The Rights of Youth: American Colleges and Student Revolt, 1798–1815* (Cambridge, Mass.: Harvard University Press, 1977), 24–25; Coulter, *College Life in the Old South*, 88; Henry and Scharff, *College as It Is*, 175; Rodney Hessinger, "'The Most Powerful Instrument of College Discipline': Student Disorder and the Growth of Meritocracy in the Colleges of the Early Republic," *HEQ* 39:3 (Fall 1999), 237–62, at 248, 254 (U. of Penn.); Rudolph, *Curriculum*, 85 (Union).

❁ ❁ ❁

Faculty attempts to correct disorderly behavior often ran up against two different student notions of honor, particularly when several perpetrators were involved. One notion was the collegiate equivalent of "honor among thieves." If a "combination" of students committed a major offense, such as bombing or defiling the chapel, college officials sought to punish all guilty parties. But when asked to finger the perpetrators or their co-conspirators, even innocent students closed ranks and refused to "squeal." As the president of Dickinson College explained to his trustees, "A spirit of loyalty to the [students' graduating] classes is deemed of higher obligation than loyalty to the Faculty and Laws."[105] The only recourse then was to dismiss or expel the suspects' whole class or dorm mates, an action with potentially serious consequences for budget, discipline, institutional reputation, and future enrollments.

The second notion of honor was particularly strong in southern colleges and in northern ones that admitted significant numbers of Southerners.[106] The southern code of male honor expected men of all classes, but particularly those of the elite planter class, to exhibit personae of duty, respect, and honesty. Public image was more important than actual content, but if anyone questioned that image, the man of honor was insulted and often ready to defend his public face with his life. The problem for college officials was that most of their students were not yet men and often behaved like adolescent schoolboys. Although the average age of matriculation in southern colleges was fifteen, most southern students assumed a heightened sense of adult honor. They felt that honor threatened in their new collegiate settings, where they were prohibited from bringing their horses, dogs, servants, rifles, pistols, swords, and knives—the accoutrements of white planter privilege in a slave society.

Often rich, spoiled, and high-spirited, these scions of the "master race" bridled at the rough hand of an arresting officer and the mere questioning of their involvement in college disorders. "Challenging

105 Sack, "Student Life in the Nineteenth Century," 262.

106 Nearly 40 percent of Princeton's undergraduates between 1820 and 1860 came from the South. Knight, *DHES* 4:249–50; Henry and Scharff, *College as It Is*, 246n5.

FIGURE 15. A haughty southern student, standing on his "honor" as a "gentleman" in opposition to college discipline. Portrait by Porte Crayon, in *Harper's New Monthly Magazine* (August 1836).

students' honor was tantamount to challenging their self-concept, and that challenge need not be serious for it to be taken seriously."[107] As an aggrieved University of Georgia student explained in 1855, it

107 Pace, *Halls of Honor*, 4–9, at 8; Jennings L. Wagoner, Jr., "Honor and Dishonor at Mr. Jefferson's University: The Antebellum Years," *History of Education Quarterly* 26:2 (Summer 1986), 155–79, esp. 166–67, 171, 174; Stephen Tomlinson and Kevin Windham, "Northern Piety and Southern Honor: Alva Woods and the Problem of Discipline at the University of Alabama, 1831–1837, " *Perspectives on the History of Higher Education* 25 (2006), 1–42, esp. 5–6, 15–16, 24–25.

was "mortifying to the feelings of the young men to have their words doubted, and must beget within them a sort of contempt and hatred for the Faculty. No graver insult could be offered to a gentleman than this."[108] Presidents and professors brought up in the North or abroad had little understanding of or patience with the adolescent resort to honor. As President Thomas Cooper of South Carolina College complained in 1822 to Thomas Jefferson, "Every student in College holds himself bound to conceal any offence against the Laws of the Land as well as the Laws of the College." "If you doubted their honor . . . [they] would never forgive you," although the English-born and Oxford-educated Cooper was convinced that their claim to honor was "little else than an insolent cover for falsehood for many of them."[109]

❁ ❁ ❁

Youth and overindulgent upbringing were far from the only causes of antebellum high jinks and hell-raising. Critics then and historians a century later were quick to blame two other contributions to student restlessness. One was the lack of organized sports, which became popular and conducive to relative campus calm after the Civil War. Intercollegiate, even intramural, baseball, football, and other sports' teams and games were *future* gifts to student morale and exercise. Many college laws actually barred the playing of sports on campus for fear that college buildings (especially windows) would be damaged (as they were in the handball games played against exterior walls) and student studiousness would be compromised by the noise outside.[110]

108 Coulter, *College Life in the Old South*, 65.

109 Hollis, *South Carolina College*, 89. In drafting the laws for the University of Virginia two years later, Rector Jefferson and the other trustees (including James Madison and James Monroe) asserted that "when testimony is required from a student, it shall be voluntary and not on oath. And the obligation to give it shall . . . be left to his own sense of right." After an early period of student mayhem and rebellion, they backed off their benign philosophy and instituted a tougher regime of laws and discipline. In 1836 and 1845, the militia had to be called in. Knight, *DHES* 3:154; Wagoner, "Honor and Dishonor," 175–76; Bowman and Santos, *Rot, Riot, and Rebellion*.

110 Folmsbee, "Campus Life at the University of Tennessee," 31; Knight, *DHES* 3:280 (University of North Carolina, 1838).

The harmless ways most students found to release their pent-up energy and to relieve the tedium of six prescribed in-dorm hours of study were impromptu "football" (soccer style) and "shinny" (field hockey–like) scrimmages, innings of "wicket," or cricket, seasonal swims and ice-skating, long walks, jumping (running and standing) contests, marble games (good for writing cramps and stiff knees mostly), and, lest we forget the realities of the day, wood sawing and chopping to feed dorm-room fireplaces. At Princeton, cannon-ball bowling in Nassau Hall was mildly enervating but more amusing when the balls were heated and rolled into the hands of a tutor-policeman. A number of colleges in the South, and even Harvard, had cadet corps and provided military exercises in lieu of the sportier war games.[111] Gymnasia were latecomers. Amherst, Harvard, and Yale all built proper gyms in 1859, though Amherst had an outdoor facility by the late 1840s in a grove behind the college that contained a circular running track, a wooden horse and springboard, and a variety of swings.[112]

Some students at colleges on or near lakes, rivers, or canals wondered why their institutions were tardy in taking advantage of the water for recreational and competitive rowing. A Harvard alumnus from the class of 1847 remembered "when there was but one boat owned by a Cambridge student, and that boat was soon reported

111 Amherst students also pitched 2- to 3-lb. quoits called loggerheads. William Gardiner Hammond, *Remembrance of Amherst: An Undergraduate's Diary, 1846–1848*, ed. George F. Whicher (New York: Columbia University Press, 1946), 16, 25, 32, 288n2; *College Days at Old Miami: The Diary of T. C. Hibbett, 1851–1854*, ed. William Pratt (Oxford, Ohio: Miami University, 1984), 49, 54, 57, 63, 92; Henry and Scharff, *College as It Is*, xxii, 202–204; Knight, *DHES* 3:155, 267, 280; 4:149–243; Hollis, *South Carolina College*, 120, 199; *Charleston Goes to Harvard: The Diary of a Harvard Student* [Jacob Motte] *in 1831*, ed. Arthur H. Cole (Cambridge, Mass.: Harvard University Press, 1940), 49, 50, 56, 92; Sellers, "Student Life at the University of Alabama," 287–88; Tomlinson and Windham, "Northern Piety and Southern Honor," 30, 42n130.

112 Larry Owens, "Pure and Sound Government: Laboratories, Playing Fields, and Gymnasia in the Nineteenth-Century Search for Order," *Isis* 76:2 (June 1985), 182–94, at 188; Hammond, *Remembrance of Amherst*, 16, 27, 35, 180, 288n3. The University of Georgia planned a gym in 1831 and again in 1849, but nothing came of it until later. Coulter, *College Life in the Old South*, 100. See Turner, *Campus*, 159 (fig. 165) for a drawing of outdoor gymnastics at the University of Virginia in 1856.

to have been suppressed by the Faculty, on the plea that there was a college law against a student's keeping domestic animals, and a boat was a domestic animal within the meaning of the statute." In 1853 Princetonians thought of increasing the number of outdoor sports by seeking permission from the directors of the large Raritan and Delaware Canal nearby "to keep two or three boats in the water, and to form boat-clubs, in imitation of the Cantabs of Cambridge University."[113]

The second—alleged—cause of student disorder was the curriculum and its pedagogy. The critics' first error was in thinking that the *prescribed* curriculum was a *static* curriculum; the second was that *recitations* dominated the curriculum, were boring in the extreme, and created powerful student urges for excitement or revenge. To begin with the latter, there is no documentary evidence that recitations and student lawbreaking were related. In fact, the evidence points in the opposite direction. The only possible connection between the two is the role of tutors in both. Of key importance, tutors were in the closest rank of faculty police, living in the dorms among the students, spying on their illicit activities, and feeling the brunt of some of their meanest pranks and persecutions. Less irritating was their role in teaching the introductory courses of the first two years, such as Latin, Greek, and math from textbooks. The method they used—because they were often recent graduates themselves and no specialists in any subject—was the recitation. The object of such classes was mastery of the textbook—its basic information and disciplinary principles, such as grammar, vocabulary, axioms, and formulae. The efficient way to "teach the text" was to drill and question the students with texts in hand to see if they understood the day's lesson.

Because the teacher was largely a listener and not a conduit of content, he mostly had to ask questions of the students in turn and to indicate whether their answers were correct or not, assigning marks for each in a grading book. If he could, he might provide

113 They had to wait until 1870 to form a boat club and two more years for competitions to start. Owens, "Pure and Sound Government," 188; Henry and Scharff, *College as It Is*, 203–204n16.

elucidation, examples, and other guidance, but it was not mandatory or usual. A serious Yale student (and future professor himself), who appreciated the largely nonconversational drill he received in his recitation classes, also noted that the tutors "could hardly be said to teach at all, their duties being to subject every pupil three times a day to so searching a scrutiny before the whole division [of his class] as to make it apparent to himself and all his fellows either that he did or did not understand his lessons."[114] Indeed, the public performance of reciting was a major spur to serious application during the daily prescribed study hours. Getting caught out by the quiz master (or "wool'd" in student slang) was cause for noisy disapprobation from one's classmates. At Princeton it took the form of "a [foot] stamp of ridicule" and a slangy reminder that one had either "fizzled" (answered poorly) or "stumped" (failed to respond at all when summoned).[115] At the University of Nashville, a math student who couldn't explain the geometrical figure he had drawn on the blackboard was openly "laughed at," at no small cost to his midwestern self-consciousness or southern honor.[116]

Although recitations would not have been voted the students' favorite classes, they did promote thoroughness, precision, and daily application. A first-generation student from a Tennessee farm was keenly aware by his first spring on the Miami University campus that "my lessons were to be *learned* before my recitations would come off," even if it meant staying up late or rising early.[117] There was nothing intrinsically boring about that preparation, and the uncertainty of when a question might be directed at any student contributed to

114 Sturtevant, *Autobiography*, 85–86.

115 Henry and Scharff, *College as It Is*, 31, 37–38, 111, 113–14. "Fizzle" was also popular at Amherst. Hammond, *Remembrance of Amherst*, 35, 42, 44, 58, 127. Students all over America quickly shared slang terms, only a few of which were borrowed from British universities. The Harvard graduate Benjamin H. Hall helped their spread when he published *A Collection of College Words and Customs* in 1851 and a revised and enlarged (500-page) edition in 1856 (Cambridge, Mass.: John Bartlett).

116 "A Student at the University of Nashville: Correspondence of John Donelson Coffee, 1830–1833," ed. Aaron M. Brown, *Tennessee Historical Quarterly* 16:2 (June 1957), 141–59, at 148.

117 Hibbett, *College Days at Old Miami*, 55 (March 12, 1852).

FIGURE 16. A Harvard recitation class being put through its paces. The reciting student receives either help or ridicule from a classmate behind. The rest of the class, with few exceptions, prepares to be called upon.

the collective alertness of the class.[118] Paying attention to the tutor's serves and student returns also added a sporting note to the learning process.

There was little doubt that more learned and experienced professors could play the recitation game better than most young tutors. As a serious Amherst student commented, "No man who comes to spend only a year or so during a course of professional study [such as divinity school] in teaching is fitted to take charge of men in college during half their course [of studies]." In contrast, professors in math and the classics who substituted for absent tutors were "infinitely

118 The older "mechanical" way of running a recitation, by calling on students alphabetically or by rows, allowed students to prepare well only when they predicted that they would next have to perform. Random quizzing was pedagogically more effective. In 1825 Yale tutors gave up the alphabetical method for questioning those whose names they drew out of a box and recording the resulting performances in a black book. Rudolph, *Curriculum*, 89.

superior." The math professor "teaches very differently . . . he is not content with hearing simply what is contained in the book, but goes into the principles, traces out a subject in all its connections, illustrates it in practice, etc."[119]

What *was* sometimes tedious was not the recitations per se, but what a Brown student diarist called "the monotony of riding around upon a circular railroad of college studies, day after day and night after night." The daily sameness of academic *activities*—not thoughts awakened or content learned—caused earnest diarists to grouse and skip days or even weeks in their chronicles. A Haverford student captured the problem when he confessed to his diary, "The monotony of a college life renders it an unsuitable place for keeping a daily journal."[120] He did not say that it was a good reason to raise nocturnal hell, burn down the college privy, or take a drunken pistol shot at the president in his study.

❁ ❁ ❁

If recitations were not the cause of student mayhem, still less was the curriculum itself. College curricula changed and adjusted throughout the antebellum period, especially after 1820, for several reasons. One reason was student and parental demand for new, often more "practical" or "useful," subjects. Students who intended to enter the ministry, law, or medicine had little complaint about the familiar subjects of the so-called classical curriculum, which (in new permutations) prepared them well for further study or apprenticeships with practitioners. But students who thought they should or could prepare more directly for the commercial realities and political economy of Jacksonian America were eager to study more modern subjects, such as sciences beyond physics, civil and mechanical engineering, "drawing" (drafting), modern languages and literatures, political economy, American history, and constitutional law.

119 Hammond, *Remembrance of Amherst*, 87, 163, 177.

120 Eschenbacher, "When Brown Was Less Than a University," 30 (c. 1846); Sack, "Student Life in the Nineteenth Century," 268.

Yet these requests rarely came as surprises to—nor were always unwelcomed by—college faculties, because the latter did not live in proverbial ivory towers. They felt the same social, cultural, and intellectual impulses and pressures felt by their students' families, often directly before they chose to teach for a living. All American colleges, whatever their funding, fulfilled a public function, producing citizens of a democratic republic and responsive to multiple constituencies, local, regional, and national. Because stasis was as bad for academic business as it was for professional health, their faculties pushed for curricular changes often before any other constituency did. Professors did not have to be dragged kicking into the "modern world" because they already lived there and were keenly aware of its academic possibilities and student attractions. But since newspaper headlines did not (and still do not) automatically translate into academic disciplines, curricular change often had to wait upon the development of sufficient scholarship—accumulated research, journal articles, textbooks, reference works—to warrant and enable the addition of new subjects and courses to the curriculum.

As new technologies, long-distance communication and transportation, industrialization, urbanization, and immigration remade the face of America, higher educators were increasingly asked to provide the intellectual, and some of the practical, tools needed to move those forces forward. Familiar subjects such as science, mathematics, and languages were now asked to make room for cognates with adjectives such as *applied*, *practical*, and *modern*. Graduates who chose the older learned professions were now joined by students who foresaw futures in newer careers and sought at least some curricular attention to, and academic blessing upon, engineering, scientific agriculture, commerce, and secondary teaching. As the nation's evolution accelerated before the Civil War, the demand for these new subjects outpaced the academic supply.

One solution was the establishment of separate specialized institutions, such as engineering-heavy West Point (1802), Rensselaer Polytechnic Institute (1824), and scientific schools at Yale and Harvard (1847). Another was the addition of parallel and partial college courses for those in a hurry who wanted differently "useful" studies in their native tongue. A third approach, admittedly a stopgap, was to squeeze into the traditional curriculum courses that did not give up the venerable goal of mental "discipline" but added some new factual "furniture" or content (in the words of the famous, mostly conservative, and widely approved Yale Reports of 1828).[121]

❋ ❋ ❋

Two major academic changes enabled the introduction of popular reforms and quietly produced others that sustained the collegiate equilibrium for several decades. The first was the professionalization of the academic career, modeled first at the older, larger colleges.[122] Tutors were gradually replaced by specialized professors, who taught entire subjects rather than set books and had been increasingly prepared at German universities for advanced work.[123] Clergymen were gradually replaced by laymen. Faculty tenures lengthened, often into lifelong callings. As faculties grew in size, they organized into departments by discipline. A recognizable career ladder was established, initially in the larger colleges, by adding new ranks such as instructor, assistant professor, and associate professor.[124] Sustained scholarship and publications resulting from it were slowly added to teaching effectiveness as criteria for promotion. As extra-local reputations rose, so did salaries and professional mobility. Policing took a back seat to more refined pedagogy.[125]

121 Potts, *Liberal Education for a Land of Colleges*, 42–47.

122 For Harvard's evolution, see McCaughey, "Transformation of American Academic Life."

123 See below, ch. 5. At least 300 Americans studied in Germany in the 1850s alone. Only 55 had gone in the previous forty years. Many were subsidized by their new institutions to receive postgraduate training. Finkelstein, "From Tutor to Specialized Scholar," 110.

124 In 1850 extra-popular Yale's 432 undergraduates and 123 graduate students were taught by a total of 22 faculty: two assistant professors, 3 instructors, 7 tutors, and 10 professors. In contrast, the average number of faculty nationally was 7, only 4–6 in the West and South. George Wilson Pierson, *A Yale Book of Numbers: Historical Statistics of the College and University, 1701–1976* (New Haven, Conn.: Yale University, 1983), 6 (table A-1.3), 346 (table D-1.1); Barnard, "Educational Statistics," 368; Burke, *American Collegiate Populations*, 48–49.

125 Kennedy, "Changing Academic Characteristics;" Finkelstein, "From Tutor to Specialized Scholar;" Finkelstein, *American Academic Profession*, ch. 2.

A second development occurred in the various academic disciplines at the hands of professors foreign and domestic. This was the fission of generalized subjects into specialized disciplines. One such general subject was natural philosophy, which hived off into physics and astronomy; another, natural history, spawned chemistry, botany, zoology, geology, and mineralogy, each with its own distinctive scholarly organizations, research protocols, journals, and textbooks. Among the few binding agents were Benjamin Silliman's *American Journal of Science and Arts* (1818) and the American Association for the Advancement of Science (1848). As soon as each discipline developed sufficiently, faculty specialists sought to teach courses in them or in small combinations, sometimes including advanced mathematics. Along with the accompanying advent of laboratories, observatories, and collection cabinets, the colleges' push led to the noticeable growth of science faculty and requirements in already crowded classrooms and curricula. In 1830 American colleges on average made do with a science faculty member or two; by 1860 the number had doubled. More than half of Harvard's and Brown's faculties were scientists. In 1850 a third of Brown's prescribed hours of instruction were devoted to science and math, not anomalously.[126]

The influx of interest in science had the result in many colleges of leading to superficial introductions to several sciences. In 1853 Princeton seniors, sated with junior-year math, rhetoric, and Latin, regretted that "the really delightful subjects" of physics and chemistry were, "instead of being judiciously distributed over the four years," "crowded" into the final year, as were expert lectures in astronomy one day a week and elective morning short courses in botany, geology, anatomy, and zoology. In contrast, the long, generic, natural philosophy course was taught by a rather "desultory" and ad-libbing lecturer whose "rambling excursions" and "careless" delivery made it "extremely difficult to write or recollect."[127]

126 Stanley M. Guralnick, *Science and the Ante-Bellum American College*, Memoirs of the American Philosophical Society, vol. 109 (Philadelphia, 1975); Stanley M. Guralnick, "The American Scientist in Higher Education, 1820–1910," in Nathan Reingold, ed., *The Sciences in the American Context: New Perspectives* (Washington, D.C.: Smithsonian Institution, 1979), 99–141.

127 Henry and Scharff, *College as It Is*, 220–21, 224–29, at 228, 229.

As the sciences proliferated and took on new, specialized, life, the foundation of the traditional curriculum—the classical languages—were also rejuvenated by their professors in several ways that enhanced their viability for several decades. One step was to raise admission standards, to accept older students who had prepared their "small" Latin and less Greek more thoroughly. This allowed them to bypass the first year or two of elementary, almost remedial, language classes with inexperienced tutors and to begin the study of classical antiquity with older professors. Among the few hundred Americans who studied in Germany between 1810 and 1860, most were theologians or students of "oriental" languages who imbibed the New Humanist philology emanating from the universities there. They returned with a new approach to studying and teaching the classics and proselytized it zealously and broadly.[128] Many other faculty gained the same insights from study at American theological seminaries, many of whose professors had studied in Germany or absorbed German scholarship.[129]

The traditional way of teaching Latin and Greek was to emphasize vocabulary and grammar, the "osteology" of language, in artless recitations denounced by reformers as "gerund-grinding," an endless string of technicalities ending in "palpable darkness and nonsense." The existing Greek grammars and lexicons were little help, giving their explanations and annotations in Latin. The major—and almost sole—college text for Greek literature (besides the Greek New Testament) was the *Graeca Majora*, a late-eighteenth-century Scottish compilation of short, uncontextualized selections from Attic plays, poems, and histories. Its goal was more to assist the study of grammar, syntax, and vocabulary than to promote the appreciation of

128 McCaughey, "Transformation of American Academic Life," 264; Carl Diehl, *Americans and German Scholarship, 1770–1870* (New Haven, Conn.: Yale University Press, 1978), 55, 60; Caroline Winterer, *The Culture of Classicism: Ancient Greece and Rome in American Intellectual Life, 1780–1910* (Baltimore, Md.: Johns Hopkins University Press, 2002), 50–62, 83–84.

129 Turner, *Philology*, chs. 5, 13; Jerry Wayne Brown, *The Rise of Biblical Criticism in America, 1800–1870: The New England Scholars* (Middletown, Conn.: Wesleyan University Press, 1969), 7–59, 75–76; Jurgen Herbst, *The German Historical School in American Scholarship: A Study in the Transfer of Culture* (Ithaca, N.Y.: Cornell University Press, 1965), ch. 4.

Greek literature or culture.[130] The German philologists and their American disciples sought to shift the emphasis "from *words* to *worlds*," to the historical context and meaning of the ancient texts as *wholes*, not snippets. Although the *Graeca Majora* continued to sell in decreasing numbers until 1860, from the 1820s on, faculty increasingly assigned complete texts of Homer, Demosthenes, Plato, Herodotus, Thucydides, Aeschylus, Sophocles, and Euripides, often edited for American readers from the best German editions.[131]

The historicist German approach to classical civilization (*Altertumswissenschaft*) went hand in glove with an American shift in the 1820s toward Greek and away from Latin. While the Roman Empire served as a flattering "mirror" for the young transcontinental republic that had similarly conquered geography and native tribes, fifth-century Athens was seen as an "antidote" to Jacksonian America's anti-intellectualism, demagogic and factionalized politics, civic corruption, uncouth oratory, rampant materialism, and "banality of incipient industrialism."[132] The new studies also imbibed the German Romantic notion of *Bildung*, or self-cultivation. The new students of classical civilization were not merely to read *about* the admirable Greeks, they were to "become Greeks" in mind and spirit. As the Harvard professor Cornelius Felton implored, they were no longer to "summon [the Greek] Shades to appear before us" so that they might judge them by modern standards, but to "transport ourselves back to the time when they lived," to be judged and elevated by their still-powerful ideals and standards.[133]

❊ ❊ ❊

130 Winterer, *Culture of Classicism*, ch. 1, at 34, 59 (quotations); Caroline Winterer, "The Humanist Revolution in America, 1820–1860: Classical Antiquity in the Colleges," *History of Higher Education Annual* 18 (1998), 111–29, at 112–16.

131 Winterer, *Culture of Classicism*, ch. 3; Winterer, "Humanist Revolution in America," 116–22.

132 Winterer, *Culture of Classicism*, 68–76, at 68, 76; Winterer, "Humanist Revolution in America," 120.

133 Winterer, *Culture of Classicism*, 77–83; Winterer, "Humanist Revolution in America," 118–19.

The new studies also entailed a new pedagogy. Even introductory recitations had to offer more than memorization of words and rules. Likewise, upper class courses offered by newly trained or inspired professors turned increasingly to planned or impromptu lectures to elicit the rich contexts and fullest meanings of the words and passages, entailing forays into classical art, archaeology, politics, history, mythology, religion, sociology, and demography as well as stagecraft, sports and games, and domestic life.

One of the signal practitioners of the new teaching was William S. Tyler of Amherst College, where he taught successfully for fifty-seven years. Although he never made the pilgrimage to Germany (two years at the Andover Seminary was sufficient), his career neatly summarized the self-wrought reforms in the humanistic faculties of the period's leading colleges, all of which, in one way or another, were informed by the spirit of German philology. For ten years after his promotion to professor in 1836, he taught both Latin and Greek, along with Hebrew classes in several years. But the load was "quite too much," he admitted, "more than anyone could successfully perform." So "as soon as the resources of the college permitted what the increasing number of students and the principle of division of labor demanded," he relinquished Latin and Hebrew to others and confined his teaching and scholarship to Greek. Upon taking charge of the department, he put aside the *Graeca Majora* and "introduced the study of separate and entire authors." Henceforth, the department's motto was (in Latin) "It is better to read much than many books and authors."[134]

With reform of the syllabus came pedagogical clarity and confidence. In all of his teaching, Tyler used Socratic questioning "not to teach the lessons only or the language only, or the literature only, or the life of the Greeks only," but also "the life . . . of mankind as illustrated by that of the Greeks." His goal was to make not

134 Tyler, *Autobiography*, 67–68. Isaac W. Stuart, a Yale-trained philologist, taught Greek the same new way at South Carolina College between 1835 and 1839, although he proposed to reinstate the *Graeca Majora* rather than spend a whole year reading Homer, whose single dialect and idiom he thought limiting. Wayne K. Durrill, "The Power of Ancient Words: Classical Teaching and Social Change at South Carolina College, 1804–1860," *Journal of Southern History* 65:3 (Aug. 1999), 469–98, at 484–85.

only "Grecians and scholars" but also "men" and Christians. Although he was not hostile to textbooks or recitations if done well, he was partial to lectures on the works, authors, and the times—"one carefully written lecture every week to each class," whether freshman or senior. At the beginning of every new class, he sought to give them "some idea of the nature of language . . . and of the history and philosophy of the Greek language and its genetic and vital relation to the language, literature, art and science of the civilized world." A German Ph.D. couldn't have said—or practiced—it better.[135]

❁ ❁ ❁

The multiple changes occurring in the antebellum professoriate are relatively easy to summarize but harder to personalize. Professors were simply not given to keeping diaries, as some of their students were. Perhaps most revealing of the trends that were altering and improving the country's colleges was the unusual diary of James Hadley, a Yale graduate in 1842 who stayed on for both graduate and theological study before becoming a tutor in 1845, an assistant professor of Greek in 1848, and a full professor three years later. In his maturity he was regarded as "America's best and soundest philologist." But he was equally advanced in mathematics; Yale's president once asked him for help in revising his algebra textbook.[136] His diary, even with several gaps and missing leaves, is the richest published account we have of the academic life of an antebellum faculty member. Although its setting is Yale, one of the biggest and best colleges in the country, the diary conveys a sense of the numerous and arduous duties most contemporary faculty performed. That Yale College was well on its way to becoming a true university, with nearly 150 graduate students enrolled in its theology, medicine, law, and philosophy and arts "departments" in 1850, makes it an apt (if leading) example of many of the forces moving the saga of American higher education into a new chapter.

135 Tyler, *Autobiography*, 68, 72–73.
136 Hadley, *Diary*, vii–viii.

Two years into his assistant professorship, Hadley summed up a typical work week. "My College duties occupy me in lessons and preparations about 36 hours a week, or 6 a day. College business, such as reporting [grades and discipline cases], attending Chapel, hearing excuses, occasional examinations, etc., perhaps 6 hours more, making 7 in a day." In lieu of the heavy police duties of peers elsewhere, he spent another six hours in recitation learning Sanskrit and Moesogothic from his senior colleague, William Dwight Whitney, for which he thought he "ought to spend 24 in preparation. This would make 12 hours a day of regular business," or a sixty-hour work week. The largely complete diaries for 1850–52 reify his numbers by documenting his broad, but not atypical, range of academic activities.[137]

Conscientious teaching dominated the majority of his time, as it did that of his sixteen colleagues who attended to the college's 386 undergraduates. Partly in order to foster his own religious knowledge, he instituted a freshman Bible class on Sunday. Whenever he (rarely) slipped up or prepared inadequately for that or any other class, he was the first to upbraid himself for "winging" or "dodging" it. At the end of each term, he spent numerous hours calculating the averages in his freshman recitation classes in Greek, "no small job with so large a class [134]." Then came oral exams and soon their replacements, writtens. The former required six hours a day to go around the class twice with questions in three divisions: "tedious" was his only word for it.

Written exams had to be prepared for the printer and proofread as well as graded. In math, which he still taught as a junior professor, the geometrical figures had to be hand drawn or, absent photocopying, cut out of his own books. The modern ubiquity of exams clearly had an early start. Matriculation exams, given orally to fifty or more candidates at least twice a year, lasted 1½ hours in each of four sessions over several days. Understandably, they earned a faculty reputation as a great "weariness of the flesh." At the end of the academic year, written exams for prizes and scholarships had to be graded: the translations were usually "a tedious affair." Faculty also took turns

137 Ibid., xi, 59–60.

presiding over the weekly junior class "disputes," the lineal descendants of medieval disputations. After reading the essays on both sides of the chosen "question," Hadley, often after some research of his own, rendered his decision, in which he reviewed the various arguments made and gave his own opinion. In a short span in the spring of 1848, he made decisions in disputes regarding Cato's suicide, the school at West Point, and Puritan policy toward the Indians.[138]

In the interstices of teaching, Hadley led an active scholarly life, as many of his contemporaries at smaller, less ambitious, or less well endowed institutions could or did not. Seven weeks into the spring term of 1849, he reminded himself that he was eager to read the works of the German philologist Georg Curtius, a German-authored *Comparative Grammar*, and another German book on Latin and Greek etymologies, and to make more progress in Sanskrit and Anglo-Saxon. A year later he was "pulling steadily" at Sanskrit, Moesogothic, Aristophanes, and Greek history—his "four regular studies." The following year he resolved to "contract my range of study so as to include only . . . Greek philology, interpretation of the Scriptures, and history."[139]

His elective studies regularly resulted in articles (early ones on Tennyson and Greek verbs), book reviews in national publications, and, soon enough, his own books, principally the popular *Greek Grammar for Schools and Colleges* (1860), *Introduction to Roman Law* (1873), and *Essays Philological and Critical* (1873). He was also a faithful attendee of learned society meetings—the Connecticut Academy of Arts and Sciences, the American Oriental Society, the (local) Philological Society, and the so-called Savants, the American Association for the Advancement of Science.[140] In his "spare" time he served as the corresponding secretary of the Yale chapter of Phi Beta Kappa, of which he had become an undergraduate member. As an alumnus of the Linonia literary society, he remained abreast of its affairs and frequently consulted or borrowed its books.[141]

138 Ibid., ix, x, 11–13, 15, 28, 34–35, 63, 69–70, 80, 85–86, 88, 116, 124, 144, 166.

139 Ibid., 20, 59, 174.

140 Ibid., viii, 43, 65, 75, 92–97.

141 Ibid., 84, 89, 115, 169, 220, 282–83.

Happily for the sake of his teaching preparation and scholarship, he was not much involved even as an assistant professor in policing, leaving that chore to the seven or eight tutors. Although until his marriage in 1851 he roomed in North College on the famous Brick Row, only occasionally did he have to report students for excessive noise, drinking, or "footballing on the Green." Most of his disciplinary energies were expended in academic cases, which often entailed letters to the "parents and guardians of our dullards" with warnings, suspensions, or expulsions.[142]

❁ ❁ ❁

Despite their scattered sites, energies, and endowments, antebellum colleges needed books to do their intellectual work as much as did medieval Paris, Tudor Oxbridge, and colonial Harvard. But given the narrowly prescribed and introductory nature of much of the unreformed curriculum, the poverty of many colleges, and the enervating workload of the average faculty member, it is not surprising that antebellum libraries were circumscribed and scarcely as central to the educational program as they are today. A former president of the University of Nebraska and Ohio State University, who retired to become the librarian of Columbia University in New York, testified that the college library of the 1850s was "almost an aside in education. Indeed, it was like the sentence which we enclose in brackets."[143] As if to anticipate his colleague, the acting president of the University of Missouri noted in 1849 that his trustees agreed that "of course" a library was of "very secondary importance" in the development of even an eight-year-old aspiring university, "scientific equipment being far more important." Pronounced sectarian opposition to the "godless" institution in Columbia doubtless informed their preference for the objective solace

142 Ibid., 15, 24–25, 47, 59, 86–87, 128, 132–33, 160, 162, 176, 186, 235, 271.

143 James Hulme Canfield, 1902, quoted in Arthur T. Hamlin, *The University Library in the United States: Its Origins and Development* (Philadelphia: University of Pennsylvania Press, 1981), 44.

of science than for the subjective difficulty of books, which were often written in "dead" or foreign tongues.[144]

In similar religious climates and strained economic circumstances, most antebellum colleges could ill afford to build, stock, and maintain libraries of any significant size. Colleges with large numbers of preparatory students had even less need. A small handful of the more ambitious and better-funded colleges thought themselves in competition with the best European or, more realistically, the best American libraries. Even venerable Harvard, with a huge jump on its American successors, envied Göttingen's 250,000 volumes and liberal lending policies. Until his death in 1826, the founder, architect, and rector of the University of Virginia, Thomas Jefferson, always thought of making it equal to Europe's and the Northeast's finest, whether in faculty talent or library holdings and housing. When South Carolina College pleaded with the legislature in 1838 for additional funds to upgrade its already substantial library holdings, the state responded handsomely with at least $3,000 a year until the war broke out. The arguments that appealed to state officials emphasized, among other things, state pride in erecting a library capable of attracting the "estimation of posterity" and of "intelligent foreigners," as well as retaining outstanding faculty and students who might jump to other states, particularly in the North, for higher "literary" learning.[145] But in frontier regions as well, *any* collection of books, no matter how small, carried symbolic force, even when they were seldom or never read.[146]

144 Ibid., 26, quoting W. W. Hudson; Tewksbury, *Founding of American Colleges*, 198–99. Rev. Alva Wood, the New England-bred founding president of the University of Alabama in 1831, was also persuaded that scientific studies were the best way to acquire "mental discipline," which the Yale Reports had deemed "the great object of education" three years before. Tomlinson and Windham, "Northern Piety and Southern Honor," 11, 14.

145 Howard Clayton, "The American College Library: 1800–1860," *Journal of Library History* 3:2 (April 1968), 120–37, at 129; Harry Clemons, *The University of Virginia Library, 1825–1950: Story of a Jeffersonian Foundation* (Charlottesville: University of Virginia Library, 1954), ch. 1; Frances B. Everhart, "The South Carolina College Library," *Journal of Library History* 3:3 (July 1968), 221–41, at 228.

146 Charles C. Calhoun, *A Small College in Maine: Two Hundred Years of Bowdoin* (Brunswick, Maine: Bowdoin College, 1993), 106.

In 1849 a detailed survey of 33 of the *better* college libraries revealed even their modest size.[147] Only nine—and only three of the ten nominal universities—possessed more than 10,000 books. Harvard was far in the lead with 56,000 volumes, followed by Georgetown [Washington, D.C.] College (25,000), Brown (23,000), and Yale (20,500). Emory College in Georgia and Norwich University in Vermont, both chartered in the mid-1830s, brought up the above-average rear with only a thousand volumes each. Nor were books being added to these collections in any volume: an annual average of 200 titles. Part of the reason for such paucity was the lack of regular funding for book purchases: an average of $200, mostly generated from student user fees ($1–2 a year) and overdue fines (often graduated according to book size). Very few libraries had special endowments: Yale's $27,000 and Brown's $25,000 funds were unusual.[148] Most books were donated by friends, faculty, and alumni. Charles Jewett, Brown's librarian and the author of the 1849 survey, concluded that the vast majority of collections were "the chance aggregations of the gifts of charity: too many of them discarded, as well-nigh worthless, from the shelves of the donors."[149] Since many donors were clergymen, their gifts had a decidedly theological cast, "mostly polemical and controversial—and very unattractive to the ordinary lad," remembered one such student from Princeton.[150]

The small size of the library collections meant that they were usually relegated to cramped, vestigial quarters without adequate heating, lighting, or study space. An upper floor of the chapel, museum, or main academic building was the likely spot until the collections grew large enough to command separate buildings. Even older eastern colleges shared the experiences of the newer, less favored, frontier colleges. Princeton's "not large" library began in 1756 in a second-floor

147 Charles Coffin Jewett, *Report on the Public Libraries of the United States of America, January 1, 1850* (Washington, D.C., 1850), digested in Hamlin, *University Library*, 230–31 (app. I).

148 W. N. Chattin Carlton, "College Libraries in the Mid-Nineteenth Century," *Library Journal* 32 (Nov. 1907), 479–86, at 481–82.

149 Quoted in Clayton, "American College Library," 123.

150 "'An Awfully Poor Place': Edward Shippen's Memoir of the College of New Jersey in the 1840s," ed. J. Jefferson Looney, *Princeton University Library Chronicle* 59:1 (Autumn 1997), 8–57, at 42.

room (c. 35 by 20 feet) of the all-purpose Nassau Hall, before moving in 1805 to a sturdy fieldstone structure that also housed the two literary societies and some classrooms. In 1860 it returned to Nassau Hall in a new rear wing, which it shared with several mineral cabinets and a bevy of skeletal and stuffed critters in the natural-history collection.[151] Williams College's first academic building (1793) harbored on its third floor a library room "so small that it was possible to stand in the middle . . . and reach all the books." Short of fresh air and space, the books moved in 1828 to a new brick chapel before being translated nineteen years later to a single-purpose octagonal building, where a centrally seated librarian could see and micro-manage all of its patrons. Bowdoin's books also shared holy space with "philosophical apparatus" on the second floor of the "Old College Chapel" (1790) until they were shifted to somewhat larger quarters in a hall behind the new chapel (1855). Those precincts, too, were soon declared lacking in "study and shelf space, adequate light and ventilation, and an atmosphere conducive to academic activity."[152]

Before South Carolina College's library inherited a splendid new building all to itself in 1840, it had been assigned space in a balcony-type room on the second floor of the chapel and, after 1817, on the same floor in a new science hall.[153] The University of Virginia was exceptional in erecting in 1826 the handsome, domed Rotunda to house its inaugural library of over 8,000 books. Equally exceptional was little Marshall College in Mercersburg, Pennsylvania, all of whose library was stashed in its professors' offices and homes.[154]

151 Alexander Leitch, *A Princeton Companion* (Princeton, N.J.: Princeton University Press, 1978), 286, 329, 332; W. Barksdale Maynard, *Princeton: America's Campus* (University Park: Penn State University Press, 2012), 15, 19, 33; Wheaton J. Lane, ed., *Pictorial History of Princeton* (Princeton, N.J.: Princeton University Press, 1947), 10–11, 29, 31, 36.

152 Tolles, *Architecture & Academe*, 75, 77, 80 (fig. 3–15), 83, 90–91 (fig. 3–26). After 1825, Trinity College in Hartford, Connecticut also housed its 5,000-volume library in a Greek-revival chapel, beside "mineral cabinets, philosophical chamber, laboratory and recitation rooms." Ibid., 137.

153 Everhart, "South Carolina College Library," 222–23.

154 As late as 1850, only the third floor and dome of the Rotunda were used for library purposes; the rest was taken up with laboratories, classrooms, and a museum.

If an intriguing topic was raised or a title mentioned in recitation or lecture, or if material was needed to prepare an essay or debate for a literary society, eager students had sufficient cause to visit their college libraries. But such a trip was daunting because they invariably encountered formidable barriers. The first was the librarian of the day, whose operating principle was "preservation before circulation." Virtually all librarians were full-time professors, whose library hours had to accommodate their teaching duties. Thus most libraries were open only once or twice a week for an hour or less each time, usually for the sole purpose of receiving and returning books.[155] Tables and chairs were at such a premium that in-house study or reference work was nearly impossible. So was browsing in the alcoves ("stacks" were a future feature). In most libraries, students were not allowed beyond the librarian's desk or railing. This impediment assumed that borrowers knew which books they needed and that they were on the shelves, no easy matter. Most libraries had printed or manuscript catalogues (usually alphabetical and out of date) and the librarian's keen memory as finding aids; subject catalogues came later. If by happy chance students were allowed into the inner sanctum, they might—even at Harvard—be stopped by a gate across every alcove entrance. In the interest of preservation, only library personnel could take books from the shelves, which meant that serendipitous discoveries were out of the question.

Once a student's titular hunt was completed, he could check out a limited number of books—of an acceptable sort. Books containing

---

Clemons, *University of Virginia Library*, 5; Carlton, "College Libraries," 480. The University of Alabama copied Virginia's Rotunda for its own library, only to discover that the acoustics were "terrible" for study. Tomlinson and Windham, "Northern Piety and Southern Honor," 4, 34n19.

155 See the list of hours for the 33 better libraries in Hamlin, *University Library*, 230–31. Harvard's was open 30 hours a week, followed by Yale's and South Carolina's 24. The rest were in the low single digits. An additional reason for short library hours, often around lunchtime or late afternoon after the last classes, was the need for natural light. Fire was a librarian's nightmare, as much for water as for flame. Lamps and candles were therefore prohibited, even for the occasional librarian who lived in the library. Electrification later in the century was a godsend and led to longer hours of operation.

valuable prints or plates, anatomical texts, reference works, "lascivious" novels (what few there were likely to be among the largely clerical donations), certain popular magazines and reviews, and especially English translations of the Latin and Greek mainstays of the curriculum—all were confined to quarters as being too expensive to replace or too unseemly, or their use illegitimate.[156] More acceptable titles could be taken out in small doses, usually three at a time. For a time, Harvard and Yale freshmen and sophomores were not allowed to borrow at all, but elsewhere all students had permission to do so. At South Carolina College and Brown, student withdrawals were sensibly limited by the size of the volume. A big folio could be kept for four weeks, a smaller quarto for three; *two* duodecimos were available for a week.[157] Sometimes a small charge was levied on each volume, another damper on scholarship. At Yale each book cost the borrower between 6 and 12 cents, at Brown only 4 and 10 cents, again depending on size. Overdue fines followed the same rationale in many colleges.[158]

❁ ❁ ❁

The hard facts about antebellum libraries amply document their limitations, but their undergraduate users should have the last word. Most of these voices belonged to students serious enough to want to go beyond their required textbooks and to pursue ideas into different and deeper sources. Modern students with unlimited access to vast print and digital collections can only imagine the obstacles their early predecessors met in trying to use their college libraries for those purposes. Basil Gildersleeve, who graduated fourth in his Princeton class of 1849 at seventeen, found the college library

156 See the Harvard list of prohibited books c. 1830 in Keyes D. Metcalf, "The Undergraduate and the Harvard Library, 1765–1877," *Harvard Library Bulletin* 1:1 (Winter 1947), 29–51, at 50; also Knight, *DHES* 3:262 (University of Alabama, 1830s).

157 At South Carolina, each volume was wrapped in "clean thick paper" before being released into undergraduate hands. Everhart, "South Carolina College Library," 226.

158 Hamlin, *University Library*, 30–31, 35–36; Carlton, "College Libraries," 483–84; Knight, *DHES* 3:156–57 (University of Virginia, 1824).

"wretchedly meagre," but that did not prevent him from delving into its "unfrequented shelves" during its two open hours a week. Near-contemporary Edward Shippen may have been speaking from personal experience (he graduated 48th in a class of 51) when he seconded Gildersleeve's indictment that the Princeton library was "very seldom visited by the students" because it "seemed to consist of dusty tomes." Despite the $500 for books generated by student fees annually, two able seniors four years later found Princeton's 9,800 books "mostly old, and modern works . . . very scarce indeed." Even the collection of dictionaries, which they thought "should form the nucleus of every Library," was "not very complete." A missing Portuguese lexicon particularly irked them for some reason.[159]

The Amherst salutatorian William Hammond made sporadic resort to his college's 5,700-volume library during his two years there, checking out three or four books at a time. During a summer visit to the imposing Harvard library in 1847, however, he discovered that even Harvard students had undue difficulty accessing its bibliographical wealth, despite its thirty operating hours a week. This prompted him to get himself appointed assistant to Amherst's professor-librarian, "not so much from a disinterested regard for the public welfare," he confessed, "as that I might have free access to its stores, which are now all but inaccessible" during the library's sole weekly opening. The following January, the librarian was persuaded to open briefly on Monday mornings as well. On opening day his eager assistant celebrated by checking out a French history of mathematics.[160]

A year after Hammond's visit, Walter Mitchell, a Harvard graduate (1846) and a current Harvard law student, sent President Edward Everett a long description of the library's inaccessibility and the staff's cool behavior toward its would-be users. To begin, he wrote, the seemingly ample hours of operation were greatly reduced by "the constant encroachments of the lecture and the recitation." During one term in his junior year, Mitchell was left with only two free hours

159 Gildersleeve, "The College in the Forties," in Briggs, *Soldier and Scholar*, 64–65; Shippen, "'An Awfully Poor Place,'" 42; Henry and Scharff, *College as It Is*, 97.

160 Hammond, *Remembrance of Amherst*, 54, 103, 155, 179, 213.

in which to obtain books. Second, "the days—when it would be most accessible to the student"—Friday afternoon and Saturday—were not "library days." Once access was gained, the seven or eight large volumes of the alphabetical catalogue were impossible to use long enough when a whole class had just been admitted to the library, as they often were. If the student discovered a dozen or more titles that he wanted to consult, he had to depend on the good will and dispatch of a library official to fetch them from the shelves and whose patient kindness might well cease after the first few volumes. If the student did manage to obtain access to the interior, the bar across every alcove prevented browsing. Moreover, he was made to feel like a "pickpocket" by the requirement that he "leave his cloak and cap at the door." Yet despite "the sleepless vigilance of three lynx-eyed librarians and an assistant porter," "no small proportion of the books that leave the library leave it clandestinely," he admitted, because the students were denied "the privilege of using the books on the spot," from browsing and returning the books to the shelves when finished. In sum, Mitchell told the president, "the labor of getting *one* reference, given us in the recitation, was rendered too tedious and formidable by the restrictions of the library."[161] Most antebellum collegians could have said similar things about their own libraries.

But they also had a partial solution of their own making. Their ubiquitous literary societies all had libraries. By 1849 at 10 of the 33 better colleges, the combined society libraries outnumbered the college's holdings. At Yale, the stock of the Linonia and Brothers in Unity libraries led the college, 27,200 volumes to 20,500. The University of North Carolina societies housed 8,800 volumes, the college only 3,500.[162]

The advantages of these student libraries, housed in their own halls or meeting rooms, were several. Because every member had a key, the society libraries were often accessible around the clock. During the day they were normally available to members of rival societies and faculty, and occasionally to townspeople. But with busy student librarians, their checkout times and limits were not always more convenient or generous than the college's. In the heavy police climate of

161 Metcalf, "Undergraduate and the Harvard Library," 39–46.

162 Hamlin, *University Library*, 230–31.

the colleges, a self-checkout honor system did not seem to suggest itself. Nonetheless, overdue fines and society dues served to keep the shelves supplied with up-to-date titles and subscriptions to popular journals and literary reviews, English and American.

Since the collections were designed primarily to help members prepare essays and debates for their weekly meetings, most included a serviceable reference section and a broad range of subject matter, largely in English. The societies invested heavily in the latest belles lettres and social sciences, as well as literary classics of the academic sort. Novels (Sir Walter Scott, James Fenimore Cooper, Henry Fielding), poetry (Lord Byron, John Keats, William Cullen Bryant), plays, histories (European and American), biographies, essays, and travel books circulated best, quite different from the college "favorites" in Latin and Greek.[163] As the Loganian Society at Haverford College concluded, the societies in their literary activities and libraries did a great deal to foster "a desire for good books and an affection for the intellectual life."[164] When American higher education added research and graduate education to its portfolio after the Civil War, many society libraries were folded into the college collections to form firm foundations for the much larger and richer libraries needed to serve the new era's needs.

But even before those major postbellum changes, a few universities and colleges sought to enlarge and improve their libraries to serve the needs not only of their serious students but especially of their faculties. Their arguments underlined the easily ignored realities of contemporary teaching, particularly of upper class courses, while pointing toward revised job descriptions of the future professoriate. As early as 1823, the trustees of South Carolina College sought to use a liberal grant from the legislature to augment the library's holdings in ancient and classical literature, science and natural history, modern European languages and literatures, and the discovery and early history of the Americas. They argued that college libraries should "comprehend all the pursuits of Man" and

163 Thomas S. Harding, *College Literary Societies: Their Contribution to Higher Education in the United States, 1815–1876* (New York: Pageant Press, 1971), chs. 3, 5, 7, 9, 11, 13; Hamlin, *University Library*, 37–41.

164 Carlton, "College Libraries," 486.

that teachers must be lifelong learners to "keep their minds in a state of constant improvement." "Those who are expected to instruct in the knowledge of the age, ought to have access to the Literature of the age." "The Speculative Sciences, where opinions are the result of abstract induction," can get along with relatively few books. But the more factual sciences require many more. A conscientious professor in those fields "may have occasion in a single lecture to refer to fifty Authorities."[165] The trustees also knew better than anyone that professors were not paid enough to accumulate personal libraries large enough for their research needs and pedagogical purposes.

In 1856 the trustees of the seven-year-old University of Mississippi made several of the same points in an effort to garner greater and more regular appropriations from their state legislature. Although the nascent university was short on buildings, faculty, scientific apparatus, and natural history cabinets, the trustees—unlike their counterparts in Missouri—put their emphasis on the needs of the library, which was only "the beginning of a collection of books." They were quick to acknowledge that it was "much more in reference to college faculties than to college students that comprehensive Libraries are desirable." "To be a successful teacher, even of the elements of knowledge," they argued, "a man must himself know much besides those elements." For "without unrestrained access to books," the professor "is in danger of intellectual stagnation." And "the reputation of colleges is to a great extent dependent upon the personal reputation for talents and learning of the professors who conduct them." "A college without a copious library can rarely count on the great advantage of embracing in its faculty a man, whose name is familiar to the learned world." This was a shame because when "people look for authoritative opinions in all those abstruser matters with which the mass of men are unfamiliar," they turn to the faculties of "our colleges and universities." In short, the trustees concluded, the "Ole Miss" library "offers no aid at all for the prosecution of such researches in the different branches of knowledge as are necessary to perfect the instructors themselves, to promote their usefulness to

165 Knight, *DHES* 3:218–21.

the University, and to enable them to connect their names honorably with the intellectual history of the age."[166] Few antebellum trustees were as enlightened as these, but many of their postwar successors had to be if their institutions were to survive and thrive.

❁ ❁ ❁

Although antebellum America was well known as "a land of colleges," its higher-educational rolls contained a surprising number of nominal universities. Among the 241 colleges thought to have existed—by charter, at least—before 1860, 43 (18 percent) carried the "university" title. Several were public institutions created by states. Several of those early "flagships" were founded to superintend the whole educational system of the state, from common schools and academies to colleges and university, a task at which they invariably failed. The earliest—the Universities of North Carolina and Georgia—have long competed for the dubious title of first state university.[167] Later institutions to which the university label was applied were much more varied. An assortment of at least 53 academies, female schools, grammar schools, and preparatory departments—some chimerical, most short lived—made an appearance as "universities" in various records.[168]

Besides visiting Europeans, several American observers were uneasy with the titular inflation. Some attributed it to American inferiority and a compensatory search for grandiosity. Others, like the Harvard historian (and future president) Jared Sparks, were simply dismissive. In a letter to George Bancroft in 1829, he wrote, "It is a great mistake . . . to call any of our institutions by the name of Universities. They are neither such, nor can ever be, without a radical

166 Knight, *DHES* 3:414–19.

167 Tewksbury, *Founding of American Colleges*, 34, 35. William S. Powell's *The First State University: A Pictorial History of the University of North Carolina* (Chapel Hill: University of North Carolina Press, 1972), 5, acknowledges that while Georgia was chartered four years before UNC (1785 vs. 1789), UNC held classes and graduated its first class sooner (1795 and 1798 vs. 1801 and 1804).

168 Burke, *American Collegiate Populations*, app. B.

change. . . . I do not believe that a university can be engrafted on any of our old colleges. Something must be done *de novo*, before any success can be hoped."[169] In resisting a change of title for South Carolina College, President James Thornwell declared in 1853 that *University* simply "sounds more imposing, and carries the appearance of greater dignity. But the truth is," he countered, "there is hardly a more equivocal word in the language. . . . In its ordinary acceptation in this country it is either synonymous with college as an institution of higher education . . . or it denotes a college with professional schools attached."[170] He knew whereof he spoke. Although most medical schools were independent, at least 23 medical departments or schools were attracted to putative universities before 1860, as were 16 law schools.[171]

President Philip Lindsley was also up on his academic usages. In 1826 he made the case for changing the name of his Cumberland College (mostly to avoid confusion with a Presbyterian interloper of the same name) to the University of Tennessee and, when that failed in the legislature, the University of Nashville. In the newspaper essay "Colleges and Universities," he informed his urban-frontier readers that "every institution in Europe, which confers degrees of any kind, is styled a University. In America," by contrast, "College and University are used as synonymous. Their charters grant them all equal powers and privileges. . . . Cumberland College can now do all that any University in America is authorized to do," just as Harvard could legally use College or University in its public acts.[172]

169 "Correspondence of George Bancroft and Jared Sparks, 1823–1832," ed. John Spencer Bassett, *Smith College Studies in History* 2:2 (Jan. 1917), 136 (June 10, 1829).

170 Knight, *DHES* 3:363.

171 Divinity schools also tended to be freestanding; many normal schools or departments were more comfortable attaching themselves to private coed or female colleges. Burke, *American Collegiate Populations*, app. A. Burke also suggests that the legal statutes of universities "allowed direct association with professional schools." Ibid., 268n38.

172 *National Banner and Nashville Whig*, Oct. 11, 1826, p. 2, cited in David Mathis, "Image, Institution, and Leadership: Philip Lindsley and the Modern University Presidency, 1825–1850"(Ed.D. diss., School of Education, College of William & Mary, 1985), 47.

Other American academics wanted to preserve the European notion of a "real" university. In 1842 the president of Brown, Francis Wayland, defined it as "a place of education in all the most important branches of human learning . . . professional as well as ante-professional science." Nine years later, Henry Tappan, president of the University of Michigan, called universities "*Cyclopaedias* of education: where . . . provision is made for studying every branch of knowledge in full, for carrying forward all scientific investigation; where study may be extended without limit."[173] Although in later American usage *university* was "usually applied to institutions with graduate or professional schools," it was before the Civil War "often used loosely of a college." Loosely and simplemindedly. When the founding president of Otterbein University, a United Brethren college in Westerville, Ohio, was asked why the bigger title was chosen, he explained, "We did not just know the difference between a college and a university. We thought, somehow, that a university meant more than a college; so we took it all in and called it Otterbein University."[174] Probably many college founders, presidents, and trustees were perplexed by the same choice.

Some of the oldest and best colleges resisted the temptation to go grand prematurely, unlike Harvard (1780) and Brown (1804), which succumbed before they had grown into the European definition of a "real" (English or German) university. Yale waited until 1887, the year after its conservative president Noah Porter passed from the scene, to become Yale University. It might have done so fifteen years earlier, when the governing board resolved that "Yale College has . . . attained the form of a university," since it had long comprised "the four departments of which a university is commonly to consist, *viz.*, the Department of Theology, of Law, of Medicine, and

173 Francis Wayland, *Thoughts on the Present Collegiate System in the United States* (Boston, 1842), in Hofstadter and Wilson, eds., *American Higher Education* 1:358; Henry P. Tappan, *University Education* (New York: George P. Putnam, 1851), 68.

174 Kenneth H. Wheeler, *Cultivating Regionalism: Higher Education and the Making of the American Midwest* (DeKalb: Northern Illinois University Press, 2011), 49–50; *A Dictionary of American English on Historical Principles*, comp. Sir William A. Craigie and James R. Hulbert, 4 vols. (Chicago: University of Chicago Press, 1938), 4:2395.

of Philosophy and the Arts" (the graduate department established in 1847, which awarded the first three American Ph.D.s in 1861.)[175]

In the decades after the Union was preserved in fratricidal war, liberal arts colleges would not only persist in modified form and continue to multiply, but bona fide universities would arise, less like mushrooms and more like truffles, as expensive as they were choice. Together with other multipurpose institutions, America's numerous colleges would not only mark a major departure from European patterns of higher education but also constitute a key and enduring element of a distinctively American pattern, even as the latter adapted several European practices after the Civil War. [176]

175 William L. Kingsley, *Yale College: A Sketch of Its History*, 2 vols. (New York, 1879), 1:161.

176 Roger L. Geiger, "The Era of Multipurpose Colleges in American Higher Education, 1850–1890," in Geiger, ed., *The American College in the Nineteenth Century* (Nashville, Tenn.: Vanderbilt University Press, 2000), 127–52.

CHAPTER FIVE

The German Impress

Influence is Clio's most elusive child.

FRANCESCO CORDASCO

AS THE MIDDLE of the nineteenth century passed, many American educators were concerned that the nation's sprawling non-system of higher education did not reach high enough. It was, they feared, not keeping pace with the fast-moving century or meeting the rising standards of the learned world. The United States had spanned the continent, connecting the coasts with iron rails and telegraph wire. It had grown in economic and social strength, attracting new waves of immigrants to its frontiers, farms, and cities. It had abolished chattel slavery and preserved the union in a civil war. And, willy-nilly, it sought to create or strengthen educational institutions to keep up with the ideas, inventions, and scholarship emanating from Europe. But its plethora of colleges and even its nominal universities, little different from colleges, were not equal to that challenge. Only a true chauvinist could argue that mid-century America had "grown as fast intellectually as England, or France, or Germany."[1]

The problem, according to critics and reformers, was twofold. First, America lacked a sufficiently extensive and rigorous system of secondary education. Without better student preparation, the colleges could not raise their standards for admission and graduation. As the Yale Reports of 1828 admitted, "The first and great improvement which we wish to see made, is an elevation in the

1 James Morgan Hart, "The Higher Education in America," *The Galaxy: A Magazine of Entertaining Reading* 11:3 (March 1871), 369–86, at 369.

standard of attainment for admission."[2] Unfortunately, widespread improvement in that quarter had to wait until after the Civil War, when America got serious, locality by locality, about establishing and funding public high schools for all, work- or college-bound, and preparatory schools were founded in numbers, either independently or as additions to existing colleges.[3] Yet even had they been able to attract better students, college faculties were not ready to raise classroom standards and performance without much better preparation on their own parts.

Forced by presidents and trustees to submit to prescribed foundational curricula, which were still dominated by ancient languages, mathematics, and science, most college professors had little need or encouragement to advance their own learning. Yoked to paternalistic institutional goals of piety maintenance and character building, they had even less opportunity or energy for it. In 1874 Princeton-born-and-educated James Morgan Hart lamented that the chief impediment for American professors was their regular assignment to "police-duty and discipline" in what amounted to "reformatory school[s]."[4] At a time when many faculty were future clergymen, and virtually all presidents were current or former ones, college teaching could be regarded as another form of ministry to the weak or fallen. But for those who sought more secular careers in *higher* education, by advancing their own and their students'

2 *Reports on the Course of Instruction in Yale College; By a Committee of the Corporation and the Academical Faculty* (New Haven, Conn.: Hezekiah Howe, 1828), 23; reprinted in David B. Potts, *Liberal Education for a Land of Colleges: Yale's* Reports *of 1828* (New York: Palgrave Macmillan, 2010).

3 William J. Reese, *The Origins of the American High School* (New Haven, Conn.: Yale University Press, 1995); James McLachlan, *American Boarding Schools: A Historical Study* (New York: Charles Scribner's Sons, 1970); W. Bruce Leslie, *Gentlemen and Scholars: College and Community in the 'Age of the University,' 1865–1917* (University Park: Pennsylvania State University Press, 1992), 161–62, 213–24; Frederick Rudolph, *The American College and University: A History* (New York: Alfred A. Knopf, 1962), 281–82, 284–86.

4 James Morgan Hart, *German Universities: A Narrative of Personal Experience* (New York: G. P. Putnam's Sons, 1874), 273, 318.

intellectual development and liberation, academic life often disappointed.[5] Most of them spent too much time in "weary repetition of the rudiment" and, as the jaded Professor Hart put it, "cudgeling the wits of refractory or listless reciters." Too many remained all-purpose "schoolmasters" because the typical collegian was "simply a school-boy of larger growth."[6]

The crux of the matter, as the University of Michigan president, Henry Tappan, lamented in 1856, was that "the graduate of a College is not prepared to become a College Professor." No longer, it was argued, in a society "continually expanding and embracing more elevated objects of research," should "the retired preacher suffering from bronchitis . . . be chosen to teach Biology, or the returned missionary, who has spent most of his days learning Japanese, . . . be chosen to teach English."[7] Professors with only an undergraduate education from a typically small, underfunded college, perhaps followed by a year or two in seminary or as a tutor leading drills in the same courses he had just taken, were prepared only to preserve and pass on elementary outlines of past worlds and disciplines. They were ill equipped to introduce young Americans to the rapidly changing and increasingly complex world that lay beyond their campuses, communities, and shores or to refine and contribute new discoveries to the accepted knowledge of it.

5 Hart, then professor of modern languages at Cornell after two stints of study and research in Germany, explored the confused meanings of the term "higher education" in America and its virtual absence in Europe in "Higher Education," *Lippincott's Magazine of Popular Literature and Science* 18 (Nov. 1876), 573–84.

6 Franklin Carter, *The College as Distinguished from the University: An Inaugural Address* (New Haven, Conn.: Tuttle Morehouse & Taylor, 1881), 17; Hart, *German Universities*, 268, 287; Samuel Sheldon, "Why Our Science Students Go to Germany," *Atlantic Monthly* 63 (April 1889), 463–66, at 463; Charles Phelps Taft, *The German University and the American College: An Essay Delivered before the Cincinnati Literary Club, January 7, 1871* (Cincinnati: Robert Clarke, 1871), 27; Francis Greenwood Peabody, *Reminiscences of Present-Day Saints* (Boston: Houghton Mifflin, 1927), 26.

7 Quoted in Richard J. Storr, *The Beginnings of Graduate Education in America* (Chicago: University of Chicago Press, 1953), 20 (Harvard report of 1824), 114 (Tappan); Carter, *College as Distinguished from University*, 24.

The solution to this dilemma, the reformers argued, could only come, at least for the foreseeable future, from abroad. "The Universities of Europe are, at this moment," said Tappan, "furnishing us with this supply. Many of our young men are educated there. Their scholars are transplanted here. We depend upon the scientific and critical labors of their learned men, who furnish the original works from whence our editions of the Classics and our own scientific works are derived."[8] Tappan and particularly later, younger, reformers were not referring to all of Europe, but almost exclusively to Germany, where many of them had done advanced work after college. In contrast, Oxford and Cambridge, both badly in need of reform, did not offer Ph.D.s until 1917 and 1920, respectively, mostly as a gesture to credential-seeking Americans.[9] The best English scholarship in classical philology largely followed German leads, historical studies were hopelessly old-fashioned, and science was pursued largely outside the universities. French science was also not conducted in the university but in national institutes or private laboratories, and the *grandes écoles* were not suited to American postgraduates.[10]

8 Quoted in Storr, *Beginnings of Graduate Education*, 114. See also Daniel Coit Gilman's remarks during his interview for the presidency of Johns Hopkins University in December 1874: "American graduates who would like to pursue certain lines of culture to their latest limits are compelled every year either to go abroad or content themselves with the necessarily imperfect aid which they can get in the post-graduate courses from overworked and half-paid professors who are doing the duty of schoolmasters." Abraham Flexner, *Daniel Coit Gilman: Creator of the American Type of University* (New York: Harcourt, Brace, 1946), 50–51.

9 Renate Simpson, *How the PhD Came to Britain: A Century of Struggle for Postgraduate Education* (Guildford, UK: Society for Research into Higher Education, 1983).

10 Samuel H. Bishop, "University Study at Berlin and at Oxford," *Educational Review* 15 (April 1898), 351–62, at 360; E. D. Perry, "The Universities of Germany," *Educational Review* 7 (March 1894), 209–31, at 211–13; Basil Gildersleeve, "English and German Scholarship," in Charles William Emil Miller, ed., *Selections from the Brief Mentions of Basil Lanneau Gildersleeve* (Baltimore: Johns Hopkins University Press, 1930), 364–76; William Berryman Scott, *Some Memories of a Palaeontologist* (Princeton, N.J.: Princeton University Press, 1939), 126, 128; James Washington Bell, "German Universities," *Education* [Syracuse, N.Y.] 2 (Sept. 1881), 49–64, at 50–51; Jurgen Herbst, *The German Historical School in American Scholarship: A Study in the Transfer of Culture*

Beginning slowly in the 1810s and accelerating throughout the century, ambitious American academics and would-be scholars regarded Germany as mecca where they found the best tonic for America's weakness in higher education. For what America's vertical system of education lacked—with the partial exception of the theological seminaries—was a top layer, a qualitatively higher institution to stimulate the ambitions of its colleges and to provide a different, efficient, and prestigious way to serve the nation's new wants and needs.[11] Growing numbers of reformers decided that America needed numerous iterations of the true university, which they thought Germany had developed to near perfection since the late eighteenth century. But what the country most needed, they quickly realized after experiencing German academic life, was the university feature devoted not to undergraduate or professional education, but to the advanced training of faculty for both colleges and the university itself. This President Tappan called its "direct object." Because the German system had no exact equivalent of America's colleges, and its universities offered only one nonprofessional degree, the Ph.D., the American university would have to fashion what was soon called the *graduate school*.[12]

(Ithaca, N.Y.: Cornell University Press, 1965), 10–13; Christophe Charle, "Patterns," in Walter Rüegg, ed., *Universities in the Nineteenth and Early Twentieth Centuries (1800–1945)*, vol. 3 of *A History of the University in Europe* [*HUE*], gen. ed. Walter Rüegg, 4 vols. (Cambridge: Cambridge University Press, 2004), 44–46, 53–57, 61–63.

11 Natalie A. Naylor, in "The Theological Seminary in the Configuration of American Higher Education: The Ante-Bellum Years," *History of Education Quarterly* 17:1 (Spring 1977), 17–30, and Elizabeth A. Clark, in *Founding the Fathers: Early Church History and Protestant Professors in Nineteenth-Century America* (Philadelphia: University of Pennsylvania Press, 2011), argue that elite institutions such as the Princeton Theological Seminary, Union Theological Seminary, and the Yale and Harvard divinity schools served as America's only postgraduate schools in the humanities until university graduate schools were established. By requiring their matriculants to have liberal arts degrees, they also helped establish and support academies and colleges throughout the country.

12 Storr, *Beginnings of Graduate Education*, 114–15 (Tappan), 129–34; Richard J. Storr, *The Beginning of the Future: A Historical Approach to Graduate Education in the Arts and Sciences* (New York: McGraw-Hill, 1973), ch. 4.

❋ ❋ ❋

In the relative absence of native graduate schools, large cohorts of American college graduates chose to attend German universities to prepare for learned careers. By the First World War, some 9,000 Americans had made the pilgrimage to Germany.[13] Looking back from the mid-1880s, the president of Columbia College, Frederick Barnard, observed that American graduates "with aspirations for making a career in a learned or scientific profession, or in the educational field," "almost universally" felt that "a residence of one or more years at a German university was indispensable to anything like signal success."[14] Each decade after the Civil War witnessed a new flood tide of academic migration. In the 1870s, a Harvard professor remembered two decades later, his generation "dreamed of nothing but the German University. . . . German scholarship was our master and our guide." For their part, a graduate of Williams College countered, "Us young fellows in the eighteen-eighties" never doubted that "Germany possessed the sole secret of scholarship." As late as 1898 it could be said, with pardonable exaggeration, that "the procession of American students"—"thousands" every year—"to the universities of Europe, and especially to those of Germany, has come to have a significance somewhat like that of the migration of a race."[15] Even after taking a Ph.D. before leaving for a year abroad, a future university president testified that "to come under the influence of a . . . German university, was then the height of academic ambition." His brief visit "left an ineffaceable impression of what scholarship meant, of what a university was and of what a long road higher education in America had to travel before it could hope to reach a plane of equal elevation."[16]

13 Herbst, *German Historical School*, 1–2n1.

14 William F. Russell and Edward C. Elliott, eds., *The Rise of a University*, 2 vols. (New York: Columbia University Press, 1937), 1:376.

15 The high point of American matriculations in German universities was 517 in 1895–96, after which they declined slowly until WW I. Konrad Jarausch, "The Universities: An American View," in *Another Germany: A Reconsideration of the Imperial Era*, ed. J. Dukes and J. Remak (Boulder, Colo.: Westview, 1988), 185.

16 Josiah Royce, "Present Ideals of American University Life," *Scribner's Magazine* 10:3 (Sept. 1891), 376–88, at 382–83; Bliss Perry, *And Gladly Teach: Reminiscences*

If going to Germany became something of an academic "fetich," as one returnee called (and spelled) it, the supplicants' reasons for going were not all the same.[17] Some went for an updated—academic—version of the Grand Tour, where they collected colorful memories of scar-cheeked duelists at Leipzig, beer drinking with student princes at Heidelberg, and world-famous (if eccentric and unintelligible) lecturers at Berlin. A few went to pursue marriageable young women sent from the States for musical or artistic training; many followed friends, classmates, or relatives, some with more burning academic ambitions than their own. If they persisted and returned to academic settings, the networks formed abroad served them well in the search for first jobs or career enhancement.[18]

The vast majority headed to German universities to prepare for and launch American careers in academe. Many received advice from previous students, either in popular books and articles, or from the mouths of fathers and favorite professors. Charles F. Smith's Greek professor at Harvard—a Leipzig Ph.D.—told him in the mid-1870s, "If you want to be a scholar, you must go to Germany." Bliss Perry's advisor was even closer. After five years of teaching at Williams College, his alma mater, the newly promoted Perry set off for Berlin and Strassburg to prepare seriously to teach early English literature. He was prompted not only by his professor-father, a student at Heidelberg twenty-five years earlier, but also by a Smith College fiancée headed for Berlin to study literature and music and the discovery that "the very few graduate courses offered in my field in American universities were chiefly

(Boston: Houghton Mifflin, 1935), 88–89; Bishop, "University Study," 351; Nicholas Murray Butler, *Across the Busy Years: Recollections and Reflections*, 2 vols. (New York: Charles Scribner's Sons, 1939), 1:127 (quotation).

17 James Mark Baldwin, *Between Two Wars, 1862–1921*, 2 vols. (Boston: Stratford, 1926), 1:35–36.

18 Anja Becker, "Southern Academic Ambitions Meet German Scholarship: The Leipzig Networks of Vanderbilt University's James H. Kirkland in the Late Nineteenth Century," *Journal of Southern History* 74:4 (Nov. 2008), 855–86; Carl Diehl, *Americans and German Scholarship, 1770–1870* (New Haven, Conn.: Yale University Press, 1978), 141.

modeled upon German methods and given by men who had received their own training abroad." None were yet to be had at Oxbridge or in France.[19]

Perry's two-year leave for "graduate study" abroad was partially underwritten by Williams, an example of how many American colleges and universities dealt with the national paucity of postgraduate courses and programs until the turn of the century. If faculty could not be professionally prepared before being hired, they would have to be some time after. Although Harvard did not institute the first formal sabbatical system until 1880, informal arrangements for faculty study leaves had famously (though inconclusively) begun in 1815, when Harvard's president, John Kirkland, encouraged four (and subsidized two) current and future faculty members to attend Göttingen to enhance the American college's prestige and its offerings in language and literature.[20] Much later, graduate fellowships also sent aspiring scholar-teachers abroad before local graduate programs or schools could be fully implemented. Having graduated from Princeton in 1877 at the head of his class, twenty-year-old William "Wink" Scott stayed at Princeton with three classmates for his first fellowship year to take advantage of President James McCosh's earnest start of graduate work. But for his second year, McCosh advised the would-be paleontologist, in so many words: "Go to England and study something with somebody, and then go to Germany and study something else with some other body." After productive studies in London with T. H. Huxley and in Cambridge, Scott went on to take

19 Becker, "Southern Academic Ambitions," 861, 863; Perry, *And Gladly Teach*, 71, 83, 87–88, 91. In 1871 John W. Burgess, a graduate of Amherst College, decided to study at Göttingen "after looking over the catalogues of all of the American colleges and finding no adequate provisions for the study of history, public law, and political science anywhere." *Reminiscences of an American Scholar: The Beginnings of Columbia University* (New York: Columbia University Press, 1934), 85.

20 Walter Crosby Eells, "The Origin and Early History of Sabbatical Leave," *Bulletin of the American Association of University Professors* 48 (Autumn 1962), 253–56; Diehl, *Americans and German Scholarship*, ch. 3, 172n21; Orie William Long, *Literary Pioneers: Early American Explorers of European Culture* (Cambridge, Mass.: Harvard University Press, 1935), chs. 1–4; Lilian Handlin, "Harvard and Göttingen, 1815," *Proceedings of the Massachusetts Historical Society* 95 (1983), 67–87.

FIGURE 17. When Harvard's president sent four young faculty members to Germany for advanced study in 1814, they all went to the University of Göttingen in Lower Saxony. Founded in 1734 by King George II of Hanover and Great Britain, it opened for classes in 1737 with an Enlightenment curriculum. By 1812 its library already held more than 250,000 volumes, strong in law, mathematics, and science. This 1815 engraving by H. Chr. Grape features the main university building and the library.

a Ph.D. in one year at Heidelberg before returning to the Princeton faculty.[21]

Although most American students bound for Germany had some kind of career-making in mind, their goals were seldom well defined. They were therefore surprised and usually pleased to discover aspects

21 Scott, *Memories of a Palaeontologist*, 71–72, 81–82, 85 (quotation). When Josiah Royce graduated from the underfunded University of California in 1875, President Daniel Coit Gilman persuaded a group of concerned townsmen to fund Royce's postgraduate studies in Germany. John Clendenning, ed., *The Letters of Josiah Royce* (Chicago: University of Chicago Press, 1970), 16. In the 1870s, American theological seminaries also sent some of their most promising graduates and faculty members to Germany. Clark, *Founding the Fathers*, 16, 365n112.

of the German universities that contributed to their larger vocational purpose. Their primary reason for choosing Germany was the international reputation of its university faculties. They wanted to study with some of the world's best scholars, whose writings they had read, heard mentioned, or assigned in their college classes. Although for most of them it was the fame of the universities that took them to Germany, that renown rested largely on the stooped shoulders of its famous senior professors—Mommsen, Grimm, Boeckh, Curtius, Helmholtz, Treitschke, Wilamowitz, Ranke. After a semester at Berlin, where many Americans liked to sit in on lectures by "some world-famous scholar upon subjects of which we knew little," Bliss Perry left for three semesters at Strassburg. He was drawn there by "the fame of that great scholar and delightful teacher, Bernhard ten Brink, . . . unquestionably the foremost Chaucerian upon the Continent." Perry's cohort consisted of six other Americans attracted by the same force.[22]

While buckling down to their studies, the visitors soon discovered that the German university provided many best practices and conditions for advanced work, which gave them additional, more defined, reasons for coming and for persuading other Americans to follow. One of the most noticeable, because it differed so markedly from conditions in the typical American college, was the freedom (*Freiheit*) enjoyed by both students and professors.[23] Students not only chose their living and dining arrangements (dormitories and refectories were nonexistent) but also studied what, where, and with

22 Scott, *Memories of a Palaeontologist*, 126; Perry, *And Gladly Teach*, 98, 102. For the American "colony" at Göttingen, see Daniel Bussey Shumway, "The American Students at the University of Göttingen," *German American Annals* n.s. 8: 5–6 (Sept.–Dec. 1910), 171–254; Konrad H. Jarausch, "American Students in Germany, 1815–1914: The Structure of German and U.S. Matriculants at Göttingen University," in Henry Geitz, Jürgen Heideking, and Jurgen Herbst, eds., *German Influences on Education in the United States to 1917*, (Washington, D.C.: German Historical Institute and Cambridge University Press, 1995), 195–211.

23 Hart, *German Universities*, 250, 259–60; Friedrich Paulsen, *The German Universities: Their Character and Historical Development*, trans. Edward Delavan Perry (New York: Macmillan, 1895), 97, 135, 161–73, 186–89, 201–10; Herbst, *German Historical School*, 19–22, 30.

whom they wished (*Lebens- und Lernfreiheit*).[24] The curriculum was predominantly elective, not prescribed; if they could not find a professor or curriculum to their liking, they could simply migrate to another of the twenty-some German universities in the national system. Their signed lecture book—like a passport—ensured the acceptance of their degree work at the last—or the first—university they attended. For the faculty, *Lehrfreiheit*, the freedom to teach what and how they thought best without outside interference, was similarly guarded by the state ministries of education, professional mobility, and secure state pensions.[25] Even though J. Mark Baldwin stayed only one semester at each of three universities, to which he was "attracted by the names of certain professors," he said that "the year was mainly profitable as affording new inspiration" for his psychological studies, "due to the freedom and range of graduate study."[26]

24 Jarausch, "Universities: An American View," 181–206, at 193; *The Autobiography of Lincoln Steffens* (New York: Harcourt, Brace, 1931), 133. During G. Stanley Hall's first 15–17 months in Germany, the strictly and rurally raised student in his mid-twenties "fairly reveled in a freedom unknown before." He discovered playful Sundays, beer, women, and sex, as well as "intellectual creativeness" and academic freedom. In his late twenties, Baptist William Dodd settled for a "mild revolt against his [Southern] puritan upbringing" by acquiring a taste for pale German ale and opera. Hall, *Life and Confessions of a Psychologist* (New York: D. Appleton, 1923), 219–23; Robert Dallek, *Democrat and Diplomat: The Life of William E. Dodd* (New York: Oxford University Press, 1968), 17. Dorothy Ross, in *G. Stanley Hall: The Psychologist as Prophet* (Chicago: University of Chicago Press, 1972), 41 and 41n39, corrects the impression Hall tried to give of having spent three years in Germany.

25 "In no country, probably, is the professor so untrammeled. . . . Government interference with the What and the How of university instruction, except of course in certain political respects, has long since ceased." E. D. Perry, "The Universities of Germany," *Educational Review* 7 (March 1894), 209–31, at 218–19. Lincoln Steffens noted that "A teacher in Germany may be sure of the . . . broadest freedom of thought." *The Letters of Lincoln Steffens*, ed. Ella Winter and Granville Hicks, 2 vols. (New York: Harcourt, Brace, 1938), 1:37. See also *Life, Letters, and Journals of George Ticknor*, ed. George S. Hillard et al., 2 vols. (Boston: J. R. Osgood, 1876), 1:98–99, for much earlier testimony.

26 Baldwin, *Between Two Wars*, 1:32. Richard T. Ely said that when he first went to Germany in 1877, he "seemed to breathe a new and exhilarating atmosphere of freedom." *Ground under Our Feet: An Autobiography* (New York: Macmillan, 1938), 124.

❁ ❁ ❁

Many students returned to America, as Baldwin did to Princeton, steeped in the "methods and principal researches" of the well-equipped laboratories and seminars in which they worked and the "full outfit[s] of ideas" growing from them. State-of-the-art science labs were funded by the state in separately administered institutes, most with their own journal-rich research libraries and some with complementary museums. When James Cattell returned home after earning a Ph.D. in Wilhelm Wundt's new psychology lab in Leipzig, his baggage held several pieces of experimental apparatus he had bought or had made by precision machinists at his own expense.[27] In the Philosophy Faculty—encompassing all of what we would call the nonprofessional liberal arts, sciences, and social sciences—most full professors, or "chairs," commonly had a seminar, outfitted with study tables and a substantial reference library, in which to conduct their research classes of hand-picked advanced students.[28]

The central university libraries, which were state-funded and served advanced clienteles, exceeded all but the largest American college libraries in size as well as depth of holdings. New American universities sometimes purchased the complete stock of a German

27 Sheldon, "Why Our Science Students Go to Germany," 464–65 (quotation); *An Education in Psychology: James McKeen Cattell's Journal and Letters from Germany and England, 1880–1888*, ed. Michael M. Sokal (Cambridge, Mass.: MIT Press, 1981), 127, 137, 159; Charles E. McClelland, *State, Society, and University in Germany, 1700–1914* (New York: Cambridge University Press, 1980), 279–87; Joseph Ben-David, "The Universities and the Growth of Science in Germany and the United States," *Minerva: A Review of Science, Learning, and Policy* 7:1–2 (Autumn–Winter 1968–69), 1–35, esp. 2–6.

28 Fred M. Fling, "The German Historical Seminar," *The Academy* (Syracuse, N.Y,=.) 4 (1889), 129–39, 212–19; Frank Hugh Foster, *The Seminary Method of Original Study in the Historical Sciences, Illustrated from Church History* (New York: C. Scribner's Sons, 1888); Ephraim Emerton, "The Historical Seminary in American Teaching," in G. Stanley Hall, ed., *Methods of Teaching History* (Boston: Ginn, Heath, 1884), 191–200; Bonnie G. Smith, "Gender and the Practice of Scientific History: The Seminar and Archival Research in the Nineteenth Century," *American Historical Review* 100:4 (Oct. 1995), 1150–76. On the origins of the seminar, see William Clark, *Academic Charisma and the Origins of the Research University* (Chicago: University of Chicago Press, 2006), ch. 5.

bookseller (as did the University of Chicago when it acquired nearly 97,000 volumes of a Berlin dealer) or the working libraries of famous scholars (as did Syracuse University when it bought Leopold von Ranke's 20,000 volumes, along with his desk and chair). When outfitting his new philology seminar at Johns Hopkins University, Basil Gildersleeve relied on the catalogue of Wilhelm Studemund's 4,000-volume *Seminarium* at Strassburg.[29]

The Americans' third discovery was that the object of the German university was "not to afford general culture," as it was in the American college, "but special training." "Everything," warned J. M. Hart, "is made subservient to minuteness and thoroughness of research."[30] The ultimate goal of advanced study (for which most Americans came) was less comprehensive control of the known facts—the "literature"—than it was original research in a specialized subject resulting in publication. Although hearing lectures ideally gave auditors a conspectus of the wider subject and an introduction to the disciplinary tools for prying it open, it was the specialized seminars and labs (from which the exceptional women were usually excluded) that led the journeyman scholar, under the eye of a master,

29 A Strassburg archaeologist also promised to provide a collection of plaster casts of ancient sculptures when Hopkins could afford them. Charles Franklin Thwing, *The American and the German University: One Hundred Years of History* (New York: Macmillan, 1928), 130–33; Robert Rosenthal, "The Berlin Collection: A History" (http://www.lib.uchicago.edu/e/spcl/excat/berlin/history.html); William Freeman Galpin, *Syracuse University, Vol. 1: The Pioneer Days* (Syracuse, N.Y.: Syracuse University Press, 1952), 88–93; Basil Gildersleeve, *The Letters of Basil Lanneau Gildersleeve*, ed. Ward W. Briggs, Jr. (Baltimore, Md.: Johns Hopkins University Press, 1987), 116–17. In 1882 Herbert Baxter Adams brought the working library of his former Heidelberg mentor, J. K. Bluntschli, to Johns Hopkins to form the nucleus of the history and political science seminar library. Emil Hübner's library went to New York University. Raymond J. Cunningham, "The German Historical World of Herbert Baxter Adams: 1874–1876," *Journal of American History* 68:2 (Sept. 1981), 261–75, at 275; Ernest G. Sihler, *From Maumee to Thames and Tiber: The Life Story of an American Classical Scholar* (New York: New York University Press, 1930), 164. The libraries of several theological seminaries were similarly augmented by those of German scholars. Clark, *Founding the Fathers*, 88–89, 92.

30 Thwing, *American and the German University*, 58, 60–61 (quotation), 62–63; Hart, *German Universities*, 385.

to his own discoveries and contributions. Reading widely, deeply, and thoroughly in his field was certainly expected: he would face a grueling oral exam from several professors if he wanted a degree. But the student was soon "encouraged to produce, to try his own powers, to see facts for himself, and then to begin investigation."[31]

From the last quarter of the eighteenth century, the German universities had put a premium on published scholarship as the coin of their realm. In hiring and promotion, the candidate's "dossier"—the now-ubiquitous *curriculum vitae*—became the key element in the deliberations of the faculty and the minister of education, who had the final word.[32] This emphasis on original scholarship worked its way into the curriculum as the Dr.phil. (or Ph.D.). The doctorate required the research, writing, and publication in copious copies of a relatively short dissertation (more article than book), which was expected to "contribute in some measure, small though it may be, to human knowledge."[33]

Very few German students—estimates range between 10 and 25 percent—took the Ph.D.; most who did, did so because they were interested in a teaching career in the rigorous classical *Gymnasia* or a university.[34] Most of the rest took a self-selection of courses in hopes

31 A. C. Armstrong, "German Culture and the Universities," *Educational Review* 45 (April 1913), 325–38, at 331–32; Cattell, *Education in Psychology*, 67–68, 158; Ely, *Ground under Our Feet*, 43 ("You learn here, and only here, how to do independent, real scientific work.")

32 R. Steven Turner, "The Growth of Research in Prussia, 1818 to 1848—Causes and Context," *Historical Studies in the Physical Sciences* 3 (1971), 137–82; R. Steven Turner, "The Prussian Universities and the Concept of Research," *Internationales für Sozialgeschichte der deutschen Literatur* 5 (1980), 68–93; Clark, *Academic Charisma*, chs. 5, 7.

33 Thwing, *American and the German University*, 61 (quotation); Clark, *Academic Charisma*, ch. 6. Wink Scott was obliged to give 180 copies of his dissertation to the university for distribution to German universities and public libraries; James Cattell and Williston Walker each gave 210 to Leipzig, William Dodd only 100. Scott, *Memories of a Palaeontologist*, 141; Cattell, *Education in Psychology*, 210; Williston Walker, "Notes from a German University," *Andover Review* 9:53 (May 1888), 491–99, at 496; Dallek, *Democrat and Diplomat*, 23.

34 E. D. Perry, "Universities of Germany," 230 (10 percent); Walker, "Notes from a German University," 493 (14 percent); Curtis, "Present Condition of German Universities," 29 (20–25 percent). For the *Gymnasia*, see James C. Albisetti, *Secondary*

of passing the state examinations for entry into the other learned professions, including diplomacy. In that sense, the German university was a thorough professional school, not unlike the medieval university.[35] American matriculants appear to have taken the degree no more frequently than their German contemporaries, even though the great majority were "picked men—honor-men, fellows, and special investigators from American colleges and universities"—and quite focused on their career objectives.[36] Some who went home without a degree chose to do so because the final oral examination covered two subsidiary fields outside their special subject and they wanted to concentrate. Some who completed the work successfully could not afford the steep examination and dissertation fees for the degree or to have the dissertation published, commercially, at their

---

School Reform in Imperial Germany (Princeton, N.J.: Princeton University Press, 1983), esp. ch. 2; James E. Russell, *German Higher Schools: The History, Organization and Methods of Secondary Education in Germany*, 2nd ed. (New York: Longmans, Green, 1905); Harold Dean Cater, "Henry Adams Reports on a German Gymnasium," *American Historical Review* 53:1 (Oct. 1947), 59–74; Friedrich Paulsen, *An Autobiography*, trans. Theodor Lorenz (New York: Columbia University Press, 1938), 125–70; Hart, *German Universities*, 296–302.

35 Richard T. Ely, "American Colleges and German Universities," *Harper's New Monthly Magazine* 61 (July 1880), 253–60, at 254; Ely, *Ground under Our Feet*, 53–54; E. D. Perry, "Universities of Germany," 227; Johannes Conrad, *The German Universities for the Last Fifty Years*, trans. John Hutchison (Glasgow, UK: D. Bryce and Son, 1885), xxi, 217, 319–23.

36 Bishop, "University Study," 351 (quotation); Diehl, "Innocents Abroad: American Students in German Universities, 1810–1870," *History of Education Quarterly* 16:3 (Autumn 1976), 321–41, at 338 (20–25 percent before 1870); John T. Krumpelmann, "The American Students of Heidelberg University, 1830–1870," *Jahrbuch für Amerikastudien* 14 (Heidelberg, 1969), 167–84 (10 percent, my computation); Hart, "Higher Education in America," 386 (< 20 percent); Anja Becker, "For the Sake of Old Leipzig Days . . ." Academic Networks of American Students at a German University, 1781–1914" (Dr. phil. diss., philologischen Fakultät, Universität Leipzig, 2006), 334–35 (10–12 percent at Leipzig, 5 percent at Göttingen); Becker's (now Werner's) dissertation has been revised and enlarged as *The Transatlantic World of Higher Education: Americans at German Universities, 1776–1914* (New York: Berghahn Books, 2013). In 1890 Lincoln Steffens exaggerated when he told his father that "only one . . . in a hundred" Americans took the degree. "They come here, get what they want in knowledge, and go home." *Letters of Lincoln Steffens*, 1:64.

own expense. Others thought of skipping the degree because they considered scholarly articles in impressive-sounding German journals worth more than three small letters after their name.[37]

As the numbers of American students in German universities climbed between 1870 and the century's end, however, the professional value of the Ph.D. and the foreign study it connoted rose steadily back home. And as more German-educated academics returned in search of appointments commensurate with their new qualifications, both older elite colleges and newly ambitious universities sought their services, often through the extensive social networks formed abroad. Some institutions were happy to secure anyone with German experience, of whatever length. But increasingly it was possession of the German Ph.D. that enhanced the job seeker's chances, even after American universities began to offer their own versions. The German doctorate seemed to accumulate prestige the less its actual requirements and local import, like its language, were understood. But until at least 1900, its relative novelty in America preserved its mystery and desirability.

Before the Civil War, Americans were not overly impressed by German credentials. When Basil Gildersleeve returned to Virginia with a Bonn Ph.D. in 1853, he had "a paucity of prospects." Writing to a German friend the following year, he lamented that academic "success is not so easy in our country, and [although] my foreign education may give me a local reputation, the reputation is not worth the fees for the Doctor's hat. Richmond can show two doctors of philosophy besides myself. . . . In a few years," he predicted, "German diplomas will be a drug on the market, but in a few years I hope to be beyond the necessity of employing such extrinsic recommendation." Three years passed before he was hired by the University of Virginia as a professor of Greek. In the end, his

37 Horace M. Kennedy, "Studying in Germany," *Popular Science Monthly* 26 (Jan. 1885), 347–52, at 351; Cunningham, "German Historical World," 268; S. H. Rowe, "Student Life at Jena," *Educational Review* 15 (Feb. 1898), 136–46, at 140; Walker, "Notes from a German University," 498; Becker, "Old Leipzig Days," 334; Cattell, *Education in Psychology*, 119, 120, 152 ("It is really more of an honor to have my paper printed by Wundt [in his journal] than to get the PhD."), 153, 167, 192–93, 194.

Ph.D. narrowly overcame the trustees' sole objection that his was "a non-Virginian name."[38]

In the next thirty years, the market for German Ph.D.s changed dramatically. Although they never became an economic "drug," they did provide many cures for unemployment. As late as the 1880s, some American students were initially undecided about the value of taking the German degree. Bliss Perry and two American colleagues at Strasburg "spent long hours . . . discussing the professional value of the Ph.D. degree. We had taken enough courses for it, and the requirements for a dissertation and oral examination were not, in that period, particularly severe." Although their major professor wished all three to become candidates, only one did so. Since Perry had a small-college job waiting for him at home, "where," he said, "I expected to spend my life," he passed on it. He knew that a Ph.D. was "a pleasant ornament to one's name in a college catalogue," but he wanted to "grapple with ideas" rather than minute textual criticism "very much more. None of us dreamed, of course," he wrote in 1935, "that within the *next* thirty years American colleges would insist upon a Ph.D. as a requisite for promotion, that its commercial value would consequently be reckoned with the precision of an actuarial table, and that all the academic 'go-getters' would take it in their stride."[39]

Wink Scott, a Princeton graduate fellow at Heidelberg, and James Cattell, a Lafayette College alumnus at Leipzig, were equally nonchalant about the degree and were happy to let their scientific researches speak to their readiness for academic employment back home. At least they were until their American mentors and sponsors, who obviously held a much higher opinion of the degree, firmly urged them to take it. In the end they were glad they did. When Scott received fourteen copies of his *summa cum laude* diploma in 1880, he sent most of them to "interested friends." Such German papers added to a growing reputation at home. The president of a

38 He was from South Carolina. Ward W. Briggs, Jr., "Basil L. Gildersleeve," in *Classical Scholarship: A Biographical Encyclopedia*, ed. Ward W. Briggs, Jr., and William M. Calder III (New York: Garland, 1990), 93–118, at 97–98; Gildersleeve, *Letters*, 17.

39 Perry, *And Gladly Teach*, 113 (my emphasis).

woman's college in New England made him a job offer sight unseen. But not until after President McCosh had announced at Princeton's commencement that Scott, who "has made some original researches in biology, which have attracted the attention of scientific men abroad," would be coming home to an instructorship in geology. Similarly, after Cattell's father, the president of Lafayette, hinted that in American academic circles a doctorate would be more intelligible and impressive than a number of German-language offprints, the wise son not only took the degree but also secured a lectureship at the University of Pennsylvania (and an English wife who had studied music at the Leipzig Conservatory).[40]

The American opinion of German universities and scholarship remained high at least through the 1890s, when American attendance peaked. Mattoon Curtis at Leipzig believed that "four out of every five students who have been more than one year in the German university will ultimately justify their sojourn there on the ground that a German degree is worth more and counts for more than an American degree." As short a stay as a year gave Mark Baldwin, "as to so many American graduate students . . . , a distinct advantage in the professorial race at home." By the late 1880s, he noted, with some exaggeration, "A German Ph.D., or at least a residence in Germany for study, was almost indispensable to a young American teacher, wishing a post of college grade."[41]

❁ ❁ ❁

As important as German universities were for advanced scholarship and their increasingly indispensable degree, they offered ambitious

40 Scott, *Memories of a Palaeontologist*, 113, 122–23; Cattell, *Education in Psychology*, 118, 206, 267, 275. Herbert Baxter Adams (Amherst 1872) had to be persuaded and funded by his older brother, a New York lawyer, to take the degree from Heidelberg, which he did *summa cum laude* in 1876 after fifteen more months of hard study. Cunningham, "German Historical World," 268.

41 Mattoon M. Curtis, "The Present Condition of German Universities," *Educational Review* 2 (June 1891), 28–39, at 39; Baldwin, *Between Two Wars*, 1:35–36. See also Sheldon, "Why Our Science Students Go to Germany," 463: "Many may go relying upon the mere fact of their having studied in Germany, or their having obtained a German degree, to secure them a good position upon their return."

American academics an invaluable ancillary benefit. Their professors, particularly the senior ones to whom they gravitated, served as models of the "professionalism of the professorship," of how to fashion a lifelong career in higher education. When seventeen-year-old Basil Gildersleeve graduated from Princeton in 1849, he, like most of his classmates, lacked a definite plan for adulthood. Ranked fourth in his class, he thought of teaching "as a temporary means of support [but] not as a vocation for life." Indeed, "there was no such thing in America as training for a college or university professorship." That a young man would deliberately select a professorship as a career smacked of presumption. To avoid ridicule for such "uppishness," "the only wise course . . . was to flee the country and seek refuge in lands where such an aspiration was not considered absurd," namely Germany. Even after receiving a Ph.D. and a professorship, the new classical philologist confessed, "I had fixed in my mind twenty years as the limit of my service." Fortunately, when he was picked as the first senior professor at the new graduate-oriented Johns Hopkins University in 1875, just shy of his expected stay in teaching, he realized he was witnessing "the beginning of a new era in professorial life, the institution of a regular career for a man who would aspire to a part in the higher ranges of educational work." Now, in America, a young man could lay plans to become a professor "in much the same way as his companions do to become doctors or clergymen," in large part because predecessors such as Gildersleeve had taken lessons and heart from German academics doing the same thing.[42]

The German example was also important for Americans because German professors modeled an appealing synergy of research and teaching in their workaday lives. American academics were experienced teachers, although most were forced to teach too many courses at an elementary level. What they lacked was the institutional time and encouragement to pursue their own scholarship at higher levels. Observing German professors closely, particularly in their institute

42 Ward W. Briggs, Jr., ed., *Soldier and Scholar: Basil Lanneau Gildersleeve and the Civil War* (Charlottesville: University Press of Virginia, 1998), 43, 67, 87; Gildersleeve, *Letters*, 319; Basil Gildersleeve, *The Selected Classical Papers of Basil Lanneau Gildersleeve*, ed. Ward W. Briggs (Atlanta, Ga.: Scholars Press, 1992), 82.

FIGURE 18. Basil Lanneau Gildersleeve, Johns Hopkins University professor of classics. He went to Germany at eighteen as a confirmed "Germanophile," but was later critical of the guidance he failed to receive and of several aspects of German philological scholarship and teaching. Portrait by Thomas Cromwell Corner. Virginia Historical Society.

labs or during seminars in their own home libraries, provided exemplars who were at once scholars and teachers and paid to be. When new American Ph.D.s returned home, they remembered and sought to reproduce institutions that promoted "the continual union of investigation and instruction."[43]

❁ ❁ ❁

For all the memorable and emulous features of the German universities, those and others were not without flaws or drawbacks in the eyes of American students. The most difficult to overcome was the very language in which academic business was conducted. Unless the student had taken some German in college or had grown up around one of the many German-speaking rural communities and urban neighborhoods, his first necessity was to learn enough to arrange for room and board, matriculate, understand lectures, participate in the give-and-take of seminars or labs, write a dissertation, and pass a long oral exam.[44] But newcomers were wont to damn the local tongue as "one Hell of a language," "an invention of the devil." It featured not only the guttural *R* and strange umlauts but also "no end of contrivances of ingenious villainy," such as "monstrous compounds, violent inversions, [and] subsidiary clauses." After visiting Heidelberg in 1878, Samuel Clemens (alias Mark Twain) quipped

43 Paulsen, *German Universities*, 5, 140; Bell, "German Universities," 58, 60 (quotation); Jarausch, "Universities: An American View," 188; Armstrong, "German Culture and the Universities," 333. German dossiers of candidates for academic positions contained not only publications and reviews thereof but also testimonials from current and former students and evidence of the size of one's classes. Clark, *Academic Charisma*, 259, 295. See also Veysey, *Emergence of the American University*, ch. 3, esp. 125–33.

44 German emigration to America surged to 1.5 million between 1820 and 1860 and reached 5 million by 1900. Middle-class American families sang German lieder, and bookstores and libraries stocked and prominently displayed German titles. Several Midwestern cities, such as Fort Wayne, Indiana, and Milwaukee, Wisconsin, had their own *Gymnasia*, taught in many instances by German-educated teachers. Before German- and Johns Hopkins-educated Ernest Sihler could find a satisfactory university post, he taught in two American *Gymnasia* without any diminution of his self-respect. Sihler, *From Maumee*, 29–39, 45, 136, 139–45.

that "In the hospital, yesterday, a word of thirteen syllables was successfully removed from a patient."[45]

Regional dialects and books printed in black-letter German *Schrift* (**gothic** script) also added to the difficulty of learning the language, particularly for those without any previous exposure. Until Germany's military and economic ascent after 1870, American college courses in the language were few, often extracurricular, and ill taught.[46] Most postgraduates therefore had to acquire the basics through pre-class immersion in German country villages, with tutors, or with patient landladies and their children. Of little help and some hindrance were the "colonies" of Americans (and English) who had matriculated in previous years and happily spoke English whenever possible. Students determined to master German quickly went out of their way to room and board with monolingual German families. During his long year in Heidelberg, Wink Scott avoided the Anglo-American Club, associated "almost exclusively with Germans," and "steeped" himself in the language by reading German publications and attending the theater. Although for a long time he

45 Anja Becker, "US-American Students in Leipzig and Their Struggle with the German Tongue, 1827 to 1909," in Hartmut Keil, ed., *Transatlantic Cultural Contexts: Essays in Honor of Eberhard Brüning* (Tübingen: Stauffenburg, 2005), 165–86, at 167–73, 182; Mark Twain, "The Awful German Language," in *A Tramp Abroad, Following the Equator, Other Travels*, ed. Roy Blount, Jr. (New York: Library of America, 2010), app. D, at 384; also *Hart*, *German Universities*, ch. 2. Erwin Panofsky, exiled by the Nazis from his art history chair at Hamburg, wrote that "the German language, unfortunately, permits a fairly trivial thought to declaim from behind a woolen curtain of apparent profundity and, conversely, a multitude of meanings to lurk behind one term." *Meaning in the Visual Arts: Papers in and on Art History* (Garden City, N.Y.: Doubleday, 1956), 319.

46 Becker, "US-American Students in Leipzig," 166; Hart, *German Universities*, 99; Butler, *Across the Busy Years*, 113–14. Basil Gildersleeve was unusual in succumbing to "Teutonomania" in college and immersing himself in the language and literature before leaving for Germany in 1850. But he was mostly self-taught because Princeton employed a succession of short-term "second-rate" teachers at a low salary, who gave lessons twice a week in "two or three different languages," for a fee, to all who chose to attend, for no grade or credit. Briggs, *Soldier and Scholar*, 40, 43, 45, 62; James Buchanan Henry and Christian Henry Scharff, *College as It Is, or, The Collegian's Manual in 1853*, ed. J. Jefferson Looney (Princeton, N.J.: Princeton University Libraries, 1996), 233.

Die Argonauten.
(Gravüre von einem etruskischen Schmuckkästchen aus Bronze.)

Drittes Buch.

Die Argonautensage.

Jason und Pelias.

Von Äson, dem Sohne des Kretheus,*) stammte Jason ab. Sein Großvater hatte in einer Bucht des Landes Thessalien die Stadt und das Königreich Jolkos gegründet und dasselbe seinem Sohne Äson hinterlassen. Aber der jüngere Sohn, Pelias, bemächtigte sich des Thrones; Äson starb, und Jason, sein Kind, war zu Chiron dem Centauren, dem Erzieher vieler großen Helden, geflüchtet worden, wo er in guter Heldenzucht aufwuchs. Als Pelias schon alt war, wurde er durch einen dunkeln Orakelspruch geängstigt, welcher ihn warnte, er solle sich vor dem Einschuhigen hüten. Pelias grübelte vergeblich über dem Sinne dieses Worts, als Jason, der jetzt zwanzig Jahre den Unterricht und die Erziehung des Chiron genossen hatte, sich heimlich aufmachte, nach Jolkos in seine Heimat zu wandern und das Thronrecht seines Geschlechtes gegen Pelias zu behaupten. Nach Art der alten Helden war er mit zwei Speeren, den einen zum Werfen, den andern zum Stoßen, ausgerüstet; er trug ein Reisekleid und darüber die Haut von einem Panther, den er erwürgt hatte; sein ungeschorenes Haar hing lang über die Schultern

*) Vgl. Anm. zu S. 105.

FIGURE 19. A typical page of black-letter Gothic *Schrift* that flummoxed many American students who attempted to learn German, particularly in Germany. From Gustav Schwab, *Die schonsten sagen des klassischen Alturtums*, 3 vols. (Gütersloh: C. Bertelsman, 1894), 1:119.

seemed to make no progress, he suddenly "had the language by the tail," speaking fluently, thinking, and even dreaming in German. He concluded that this facility was perhaps "the most valuable result of my life in Heidelberg, though the benefits were many," including a Ph.D.[47]

Those who put in less effort struggled longer and missed educational opportunities: lectures moved too fast for effective note-taking, the nuances of seminar discussions went unnoticed, and working relationships with German lab partners remained half-formed. After nearly four years in Leipzig, James Cattell was still unsure of his command of German. He was forced to write his dissertation in English, dictate it in halting German to a German colleague for correction (which he feared might take a hundred hours to complete), and received "a good lot of corrections—nearly all verbal" from his major professor, who knocked the final grade down a peg because of them. In his oral exam, he confessed to his parents, he was "considerably troubled by the foreign language, often not being able to express myself, or worse, saying the opposite of what I meant." His linguistic ineptitude—and inattention to the second of his minor fields—earned him a mere *cum laude* when he expected better.[48]

❁ ❁ ❁

Once the Americans began to function in German reasonably well, they discovered that several aspects of their new academic existence did not meet all of their hopes or expectations. As admirable as they were, all three major modalities of the German curriculum—lectures,

47 Scott, *Memories of a Palaeontologist*, 112, 118, 124, 126; Butler, *Across the Busy Years*, 118–19; Dallek, *Democrat and Diplomat*, 16–17; Walker, "Notes from a German University," 497, 498; *Letters of Lincoln Steffens*, 1:11, 16, 21.

48 Cattell, *Education in Psychology*, 149, 164, 202, 205, 206. William Dodd's history advisor at Leipzig was similarly critical of his written German and for the same reasons gave him a *cum laude*. The Leipzig rules demanded as "absolutely necessary conditions . . . a good form and correct language." Fred Arthur Bailey, *William Edward Dodd: The South's Yeoman Scholar* (Charlottesville: University Press of Virginia, 1997)), 20–21; Edmund J. James, "The Degree of Ph.D. in Germany," *Andover Review* 9:54 (June 1888), 611–23, at 616.

seminars, and labs—came in for criticism. Lecture halls, located in dowdy urban buildings, were routinely described as "dingy rooms filled with the commonest wooden benches" and "foul air."[49] Attendance was sporadic because of the student tendency to migrate between lecturers and universities and to play truant in courses that seemed to have no direct relation to the entrance exams for the learned professions (*Brotstudium*, "bread studies").[50] The stars of the show, often bedecked in academic gowns, lectured from a dais or desk, usually from notes or full texts. The goal of the student was to leave the course with a full and complete "*Heft* or body of notes for future reference." New American students often sat in the front rows in order to hear more clearly. But in delivery, Stanley Hall noted, "German professors . . . had almost every excellence and every defect." Some virtually dictated their texts, "book[s] doled out in small slices," as if Gutenberg hadn't been born. Others exhibited so many "crotchets" and idiosyncrasies that the concentration of auditors was sorely challenged.[51]

The large Berlin and Leipzig faculties, among the nation's best, harbored some of the worst offenders, despite their published command of their subjects. In the 1850s, Gildersleeve recalled, "the discourses of many of the teachers were dullness itself,—certainly to the novice. Long lists of books read off in a droning voice . . . , infinite discussions of infinitesimal points, endless divagations, hateful polemics, poor jokes" were standard fare. When he tried to listen to Ranke, the great historian, his sputtering, contorted, "torrential delivery" of German vocables defeated even native listeners. Thirty years later, the equally renowned Treitschke's performance

49 Bell, "German Universities," 49; Perry, *And Gladly Teach*, 97; Cattell, *Education in Psychology*, 136. Despite other improvements, the benches were still there in 1913. Armstrong, "German Culture and the Universities," 330.

50 Paulsen, *German Universities*, 219–23; Bell, "German Universities," 52; Ely, "American Colleges and German Universities," 254–55; Herbst, *German Historical School*, 22, 31; Abraham Flexner, *Universities: American, English, German* (New York: Oxford University Press, 1930), 320–21, 349.

51 Walker, "Notes from a German University," 492–93; Hall, *Life and Confessions*, 211–14; Gildersleeve, *Selected Classical Papers*, 125; Taft, *German University and the American College*, 10.

FIGURE 20. An 1867 portrait of Leopold von Ranke (1795–1886), a leading German historian, long-time professor at the University of Berlin, and the first honorary member of the American Historical Association (1884). A graduate in philology of the University of Leipzig, he was appointed Prussia's royal historiographer in 1841, ennobled in 1865, and made a privy councilor in 1882. His research seminar at Berlin was a major draw for American students, as were his deeply researched multivolume histories.

drove Frederic Bancroft from the hall to a friend's course notes. Increasingly deaf, the *Politik* master's talk ran all sentences together and consisted of the "most distressing sobbing." Stanley Hall witnessed a Leipzig master who "habitually gazed at a peculiar knot in a tree outside and was upset when the tree was felled." Another "sank down in his chair as if abstracted, looking toward his feet, and seemed soliloquizing, sometimes clucking and bringing his heavy hand down with a blow upon the desk." An epistemologist began his lectures with "a thin falsetto, baby voice and ended in stentorian." Hall speculated facetiously that the faculty may have thought that "the students would love the truth all the more because of the difficulties they had to obtain it."[52]

For most American postgraduates in the philosophy faculty, the advanced research seminars were regarded as "the best a German university has to offer." It was there that "the merits of German methods and the spirit of the great German teachers are best learned."[53] But they, too, had downsides. In some subjects in the larger universities, the enrollments could be excessive. In 1889, 56 were registered for the history seminar at Leipzig. The modern section of 28 extremely diverse members met weekly in the history seminary rather than the professor's home library, as was often the custom.[54] Unlike lectures, the success of seminars depended as much on the student members

52 Briggs, *Soldier and Scholar*, 68, 86–91; Gildersleeve, *Selected Classical Papers*, 125, 144, 291, 295; Hall, *Life and Confessions*, 213–14; Frederic Bancroft, Berlin, to H. B. Adams, Jan. 17, 1886, in W. Stull Holt, ed., *Historical Scholarship in the United States, 1876–1901: As Revealed in the Correspondence of Herbert B. Adams*, Johns Hopkins University Studies in Historical and Political Science, ser. 56, no. 4 (Baltimore, Md.: Johns Hopkins University Press, 1938), 76; Burgess, *Reminiscences of an American Scholar*, 109. Professors were no more exempt from American criticism in Heidelberg. Wink Scott said that they "not only attached no importance to ease and grace in speaking, but most of them actually disapproved of those qualities in the lecture-room." *Memories of a Palaeontologist*, 111–12.

53 Bishop, "University Study," 358.

54 Fling, "German Historical Seminar," 136, 213. Walter L. Hervey, in "The Study of Education at the German Universities," *Educational Review* 16 (Oct. 1898), 220–32, at 222, reported a Leipzig education seminar of 60. By 1906 rumors of 150- to 200-member "seminars" filtered back to the United States. Jesse, "Impressions of German Universities," 441.

as on the genius of the director. The students came in four varieties: full members, associate members, aspirants, and listeners. Seminars were powerful research labs for the humanities and social sciences, but they often failed to develop in the students the "power of presentation." Early in the German seminars' development from training for *Gymnasium* teaching to serious research, Gildersleeve later lamented, philology seminars did not promote clear exegesis of texts or a prevent a great deal of "juvenile" criticism, which was largely of the "conjectural sort," with only "slight palaeographical knowledge" and "second-hand views concerning families of manuscripts." Too many research topics were "hopelessly microscopic and hopelessly dry." By 1880 he had learned from German colleagues that American students had become "more German than the Germans in their mode of presentation, in the cumbrousness of their apparatus, in the thinness of conclusions as compared with the thickness of material, in a certain routine criticism."[55]

Seminars in history and English literature were no more immune to disappointing performances. In the bloated Leipzig seminar, student reports on the primary sources and historiography pertaining to short episodes of the German past were soporific. The work was "scientific and thorough"—the German scholarly ideal—but there was "no debate, no lively interest in the questions discussed, and no one attempted to conceal the fact that the exercise was decidedly long and tiresome." Even the professor "covered his face with his hand, now and then, to conceal—or attempt to conceal—the big yawn that he could not restrain." The majority of attendees were "silent spectators, not even taking notes." Other, more experienced, reporters often performed no better. One "old boy" dug out a vast amount of material, but "he did not know what he had, where to begin, or where to end, what facts were great or what were small. He

55 Gildersleeve, *Selected Classical Papers*, 128–31; Gildersleeve, *Letters*, 119–20. Ernest Sihler of Indiana, German-educated and later a fellow at Johns Hopkins University, testified that Gildersleeve was a master of presentation in both class and print. "In Berlin and Leipzig," Sihler wrote, "I had listened to and carefully observed many classical scholars of ponderous erudition, but none whose faculty of presentation inspired me so much." *From Maumee*, 104–106 .

frequently came to a dead halt, stared wildly into vacancy, chewed his mustache, and was apparently at his wit's end." Clearly, the seminar's leading light did nothing to teach or model the art of presentation. At the end of the interminable semester, "there was no final summing up or survey of the entire ground that had been traversed" and "on the last evening work was dropped just where it was."[56]

At Strassburg, Bliss Perry thought that ten Brink's lectures on Shakespeare showed "the imaginative insight of a born man of letters as well as consummate technical scholarship." But his seminars on the Bard were devoted largely to a minute comparison of the quarto and folio texts of *Othello* and *Lear*, in which the variant English scripts had to be translated into German for discussion. Perry was disappointed that "we [older] Americans wasted a great deal of time over mere mixing of mortar and sorting of bricks. We never saw the palace of Shakespeare's mind from those Seminar windows." Their research papers, built on the seminar's "remorseless methods," were equally off-putting. "We murdered to dissect," but they lacked their master's creative imagination to "make every dry bone live again." Unsure that they would ever have his gifts, they tried in the meantime to "handle the literary microscope and scalpel with Germanic thoroughness."[57]

Wink Scott also wielded a mean scalpel in his Heidelberg lab, where he studied the embryology of lamprey eels under Carl Gegenbaur, one of the country's great scientists and a member of the medical faculty. Scott, however, may have felt like using his blade on his supervisor, who, after a generous welcome, soon showed him nothing but "rudeness and insolence." At their morning progress reports, the good *Doktor* was "positively insulting, said all the sneering, derogatory things he could think of, browbeating me for every mistake in German that I made (he knew English well, but would not permit any of his students to speak it to him)." Understandably, the young American was "deeply angered and much bewildered" and drew into his shell. Fortunately, the siege lifted after two months and the master inexplicably became warm, friendly, and helpful, which he

56 Fling, "German Historical Seminar," 212–19.

57 Perry, *And Gladly Teach*, 111–12.

remained for the rest of his life. One of Scott's lab partners explained that the professor had taken an extreme dislike to Scott's predecessor, another American who, like Scott, had come from England with a letter of introduction from Huxley. His rough demeanor was a test to see if Scott had the "pluck and determination" to stick to his work despite "unpleasant features." Hazing occurred not only in the less serious student dueling and drinking societies. Fortunately, it was rare and the older, focused Americans were usually well received and regarded by their German mentors.[58]

Beyond their main instructional systems, German universities drew a miscellany of American complaints. The central university and once-ducal national libraries, while impressively stocked, were usually closed-stacked, slow on delivery, cold in winter, and often lacked card catalogues (only "a set of huge folios in which were pasted the titles of the acquisitions of each year").[59] German historians and American students alike lamented the relative lack of sources for pursuing American history. In 1878 Hermann von Holst, who would eventually leave Freiburg for the new University of Chicago, noted "how *very* hard it is in Germany to get hold of the most necessary materials" for reconstructing America's political and constitutional

58 Scott, *Memories of a Palaeontologist*, 108–109; Bishop, "University Study," 355; Rowe, "Student Life at Jena," 143; Ely, *Ground under Our Feet*, 40, 43; Royce, "Present Ideals," 383.

59 Perry, *And Gladly Teach*, 98; Walker, "Notes from a German University," 494; Hugo Kunoff, *The Foundations of the German Academic Library* (Chicago: American Library Association, 1982), chs. 5–6. By 1800 Göttingen had 200,000 books and was the largest academic library in Germany. It was ten times larger than the largest American college library. Thwing, *German and the American University*, 130–33; Clark, *Academic Charisma*, ch. 8, esp. 317, 332. See also Paul Gerbod, "Resources and Management," in *HUE* 3:106 (table 4.1); Hervey, "Study of Education," 227, 229. In the mid-1880s, the experienced librarian, historical researcher, and doctoral student George Lincoln Burr lamented Leipzig's "ridiculously small" reading room (about the size of Cornell's faculty room), its constricted hours (3 hours daily, book delivery only 2), and antiquated procedures (titles written on call slips, deposited in a box outside the library the previous night). "The lacunae," even in European history, "are astounding," he told the Cornell president, Andrew D. White. *George Lincoln Burr: His Life. By Roland H. Bainton [and] Selections from His Writings*, ed. Lois Oliphant Gibbons (Ithaca, N.Y.: Cornell University Press, 1943), 27.

history. "International ignorance," he suggested, "is with us as yet in a most flourishing condition with regard to the United States." To complete his 83-page Leipzig thesis, "Jefferson's Return to Politics in 1796" (1900), William Dodd had to spend six weeks in the British Museum and additional time in Berlin. In the 1930s, the now ambassador Dodd still had difficulty locating materials in Berlin for his history of the Old South.[60]

❁ ❁ ❁

One relatively small but not insignificant group of Americans was mightily frustrated by their experiences in German universities. Scholarly women, all of whom had graduated from American universities, women's colleges, or medical schools, found it difficult to replicate in Germany their previous educational opportunities. Until 1910, women were officially prohibited from matriculating at or receiving degrees from the full range of German universities. From the 1870s, a few universities did allow women to audit lectures and fewer still to participate in seminars and labs. Early on, Göttingen somehow managed to graduate a couple of women, as did Leipzig, but later raised the drawbridge and forbade them to take classes. Munich and Strassburg were adamant in all regards, Berlin and Heidelberg not much less so. Leipzig, with its large male American contingent, was the most accommodating because many of its professors winked at the rules and allowed serious American women—thirty-eight in the 1870s alone—to audit lectures, join their seminars, and use the university and seminar libraries. But even it did not award degrees to women until 1906. Female physicians who wanted advanced work in German university hospitals were mostly out of luck and advised to go to Vienna or Zürich. Without influence exercised by American diplomats, relatives, and alumni, the women's numbers would have been even smaller.[61]

60 Holt, *Historical Scholarship*, 35; Bailey, *William Edward Dodd*, 20–21; Erik Larson, *In the Garden of Beasts* (New York: Crown, 2011), 133.

61 Patricia M. Mazón, *Gender and the Modern Research University: The Admission of Women to German Higher Education, 1865–1914* (Stanford, Calif.: Stanford University

The misadventures of a strong American woman convey the flavor of the German universities' resistance to women in general. M. Carey Thomas, a star graduate of Cornell University, initially thought she could prepare for a professorial career in philology by attending newly founded Johns Hopkins University in her native Baltimore. Although her father was a trustee, she—because of her gender—was not allowed to take the small graduate classes. At best she could attend certain public lectures and receive suggestions for reading from willing professors such as Basil Gildersleeve. Rather than acquire the latest German methods indirectly and with maximum difficulty, she set off for Germany with a like-minded friend to sup at the scholarly source.

Although she knew that degrees for women were exceedingly rare, she did gain entry to several Leipzig lectures and, in her second year, to two key seminars through the influence of former Cornell president Andrew D. White, then the U.S. minister in Berlin. Eventually, despite the aggressive stares and rudeness of male students, she and a few other American auditors earned their "contemptuous affection" as "established nuisances." Sticking to her lasts, she filled *heft* notebooks in lectures four hours a day and ransacked the shelves of the library, resorting to interlibrary loans for more fugitive titles. What she could not enjoy, of course, was the mutual aid of fellow students in lending books, studying together, reading each other's papers, or brainstorming over beers at local taverns.

After two and a half years of hard study, she visited Göttingen in hopes of being allowed to take a degree there. But poor advice about her dissertation topic, and a "savage" ruling that all forty-three professors in the philosophy faculty had to agree to her candidacy, sent

---

Press, 2003); James C. Albisetti, "German Influence on the Higher Education of American Women, 1865–1914," in Geitz, Heideking, and Herbst, eds., *German Influence on Education*, 227–44, esp. 240–44; Anja Becker, "How Daring She Was! The 'Female American Colony' at Leipzig University, 1877–1914," in Anke Ortlepp and Christoph Ribbat, eds., *Taking Up Space: New Approaches to American History* (Trier, Germany: Wissenschaftlicher Verlag Trier, 2004), 31–46; Helen Lefkowitz Horowitz, *The Power and Passion of M. Carey Thomas* (New York: Alfred A. Knopf, 1994), 111, 119. See also Sandra L. Singer, *Adventures Abroad: North American Women at German-Speaking Universities, 1868–1915* (Westport, Conn.: Praeger, 2003).

her packing to much friendlier Zürich. There she put in four additional months to prepare for an even harder final test than the German universities required. After her dissertation (written in Leipzig) was accepted and printed, she tackled a six-hour written exam on German philology, another thesis written in three days with the aid of reference books, and a three-hour grilling from a *dozen* male specialists. When they awarded her the Ph.D. *summa cum laude*, she could legitimately boast that she was the first woman in the university's history to earn not only a Ph.D. in philology but highest honors, which men rarely achieved.[62]

❁ ❁ ❁

Despite their reservations about certain features of the German universities, American returnees, many sporting Ph.D.s, sustained their enthusiasm for and appreciation of their academic experiences abroad. Understandably, most of them wished to repair America's higher-educational weaknesses with Germany's institutional strengths, and many of them worked to do so. But no matter how fervent their faith in German solutions, America's particular problems could not be solved by wholesale imports. Germany's and

62 Horowitz, *Power and Passion*, chs. 4, 6; Marjorie Housepian Dobkin, ed., *The Making of a Feminist: Early Journals and Letters of M. Carey Thomas* (Kent, Ohio: Kent State University Press, 1979), ch. 2. A similar story of obstruction and "thinly veiled contempt" for female American scholars was told by Alice Hamilton, an M.D. from the University of Michigan, who traveled to Germany in 1885–86 with her older sister, Edith, a graduate of Bryn Mawr College. Alice had less trouble finding work in labs and attending scientific lectures and meetings, but at Roman Catholic Munich University, Edith was allowed to attend one lecture only by being seated on the stage next to the professor, facing the hostile all-male audience. Despite their setbacks, Alice became the first female professor at Harvard and Edith an elite-prep-school mistress and a hugely popular interpreter of classical culture. Alice Hamilton, "Edith and Alice Hamilton: Students in Germany," *Atlantic Monthly* 215:3 (March 1965), 129–32; Alice Hamilton, *Exploring the Dangerous Trades: The Autobiography of Alice Hamilton, M.D.* (Boston: Northeastern University Press, 1985; Little, Brown, 1943), 44–50; Barbara Sicherman, *Alice Hamilton: A Life in Letters* (Cambridge, Mass.: Harvard University Press, 1984); Doris Fielding Reid, *Edith Hamilton: An Intimate Portrait* (New York: W. W. Norton, 1967).

America's cultures, social structures, institutions, economies, religions, and histories were just too different. Even 9,000 missionaries could not convert America's maturing colleges and universities to a German model, either quickly or thoroughly. Reformers were forced to move slowly, borrow selectively, and adapt constantly to the fluid realities of American life and changing times.

As early as 1828, Yale's president doubted that German universities were appropriate "models to be copied in every feature, by our American colleges." The colleges could improve, he admitted, by "cautiously introducing, with proper modifications, such parts of their plans as are suited to our peculiar situation and character." Thirty-six years later, while on a sabbatical to study chemistry at the small University of Marburg, Harvard's future president Charles W. Eliot could not admit even that much. He wrote home to opine that it was "quite clear—a German University would suit the 150 young men who enter Freshmen every year, about as well as a barn-yard would suit a whale. . . . The system is utterly inapplicable to us."[63]

Similar warnings echoed through the rest of the century and into the next. In 1876, eight years after returning with a J.D. from Göttingen, J. M. Hart confessed that newly returned Ph.D.s tended to regard their German alma maters as "*ne plus ultra*." But as they felt "the sharp corners of American prejudices and peculiarities" and renewed their familiarity with American life, they gradually realized that "a German university is not a thing to be plucked up by the roots and transplanted bodily to American soil. We have rather to take our native stock as we find it, and engraft upon it a slip from the German." One-time "Teutonomaniac" Gildersleeve agreed. "The traditions of our older institutions of learning and the circumstances of our nationality necessarily modify the conception of university work" in America. "University as well as college should be American, meet the needs of our civilization, and bear the stamp of our national character." On the eve of World War I, Wesleyan University professor A. C. Armstrong still felt obliged to warn American

63 Potts, *Liberal Education*, 21, 22–23. Henry James, *Charles W. Eliot, President of Harvard University, 1869–1909*, 2 vols. (Boston: Houghton Mifflin, 1930), 1:136–37 (Oct. 30, 1864).

educators that "Loyalty to our German preceptors does not exclude devotion to the best elements of our own inheritance. Rather," he insisted, "we shall manifest the deepest loyalty by uniting the lessons of their teaching with the promptings of our national genius."[64]

Another reason Americans could not import the German university wholesale was because there was no such thing: there were twenty-some versions of it, each different from the others, each constantly changing. Moreover, American visitors brought their own preconceptions, expectations, and astigmatisms to the universities they attended, often just one, rarely more than three. Some American students misunderstood what they saw, others idealized it. A few, like attentive anthropologists making cultural comparisons, exhibited "keen perceptiveness," inaccessible even to German insiders. But no one, not even the most objectively intended, brought a totally "innocent eye" without goals and intentions. They "picked out as salient features of German universities . . . what rubbed hardest against their own discontents with American higher education." Their motives were less to emulate Germany than to "improve their own colleges" or the new universities and graduate schools they envisioned. And what features they did borrow, they reworked, making them fit the American ideals that had informed their journeys abroad and the realities that now constrained their reforms at home.[65] J. M. Hart was wise to counsel American academics not to

64 James Morgan Hart, "Professor and Teacher," *Lippincott's Magazine of Popular Literature and Science* 17 (Feb. 1876), 193–203, at 202; Basil Gildersleeve, "University Work in America and Classical Philology" (1879), in Gildersleeve, *Selected Classical Papers*, 113–14; Armstrong, "German Culture and the Universities," 338. See also Daniel C. Gilman, "The Idea of the University," *North American Review* 133 (Oct. 1881), 353–67, at 356; Bishop, "University Study," 354; N. M. Butler, in Paulsen, *German Universities*, xiii; J. M. Hart, review of Paulsen, *The German Universities*, in *Nation* 61 (Aug. 1, 1895), 86.

65 Thomas A. Howard, *Protestant Theology and the Making of the Modern German University* (New York: Oxford University Press, 2006), 349 (quotation), 378; James Turner and Paul Bernard, "The 'German Model' and the Graduate School: The University of Michigan and the Origin Myth of the American University," *History of Higher Education Annual* 13 (1993), 69–98, at 70–71. See also Ben-David, "Universities and the Growth of Science," 7–8; Nathan Reingold, "Graduate School and Doctoral Degree: European Models and American Realities," in Nathan Reingold and Marc

go to Germany before they were "fully ripe," before they knew "what to take and what to leave."[66]

❁ ❁ ❁

Among the easiest things to take home were the three German teaching methods—lectures, seminars, and labs. Lectures and labs were not unknown in America, but their purposes were different from those of their German cognates. In the curricula of traditional colleges, upper class lectures on new or advanced subjects were outnumbered by recitations and drills in foundational subjects such as classical languages and mathematics. Moreover, the material being conveyed—at second- or thirdhand—was largely *received* knowledge, not *new* knowledge that the lecturer had discovered or made his own. It could have come from a textbook (including one in progress) and often did. Memorizing and repetition were expected of the students, less so critical engagement with the sources of that knowledge or its authors. Nor was the traditional college lecturer expected to provide a prospect of a whole field, as the German *Ordinary*, or full professor, was. Similarly, the rare and rudimentary college labs were used for *demonstrations* rather than *investigations* by either professor or students.

Although some German lecturers had their critics, many returning Americans touted the value of lectures given the German way. Andrew White, a professor of history who attended many in Berlin in the fall and winter of 1854–55, galvanized both students and other faculty at the University of Michigan after he replaced recitations

---

Rothenberg, eds., *Scientific Colonialism* (Washington, D.C.: Smithsonian Institution Press, 1986), 129–49, at 130; Jarausch, "Universities: An American View," 197–98; Gabriele Lingelbach, "Cultural Borrowing or Autonomous Development: American and German Universities in the Late Nineteenth Century, " in Thomas Adam and Ruth Gross, eds., *Traveling between Worlds: German-American Encounters* (College Station: Texas A&M University Press, 2006), 100–123; Walter P. Metzger, "The German Contribution to the American Theory of Academic Freedom," *Bulletin of the American Association of University Professors* 41:2 (Summer 1955), 214–30, at 214, 230; Veysey, *Emergence of the American University*, 125–33 at 126, 128, 132.

66 Hart, *German Universities*, 393.

with lectures two years later. By the time he become the founding president of Cornell University in 1869, lectures had infiltrated institutions large and small around the country. Their novel value was manifest, if managed right. "A course of lectures," argued Columbia's Edward D. Perry, "should give in a continuous series the lecturer's personal views, gained by investigation at first hand, of the totality of some branch of science [knowledge, *Wissenschaft*], of its main problems and leading ideas, of its most important content and the method of its acquisition, of its relations to science as a whole." Granted, all of that could be put in a book. But if it were, it could not be constantly revised or added to, as lectures could. "By comparison with personal communication a book is a lifeless thing." It was the "personal element" in the lecture system that was of "paramount importance." At the same time, lectures were economical: they could engage large numbers with only one teacher. In cash-strapped and faculty-short colleges, lectures recommended themselves on that basis better than medium-sized recitations and certainly better than Oxbridge-style tutorials. By 1906, President R. H. Jesse of the University of Missouri could say, without fear of contradiction, "now every institution of learning has lectures."[67]

The large-scale adoption of lectures in America also fostered some amendments and criticisms. One amendment was that American professors were not paid from fees levied on each auditor but from general tuition charges. Another was the division of large lecture classes into discussion sections, in order to promote closer student-faculty contact and "harder work." Sections added costs because they had to be manned by additional teachers, often junior professors, later by graduate students in training for teaching careers, but it was a price Americans were largely willing to pay.[68] A major criticism that arose

67 Turner and Bernard, "'German Model,'" 78, 94n56; *The Diaries of Andrew D. White*, ed. Robert Morris Ogden (Ithaca, N.Y.: Cornell University Library, 1959), 97–108; Perry, "Universities of Germany," 222–23; Jesse, "Impressions of German Universities," 435–36.

68 Jesse, "Impressions of German Universities," 435–36; Veysey, *Emergence of the American University*, 153, 339n240; Frederick Rudolph, *Curriculum: A History of the American Undergraduate Course of Study Since 1636* (San Francisco: Jossey-Bass, 1977), 144–45, 232–33.

when lecturing became nearly universal was that many professors were not the equals of their German inspirations. In 1928 Charles F. Thwing, long-time president of Western Reserve University, deemed the American lecture system to be largely a failure because it was not supported by "the energetic productive scholarship of the lecturing professor." Although the lecturer had usually "learned the facts," he had not made himself the "active master of scholarly method" and therefore lacked the self-confidence and authority gained from "prolonged and independent investigation." Furthermore, the cost of student passivity in large lectures was seldom met by what one Amherst student called "the personal magnetism of the speaker." Perhaps most serious of all, in Thwing's eyes, was that "the American college man" could not fully absorb the (dubious) benefits of the lecture system. He lacked "the intellectual maturity of the German student of the same age," who had been groomed for the university by the classical *Gymnasium*. The American's "earlier education has been less well directed in both aim and content. . . . He enters college still a boy." Ideal German lectures were for men, not boys.[69]

Although most college laboratories were used for demonstrations of scientific principles and known results, those at the new universities and some of the elite colleges were often well equipped for the day and capable of supporting the scholarly research of their faculty, thanks in large part to the efforts of German returnees. By 1906 President Jesse could even worry that "American men of science, generally—not universally—are excessive in their devotion to the laboratory," not unlike their German contemporaries.[70] In 1825 Justus Liebig, at the University of Giessen, had established the first research lab for chemistry in Germany. In the next fifty years he trained a number of America's best academic chemists, including Eben Horsford, who in 1848 established the first teaching lab for the Lawrence Scientific School at Harvard. Munich (where Liebig

69 Thwing, *American and the German University*, 122–26; *Amherst Student* (March 10, 1877), 126–27, quoted in Fred M. Newmann, "The Influence of German Universities on Amherst College, 1854–1911" (B.A. honors thesis, Dept. of American Studies, Amherst College, April 27, 1957), 90 (many thanks to Professor Newmann for a copy).

70 Jesse, "Impressions of German Universities," 436.

finished his career), Göttingen, and later Leipzig were equally productive of American scientists and famous for their laboratories in numerous sciences.[71]

Ira Remsen, one of the six founding faculty at Johns Hopkins, had a Ph.D. from Göttingen (1870), as did his assistant (1875). When Remsen asked for a small room for a private lab at Williams College, his first faculty appointment, the president warned him to "keep in mind that this is a college and not a technical school." After moving eagerly to Baltimore, he toured a number of American chemistry labs before planning what many considered the best one in the country. Although he had been an instructor and lab assistant at Tübingen for two years before returning home, he introduced lab work carefully rather than assuming that a German import would be instantly successful or welcomed. He cautioned American colleagues to be "as watchful in the laboratory as in the recitation-room" and "as exacting in regard to the experimental work as the teacher of languages is in regard to the words of a lesson."[72]

Graduate-oriented universities could be expected to build first-rate laboratories, but some smaller eastern colleges were even sooner off the mark. In the last half of the nineteenth century, all of the Amherst departments in natural science built or expanded and used labs to actively engage students in the scientific process. The faculty most responsible for the labs' development were, to a man, German trained. William S. Clark, '48, the first Amherst alumnus to earn a Ph.D., did so in chemistry at Göttingen in 1852. Three years later he introduced lab work in his advanced classes, for which a new lab was quickly built. When Clark resigned in 1868, his successor, Elijah Harris '55, another Göttingen Ph.D. (1859), began to turn out scientific scholars in abundance. By 1907 he had produced 35 future

71 Samuel Eliot Morison, ed., *The Development of Harvard University Since the Inauguration of President Eliot, 1868–1929* (Cambridge, Mass.: Harvard University Press, 1930), 414, 417. Between 1830 and 1870, Heidelberg, too, matriculated 48 Americans in chemistry and another dozen in other sciences. Krumpelmann, "American Students of Heidelberg."

72 Hugh Hawkins, *Pioneer: A History of the Johns Hopkins University, 1874–1889* (Ithaca, N.Y.: Cornell University Press, 1960), 47–48, 60, 223.

professors of chemistry, at least 13 of whom had followed him to Göttingen for doctorates. A new lab in 1893 allowed Harris to offer lab work to every student, thus raising the chemistry department "from a minor place in the classical education of young ministers to a training school for scientists." The Amherst departments of geology, biology, and physics were similarly guided into modernity by professors who had studied in Germany and been trained in enviable university labs. If the students were not expected to make original discoveries, they were introduced to "the independent attitude in research which university life inculcates."[73]

❃ ❃ ❃

As German-style laboratories were to American sciences, German-inspired seminars were to the humanities and social sciences. Even more than lectures and labs, which were at least known in America, seminars caught the imaginations of large numbers of students in Germany and held them when they returned home. The first American seminars appeared at the University of Michigan and Harvard in the early 1870s, but they really caught on in the 1880s, encouraged by their fame as graduate classes at Johns Hopkins. By 1894 it could be said that "the institution has been carefully transplanted, and has taken firm root," in undergraduate colleges and nascent graduate schools alike.[74]

Although their methods, tone, and efficacy differed considerably, almost all seminars were aimed at "the training of the investigator" in the discovery of *new* knowledge—new to the student in undergraduate classes and to the learned world in graduate courses.

73 Newmann, "Influence of German Universities," 82–89, at 84, 87. See also Hugh Hawkins, "Transatlantic Discipleship: Two American Biologists and Their German Mentor," *Isis* 71:2 (June 1980), 196–210. In 1952 a study of 18,000 scientists, educated mainly in the 1920s and '30s, found that 34 of the top 50 undergraduate producers were liberal arts colleges. R. H. Knapp and H. B. Goodrich, *Origins of American Scientists: A Study Made under the Direction of a Committee of the Faculty of Wesleyan University* (Chicago: University of Chicago Press for Wesleyan University, 1952), 22.

74 Veysey, *Emergence of the American University*, 154–57; Thwing, *American and the German University*, 120–22, 126–29; Herbst, *German Historical School*, 34–37; E. D. Perry, "Universities of Germany," 224.

Enrolling groups of three to thirty advanced students, seminars focused on primary sources—literary texts, public documents, *objets d'art*, archaeological remains—and usually resulted in independent, if not always original, essays, which were then presented to the class and the professor for critique. Like lectures, they depended greatly on the pedagogical skill and personal charisma of the "master" in charge for their success. In the best graduate seminars, such as Gildersleeve's, the students were also prepared for their future roles as teachers. Seminars also served, as they did in Germany, as sites of networking for future career-building.[75]

As seminars became entrenched in graduate teaching, they also penetrated undergraduate curricula. At the University of Michigan, the Germanophile president Henry Tappan (1852–63) seems to have ignored the seminar in his unsuccessful bid to Prussianize the undergraduate curriculum. But his second successor, James B. Angell (1871–1909), and the historian Charles K. Adams instituted seminars at both the graduate and undergraduate levels, where they remain. Several New England colleges kept pace with the larger universities. The 1881 introduction of a seminar in British literature inaugurated Wesleyan University's rapid adoption of the German imports in the early 1890s.[76]

Amherst began to offer seminars in 1874–75, when John Burgess returned from three years in Göttingen, Leipzig, and Berlin to teach history and political science. At the request of seven new graduates, he offered a postgraduate seminar on modern European political history according to "the methods of the German seminar." At the end of the year, he "advised them all to go to Germany and study further in Berlin University or in some other German university of the first class," which they and two more classmates did. Although graduate courses and degrees never caught on there and Burgess left for Columbia a year later, "the seminar came to Amherst in letter and spirit." In 1886, Anson Morse '71, a recent graduate of Heidelberg, reintroduced the historical seminar, emphasizing the use of sources, class discussion, and interpretive essays. He told the trustees

75 Hawkins, *Pioneer*, 224–32, at 225; Turner and Bernard, "'German Model.,'" 79.

76 Turner and Bernard, "'German Model,'" 73–79; David B. Potts, *Wesleyan University, 1831–1910: Collegiate Enterprise in New England* (New Haven, Conn.: Yale University Press, 1992), 130.

that he had made "only a beginning of the methods of the German seminar." But he soon had company because five of his six colleagues in the department were German-trained and several other faculty adopted the new class format, especially in English and philosophy.[77]

❁ ❁ ❁

The new taste of freedom in the classroom and lab reminded German-trained American faculty of the even greater *Freiheit* enjoyed by their German colleagues, both student and professorial. Eager to bring German solutions to America's educational problems, German veterans spearheaded the homegrown push for greater choice of courses for students and more specialization for faculty. The public leader of the movement was Harvard's president Charles W. Eliot, who had studied chemistry and higher education in Germany before his elevation in 1869. In his inaugural address, he joined Cornell's president Andrew White and others in declaring war on the prescribed curricula of the older colleges, saying that a university should be open to all studies and disciplines. "We would have them all," he said, "and at their best." He also attacked the "faculty psychology," the fundament of the prescribed curriculum, by urging democratic America to pay attention to "the individual traits of different minds."[78] His was a clarion call to faculties everywhere who sought greater interest

77 Burgess, *Reminiscences of an American Scholar*, 140–46; Newmann, "Influence of German Universities," 68–69, 73–82. For the spread of seminars in America, see Everett Emerton, "The Historical Seminary in American Teaching," in *Methods of Teaching History*, Pedagogical Library, ed. G. Stanley Hall, vol. 1 (Boston: Ginn, Heath, 1883), 191–200, and Herbert B. Adams, "Methods of Historical Study," *Johns Hopkins University Studies in Historical and Political Science* (2nd ser.) vols. 1–2 (Baltimore, Md., Jan.–Feb. 1884), 87–109.

78 The "faculty psychology" posited that the mind was composed of several muscle-like "faculties" (such as reasoning, taste, memory, imagination, and eloquence) all of which needed to be "brought into exercise" in order to receive a balanced liberal education. Specific subjects were presumed to develop certain mental muscles: ancient literature was thought best for taste; logic and mental philosophy for thinking; physical sciences for facts, induction, and probable evidence. Rudolph, *Curriculum*, 68–69, 209–10.

in their teaching, more motivation in their students, and more time and openings for their scholarship.[79]

Harvard also showed the way in granting students increased choice in their courses. All course requirements were dropped for seniors in 1872, for juniors in 1879, and for sophomores in 1884. Ten years later, the freshmen faced prescribed courses only in rhetoric and a modern language. All of this choice and concomitant specialization was made possible by Harvard's burgeoning endowment and faculty, which few colleges and universities enjoyed. In 1870, 32 professors taught 73 courses; by 1910, 169 professors taught 401 courses. Few universities were as bullish on electives. By 1897, Cornell and Stanford were, but Yale, Princeton, Columbia, and Brown hung back. Yet every "reputable college" had adopted electives "in some measure." By 1901, a survey of 97 colleges found 34 with at least 70 percent elective curricula and another dozen with 50–70 percent.[80]

The elective system had many beneficiaries, which accounts for its popularity. The students tasted some of the *Lernfreiheit* enjoyed by their German contemporaries, even though they could not move freely between institutions. Colleges and universities benefitted from the great boost in faculty and student morale and in reputation for increasing their democratic and utilitarian coverage of the new learning, particularly in the natural and social sciences. But the faculty gained the most. As Eliot proclaimed on the eve of his retirement in 1908, "The largest effect of the elective system is that it makes scholarship possible, not only among undergraduates, but among graduate students and college teachers." It engaged all three groups in the search for discoveries and made them "no longer enemies, but friends." At the same time, it allowed faculty to deepen

79 Rudolph, *American College and University*, ch. 14, esp. 290–95; Rudolph, *Curriculum*, 191–96, 206–208.

80 Rudolph, *Curriculum*, 194, 196, 206; R. Freeman Butts, *The College Charts Its Course: Historical Conceptions and Current Proposals* (New York: McGraw-Hill, 1939), ch. 10, esp. 239–43; Harold A. Larrabee, "Electives Before Eliot," *Harvard Alumni Bulletin* (April 1940), 893–97; Albert Perry Brigham, "Present Status of the Elective System in American Colleges," *Educational Review* 14 (Nov. 1897), 360–69, at 360; E. D. Phillips, "The Elective System in American Education," *Pedagogical Seminary* 8 (June 1901), 206–30.

their teaching and scholarship by specializing and made possible the creation of "scholarly professions, above the old schoolmaster's trade." Above all, it was the major instrument that enabled colleges, no matter how small or poorly endowed, to improve their student and public appeal and the more ambitious, better-endowed colleges to evolve into full-fledged universities.[81]

Yet the elective system was not a panacea because German *Lernfreiheit* came freighted with its own weaknesses, which American observers were quick to notice. Simply put, allowing students a virtually unlimited choice of studies led to curricular chaos, loss of focus, and a sad waste of time and effort. Richard Ely warned that "many American educators and presidents of American universities . . . erred seriously in imagining that they were turning American colleges into German universities by making studies elective and optional." They were misled by thinking that "all work in a German university was elective," but they failed to recognize that the German university was "a professional school." "Each student had in mind an examination which was to admit him to a means of livelihood and he pursued only the studies required for passing it, and pursued them no farther than was demanded." *Lernfreiheit*, therefore, was largely "the freedom given to men of selecting their own professions."[82] The American preference for coherent educational breadth was foreign to the German university.

Perhaps because of his twenty years on the faculty of the precociously elective University of Virginia, Basil Gildersleeve was dismayed that German universities were "not so organized as to give the student a systematic training." He rued his own "haphazard course" of studies at Berlin where, as an 18-year-old novice, he had "no plan" and "no mentor." He had picked out courses blindly from the thick *Index Lectionum* (course book) "guided simply by the great names of which I knew something dimly." Like most assiduous Americans, he

81 Rudolph, *American College and University*, 304–305; G. W. Pierson, "The Elective System and the Difficulties of College Planning, 1870–1940," *Journal of General Education* 4 (April 1950), 165–74, at 172.

82 Ely, *Ground under Our Feet*, 53–54; Ely, "American Colleges and German Universities," 255.

accumulated a "whole shelf" of lecture notes, but he later admitted that "it is seldom visited." Stanley Hall was equally dismayed by the lack of coherence in his choice of "wild electives" at the same model university two decades later. In his five semesters there, he attended a number of unrelated lectures several hours a day. But, he confessed, "I had too little experience in note-taking at first to get much benefit from most of them, and some, even those I had paid for, were sooner or later abandoned." German students, released from their "strictly controlled" and totally prescribed *Gymnasia*, were even more prone to waste one or more years in the "licentious" freedom of elective curricula and family-free living arrangements. As another American Berliner recognized, "There is no force in a German university, as an institution, which tends to fix and concentrate wandering and scattered mental ambitions and energies."[83]

American educators, including German veterans, therefore pulled back from the *über*-elective brink in their postbellum reforms, tantalized by, but ultimately wary of, Teutonic *Freiheit*, particularly for American undergraduates. The majority of colleges and universities offered less than half of their courses as electives, and the great majority sought various compromises between license and prescription. The middle ground, typically, offered modest choices in the under class years and more in the upper class, often between groups of cognate courses rather than between individual courses. By the time widespread reaction against the elective system set in around 1910, curricular devices such as majors and minors, honors programs, distributional requirements, and comprehensive exams had begun to domesticate still further the "wild" Germanic import.[84]

American professors with German experience were more envious of their mentors' *Lehrfreiheit*, the virtually unlimited freedom to teach what and how they liked. In Germany that freedom was safeguarded by state ministers of education, faculty status as civil servants, and established traditions of university autonomy and faculty

83 Gildersleeve, in Miller, ed., *Selections from the Brief Mentions*, 107, 372–73; Briggs, *Soldier and Scholar*, 70; Hall, *Life and Confessions*, 190; Bishop, "University Study at Berlin and Oxford," 354–55.

84 Rudolph, *Curriculum*, 196, 227f.; Butts, *College Charts Its Course*, 408–16.

mobility. It did not automatically extend to political activity or speech outside the university, in which academics were discouraged from indulging by the idealistic belief that politics destroyed scholarly objectivity. But without the faculty's (and the students') essential freedom, testified J. M. Hart, an institution, "no matter how richly endowed, no matter how numerous its students, no matter how imposing its buildings, is not, in the eye of a German, a *university*."[85]

In America, however, two major impediments prevented the direct transplantation of *Lehrfreiheit*: legally supreme boards of trustees, representing "the public," and powerful presidents. Heavily dependent on private, often denominational, donors, alumni, or populist state legislatures for support, colleges and universities could ill afford to alienate or to get too far ahead of public opinion in their teachings or advocacy. Faculty were expected to practice strict neutrality in the classroom and to expect no extension of their limited protections in outside political activities, in which they were more active than their German counterparts. Until American universities grew in sufficient number and national importance and their faculties in size and professional strength, professors failed to earn the robust academic freedom their German colleagues enjoyed. Small-college faculties took even longer.

The first national effort to secure academic freedom—along with its strongest guarantee, tenure—came only in 1915, when the American Association of University Professors was founded during prewar tensions over loyalty and free speech. The organization's Declaration of Principles alluded to both "*Lehrfreiheit* and *Lernfreiheit*" in its opening sentence before limiting itself to the former. It was no coincidence that eight of the thirteen signers of the report had studied in Germany, as had a good proportion of the leaders and targets in academic freedom cases from the 1890s to the First World War. In America, as the bloom on the elective rose faded, the educational promise of *Lernfreiheit* was subordinated to the institutional and public threat to *Lehrfreiheit*.[86]

85 Hart, *German Universities*, 250; Paulsen, *German Universities*, 97, 161.

86 Richard Hofstadter and Walter P. Metzger, *The Development of Academic Freedom in the United States* (New York: Columbia University Press, 1955), ch. 8; Metzger, "German Contribution," 214–30; Walter P. Metzger, ed., *The American Concept of*

❁ ❁ ❁

Of all the academic imports from Germany, the one most needed to complete America's higher educational "system," and to take a giant step toward the country's intellectual independence from Europe, was the Ph.D. Equally necessary was the development of an indigenous institution to produce doctorates in numbers, the graduate school. Unless the United States could train its own faculties for higher college teaching and advanced university research, it would remain forever dependent on strangers and maladapted institutions to do the job. As much as they profited from their foreign experiences, returning veterans of the German system led the campaign to establish fully developed universities that caught some of the spirit of German universities but were better adapted to American needs, ambitions, and conditions.

America made a slow start in 1861 when Yale's Sheffield Scientific School, through a new Department of Philosophy and the Arts (reminiscent of the German philosophy faculty), awarded three earned doctorates in classics, physics, and philosophy and psychology. The degree program had been instituted, with the encouragement of Berlin-trained professor of geography Daniel C. Gilman, to offer the familiar German degree in order to "retain in this country many young men, and especially students of Science, who now resort to German Universities for advantages of study no greater than we are able to afford." Although possession of a bachelor's degree was not strictly necessary, a firm knowledge of Latin and Greek was. (No one until 1890 presented himself without one, and then the candidate was, ironically, a German, a future dean of the Yale Graduate School.) At least two years of resident study, a comprehensive exam, and a thesis giving evidence of "high attainment," preferably some degree of originality, in the studies pursued were the main hurdles to be cleared.[87]

Academic Freedom in Formation: A Collection of Essays and Reports (New York: Arno Press, 1977), essay 10, p. 20.

87 Kelley, *Yale*, 185–86, 504n41; Russell H. Chittenden, *History of the Sheffield Scientific School of Yale University, 1846–1922*, 2 vols. (New Haven, Conn.: Yale University Press), 1:84–89.

Yale awarded several more Ph.D.s before her eastern rivals issued their first: the University of Pennsylvania in 1871, Cornell in 1872, Harvard in 1873, Columbia in 1875, and Princeton in 1879. All of these colleges had added postgraduate students to their undergraduate departments without organizing full-fledged graduate schools to serve them.[88] Yet by 1894, more than 3,000 students had received Ph.D.s (some of them honorary) at American universities, most of them private institutions but an increasing number public in the West and Midwest. Between 1898 and 1909, 3,471 new doctors joined them, so many that the Harvard philosopher William James deplored "the Ph.D. Octopus" of rampant credentialism.[89]

A few universities were created with the sole intent of producing Ph.D.s for the American academic market. Johns Hopkins in Baltimore opened its doors and German-style seminars and labs in 1876; eight of its original thirteen professors were German-trained, as was President Gilman. Although it quickly added undergraduates to serve the region and to provide well-prepared candidates for its graduate classes, the graduate student Woodrow Wilson was not far from the mark in regarding the university as a "high normal school for special[ized] professional teachers." By 1891, 184 of its 212 Ph.D.s—who outnumbered Harvard's and Yale's combined totals—were teaching, the great majority in colleges and universities.[90] In 1889, the year before Harvard formed its graduate school, Clark University and the Catholic University of America (its full title) also began operations for graduates only. But Clark's namesake-benefactor eventually foiled President Stanley Hall's plans to transplant a small,

88 Robert E. Kohler, "The PhD Machine: Building on the Collegiate Base," *Isis* 81:4 (Dec. 1990), 638–62.

89 Edgar S. Furniss, *The Graduate School of Yale: A Brief History* (New Haven, Conn.: Yale Graduate School, 1965), 26; Reingold, "Graduate School and Doctoral Degree," 136; Edwin E. Slosson, *Great American Universities* (New York: Macmillan, 1910), 317; William James, "The Ph.D. Octopus," *Harvard Monthly* 36:1 (March 1903), 1–9, in James, *Essays, Comments, and Reviews* (Cambridge, Mass.: Harvard University Press, 1987), 67–74.

90 Hawkins, *Pioneer*, 122, 291; W. Carson Ryan, *Studies in Early Graduate Education*, Bulletin 30 (New York: Carnegie Foundation for the Advancement of Teaching, 1939), ch. 1; Veysey, *Emergence of the American University*, 158–65.

concentrated version of a German university in Worcester, Massachusetts, by insisting on an American-style undergraduate college as well. Catholic University's focus on theology—until it, too, added undergraduates in 1904—kept it out of the lists of great American universities, though not out of the elite Association of American Universities, which was formed in 1900 to coordinate graduate standards and to make the degrees of American research universities acceptable in Europe, particularly Germany.[91]

No matter how Teutonically intended the college reformers and university builders were, they had to cut their academic patterns to accommodate the American body politic. The first modification of the German Ph.D. was to make it an exclusively postgraduate degree for graduates of four-year liberal arts colleges. This was a major innovation because, strictly speaking, there were no graduate schools in Germany—only post*secondary* institutions that gave a single nonprofessional degree.[92] The second modification was to make the degree the sole requirement for college or university teaching, which meant that a much larger percentage of (graduate) students sought and took it. In Germany, Ph.D.s could teach, after additional training, in a *Gymnasium* or *Realschule* (a less classical, more science-oriented school), but they could not begin a university career until they had written and defended a second, somewhat longer, less specialized dissertation (*Habilitation*) and obtained from the appropriate faculty the right to teach (*venia legendi*) as a *Privatdozent* (an unsalaried instructor who lectured for student fees).[93] Although early

91 Ryan, *Studies in Early Graduate Education*, ch. 2; Veysey, *Emergence of the American University*, 165–71; William A. Koelsch, *Clark University, 1887–1987: A Narrative History* (Worcester, Mass.: Clark University Press, 1987), chs. 1–3; John Tracy Ellis, *The Formative Years of the Catholic University of America* (Washington, D.C.: American Catholic Historical Association, 1946); C. Joseph Nuesse, *The Catholic University of America: A Centennial History* (Washington, D.C.: Catholic University of America Press, 1990).

92 James, "Degree of Ph.D. in Germany," 617–18, 622.

93 Ben-David, "Universities and the Growth of Science," 6–9; Reingold, "Graduate School and Doctoral Degree," 132–33, 135–39; Edward Shils and John Roberts, "The Diffusion of European Models: North America," *HUE* 3:167–74; Hart, *German Universities*, 276–86; Paulsen, *German Universities*, ch. 4; Alexander Busch, "The

American dissertations were as short as German ones—about the length of modern senior or master's theses (ca. 40–90 pages), by the 1900s they grew in size and substance to resemble the heftier *habilitation* theses (ca. 50–100 percent longer). And like their German prototypes, many dissertations were required to be printed at the candidate's expense and submitted in multiple copies.[94]

A third American feature was that graduate schools were quite distinct and separate from professional schools—somewhat as the German philosophy faculty was distinct from, though administratively engaged with, the law, theology, and medical faculties—and were thus called schools "of Arts and Sciences." At the same time, graduate and professional schools in America were both open to applied and "pure" research and teaching, much more so than they were in Germany. German and American academic subdivisions were also different. American universities spawned autonomous, multimembered *departments* (corresponding to scholarly disciplines), whereas German universities retained only four or five larger *faculties*, comprising single monocratic (often autocratic) *chairs* who represented particular disciplines or specialties in university governance. Finally, American graduate schools differed from German universities by insisting on periodic tests, papers, and grades and language requirements (primarily German and French) as a check on the more mottled academic backgrounds of their candidates than those produced by the exacting and thorough *Gymnasia*. With a few

Vicissitudes of the *Privatdozent*: Breakdown and Adaptation in the Recruitment of the German University Teacher," *Minerva* 1:3 (Spring 1963), 319–41; *Max Weber on Universities: The Power of the State and the Dignity of the Academic Calling in Imperial Germany*, ed. and trans. Edward Shils (Chicago: University of Chicago Press, 1974), 54–55.

94 Clark, *Academic Charisma*, 222, 234. Lester F. Goodchild and Margaret M. Miller, "The American Doctorate and Dissertation: Six Developmental Stages." *New Directions for Higher Education*, no. 99 (Fall 1997), 17–32. See also above, p. 234n33. The first three Yale dissertations were in the 20–30-page range, handwritten. Between 1879 and 1900, Princeton's first 26 dissertations averaged (excluding a hugely atypical 590-page monograph) 52 printed pages and appeared mostly as journal articles. Clark University's first 10 dissertations (1891–1899) averaged 61 pages. Thanks to archivists Judith Schiff of Yale, John DeLooper of Princeton, and Fordyce Williams of Clark, and to Professor R. Steven Turner for these data.

exceptions (such as Princeton's 1913 Gothic-style residential graduate college), however, they did exempt their students from quasi-parental supervision in their daily living, a touch of local *Lebenfreiheit*.[95]

❁ ❁ ❁

In the process of cherry-picking in the land of the footnote, American scholars took what they wanted and needed most for their own private and later public purposes. In doing so, they missed most of the animating spirit, or *Geist*, of the early- and mid-century German universities, what the natives called *Bildung*. This was an idealized concept that connoted "self-cultivation" or education of a "philosophical"—what we would call "liberal"—sort.[96] It referred to both "the process and the result of a person's intellectual development." As in contemporary American notions of liberal education, it also had an "implicit bias in favor of the social groups whose leisure and money permitted them to pursue the cultivation of their talents and personalities." In higher education it was associated with the notion of *Wissenschaft*, by which Germans meant "knowledge in the most exalted sense of that term, namely, the ardent, methodical, independent search after truth in any and all of its forms, but wholly irrespective of utilitarian application." *Wissenschaft* was thus

95 Veysey, *Emergence of the American University*, 320–24; Panofsky, *Meaning in the Visual Arts*, 333–44; Joseph Ben-David, *Centers of Learning: Britain, France, Germany, United States* (New York: McGraw-Hill, 1977), 46–52, 59–67; Joseph Ben-David and Awraham Zloczower, "Universities and Academic Systems in Modern Societies," *European Journal of Sociology* 3:1 (1962), 45–84, at 57, 74–75; Ben-David, "Universities and the Growth of Science," 9–13, 19–21; Reingold, "Graduate School and Doctoral Degree," 131, 144–45, 147; Paulsen, *German Universities*, 77–81; *HUE* 3:170; James Axtell, *The Making of Princeton University: From Woodrow Wilson to the Present* (Princeton, N.J.: Princeton University Press, 2006), ch. 7.

96 As a student in Berlin in 1890, Lincoln Steffens confessed his disappointment in his fellow American students. "All seem to be specialists, bread-winners (Germans say *Brot-studenten*—bread-students) and few are cultivated men, few are thinkers. . . . [They] are getting some knowledge, some training, but culture or ideas they are not getting, and the Germans remark it too." *Letters of Lincoln Steffens*, 38–39.

the chief goal and process, the "highest calling," of the scholar. Like *Bildung*, it, too, was an aesthetic and character-building enterprise.[97]

Instead of absorbing their idealistic, neohumanist connotations, practical Americans virtually ignored *Bildung* and reduced *Wissenschaft* to "research," as German academics had done in the last quarter of the century. Since they took their notion of liberal education more from Matthew Arnold than from Alexander von Humboldt and Johann Fichte, "one kind of German influence—that toward pure research—far outshone [all] others." Americans largely borrowed methods and techniques of research and an invigorating but vague "spirit of inquiry," rather than any philosophical underpinnings.[98] And they used those imports in their own ways to create professionalized academic careers at home. As late as 1871, the newly elected president, James B. Angell, told an audience at the University of Michigan that "it seems to have dawned but recently on men's minds that teaching in the College or University is a special profession." Many returnees from German universities sought to update such thinking.[99]

97 Albisetti, *Secondary School Reform in Imperial Germany*, ch. 1; McClelland, *State, Society, and University in Germany*, 123–31, at 123, chs. 5–6; Hart, *German Universities*, 250; Fritz Ringer, "Bildung and Its Implications in the German Tradition, 1890–1930," in Fritz Ringer, *Toward a Social History of Knowledge: Collected Essays* (New York: Berghahn Books, 2000), ch. 7; Chad Wellmon, *Organizing Enlightenment: Information Overload and the Invention of the Modern Research University* (Baltimore, Md.: Johns Hopkins University Press, 2015).

98 Perhaps typical were historians who, in their "scientific" search for truth and objectivity, learned from German seminars to fetishize (and even feminize) documentary archives and to regard the all-male seminars as theatres of agonistic competition for personal honor and professional standing. Smith, "Gender and the Practice of Scientific History."

99 Veysey, *Emergence of the American University*, 132, 135; Lenore O'Boyle, "Learning for Its Own Sake: The German University as Nineteenth-Century Model," *Comparative Studies in Society and History* 25:1 (Jan. 1983), 3–25, at 20n54, 21. James Turner warns that "research" in the later nineteenth and earlier twentieth centuries was not as specialized or as exclusive as ours tends to be. "Liberal culture" advocates and other polymaths pursued research as steadfastly and successfully as narrow specialists. "The Forgotten History of the Research Ideal," in *Language, Religion, Knowledge: Past and Present* (Notre Dame, Ind.: University of Notre Dame Press, 2003), ch. 5.

They did so by transplanting several aspects of German academic life. First, they elevated the importance of original research, or "investigation," in the classroom as well as on the nation's cultural agenda. With a new premium on primary sources for new knowledge and the refinement of old, libraries enjoyed a resurgence and a larger share of institutional budgets. Accessibility to their books and journals increased through longer hours, open stacks, and more liberal borrowing privileges.[100] Universities felt obliged to help disseminate the new learning by establishing publication agencies, scholarly presses (on the Oxbridge model in the absence of a German one), journals, and monograph series. As in so much, Johns Hopkins led the way with such organs as the *American Journal of Mathematics* (1878), *The Johns Hopkins University Studies in Historical and Political Science* (1882), and the evolution of the Johns Hopkins University Press (1891) from the decade-old "Publication Agency."[101]

Since published research and scholarship was increasingly the currency of academe, American universities and elite colleges could establish or ratchet up policies of "publish or perish" for promotion and, eventually, tenure. This was a bearable price to pay for meritocratic criteria for professional career building that related directly to the duties of one's job, rather than recurring attention to nepotism,

100 Thwing, *American and the German University*, 130–33; John Y. Cole, "Storehouses and Workshops: American Libraries and the Uses of Knowledge," in Alexandra Oleson and John Voss, eds., *The Organization of Knowledge in Modern America, 1860–1920* (Baltimore, Md.: Johns Hopkins University Press, 1979), 364–85; Kenneth J. Brough, *Scholar's Workshop: Evolving Conceptions of Library Service* (Boston: Gregg Press, 1972), chs. 2, 5–6; Arthur T. Hamlin, *The University Library in the United States: Its Origins and Development* (Philadelphia: University of Pennsylvania Press, 1981), chs. 3–4, 9; Potts, *Wesleyan University*, 130–32; Axtell, *Making of Princeton University*, ch. 8; Kelley, *Yale*, 291–92; Daniel Coit Gilman, *University Problems in the United States* (New York: Century, 1898), 237–61; Hawkins, *Pioneer*, 118–20.

101 Hawkins, *Pioneer*, 107–18; Richard Macksey, "Shadows of Scholars: 1878–1978," in *One Hundred Years of Scholarly Publishing, 1878–1978* (Baltimore, Md.: Johns Hopkins University Press, 1978), 1–15; Edward Shils, "The Order of Learning in the United States: The Ascendancy of the University," in Oleson and Voss, eds., *Organization of Knowledge*, 19–47, at 39–40; Daniel Coit Gilman, *The Launching of a University and Other Papers: A Sheaf of Remembrances* (New York: Dodd, Mead, 1906), ch. 7; Fabian Franklin, *The Life of Daniel Coit Gilman* (New York: Dodd, Mead, 1910), 229–33.

wealth, religion, politics, or other circumstances. The formation of specialized in-house and scholarly associations, such as the Hopkins Metaphysics Club and the American Historical Association, inevitably led faculty to stronger identification with their transnational disciplines than with their local institutions. So did the division of faculty into departments, where increasingly specialized elective courses could be given along with required introductions and surveys.[102]

Given America's populist suspicion of intellectualism, the nineteenth-century American professor could never earn the German public's near-reverence for the *Herr Doktor Professor*, a title of "high dignity" and the object of "sincere respect . . . by all classes of people."[103] After 1890 or so, however, the American's newly professionalized status could be recognized on those annual occasions when academic pomp was de rigueur and assemblies of parents, alumni, local citizens, and invited dignitaries were present. Bedecked in a theatrical array of colorful caps, gowns, and hoods, the professors

102 Shils, "Order of Learning," 32–36; Ben-David, "Universities and the Growth of Science," 20–21, 24–25.

103 Richard Hofstadter, *Anti-intellectualism in American Life* (New York: Knopf, 1963); Hart, *German Universities*, 267; Scott, *Some Memories of a Palaeontologist*, 131; "The German Professor (Old Style)," *Saturday Review of Literature, Science, and Art* [London] (July 12, 1884), 47–48; William H. Carpenter, "The Financial Status of the Professor in America and Germany," *Educational Review* 36 (Nov. 1908), 325–41; Fritz K. Ringer, *The Decline of the German Mandarins: The German Academic Community, 1890–1933* (Cambridge, Mass.: Harvard University Press, 1969), ch. 2; Winfreid Herget, "Overcoming the 'Mortifying Distance': American Impressions of German Universities in the Nineteenth and Early Twentieth Centuries," in *Transatlantische Partnerschaft: Kulturelle Aspekte der deutsch-amerikanischen Beziehungen* (Bonn: Bouvier Verlag, 1992), 195–208, at 198–200; *Letters of Lincoln Steffens*, 1:37, 39. See also Mark Twain's account in 1892 of the huge Berlin celebration by some 4,000 students, faculty, civic officials, and guests of the seventieth birthdays of the scientists Rudolph Virchow and Hermann von Helmholtz. The last guest to arrive was the classicist and historian Theodor Mommsen, whose modest appearance brought the whole house to its feet and clamorous welcome. Twain, who was not easily impressed, exclaimed: "Mommsen!—think of it! . . . Here he was, carrying the Roman world and all the Caesars in his hospitable skull and doing it as easily as that other luminous vault, the skull of the universe, carries the milky way and the constellations." Twain, *Tramp Abroad*, 992–97, at 996.

could bask in temporary limelight and dignified respect. If they owed their finery to European traditions and an Albany, New York, entrepreneur, some of those present might have remembered when they first saw it on academic display in Germany, as Bliss Perry did in 1886 when he attended the 500th-anniversary of the founding of the University of Heidelberg.[104] For the "Germany-returned," such a memory would have been only one of myriad reminders of what they owed their academic experiences there. But it also could have symbolized all they had been offered and the careful cuttings they had made for grafting upon their former colleges and future universities.

104 Perry, *And Gladly Teach*, 92; Baldwin, *Between Two Wars*, 1:58. In December 1893, the article "The Cap and Gown in America" in the *University Magazine* testified that "the custom of wearing caps and gowns on appropriate occasions is fast becoming fixed in the higher educational institutions of this country." Two years later, the custom had grown so prevalent that Princeton convened in New York an Intercollegiate Commission to standardize academic costume for its sesquicentennial celebrations the following year. Recommendations for hoods as well as caps and gowns were made, which the firm of Cotrell & Leonard in Albany immediately turned to their advantage. The article by Gardner Cotrell Leonard, Williams College '87, was reprinted by his family's firm in 1896, with numerous illustrations of its wares. See also Donald L. Drakeman, "Caps, Gowns, and a Debt to Princeton: The University's Unsung Role in Standardizing Academic Garb," http://paw.princeton.edu/issues/2011/07/06/pages/6367/index.xml.

CHAPTER SIX

Coming of Age

I would found an institution where any person
can find instruction in any study.

EZRA CORNELL, 1865

IF ANTEBELLUM AMERICA was a strapping raw youth in search of self-control, purpose, and a viable future, postbellum America learned to harness its strength and settled into an ambitious maturity. Political union having been saved—narrowly—by a costly and deadly civil war, the surging U.S. (primarily white) population turned to the business of consolidating its dominance from coast to coast and building an economy and culture worthy of a continental empire.

Between 1870 and 1900, which Mark Twain dubbed the Gilded Age, the population nearly doubled to over 76 million, bolstered by some 10 million "new immigrants" from southern and eastern Europe in search of inexpensive farmland or urban jobs. The main lure was good industrial wages, which in real terms increased 60 percent between 1870 and 1890, the year the American "frontier" allegedly vanished and U.S. manufacturing outstripped that of world-leading Great Britain. This second—American—industrial revolution rode on railroad tracks that not only spanned the continent in 1869 but tripled by 1880 and doubled again by 1920. Larger, more powerful locomotives carried newly discovered coal from the Appalachians, oil from western Pennsylvania, and iron ore from the Lake Superior region to new factories and foundries in eastern and midwestern towns and cities. There the applied technology winnowed from half a million patents, including those for electrification, the telephone, and the typewriter, produced the steel for city skyscrapers, bridges, farm machinery, and soon, on innovative assembly lines, automobiles.

The dominant form of big business became the corporation, combinations of which created pools of investment capital and manpower, efficiencies, and monopolies, or "trusts," that dominated whole industries and manipulated prices and profits, often by buying regulatory and political favors. In the process, while the American economy grew exponentially (without a serious federal income tax until 1913), so did the fortunes of many companies—U.S. Steel, Standard Oil, AT&T, Southern Pacific—and their executives, as did the disposable income of a burgeoning, particularly white-collar, middle class.[1]

One result of this auspicious growth was a major leap forward for American higher education. In the forty years after 1860, 432 four-year colleges and universities were added to the fewer than 300 that had been established since 1636. Another 200 were added before 1934.[2] Enrollment and graduation gains were even more impressive. While the U.S. population grew 2.6 times between 1880 and 1940, higher education enrollments grew 13 times and earned degrees nearly 15-fold. In the same period, the percentage of 18–24-year-olds attending college rose from 1.6 to 9.1 (15.5 percent of 18–21-year-olds).[3]

Since the rise in college matriculations far exceeded general population trends, explanations for the popularity of college attendance must be sought in other than a simple law of supply and demand. The stage for both trends was set by the dramatic increase in private and, especially, public high-school enrollments and graduates, themselves one consequence of the American shift in population from rural to urban before 1920.[4] From only 110,000

1 Between 1883 and 1913, America's gross national product (GNP) quadrupled. Jonathan R. Cole, *The Great American University* (New York: PublicAffairs, 2009), 46–47.

2 Claudia Goldin and Lawrence F. Katz, "The Shaping of Higher Education: The Formative Years in the United States, 1890 to 1940," *Journal of Economic Perspectives* 13:1 (Winter 1999), 37–62, at 42. The authors drew on a sample of 921 four-year institutions (778 private and 143 public) in existence in 1934 and surveyed by the U.S. Office of Education. Independent teacher-training institutions were excluded, but independent professional schools were included.

3 *120 Years of American Education: A Statistical Portrait*, ed. Thomas D. Snyder (Washington, D.C.: National Center for Education Statistics, 1993), 76 (table 24).

4 *Historical Statistics of the United States: Millenial Edition Online*, hsus.cambridge.org/HSUSWeb/HSUSEntryServlet. The Census Bureau defined "urban" as an incorporated place with a population over 2,500.

students in 1880, high schools enrolled more than half a million in 1900 and 6.6 million in 1940. Those who earned diplomas rose from 62,000 to well over a million in the forty years after 1900. A relatively small but growing number of graduates chose to attend college, not only for familiar intellectual, economic, and social reasons, but because current students, avid alumni, and popular media publicized and glamorized campus culture, which the Roaring Twenties glorified.[5]

Although the number of institutions only a little more than doubled between 1880 and 1940, a shift in types, incomes, and sizes enabled the 13-fold growth in college matriculations. Private four-year colleges continued to greatly outnumber public institutions, but the latter, many of which were universities in name and deed, enrolled a majority of students by 1940. The reasons for the universities' catch-up are not hard to find. Because most universities were publicly financed, they were, on average, less costly to attend and considerably larger than private institutions. As early as 1897, the median size of the student body at a private college was 505, at a public one, 787. By 1934, the median private campus, charging $265 for tuition, accommodated 2,271 students, which was dwarfed by the public enrollment of 8,181, whose tuition tab was only $61. Almost 95 percent of public students (versus 62 percent of private students) attended schools with more than 1,000 students; nearly 6 percent (and less than 0.5 percent of private students) rubbed elbows with more than 10,000 contemporaries.[6]

Although universities were, historically and for the future, greatly outnumbered by smaller colleges, they quickly captured the public's attention and respect. For Americans emerging from the Gilded Age, bigger was often equated with better, and universities were certainly bigger than any colleges to date. The trend toward bigness was promoted by the federal Morrill Act of 1862, which gave generous

5 Helen Lefkowitz Horowitz, *Campus Life: Undergraduate Cultures from the End of the Eighteenth Century to the Present* (Chicago: University of Chicago Press, 1987); Paula S. Fass, *The Damned and the Beautiful: American Youth in the 1920s* (New York: Oxford University Press, 1977).

6 Goldin and Katz, "Shaping of Higher Education," 43, 44 (table 1).

amounts of federal land to states to underwrite "at least one college where the leading object shall be, without excluding other scientific and classical studies, . . . to teach such branches of learning as are related to agriculture and the mechanic arts."[7] Growth of the numerous, particularly state, universities that resulted from this and similar enlargements of their purviews and public expectations was inevitable. As the University of Michigan's new president said in 1921, "A state university must accept happily the conclusion that it is destined to be large."[8]

Even privately endowed universities were not averse to bigness. In 1897 the president of Harvard, Charles W. Eliot, told his counterpart at much smaller Johns Hopkins that "I find that I am not content unless Harvard grows each year, in spite of the size which it has attained. . . . Quality being secured, the larger the quantity the better."[9] By the fall of 1909, Harvard's 5,558 students were second only to urban Columbia's 6,232 and not far ahead of Chicago's 5,487 and Michigan's 5,259. Johns Hopkins, graduate-heavy and impervious to Eliot's advice, trailed happily at 725.[10] Twenty-five years later, in the teeth of the Great Depression, seven public and three private universities enrolled more than 10,000 students. The trend continues. Today, the twenty largest public doctoral universities register between 40,000 and 75,000 students. The biggest private universities manage to thrive with "only" 17,000 to 44,000.[11]

7 John R. Thelin, ed., *Essential Documents in the History of American Higher Education* (Baltimore, Md.: Johns Hopkins University Press, 2014), 76–79, at 77. Before 1900, thirty states took advantage of the law to establish new state universities (A&Ms) or to augment the offerings of established institutions. Yale was once Connecticut's land-grant college, as Cornell was New York's.

8 Howard H. Peckham, *The Making of the University of Michigan, 1817–1967* (Ann Arbor: University of Michigan Press, 1967), 140 (quoting Marion Burton).

9 CWE to Daniel Coit Gilman, Oct. 20, 1897 (DCG Collection, Johns Hopkins University), quoted in Laurence R. Veysey, *The Emergence of the American University* (Chicago: University of Chicago Press, 1965), 356.

10 Edwin E. Slosson, *Great American Universities* (New York: Macmillan, 1910), 475.

11 Goldin and Katz, "Shaping of Higher Education," 44 (table 1); *Chronicle of Higher Education Almanac 2014–15* (Aug. 22, 2014), 29.

❁ ❁ ❁

The accelerated advent of universities—evolved and new—after 1890 led to a reconfiguration of the American educational "system," which lacked a national directorate like France's or even a separate seat in the president's cabinet until 1979. In outline, the system resembled a slightly truncated pyramid. On the broad base sat the nation's proliferating primary, secondary, and high schools, some private but most public. Next came, in the early decades of the twentieth century, a surge of public two-year, vocationally oriented, and urban-located "junior" (or "community") colleges. Their graduates could often transfer with advanced standing to four-year institutions, most easily to other public colleges in the same state.[12] The middle layers consisted of the abundant four-year liberal arts colleges, those that had not evolved, by choice or circumstance, into universities. At the top were not one or two icons like England's Oxford and Cambridge, but the moderate and still growing number of universities, increasingly arranged in a hierarchy based on quality as well as size. Those at the very top all had distinguished faculties, major Ph.D.-granting graduate programs if not schools, and one or more professional schools that required at least two years of undergraduate study for admission.

As soon as all of these institutions assumed their mature form, they by and large carved out specialized functions and shed those that were best served by their neighbors above or below in the pyramid. Until the advent of Advanced Placement courses in 1955, high schools did not attempt to usurp the colleges' curricula or customers. Normal schools—independent or departments of colleges—morphed

12 Steven G. Brint and Jerome Karabel, *The Diverted Dream: Community Colleges and the Promise of Educational Opportunity in America, 1900–1985* (New York: Oxford University Press, 1989); Arthur M. Cohen and F. B. Brawer, *The American Community College*, 5th ed. (San Francisco: Jossey-Bass, 2008); David O. Levine, *The American College and the Culture of Aspiration, 1915–1940* (Ithaca, N.Y.: Cornell University Press, 1986), ch. 8. By 1940, 456 junior colleges enrolled nearly 150,000 students across the country. Two years earlier, 17.6 percent of the nation's collegians were enrolled in two-year institutions (Levine, *American College*, 162).

into state teachers colleges.[13] Junior colleges offered only the first two introductory years of the college curriculum or job-ready vocational training. For their part, the liberal arts colleges largely jettisoned their preparatory departments, vocational courses, and graduate ambitions and, with some socially elite exceptions (mostly in New England and the Midwest), retained a local or regional draw, while universities tended to cast their eyes and applications upon the whole nation and even abroad.[14] Other, smaller, niches were filled by colleges for women, Catholics, African-Americans, Native Americans, and evangelical denominations, as well as by comprehensive branch campuses in newly organized state university systems. In recent decades, institutions exclusively online and for profit, "diploma mills" that offer unearned or bogus degrees for cash, and degreeless institutes for advanced study have carved out additional niches in the increasingly segmented but still coherent national system of higher education.

The emergent system of higher education was, fittingly for a laissez-faire economy and a democratic polity, not the product of federal or even state legislation, but rather of "voluntary agreements, imitation, internal competition, and generalized rules of conduct." Its strength lay in its "variety of institutions and the way they competed with each other to serve the public" and their particular constituencies.[15] Its structural integrity was owed to what a keen student called its "coherent heterogeneity," in contrast to the "incoherent homogeneity" of the antebellum college scene.[16] Yet for all its notable diversity, the system was increasingly dominated and

13 Jurgen Herbst, *And Sadly Teach: Teacher Education and Professionalization in American Culture* (Madison: University of Wisconsin Press, 1989).

14 W. Bruce Leslie, *Gentlemen and Scholars: College and Community in the "Age of the University," 1865–1917* (University Park, Pa.: Penn State University Press, 1992), ch. 10. Before 1900, twelve Ohio colleges offered a Ph.D. (often honorary); only one—Ohio State University—ended up with a doctoral program. Roger L. Geiger, *The History of American Higher Education: Learning and Culture in America, 1636 to 1940* (Princeton, N.J.: Princeton University Press, 2014), 415.

15 Arthur M. Cohen with Carrie B. Kisker, *The Shaping of American Higher Education: Emergence and Growth of the Contemporary System* (San Francisco: Jossey-Bass, 2010), 169.

16 Slosson, *Great American Universities*, 347.

stabilized by universities of a certain kind: those devoted to research and the scholarly production of new knowledge, pure and applied. When the public heard or read about the leading or "great" universities between 1890 and 1910, they were invariably introduced to large research universities that topped the newly emerging rankings of educational quality.

❁ ❁ ❁

The first organization to pick winners was the Association of American Universities, which chose its own members to carry the national banner in dealings with European, particularly German, universities. In January 1900, the presidents of Harvard, Columbia, Johns Hopkins, Chicago, and California invited their counterparts from eight other highly regarded research universities—Clark, Cornell, Michigan, Pennsylvania, Princeton, Stanford, Wisconsin, Yale, and, to show their ecumenism, promising Catholic—to confer in Chicago about three concerns: the lack of consistency and standards in American higher education, the small respect that major European universities seemed to have for American degrees, and the annoying behavior of American students who still chose to go abroad for graduate work when American universities offered research training as good or better. Of the original fourteen members, eleven were private universities and three were public. By 1909, eight more public research universities were invited to join, thereby balancing the proportions and signaling the qualitative as well as quantitative rise of public universities in all regions of the country.[17]

17 The letter of invitation to the inaugural conference is in the AAU archive in Johns Hopkins' Milton S. Eisenhower Library. It is reproduced on the AAU website (www.aau.edu), as is Ann Leigh Speicher, "The AAU: A Century of Service to Higher Education, 1900–2000." The 8 new public members were Indiana, Illinois, Iowa, Kansas, Minnesota, Missouri, Nebraska, and Virginia. In 2011 the AAU's 60 U.S. members received 58 percent ($23.5 billion) of all federal research dollars and spent $6 billion of their own. Forty-one of the top 50 academic libraries belonged to AAU schools, which also produced 46.5 percent of all U.S. doctorates, 70 percent of U.S. Nobel Prize winners, and 69 percent of National Medal of Science recipients. ("AAU By the Numbers," https://www.aau.edu/WorkArea/DownloadAsset.aspx?id=13460).

In 1910 the publication of two lists also served to shine a spotlight on the leading American universities. Kendric Babcock, former president of the University of Arizona and expert staffer at the U.S. Bureau of Education, was hired by the AAU to make a four-"class" ranking of 344 colleges and universities. After he made numerous site visits, examined student transcripts, and dug into other records, his Class I list contained 59 schools whose B.A. graduates were deemed able to take a master's degree from leading graduate schools in just one year. (Graduates of the Class IV schools, in contrast, were thought to be two years short of a "standard bachelor's [degree] of a standard college.") The former included prestigious liberal arts colleges such as Amherst, Oberlin, Haverford, and Smith as well as the undergraduate colleges of the Ancient Three (Harvard, Yale, and Princeton), California, Michigan, and Wisconsin. Four years later, the AAU rehired Babcock to make a three-tier appraisal of undergraduate producers whose graduates attended AAU-member graduate and professional schools. The list of top performers was sent to German universities to argue the high quality of American degrees.[18]

The second and more public list in 1910 was Edwin E. Slosson's 550-page book *Great American Universities*, which featured fourteen chosen from the Carnegie Foundation for the Advancement of Teaching's list of universities that spent the most money annually for instruction, "probably," the author suggested, "a fairer criterion than any other objective standard." Slosson had the academic credentials to write such a book. He was a Phi Beta Kappa graduate of the University of Kansas, a *magna cum laude* Ph.D. from the University of Chicago, and a former professor of chemistry at the University of Wyoming. Slosson spent a week at each university (attending over a hundred classes in toto), scrutinizing its history, current records, and performance. His lengthy profiles appeared monthly in *The*

18 David S. Webster, *Academic Quality Rankings of American Colleges and Universities* (Springfield, Ill.: Charles C. Thomas, 1986), ch. 4, at 36. Babcock's first list is reproduced—and misdated—in Andy Thomason, "How Did the Federal Government Rate Your College a Century Ago?" *Chronicle of Higher Education*, Aug. 6, 2014 (http://chronicle.com/blogs/ticker/how-did-the-federal-government-rate-your-college-a-century-ago/83411).

Independent (whose literary and managing editor he had been since 1903) between January 1909 and March 1910 before their appearance in book form in October. His roster featured nine endowed universities (Harvard, Yale, Princeton, Columbia, Chicago, Cornell, Penn, Stanford, and Johns Hopkins) and five state universities (Michigan, Wisconsin, Minnesota, California, and Illinois). Festooned with helpful statistical tables, graphs, and photos, his rich descriptions and spirited comparisons made it clear that the United States had plenty of reasons to take pride not only in its top research universities but also in "scores of other institutions . . . that do just as good work in collegiate and often in advanced and specialized studies" as those highlighted.[19]

Similar profiles and photos of the same league-leading universities in numerous other popular periodicals secured the universities' hold on Americans' imaginations, affections, and—not unimportantly—pocketbooks. Interspersed with admiring sketches or commencement addresses of larger-than-life presidents, those Captains of Erudition later made (in)famous by Thorstein Veblen, profiles of the leading research universities appeared frequently in the likes of *Munsey's*, *McClure's*, *The Century*, *The Outlook*, *Scribner's*, and, in the West, *Sunset*, *Overland Monthly*, and *Pacific Monthly*.[20] The rise of new members of the elite circle—Stanford, California, Wisconsin—were always popular topics, but so were women's colleges, student life and culture, athletics, fraternities, and other aspects of the burgeoning extracurricular "sideshows."[21] All served to

19 Slosson, *Great American Universities*, ix, 525. In 1921 Slosson revisited the university landscape in *The American Spirit in Education* (New Haven, Conn.: Yale University Press), a short volume in the popular Chronicles of America series. He devoted chapters to state, land-grant, and contemporary research universities, the last his clear favorites.

20 Thorstein Veblen, *The Higher Learning in America: A Memorandum on the Conduct of Universities by Business Men* (New York: Hill and Wang, 1957 [1918]), ch. 3, at 62.

21 James C. Stone and Donald P. DeNevi provide a representative sample of periodical articles in *Portraits of the American University, 1890–1910* (San Francisco: Jossey-Bass, 1971). "Sideshows" was Princeton president Woodrow Wilson's description. James Axtell, *The Making of Princeton University: From Woodrow Wilson to the Present* (Princeton, N.J.: Princeton University Press, 2006), ch. 5, at 238–42.

suggest that large research universities were the wave of America's higher-educational future because they managed to combine the best of the tried and the new.

❁ ❁ ❁

The "flowering" of the university movement in the twenty years after 1890 was marked by two parallel trends that served to stabilize the higher educational system by endowing it with enough uniformity to balance its notable diversity.[22] The first trend was a blending of the four major postbellum conceptions of the purpose of higher education: (1) mental discipline, piety, and character formation, the staples of the antebellum colleges and their lineal descendants; (2) "practical" preparation for "real life" or vocational training for "usefulness"; (3) pure research and scholarship on the assimilated German model; and (4) a more socially elite eastern goal, the cultivation of "liberal culture" for the molding of "well-rounded" persons largely through the humanities.[23] This medley of ideals was largely the product of the new university leaders who sought to make their ambitious and needy campuses appealing to potential donors, political supporters, faculty, students, and alumni. Typical was Benjamin Ide Wheeler, president of the University of California, who wrote in 1901, "The modern university . . . is an assemblage into one of all the colleges, all the courses, all the life aims, and all the generous ways of reaching them." Private university presidents also sought to please multiple constituencies. In 1907 Chicago's Harry Pratt Judson expressed his belief that the college should *not* "aim at any one kind of product. . . . No college should aim to put its hallmark upon all men in such a sense as to expect that all will be substantially alike."[24] Although the result of such philosophical mergers was too often intellectually bland, it made for anodynic commencement addresses and supple appeals for funding.

22 I borrow "flowering" from Frederick Rudolph, *The American College and University: A History* (New York: Alfred A. Knopf, 1962), ch. 16, at 329.

23 Veysey, *Emergence of the American University*, chs. 1–4 and pp. 342–45.

24 Both quoted in ibid., 344.

The second stabilizing trend was the widespread standardization of university structures and practices. Thanks to greater awareness of national trends through popular publications and new academic organizations (such as the AAU) and communications, universities became keenly aware of each other and increasingly competitive within their respective ranks. But instead of striving to be different from the rest, they sought to be better at the same things and largely in the same ways. When they had a choice, they avoided "pronounced eccentricities" at all (imagined) costs. But as the Yale president, Arthur Twining Hadley, sought to explain in 1901, even private universities with ample endowments believed they had little room to maneuver in the "highly normative universe" in which they operated.[25] "All institutions . . . have been compelled by force of circumstances to approximate toward a common type more or less independent of the wishes of those who established and controlled them."[26] The power of the norm was so great that something dubbed the Standard American University (SAU) was recognized by the National Association of State Universities in 1908 and the U.S. Commissioner of Education in 1909; Slosson's *Great American Universities* publicized it the following year.[27]

At the thirteenth annual meeting of the state-universities association in the nation's capital (a measure of its members' increasing importance), a four-man committee on "standards" reported on three years of work. Their recommendations spoke to each segment of the "organic" university system to date. The foundational college of arts and sciences, they said, should offer in the first two years "general or liberal work completing or supplementing the work of the high school" and in the last two years "special, advanced, or university instruction," suffused with the "spirit of discovery." High-school teachers were expected to have four-year B.A.s and, ideally, M.A.s

25 Ibid., 340 (first quotation). Geiger, *American Higher Education*, 538 (second quotation).

26 Quoted in Veysey, *Emergence of the American University*, 261; Charles W. Eliot, "American Universities: Their Resemblances and Their Differences," *Educational Review* (Feb. 1906), 109–34, at 109.

27 Slosson, *Great American Universities*, 522.

as well. College faculty, understandably, ought to have "a doctor's degree or its equivalent" and, above all, the "power as teachers to inspire the students with zeal for research." They could do this best by modeling their own prowess in "research and publication." Of course, given the residue of antebellum ideals, they were still responsible for "imparting knowledge" and "character building." Yet notably, inculcating piety and enforcing discipline had been dropped from their duties.

The spirit of research that permeated the SAUs was manifested in several concrete requirements. "Standard" graduate schools had to offer the Ph.D. in at least five departments. The minimum time-to-degree was one postgraduate year for the M.A. and three for the Ph.D. To render these schedules feasible, the universities had to offer at least "adequate general and departmental libraries," "modern laboratories and apparatus," museums, and proper facilities for the "educational, political, and social sciences." SAUs were also expected to have at least one "university[-level] professional school" that required at least "two years' collegiate training for admission." That standard was soon raised in practice to four years of college in tandem with the elevation of professional education in its theoretical aspects and scholarship.[28]

❁ ❁ ❁

The blueprint for the SAU sketched before 1910 only glimpsed, of course, a few of the similarities that America's actual universities came to share. The normative uniformity of the times also got a prescriptive nudge from a number of regional accrediting groups, which freely borrowed each other's standards for assessing their member colleges and universities. Between 1885 (when the New England Association was formed) and 1923 (when the Western Association began), every region of the country established an Association of Colleges and Secondary Schools, including a majority of representatives from the region's colleges and universities. Their job was to

28 *Report of the [U.S.] Commissioner of Education for . . . 1909*, vol. 1 (Washington, D.C.: Government Printing Office, 1909), 88–91.

adopt explicit standards for such things as economic viability, academic programs, degrees, classroom and lab size, and library holdings. After site visits, substantial reports, and self-studies, those institutions that passed muster had their names added to a published list; those that did not risked the loss of donations, top faculty, students, and face.[29]

Two extremely wealthy foundations applied even more pressure to maintain uniformly high standards at the top of the academic pyramid. While they kept their hands off the running of individual institutions, they used their grants to "promote a comprehensive system of higher education" in the United States by aiding the "survival of the [academically and economically] fittest" colleges and universities with endowment and salary boosts and faculty pensions. Initially focused on black education in the South, John D. Rockefeller's General Education Board (est. 1902) shifted its emphasis in 1905 to higher education in the whole country. During the next twenty-one years, the GEB spent $188 million (over $4 billion in 2015 dollars) of the Standard Oil magnate's money in an effort to reduce the supply of small, poorly located and funded colleges by requiring matching funds from the board's lucky recipients. Understandably, older, well-established liberal arts colleges and research universities fared the best.[30]

The Carnegie Foundation for the Advancement of [College] Teaching, launched by a $10-million gift from agnostic steel baron Andrew Carnegie, initially provided pensions to retired professors from private colleges, provided that their schools had at least six (later eight) full professors (which usually meant that number of departments) and endowments of at least $250,000 (later $500,000) and no debts, were free from (certain kinds of) sectarian control, and admitted only students who had completed four years of secondary

29 Cohen and Kisker, *Shaping of American Higher Education*, 167–68; William K. Selden, *Accreditation: A Struggle over Standards in Higher Education* (New York: Harper, 1960), esp. ch. 4.

30 Merle Curti and Roderick Nash, *Philanthropy in the Shaping of American Higher Education* (New Brunswick, N.J.: Rutgers University Press, 1965), 215–17. Even in the late 1920s, the GEB's aim was still to "make the peaks higher." Roger L. Geiger, *To Advance Knowledge: The Growth of American Research Universities, 1900–1940* (New York: Oxford University Press, 1986), 161.

education as measured by standardized "Carnegie units" of classroom time, the prevailing American measurement for college admissions for several decades.[31] In 1908 the foundation declared state universities eligible for pensions. Nine years later, the increase in demand led to the creation of the still-indispensable Teachers Insurance and Annuity Association (TIAA, later yoked to CREF—the College Retirement Equities Fund—to create the largest pension fund in the United States today). But pensions were no longer scot-free: professors now had to contribute 5 percent of their salary toward their golden (or at least silver-haired) years.[32]

Pressures toward uniformity from outside academe were not only directed largely at the minority of leading universities, they were also comparatively light compared to the pressures generated within. After 1890, standardization proceeded largely on the triple boosters of ambition, competition, and emulation, which filtered into all segments of higher education. But higher education was not an independent variable; it did and had to respond creatively to the larger public that helped define its purposes, sustained its operations, and hired its graduates. Some important forces for uniformity came from the universities' ambient social culture, which exerted similar pressures on other aspects of contemporary American life, such as business, schooling, the professions, and the production of knowledge.

Two important shifts in higher education followed social trends rather closely. One was the *gradual* secularization of institutional leadership, except in Catholic colleges. Unlike their antebellum and even early-postbellum college counterparts, university presidents were increasingly chosen less for their personal religiosity or clerical collars than for their leadership, administrative, and fund-raising skills. The shift was inexorable but not immediate or wholesale. Many nonclerical presidents, public and private, were liberal

31 The Carnegie unit, described as "the epitome of academic accountancy," was a one-period high-school course carried for five days a week throughout the school year. Rudolph, *American College and University*, 438.

32 Curti and Nash, *Philanthropy*, 220–23; Ellen Condliffe Lagemann, *Private Power for the Public Good: A History of the Carnegie Foundation for the Advancement of Teaching* (Middletown, Conn.: Wesleyan University Press, 1983), ch. 3.

Protestants who tried to reconcile the new science with new, less authoritarian, forms of religious practice and moral discipline.[33] Until the early decades of the twentieth century, a few presidents of even state universities were either ministers or had studied theology without pursuing a clerical career. Such backgrounds stood them in good stead when their turn came to conduct morning chapel services, which several large state and private universities required as late as World War I.[34] But more made the daily services voluntary and moved them from dawn to mid-morning, before forgoing them altogether. At the large, public University of Minnesota in Minneapolis, the charismatic president Cyrus Northrop (1884–1911) conducted chapel daily for some 200 students at 10:30 a.m., thereby catching some of the many day students who lived off campus. Although he was a Yale College and Yale Law School graduate, former newspaper editor, and long-time Yale professor of English literature, he was said to have "sanctified" the "godless" institution left to him by his predecessor with a nonsectarian but effective "evangelical religion," formed in his Congregational home and a pre-college year in seminary.[35]

The decline of clerical leaders was also notable in the composition of the boards of trustees. Antebellum, particularly denominational, college boards were heavily freighted with clerical members, nearly 40 percent in 1860. But by 1930, clergymen were in very short supply, even in private colleges and universities, such as once-orthodox Yale, Wesleyan, Princeton, and Knox. On boards that averaged in size from the low to mid-twenties, clergymen fell to 7 percent, replaced by large numbers of businessmen, bankers, and lawyers, who made up nearly 75 percent of most boards in 1930.[36] The shift

33 Julie Reuben, *The Making of the Modern University: Intellectual Transformation and the Marginalization of Morality* (Chicago: University of Chicago Press, 1996).

34 Henry T. Claus, "The Problem of College Chapel," *Educational Review* (Sept. 1913), 172–87; Earle D. Ross, "Religious Influences in the Development of State Colleges and Universities," *Indiana Magazine of History* 46:4 (Dec. 1950), 343–62.

35 James Gray, *The University of Minnesota, 1851–1951* (Minneapolis: University of Minnesota Press, 1951), 83–85.

36 Earl. J. McGrath, "The Control of Higher Education," *Educational Record* 18:2 (April 1936), 259–72, at 264–65 (tables 1 and 2).

in membership did not reflect a rise in anticlericalism so much as a growing recognition that universities in particular were becoming large corporations involving ungodly numbers of buildings and grounds, budgets and endowments, often fractious personnel (students and faculty), and administrative, political, and public challenges, all of which needed expert help in their solution. From his almost 40-year experience running Harvard, President Eliot recommended as trustees successful business or professional men who were highly educated, public spirited, and, most of all, possessed of good judgment. In public universities, he noted, the key tasks of such trustees were to persuade legislatures and voters of the university's value, especially "its merits and defects in comparison with the universities of other States," and to align their institutions with the state's particular resources and industries.[37]

Two smaller groups also made their way onto governing boards. One was not surprising: major donors or their representatives.[38] After the death of her husband and co-founder in 1893, Mrs. Leland Stanford continued as the sole trustee of the university they had created from scratch at the edge of the foothills south of San Francisco. A nominal board of 24 trustees had been named by the Stanfords in 1885 and reduced to 15 in 1899, but they were "a shadowy body without powers or duties" except to consult when asked, which was seldom. Only in 1903 did she yield full legal power to the board, to which she was elected with alacrity and some (quiet) misgivings. Similarly, John D. Rockefeller, Jr., the Rev. Frederick Gates, and Thomas W. Goodspeed, all of whom were instrumental in persuading Rockefeller Senior to found the University of Chicago as the first great Baptist-inspired university in the country, served lengthy terms on its board during its first 25 years.[39]

37 Charles W. Eliot, *University Administration* (Boston: Houghton Mifflin, 1908), ch. 1.

38 Rudolph, *American College and University*, 426–27.

39 Orrin Leslie Elliott, *Stanford University: The First Twenty-Five Years* (Stanford, Calif.: Stanford University Press, 1937), 466–67; Thomas Wakefield Goodspeed, *A History of the University of Chicago: The First Quarter-Century* (Chicago: University of Chicago Press, 1972 [1916]), 468. See also Richard J. Storr, *Harper's University: The Beginnings* (Chicago: University of Chicago Press, 1966).

The other newcomers, particularly on private college boards, were alumni.[40] Many had already been elected by virtue of their loyalty to alma mater, wealth, or experience in running successful businesses. Since the early nineteenth century, alumni of older eastern colleges had been forming graduate societies to keep the current administrations on their toes, to keep matriculation-class members together, and to raise funds for students in need. Princeton had one in 1826 (whose first president was the past U.S. President James Madison), Yale the following year, which sold a life membership for $25.[41] As soon as graduates moved to big cities in sufficient numbers, alumni clubs sprang up there for the same purposes. The first Yale club formed in wartime Cincinnati in 1864, followed by 5 others two years later. Smaller Brown had 3 city clubs by 1870. By 1886 Princeton had 17 across the country.[42] In turn, unified alumni associations sought to enlist all former students, graduates and (especially wealthy) dropouts alike, for serious fund-raising and reunion conviviality.[43] The more money they raised for the universities' new annual funds and ambitious anniversary campaigns (both now permanent fixtures in every institution), the more they sought a voice in alma mater's policies and practices.

But only after the Civil War did private institutions yield to alumni pressure to reserve specific board seats for graduates. Williams College alumni won places in 1868, as did Yale and Union graduates three years later. Princetonians had to wait until 1889,

40 State university boards were typically chosen by voters or appointed by governors. Members were frequently alumni, but seats were not reserved specifically for alumni, which required legislation or even constitutional change.

41 Thomas Jefferson Wertenbaker, *Princeton, 1746–1896* (Princeton, N.J.: Princeton University Press, 1946), 181–82; [Lyman C. Bagg], *Four Years at Yale. By a Graduate of '69* (New Haven, Conn.: Charles C. Chatfield, 1871), 678–79.

42 Bagg, *Four Years at Yale*, 685; Judith Schiff, "The First Yale Club," *Yale Alumni Magazine* 78:1 (Sept.–Oct. 2014), 28; Martha Mitchell, *Encyclopedia Brunonia* (Providence, R.I.: Brown University Library, 1993), 40–41.

43 In a survey of sixteen large universities, the median year for installing salaried alumni secretaries was 1910 for eight midwestern state universities and 1919 for eight private eastern universities (seven future Ivy League schools and NYU). Earl James McGrath, *The Evolution of Administrative Offices in Institutions of Higher Education in the United States from 1860 to 1933* [summary of Ph.D. diss., Dept. of Education, 1936] (Chicago: University of Chicago Libraries, 1938), 182, 192.

when more recent graduates managed, with former president James McCosh's help, to replace some of the unprogressive "old fogeys" on the board. Eleven years later, reorganization gave five seats to alumni, who were elected to five-year terms from two eastern and three midwestern cities. The University of California did not reserve a seat for an alumnus on the board of regents until 1917, and he was the president of the alumni association, who served only ex officio.[44]

Similar events took place all across the American university landscape. In the newest institutions, the time line was merely compressed. Founded in 1891, Stanford (then misleadingly named Leland Stanford Junior College) had a San Francisco alumni association six years later and an alumni magazine to drum up support by 1899.[45] The newly founded University of Chicago made similar speed. Opened in the fall of 1892, Chicago could hardly wait to establish an association of alumni until it awarded its first 31 degrees the following June, quickly followed by separate associations for divinity graduates, Ph.D.s, and male and female graduates. Although a few alumni of the university's namesake predecessor had been given seats on the new board, its own graduates soon sought their own places. In 1914 they got them, in part because they had, since 1896, made large class gifts at commencement. The Chicagoans simply followed a practice by then widespread in older schools, where reuning (particularly the twenty-fifth- and fiftieth-year) classes competed vigorously to exceed the gifts of their predecessors.[46]

❀ ❀ ❀

Another recognizable feature of the Standard American University was the numerical and official presence of administration. As universities

44 Rudolph, *American College and University*, 428; Wayne Somers, comp. and ed., *Encyclopedia of Union College History* (Schenectady, N.Y.: Union College Press, 2003), 43, 747; Wertenbaker, *Princeton*, 332–33, 376–77; Verne A. Stadtman, *The University of California, 1868–1968* (New York: McGraw-Hill, 1970), 200.

45 Elliott, *Stanford*, 204–5.

46 Some classes succeeded by purchasing in their youth life-insurance policies and designating alma mater as the beneficiary. Rudolph, *American College and University*, 428–29.

grew in size and population trying to serve a diversity of "interests and emphases," they also sought a semblance of unity through "the refinements, the habits, and the certainties of organization."[47] With each new jump in enrollment, each new building erected, each new department hired, and each new professional school launched, the need for administrative oversight grew commensurately. Running an antebellum college of a few hundred students and faculty was one thing, coordinating a complex university of several thousand quite another. In 1860 the median number of administrative staff needed to run an American college was four; by 1933 it was 30.5.[48] Given the size of most early twentieth-century universities, administrative "bloat" (which is assailed today for helping to raise college costs at an unsustainable rate) was not an issue. So many new functions needed to be filled and new demands met that too few—not too many—administrators were the problem. With business-savvy trustees and tightfisted legislators overseeing university budgets, extravagant spending on non-instructional staff was rare.

And yet administrative positions proliferated as students demanded new services and predictability, faculty sought release from disciplinary and other management duties in order to conduct career-building research, the president and trustees needed new volumes of statistics and information from myriad sources in order to govern, and donors and alumni wanted to know, more specifically than ever before, if the institution was sound, efficient, and worth their investment of time and treasure. Small wonder that by 1940 there was in America's colleges and universities one administrative staffer for every ten students and four for every three professors.[49]

The pilothouse of university operations was, then as now, the president's businesslike *office* (no longer bookish *study*). When Nicholas Murray Butler moved into Columbia's in 1902, he inherited three secretaries, five stenographers, and two office boys.[50] Rather

47 Ibid., ch. 20, at 423.

48 Ibid., 435; McGrath, *Evolution of Administrative Offices*, 190.

49 *120 Years of American Education*, 67, 80 (table 26).

50 Six years later, Charles W. Eliot thought that a large-university president's office, like his own at Harvard, could get along with only 2 or 3 young alumni

than a displaced scholar, Butler was an incurable correspondent and publicist. In his first year he managed to spend $800 on first-class postage (at 2 cents an ounce), which news from his secretary must have daunted Ira Remsen, the world-class chemist and inquisitive new president of cosier Johns Hopkins.[51] But in the standard university of the time, the central administration sent out deputies in all directions, seeking to impose bureaucratic order upon the cascading transactions and paper generated in the university's moving and proliferating parts. Despite a few administrators who took their rules and themselves too seriously, the university's operational rule of thumb was "business means, but not business ends." Efficiency and thrift were certainly desirable, but a good president never let his professional staff forget that education, research, and public service were the paramount goals of the institution.[52]

William Rainey Harper, the University of Chicago's first president, was one of those true "Captains of Erudition" who not only wrote his university's founding objectives but lived and vigorously upheld them until the day he died in 1906 at the age of forty-nine. Before he was enticed from his Yale chair of Semitic languages by the senior Rockefeller, he had drafted an extensive plan for a bold new university, American-style. When the university was up and running, it had so many parts and offered so many services to so many constituencies that pundits dubbed it "Harper's Bazaar" and compared it to a department store.[53] It featured five main divisions: the University Proper (Arts and Sciences); Extension; Press; Affiliations (with numerous small midwestern colleges); and Libraries,

---

"secretaries" to handle correspondence and university communications, prepare trustee business, make appointments, and work on university publications. *University Administration*, 245–46.

51 Veysey, *Emergence of the American University*, 307; John C. French, *A History of the University Founded by Johns Hopkins* (Baltimore, Md.: Johns Hopkins Press, 1946), 143. Thanks to philatelist Don Noble for the price of stamps.

52 Veysey, *Emergence of the American University*, 353–54 (quotation); Eliot, *University Administration*, 29–30; Andrew S. Draper [President of the University of Illinois], "The University Presidency," *Atlantic Monthly* 97 (Jan. 1906), 34–43, at 36.

53 Veysey, *Emergence of the American University*, 311, 353, 377, 389; Goldin and Katz, "Shaping of American Higher Education," 46.

Laboratories, and Museums. Each division had a director, thus establishing the second echelon of administrators. The first rank below the president was held by three executive officers: examiner, recorder, and registrar. Junior and senior "colleges" (the first and second pairs of undergraduate years in lieu of the more standard four-class division) in four curricular divisions, two graduate schools (one for the sciences), and the various professional schools all had deans, who were supervised by a principal dean of the faculties.[54]

Necessity soon called into being a comptroller (later titled business manager), a nondenominational chaplain (although the university had inherited a Baptist divinity school), a treasurer, a legal counsel (often an experienced trustee), house heads for residence halls, and an auditor, a key appointment because the counsel and business manager had their offices in the downtown business district rather than on campus. Although the University of Chicago was not a business corporation, like every other SAU it had to be run like one as it grew and its business-bred trustees and donors made known their expectations for its lean and smooth operation.[55]

Trevor Arnett was a perfect find for the auditor's job. He had learned accounting in large corporations before matriculating in 1896. After he graduated in just two years and added a year of graduate work, President Harper, for whom he had prepared financial statements and memos while a student, hired him to head the accounting department. In 1901 he was elevated to auditor, one of the two leaders of the increasingly vital Business Department. His conduct of the university's business was so outstanding that word spread and he was often prevailed upon to give lessons to visitors and correspondents from other institutions. In 1915 the Rockefeller-funded General Education Board asked for and got him six months of release time to write a book, *College and University Finance*.[56] Needless to

54 The office of dean (usually "of the faculty") appeared by 1900 in all sixteen of the large eastern and midwestern universities studied by Earl McGrath; the median date was 1882. McGrath, *Evolution of Administrative Offices*, 79, 192.

55 Goodspeed, *History of the University of Chicago*, 136, 138–39, 154.

56 Ibid., 151, 193, 382–87; Trevor Arnett, *College and University Finance* (New York: General Education Board, 1922).

say, the hundred employees in the Business Department benefitted from his tutelage as did the many other number crunchers who read his work. This was but one of many ways that America's universities came to bear striking resemblances to each other.

❁ ❁ ❁

Once an administrative cabinet for a new university was chosen by the trustees and president, its immediate task was to begin the university's operations in a suitable and stable location. Uniquely in America, such an academic location is called a *campus*, a usage begun in the 1770s by Princeton's president John Witherspoon, who thought that his spacious, tree-lined college grounds resembled the *Campus Martius*, the ancient military exercise site near Rome. By 1900 the vast majority of American colleges and universities had adopted the name.[57] But by then, few universities were as compact and bucolic as Princeton. Their burgeoning enrollments mandated campuses and physical footprints of considerable size, whether the institution had grown by accretion over time or had been planned, funded, and built in a short period.

Urban universities faced unusual constraints on their physical planning and growth. The scarcity and high cost of space meant that university buildings had to be built up rather than out, like—and not too different from—their neighbors. Grass was rarer than concrete. In the 1890s, the brand-new University of Chicago and Columbia University when it moved uptown in New York both started out on four-block parcels and designed quarters to fit. Chicago chose three- to five-story Collegiate Gothic quadrangles, punctuated by a towered or turreted library, chapel, and dining commons. Columbia's simple Beaux-Arts edifices were less distinctive, save for a large domed and colonnaded library at the focal point of the campus. The

57 Paul Venable Turner, *Campus: An American Planning Tradition* (Cambridge, Mass.: MIT Press, 1984), 47; Albert Matthews, "The Term 'Campus' in American Colleges," *Publications of the Colonial Society of Massachusetts* 3: *Transactions, 1895–1897* (Boston, 1900), 431–37. In 1897 Matthews found that some 320 of 359 colleges and universities used the term to describe their grounds.

FIGURE 21. Chicago architect Henry Ives Cobb's 1893 master plan for the University of Chicago, crowded into a four-block site. Seven Collegiate Gothic quadrangles echoed Oxbridge as well as Trinity College in Hartford, Connecticut. In the center axis are the chapel and a building housing the university hall and library.

University of Minnesota was squeezed into an urban bluff on the Mississippi River and responded, like Columbia, with tall structures along neoclassical lines. The University of Pittsburgh solved its space problems for a time with the striking, 42-story, Cathedral of Learning in a style pundits called Girder Gothic.[58]

Universities built from scratch in non-urban settings had freer rein to fashion distinctive campus signatures. Like its major academic model, hilltop Cornell, Stanford enjoyed a large initial endowment—$20 million—which it could use to fabricate a new university in wide-open spaces.[59] The site was ex-governor Leland Stanford's

58 Jean F. Block, *The Uses of Gothic: Planning and Building the Campus of the University of Chicago, 1892–1932* (Chicago: University of Chicago Library, 1983); Turner, *Campus*, 176–78 (figs. 179–81), 197–98 (figs. 201–202), 237 (fig. 241); Robert C. Alberts, *Pitt: The Story of the University of Pittsburgh, 1787–1987* (Pittsburgh, Pa.: University of Pittsburgh University Press, 1986), 112–13.

59 One geographically challenged New York newspaper opined that the Stanford donation would be totally wasted in an "irreclaimable desert." Another said that "to attempt to create a great university Aladdin-like out of nothing but money is as useless as would be the building of . . . an institution for the relief of destitute ship-captains in

FIGURE 22. A 2008 aerial view of the Stanford University campus, with its distinctive sandstone buildings, red tile roofs, and Spanish Mission architectural signature. The large Memorial Church stands in the foreground. The 285-foot-tall Hoover Tower, built and named in 1941 for trustee and former U.S. President Herbert Hoover, looms on the right.

8,000-acre horse farm, located near the gently rolling foothills west of Palo Alto. Although he hired Frederick Law Olmstead from New York (where he had famously designed Central Park) to produce a master plan, the founder chose instead to situate his university on a level plain that would accommodate a quadrangular arrangement of buildings and multiple future additions. When classes opened in the fall of 1891, the handsome Inner Quadrangle, consisting of one-story,

the mountains of Switzerland." *Stanford Mosaic: Reminiscences of the First Seventy Years of Stanford University*, ed. Edith R. Mirrielees (Stanford, Calif.: Stanford University Press, 1962), 26; Elliott, *Stanford*, 76. For Cornell's academic and architectural development, see Carol Kammen, *Cornell: Glorious to View* (Ithaca, N.Y.: Cornell University Library, 2003).

FIGURE 23. In the devastating Portola (or San Francisco) earthquake of 1906, Stanford University suffered a great deal of damage to its relatively new buildings. Another casualty was the statue of scientist Louis Agassiz, which fell head-first off the facade of the zoology building into the concrete below. As students would, several shook his upside-down hand in passing.

Spanish Mission–style, arcaded, sandstone buildings under red-tile roofs, was operational, as nearby were two large dormitories (one for women) and ten clapboard houses for faculty families. Although the wife of the first registrar remembered that the university appeared at first sight "exactly like a factory," the first geologist's wife thought the Inner Quad was "like a gem in a coarse setting," with the surrounding grounds under dusty construction and the quad not yet planted with islands of palm and eucalyptus. The Stanford gem grew even bigger facets in the next few years with the addition of an outsized, frieze-wrapped memorial arch, a towering church, a domed neoclassical library, a multi-chimneyed chemistry building, and what became the largest privately owned museum in the country. Almost all of them were damaged—a few beyond repair—in the devastating Portola (popularly known as the San Francisco) earthquake of 1906.

Fortunately, the Farm (as the Stanford campus is still called) rebuilt and kept adding structures and greenery to create one of the most beautiful academic sites in the United States.[60]

In 1906 Harvard president Eliot described some of the resemblances and differences between American universities. He placed among the differences, which sprang less from the "historical development of policies and ideals" than from external circumstances, the various locations and looks of college campuses.[61] But he might well have regarded them as essentially similar because they were all campuses, seats of higher learning animated by special yet kindred "spirits of place" for their respective students, alumni, neighbors, and public admirers across the country. As a loyal and learned Princetonian noted in 1879, "There is no spell more powerful to recall the memories of college life than the word Campus."[62]

While their dominant styles or medleys of architecture may have differed, universities in the late nineteenth and early twentieth centuries chose their architectural signatures from a relatively small pattern book. The philanthropist who offered Harvard a million dollars to build a dormitory in "the Turkish style" didn't get to first base.[63] State universities often had to be satisfied with bland generic patterns bought from the lowest bidder. But well-endowed universities could usually afford to hire "name" architects from the most experienced eastern firms and to build durable buildings of beauty and efficiency according to the tastes of the times and forward-looking campus plans. If some university campuses turned into vast hodgepodges, others were regarded as "cities [of learning] beautiful."[64] They all had their nostalgic loyalists.

60 Turner, *Campus*, 169–72; Margo Davis and Roxanne Nilan, *The Stanford Album: A Photographic History, 1885–1945* (Stanford, Calif.: Stanford University Press, 1989), 51 (both quotations), 97–101, 113, 116–21; Thomas A. Gaines, in *The Campus as a Work of Art* (New York: Praeger, 1991), 122–26, 155, ranked Stanford highest on its list "Top Fifty Campuses."

61 Eliot, "American Universities," 117, 126.

62 Henry J. Van Dyke, Jr. quoted in Matthews, "The Term 'Campus,'" 436.

63 Richard P. Dober, *Campus Planning* (New York: Reinhold Publishing, 1964), 34.

64 Turner, *Campus*, ch. 5.

Two prominent features of every major university were the size and specialized function of its facilities. In response to the generalized bulge in enrolments, most university buildings, even football stadiums, were nothing short of monumental. The academic competition for prestige fueled the architectural "arms race" of the time as powerfully as it does today's buildups of athletic facilities and programs. Stanford's and Chicago's well-heeled construction campaigns were atypical only in the short time they were carried out. Other research universities may have spaced their constructions out a little longer, but their final products too were calculated to impress as well as to fill vital educational and research needs.

As the sciences gained new academic and economic importance and spawned new disciplines and specialties, large, efficient, and well-equipped laboratories were required to accommodate the new faculty's teaching and research. Stanford's 60,000-square-foot chemistry building, with its twenty-some ventilating chimneys, was touted as one of the country's biggest and best when it was completed in 1903. Typically, it did not share space with any of the other sciences, each of which had its own quarters. Large lecture classes required lecture halls bigger than the older recitation rooms still prevalent in liberal arts colleges. On rural and suburban campuses, the lack of sufficient off-campus housing necessitated the erection and maintenance of multi-story dormitories both for men and for women. (The "coed" dorm was a phenomenon of the last third of the twentieth century, not coincidentally post-1960s.) When classes began in 1891, Stanford's long and handsome four-story Encina Hall for men and three-story Roble Hall for women were luxuriously equipped with electric lights, steam heat, hot and cold running water, numerous baths (in which fresh*men* would soon be dunked by upper class hazers), and excellent yet inexpensive dining rooms. Their elevated and arched main entrances made for appealing publicity photos when filled with well-dressed denizens of each, especially when the latter would brag to anyone who would listen that they lived in the most modern dorms in America.[65]

65 Davis and Nilan, *Stanford Album*, 41–42, 52, 54; Richard Joncas, David J. Neuman, and Paul V. Turner, *Stanford University: The Campus Guide*, 2nd ed. (New York:

❁ ❁ ❁

The academic buildings that felt the greatest pressure of numbers were libraries. As faculties continued to subdivide their disciplines and to carve out new specialties, books and other research materials needed to be purchased all over the world to accommodate their teaching (which emphasized more investigation than regurgitation) and their own recondite research. As classes required more demanding and discovery-based homework, the demand for library reference collections and study space increased, as did greater access to the stacks themselves. At the same time, the national and global explosion of knowledge resulted in a tremendous fallout of books, research reports, and journals, which begged to be purchased, catalogued, and housed in America's leading research libraries.[66] Since librarians were famously poor prognosticators of the volume of future publications and requisite space requirements, their best-laid plans for buildings had to be upgraded time and time again. When Princeton built the state-of-the-art, hollow-quadrangular, five-level Pyne Library in 1897, it was expected to serve the newly named university for at least a century. It was outgrown in only 28 years.[67]

On the West Coast, the University of California (Berkeley) needed a much larger specialized library to replace the combined art and library building, which had been built in 1881, as early as 1900. In that year, when the one-floor library held only 80,000 books (half as many as Michigan, one-seventh as many as Harvard), President Wheeler told the governor that California faculty who undertook "work of first-rate value" in the humanities and even in natural

---

Princeton Architectural Press, 2006 [1999]), 44–46; Cecil Mortimer Marrack, "Stanford University—The Real and the Ideal," *Sunset Magazine* (Dec. 1902), in Stone and DeNevi, *Portraits of the American University*, 99–100. Small wonder that Encina was grand: its plan was suggested to Mr. Stanford by a favorite lakeside resort in Austria. Elliott, *Stanford*, 37.

66 Arthur T. Hamlin, *The University Library in the United States: Its Origins and Development* (Philadelphia: University of Pennsylvania Press, 1981), chs. 3–4; Kenneth J. Brough, *Scholar's Workshop: Evolving Conceptions of Library Service* (Urbana: University of Illinois Press, 1953).

67 Axtell, *Making of Princeton University*, 440–43.

FIGURE 24. By 1920, the handsome neoclassical Doe Memorial Library (1911) at the University of California, Berkeley had already expanded once. Because of its monumental design, however, much of its expansion had to take place beneath the site and under surrounding green areas. In 2014 it held more than 11.5 million volumes, the fourth-largest university collection in the United States.

science found it necessary to "remove for some considerable period to the seat of an eastern or European library." "Here," he exhorted, "more than any university in the country, a great library is needed and deserved." In 1911 he finally got one in the impressive white granite, neoclassical Doe Library. But in less than six years, it, too, needed expansion, which it got again in 1927. Other libraries that emulated its scale and features, such as Harvard (1914), Michigan (1920), and Minnesota (1924), soon discovered that their buildings too were "frozen," incapable of significant exterior additions.[68] New libraries were the only solution.

68 Stadtman, *University of California*, 108–10, 211 (quotation); Kenneth G. Peterson, *The University of California Library at Berkeley, 1900–1945* (Berkeley: University of California Press, 1970), 89–99, 101. Cornell's Sage Library, built in 1892 for 400,000 volumes, was chockablock with twice as many by 1934. Rita Guerlac, "Cornell's Library," *Cornell Library Journal*, no. 2 (Spring 1967), 1–33, at 22.

Inter-university rivalries and the national spread of the student extracurriculum promoted monumentalism also in athletic facilities. Large gymnasiums for both sexes, running tracks, swimming pools, and playing fields all found early places on the new research campuses. After making do with ersatz, often dirt, football fields for several years, Stanford and California raced each other to rear giant stadiums around grassy gridirons to accommodate not only their thousands of students but also the tens of thousands of alumni and public fans who clamored for seats to view the state's annual Big Game. Stanford finished first in 1921 with a 60,000-seat, open-ended oval based on that at Pompeii (but lost the game convincingly, 42–7); additions soon raised its capacity to nearly 90,000. Not to be totally outdone by an academic upstart, California completed its own 75,000-seater two years later and celebrated with another thumping of the Cardinal Red. Both put to shame Harvard's 1903 U-shaped steel-and-concrete "Grecian" stadium around Soldier's Field. As reported in the partisan *Overland Monthly*, the vociferous spectators for the first Harvard-Yale grudge match numbered only 38,400, some standing or in a temporary bleacher in the U's opening. Although Yale in its new "Roman" coliseum—the Yale Bowl—lost *its* first Big Game (36–0) in 1914, it could boast that 32,000 more fans viewed the (lopsided) action.[69]

❁ ❁ ❁

At the center of America's research universities, the professoriate, for all their individual peculiarities, underwent its own measure of standardization. Rather than teachers first and scholars sometimes, as in the smaller liberal arts colleges, the new university professors were scholar-teachers, with increasing emphasis on the *scholar*. After 1890

69 *Chronology of Stanford University*, 54–55; Joncas, Neuman, and Turner, *Stanford*, 64–65; Stadtman, *University of California*, 288; George P. Morris, "The Harvard Stadium," *Overland Monthly* (May 1903), in Stone and DeNevi, *Portraits of the American University*, 344–45; Vincent Scully, Catherine Lyman, Erik Vogt, and Paul Goldberger, *Yale in New Haven: Architecture & Urbanism* (New Haven, Conn.: Yale University, 2004), 20–21 (fig. 9), 203–204 (figs. 188–89); Brooks Mather Kelly, *Yale: A History* (New Haven, Conn.: Yale University Press, 1974), 302–303. For more on the standardized extracurriculum, see below, pp. 310–11.

university teaching became a bona fide profession, not just a personal calling or sometime job. For admission to its ranks, a Ph.D. was required or imminent. As late as 1884, a small minority of university faculty had earned the magical three letters: only 19 of Harvard's 189, only 6 of Michigan's 88. By 1900, virtually all professors brandished them more proudly than Phi Beta Kappa keys. Honorary doctorates from one's own institution, which had flooded the commencement market in the 1870s and '80s, were replaced by the real thing in the 1890s and beyond with the help of energetic graduate schools at Johns Hopkins, Clark, Yale, and Chicago and the continuing draw of German universities.[70]

Rather than being wholly subject to the personal standards of presidents or non-academic trustees, the new professors became members of self-governing scholarly disciplines and largely autonomous academic departments. Their fissile disciplines began to coalesce as national associations after the American Philological Association formed in 1869.[71] The chemists came together in 1876, followed closely by the devotees of modern languages and literatures (1883), history (1884), economics (1885), mathematics (1888), and geology (1888). At their annual meetings they read and listened to learned papers, hired colleagues, recruited graduate students, and flew their institutional colors at dinners, "smokers," and business meetings. At each encounter they were reminded of the shared standards and best

70 Rudolph, *American College and University*, 395–97; Stephen Edward Epler, *Honorary Degrees: A Survey of Their Use and Abuse* (Washington, D.C.: American Council on Public Affairs, 1943), 59–68.

71 In 1893 Chicago's biology department split into 5 new departments: botany, zoology, anatomy, neurology, and physiology. The antebellum "moral philosophy" course spawned several of the modern social sciences, just as philology gave rise to many of the modern humanities. Goodspeed, *History of the University of Chicago*, 322; Jon H. Roberts and James Turner, *The Sacred and Secular University* (Princeton, N.J.: Princeton University Press, 2000), chs. 2, 4; Gladys Bryson, "The Emergence of the Social Sciences from Moral Philosophy," *International Journal of Ethics* 42 (1932), 304–23; Dorothy Ross, "The Development of the Social Sciences," in Alexandra Oleson and John Voss, eds., *The Organization of Knowledge in Modern America, 1860–1920* (Baltimore, Md.: Johns Hopkins University Press, 1979), 107–38; James Turner, *Philology: The Forgotten Origins of the Modern Humanities* (Princeton, N.J.: Princeton University Press, 2014).

practitioners of their peer group's distinctive methodologies, theories, and crafts. When they returned to their home campuses, they applied those standards to their department colleagues who applied for promotions, pay raises, course reductions, and, later in the twentieth century, permanent tenure.[72]

Although university faculty were expected to teach well (at least conscientiously), they were judged primarily and increasingly on the quality and quantity of their published research. As Chicago president Harper told his inaugural faculty, he expected from everyone "honest and persistent effort in the direction of contribution to the world's knowledge."[73] Most of the top universities assisted their faculties by encouraging research and its publication in several ways. One was the financing of departmental journals or research serials, variably called "studies," "transactions," or "contributions." Soon after its founding in 1876, Johns Hopkins showed the way with national journals of mathematics (1878), chemistry (1879), and philology (1880). Chicago launched seven journals in its first nine years. By 1904, Columbia's ambitious faculty could announce their findings in 35 serial publications. Not to be left too far behind in eastern dust, California began to publish series of publications in anthropology, botany, zoology, and philology.[74] As both faculty and administrators realized, without specialized research, there would be no departments, no department chairs, no internal hierarchies—only an undifferentiated assemblage of teachers whose local reputations could not attract graduate students, outside research funding, or

72 In most universities, continuous faculty employment up through the professorial ranks was assumed, unless a powerful president saw fit to terminate a junior member. In 1940, however, the American Association of University Professors, formed in 1915, issued a revised statement of principles. These spelled out the still-current "up or out" policy, namely, that after a probationary period of no more than seven years, full-time faculty "should have permanent or continuous tenure." Wilson Smith and Thomas Bender, eds., *American Higher Education Transformed, 1940–2005: Documenting the National Discourse* (Baltimore, Md.: Johns Hopkins University Press, 2008), 455–58, at 456.

73 Goodspeed, *History of the University of Chicago*, 319 (1894).

74 Geiger, *To Advance Knowledge*, 23–24 (table 1), 32–33 (table 2); Rudolph, *American College and University*, 405–406.

institutional bragging rights accruing from the new national rankings of graduate departments.[75]

To help their professors get to the point of publication, SAUs offered paid and unpaid leaves for special occasions (such as counters to offers from rival "raiders") and at least partially paid sabbaticals every seventh year.[76] Research leaves could also be used by winners of prestigious fellowships offered by such new Maecenases as the National Research Council (est. 1916), the American Council of Learned Societies (est. 1919), the Social Science Research Council (est. 1923), and the John Simon Guggenheim Memorial Foundation (est. 1923). To help in the preparation of manuscripts, the universities supplied would-be authors with newfangled typewriters or with secretaries who knew how to tame them.

Once complete, book manuscripts were ferried across campus, town, or country to university presses, which had been established by the larger universities with deeper pockets. In its current advertisements, Cornell claims to be "America's First University Press," which it was in 1869. But it closed operations in 1884 and did not reopen until 1930. The University of Pennsylvania Press (incorporated in 1890) also opened and closed—twice—before resuming business in 1927, leaving Johns Hopkins University Press as the oldest, continuously operating iteration in the country. It was founded in 1878 by President Gilman only two years after the university was founded, although it didn't publish its first book (as opposed to journals) until 1887. Chicago, as we have seen, opened a press as one of its five main academic divisions in 1891. Many other universities followed the leaders because they realized that presses were "an indispensable component of the modern research university."[77]

75 Webster, *Academic Quality Rankings*, ch. 15. The first national ranking was *A Study of the Graduate Schools of America* (Oxford, Ohio, 1925), by Raymond M. Hughes.

76 Harvard offered the first (half-paid) sabbatical in 1880. Veysey, *Emergence of the American University*, 175; Walter Crosby Eells and Ernest V. Hollis, *Sabbatical Leave in American Higher Education: Origin, Early History, and Present Practice,* Bulletin 1962, no. 17 (Washington, D.C.: U.S. Dept. of Health, Education, and Welfare, Office of Education, 1962); Bruce A. Kimball, "The Origin of the Sabbath and Its Legacy to the Modern Sabbatical," *Journal of Higher Education* 49:4 (July–Aug. 1978), 303–15.

77 Peter Givler, "University Press Publishing in the United States," in Richard E. Abel and Lyman W. Newlin, eds., *Scholarly Publishing: Books, Journals, Publishers, and*

❀ ❀ ❀

The new faculties' research agendas did not release them from old, and new teaching duties. In 1906, Yale's president, Arthur Hadley, warned the AAU representatives at their annual meeting that "senior research professorships" were a bad idea, not only for the students, who would miss their holders' exemplary guidance and sharing of fresh discoveries, but also for their younger colleagues, who would be relegated to introductory courses and shut out of research work and advanced courses in which to build their own competence and originality. He may have worried needlessly because most universities expected their faculty to teach and research symbiotically. The advent of the elective system and then majors made it possible for faculty both to teach to their strengths and to pursue research to enhance them. Those who did spend extra time in the lab, museum, archives, or observatory could find some relief by teaching a course or two fewer or by handling larger numbers in lecture courses.[78]

At big research-rich universities like Berkeley, alumni memories of great teachers were formed predominantly in large lectures. Although it had 10,000 students in 1920, making it "the largest university in the world," the future biographer and novelist Irving Stone remembered that "we were trained from the outset to compensate for size, to avail ourselves of the privileges that came from the extensive facilities and faculty." If classes appeared "large and impersonal" to some, "it was the tradition of great lecturing . . . that alone made it possible for a university as large as Berkeley to stimulate as many minds as it did." Without teaching awards or course reductions, most of Berkeley's best lecturers were also said to be its best scholars.[79]

Libraries in the Twentieth Century (New York: Wiley, 2002), ch. 6 (107–20), at 108; John Higham, "University Presses and Academic Specialization," *Scholarly Publishing* 10:1 (Oct. 1978), 36–44.

78 Arthur T. Hadley, "To What Extent Should Professors Engaged in Research Be Relieved from the Work of Instruction?" *Educational Review* 31 (April 1906), 325–32.

79 Irving Stone and Jean Stone, eds., *There Was Light: Autobiography of a University. A Collection of Essays by Alumni of the University of California, Berkeley, 1868–1996* (Berkeley: University of California, 2002 [1970, 1996]), 95, 131, 324, 333–34.

Although SAU students (predominantly coed) came in every imaginable size, age, IQ, race, ethnicity, and national origin (foreign students from Europe, Asia, and Latin America), several of their college experiences and routines were as standardized as the faculty's. The Americans were admitted after collecting a certain number of Carnegie units in high or prep school and passing a written institutional exam or earning high enough scores on the new College Entrance Examination Board (est. 1900) exams (which led to the now-dreaded Scholastic Aptitude Tests [SATs] in 1926).[80] As they registered at their new alma maters, they began their education in the arcana of credit hours, quarter or semester calendars, standard-length class periods (truncated by ten or fifteen minutes to get to the next class), required courses or electives, open courses or those with prerequisites, lab requirements, majors and minors, honors programs, and degree possibilities.

If the curriculum and its myriad regulations were handed down to the students from on high, undergraduates were resourceful and resolute in shaping their own *extra*curricula out of age-group materials that enjoyed national currency. The way they talked and dressed, the things they read and listened to on the new phonograph and radio, and the organizations they formed and joined wove patterns that covered America's campuses with surprising speed.[81]

80 Nicholas Lemann, *The Big Test: The Secret History of the American Meritocracy* (New York: Farrar, Straus, and Giroux, 1999). Numerous qualified students, however, were not admitted to several elite eastern universities, particularly in the 1920s and '30s. Jews and Blacks were discriminated against the most by the Big Three and Columbia. Princeton and Yale also barred women from their classes until 1970. Harvard, Columbia, and Brown had coordinate colleges for women even longer. Marcia Graham Synnott, *The Half-Opened Door: Discrimination and Admissions at Harvard, Yale, and Princeton, 1900–1970* (Westport, Conn.: Greenwood Press, 1979); Jerome Karabel, *The Chosen: The Hidden History of Admission and Exclusion at Harvard, Yale, and Princeton* (Boston: Houghton Mifflin, 2005).

81 Rudolph, *American College and University*, ch. 7; Fass, *Damned and the Beautiful*; Horowitz, *Campus Life*; Levine, *American College*, ch. 6; Robert Cooley Angell, *The Campus: A Study of Contemporary Undergraduate Life in the American University* (New York: D. Appleton and Co., 1928); Deirdre Clemente, *Dress Casual: How College Students Redefined American Style* (Chapel Hill: University of North Carolina Press, 2014).

College students have long created their own jargon and slang, as if to guard their thoughts, feelings, and fears from adults, officialdom, and each other. As early as 1851, the recent Harvard graduate Benjamin Hall compiled *A Collection of College Words and Customs* from England and the United States; five years later he revised and enlarged it into a 500-page book. Although he leaned heavily on sources at Harvard, Yale, Princeton, Williams, and Union, he also drew from colleges as far away as Indiana, Kentucky, and South Carolina.[82] Folklore, legends, and other traditions have also migrated from one campus to another to be absorbed into the local culture. In 1901 Professor Henry D. Sheldon of the University of Oregon published a 388-page study of *Student Life and Customs* in medieval, German, English, Scottish, and American colleges and universities. His detailed coverage included matriculation-class systems, fraternities and sororities, athletics, honor systems, hazing, debating societies, religious societies such as the YMCA, and several forms of student self-government.[83] Depending on their intellectual proclivities when they were asked to write them, alumni memoirs of university life often devoted as much or more attention to their extracurricular educations as to the "life of the mind" that faculty had hoped to cultivate, or at least seed.[84]

82 B. H. Hall, *A Collection of College Words and Customs* (Cambridge, Mass.: John Bartlett, 1856 [1851]). More recently, the University of North Carolina linguist Connie Eble has devoted most of her career to the scholarly study of college slang and its uses. Her short descriptive handbook, *College Slang 101* (Georgetown, Conn.: Spectacle Lane Press, 1989), was followed by a longer, more analytical, treatment, *Slang & Sociability: In-Group Language among College Students* (Chapel Hill: University of North Carolina Press, 1996).

83 Henry D. Sheldon, *Student Life and Customs*, International Education Series 51 (New York: D. Appleton, 1901). More recent additions to the literature are Simon J. Bronner's two rich volumes, *Piled Higher and Deeper: The Folklore of Campus Life* (Little Rock, Ark.: August House, 1990) and *Campus Traditions: Folklore from the Old-Time College to the Modern Mega-University* (Jackson: University Press of Mississippi, 2012), and Horowitz, *Campus Life*.

84 Mirrielees, *Stanford Mosaic*; Hugh Garnett Davis, *A Memoir of Union College Life, 1903–1907*, ed. C. William Huntley (Schenectady, N.Y.: Union College, 1989); Ashbel Green, ed., *My Columbia: Reminiscences of University Life* (New York: Columbia University, 2005); Carolyn B. Matalene and Katherine C. Reynolds, eds., *Carolina*

❁ ❁ ❁

The rise of ambitious, large, and populous universities depended on a steady stream of ample funding. As President A. Lawrence Lowell, Harvard's ace fund-raiser, warned in 1920, "of the needs of a university, there is, indeed, no end."[85] It mattered little whether the majority of funds came from private endowments, which thrived on good economic conditions and favorable tax laws, or from state appropriations, which grew along with rising populations, prosperity, and tax bases. Private donations and endowments were vital to both. And while older, eastern schools depended more heavily than the public schools on tuition and fees to complement endowment proceeds, state universities depended as much as the privates on foundation, donor, and alumni generosity. As the Michigan president James B. Angell reminded those who attended his inaugural in 1871, "Let it not be thought that the aid furnished by the States leaves no room for munificence."[86] Over time, the revenues of the top universities in each category were quite similar and competitive, as were their academic results. President Eliot of well-heeled and not overly modest Harvard admitted in 1906 that "it would be hard to prove that any important difference in discipline, educational policy, or scholarly ambition and gain, correspond with or accompany" the difference in the major source of income. "The two sorts of university will," he predicted accurately, "both serve the country greatly, maintaining a fine rivalry in scholarship and serviceableness."[87]

Voices: Two Hundred Years of Student Experiences (Columbia: University of South Carolina Press, 2001); Diana Dubois, ed., *My Harvard, My Yale* (New York: Random House, 1982); Jeffrey L. Lant, ed., *Our Harvard: Reflections on College Life by Twenty-Two Distinguished Graduates* (New York: Taplinger Publishing Co., 1982); Alfred de Grazia, *The Student at Chicago in Hutchins' Hey-Day* (Princeton. N.J.: Quiddity Press, 1991).

85 Harvard University, *President's Report* (1920), 33, quoted in Geiger, *To Advance Knowledge*, 56. During his presidential tenure (1909–33), Lowell's gift of "the ask" pushed Harvard's endowment from $22 million to over $128 million, which included a few million of his own. Curti and Nash, *Philanthropy*, 138, 140.

86 Quoted in Curti and Nash, *Philanthropy*, 187.

87 Eliot, "American Universities," 133–34; Geiger, *To Advance Knowledge*, 41; Cohen and Kisker, *Shaping of American Higher Education*, 174.

Building and operating funds flowed to all of the nation's research universities through many of the same channels. To judge by the growth of the endowments of sixteen top schools between 1899 and 1939, the channels were clear and ran smoothly. In all four decades, including the Depression Thirties, only two endowments managed to lose value, each once in a different decade.[88] In the five best state universities, state appropriations followed the same rising curve.[89] A few universities, such as Chicago, Clark, Stanford, Vanderbilt, and Johns Hopkins were fortunate enough to be founded by huge donations from multimillionaires, who tended to be less interested in underwriting ongoing operations and maintenance than in new buildings. That's where a much larger pool of smaller donors stepped in to raise or maintain the new institutions' bottom lines. Some were one-time givers—local businessmen seeking good will or an inside track to work-related research, will-drafting widows whose lawyers slyly mentioned their own alma maters, and heirless widowers. Since most presidents and trustees were no longer members of the frugal clerical class, they, too, were easy targets. Even a few "old-money" faculty were known to indirectly subsidize their own modest salaries by contributing generously to the annual campaigns.[90]

But the biggest targets were the thousands of alumni whose campus experiences made them grateful, nostalgic, or simply annoyed that the football team didn't win more games. The frequent publication of alumni magazines (from 1900 to 1940, Princeton published a *weekly* during the academic year), the creation of alumni secretaries

88 Geiger, *To Advance Knowledge*, 276–77 (app. D).

89 Only in Wisconsin in 1937 did the state contribution fail to exceed the 1929 appropriation. Cornell was fortunate in 1937 to receive $2.8 million from New York State to offset a $23,000 dip in endowment income. Geiger, *To Advance Knowledge*, 273–75 (app. C).

90 Chicago president Harper's close study of faculty pay at a representative sample of colleges, professional schools, and smaller state universities in 1893 strongly suggested that only full professors at the larger institutions (especially those not included in the sample) received decent salaries and even they were far from overpaid. Instructors and assistant professors were as poorly paid and badly treated as untenured adjuncts are in 2015. Harper thought that raising all faculty salaries 50 percent would not be unreasonable. W. R. Harper, "The Pay of American College Professors," *Forum* (Sept. 1893), 96–109.

and development offices, and elaborate rosters of class officers, reunion organizers, and other boosters paved the way for standardized, professionalized, fund-raising.[91]

The university's preference for all donations was that they be unrestricted as to purpose. But many donors had specific—restricted—goals in mind, such as named athletic fields or gyms, dedicated reading rooms, concert-quality auditoriums, or even anonymous endowments for ice cream or fresh orange juice to please the student palate. Several large foundations were similarly interested in restricted—and selective—generosity. They wanted to raise the "peaks" of the top universities by providing additions to endowment and venture capital for adventurous research that might pay inventive or intellectual dividends.[92] They, too, had professional staffs to select recipients with the most potential. Although foundations gave away some $220 million ($3.7 billion in 2015) by 1938, the majority of colleges and universities did not benefit. In the flush 1920s, the five largest foundations, including Carnegie and Rockefeller, gave 86 percent of their grants to just 36 institutions, all well-known, yet still hungry, "haves."[93] That America's best universities before 1940 succeeded in financing most of their ambitions is confirmed by their secure positions at the top of the most recent rankings.[94]

❁ ❁ ❁

When students, faculty, and administrators did their jobs, their academic-year-end celebrations were also remarkably standardized.

91 Rudolph, *American College and University*, 428–30; Geiger, *To Advance Knowledge*, 126–29; Curti and Nash, *Philanthropy*, 201–11. Yale's alumni magazine was the first, in 1891.

92 Jesse Brundage Sears, *Philanthropy in the History of American Higher Education* (New Brunswick, N.J.: Transaction Publishers, 1990 [1922]), ch. 5; Curti and Nash, *Philanthropy*, 191–98, 214, ch. 10, at 227; Geiger, *To Advance Knowledge*, ch. 4, at 161. See also John R. Thelin and Richard W. Trollinger, *Philanthropy and American Higher Education* (New York: Palgrave Macmillan, 2014).

93 Curti and Nash, *Philanthropy*, 222–23, 227.

94 Goldin and Katz, "The Shaping of Higher Education," 38, 54. See the prologue above, p. 000–00.

Commencements, baccalaureates, hoodings, and other ceremonies took on a predictable sameness across the institutional spectrum. After the 1895 conference in New York to regularize the academic costume for Princeton's splashy 150th anniversary and baptism as a true university the following year, caps, gowns, and hoods conformed to a negotiated code of colors, shapes, and designs while allowing each institution a few saving signs of individuality.[95] Whether caps were flat or floppy, gowns black or colored, the sartorial vocabulary turned lingua franca with time and tradition.[96] The collective award of *degrees* by presidential decree morphed into the presentation of individual *diplomas*, suitable for framing.[97] Most were in English, but colleges and universities bent on signaling their long learned ancestry resorted to Latin, all the more impressive if neither graduate nor family could read it. In the stately wash of processions, music, speeches, prizes to the brightest and best, and honorary degrees to academic eminences, major donors, or public celebrities, the graduates might well feel elated yet also humbled by the venerable pageantry playing out on their stages.

But most graduates in those early decades felt nothing like "standard" parts in America's emerging greatness of academic size and quality. At home, despite the Great Depression, their educations would launch the great majority of them into the middle class or higher. By 1940, degrees from America's best universities were recognized and honored around the globe, the fulfillment of the AAU's forty-year mission; indeed, foreigners flocked to them for credentials in rising numbers. Those universities had surpassed their one-time models in Germany, whose political leaders had just ignited a world war that would, ironically, propel the United States to even greater prominence in higher education and research.

95 See above ch. 5, p. 274–75.

96 David A. Lockmiller, *Scholars on Parade: Colleges, Universities, Costumes and Degrees* (London: Collier-Macmillan, 1969).

97 Once Johns Hopkins University designed a seal in 1885, it immediately put it on diplomas for its graduates. It had conferred degrees since 1878 but without a special piece of "parchment" to certify the act. Gowns and hoods had to wait for official sanction until 1892. French, *History of Johns Hopkins*, 365–70.

CHAPTER SEVEN

Multiversities and Beyond

The envy of the planet

ANNE MATTHEWS

THE HISTORY OF the American university pivoted decisively during and after the Second World War. Before the war, the Great Depression had eroded university income, new building, faculty salaries and morale, and graduate employment, everything but enrollments. Research was largely initiated and financed within house and conducted in the interstices of teaching and service (to institution and scholarly discipline). Even at Harvard, according to President Nathan Pusey (who must have exaggerated for effect), pre-war research used to be "a kind of professorial avocation." After the war, research became "a major joint enterprise with teaching" and often dominant.[1] More important, it became embedded in a national "ecosystem of research" that depended increasingly on federal and (comparatively decreasing) philanthropic support for basic research, industry for its technological development, and the military for both.[2]

The institutions that took full advantage of these trends achieved superiority among the nation's, indeed the world's, universities. They became known and were universally regarded as the premier producers and purveyors of knowledge in a world irrevocably beholden to new knowledge for its wealth, health, and wisdom—for the

1 Morton Keller and Phyllis Keller, *Making Harvard Modern: The Rise of America's University* (New York: Oxford University Press, 2001), 187.

2 Committee on New Models for U.S. Science & Technology Policy, American Academy of Arts and Sciences, *Restoring the Foundation: The Vital Role of Research in Preserving the American Dream: Report Brief* (Cambridge, Mass.: AAAS, 2014), 11.

essentials of its well-being and progress.[3] And once they earned top ranking, they were very hard to dislodge. Ambitious, often public, newcomers sometimes gave the predominantly private leaders a run for their money, but the familiar names seldom dropped out of the elite company they had long kept.[4]

America's research universities emerged from the war strong because the United States itself did. An ocean away from the carnage and destruction in Europe, the technically neutral United States had time to prepare for war between September 1939, when Nazi Germany invaded France and Poland, and December 1941, when the Japanese attacked the U.S. naval base at Pearl Harbor, Hawaii. This build-up did much to end the Depression sooner than elsewhere, and America's wartime production helped to make the United States the world's leading economy for the rest of the century and into the next. Moreover, no American cities, universities, or libraries were bombed or destroyed during the war, as they were so tragically in Europe and Asia.

One month after the United States declared war on the Axis countries, more than a thousand college presidents met to pledge "the total strength of our colleges and universities" to the nation's cause and to define some of the institutions' needs to fulfill their pledge. Besides endorsing the principle of the Selective Service draft of young males, they promised to accelerate academic programs, teach year-round if necessary, cope with teacher shortages, maintain academic standards in admissions and the granting of credit for

3 In 1958, the production, distribution, and consumption of knowledge in all its forms accounted for nearly 29 percent of the U.S. gross national product. From 1960 to 1980, it grew to 34 percent. In both periods it grew at about twice the rate of the rest of the economy. Fritz Machlup, *The Production and Distribution of Knowledge in the United States* (Princeton, N.J.: Princeton University Press, 1962); Michael Rogers Rubin and Mary Taylor Huber, *The Knowledge Industry in the United States, 1960–1980* (Princeton, N.J.: Princeton University Press, 1986).

4 David S. Webster, *Academic Quality Rankings of American Colleges and Universities* (Springfield, Ill.: Thomas, 1986); Webster, "America's Highest Ranked Graduate Schools, 1925–1982," *Change* 15 (May–June 1983), 14–24; Hugh Davis Graham and Nancy Diamond, *The Rise of American Research Universities: Elites and Challengers in the Postwar Era* (Baltimore, Md.: Johns Hopkins University Press, 1997).

military experience, and promote the physical fitness of students. In return they sought federal aid to facilitate acceleration and occupational deferments for selected graduate and professional students.[5]

America's universities lost large numbers of students—and therefore income—to military service and numerous faculty to wartime assignments in government, the military, and high-priority research in other university and federal laboratories.[6] But the losses were quickly reduced, though never eliminated, by the advent of military training programs conducted on college campuses. Between 1939 and 1944, the federal government spent $97 million ($636 million in 2015 dollars) in contracts with 660 institutions to provide specialized training and occasionally general or liberal education to officer candidates, navigators, cartographers, and a host of other vocational trainees in the armed forces, particularly the army and navy. Many of the same institutions were designated Key Centers of Information and Training by the U.S. Office of Education to provide education for adult civilians in such areas as first aid, air-raid detection, blood donation, democratic institutions, Western history, and international relations. The importance of federal funds during the straitened war years is suggested by their growth as "educational and general purpose" income of the cooperating institutions. In 1939–40, government dollars covered a mere 5.4 percent of that income; by 1943–44, they contributed nearly 36 percent to both public and private institutions.[7]

The refashioning of college campuses for military students, instructors, and training for two or three years captured the attention of the media and freshmen green from school. Uniformed cadets marching in platoons to class, saluting their instructors, digging foxholes in the playing fields, and enduring unsporting physical

5 David D. Henry, *Challenges Past, Challenges Present: An Analysis of American Higher Education since 1930* (San Francisco: Jossey-Bass, 1975), 40–41. Henry (1905–95) had served as president of Wayne University in Detroit through the G.I. Bill years (1945–52) and of the University of Illinois for sixteen years (1955–71).

6 Almost a third of Princeton's 358 full-time faculty left for military service or defense work. Three-quarters of the physics department was involved in atomic research. Richard D. Challener, "The Response to War," *Princeton History* no. 11 (1992), 48–65, at 63.

7 Henry, *Challenges Past*, 42, 87–88.

conditioning could be—and soon were—taken in stride as the cost of war and the price of peace. But the relatively brief militarization of America's campuses had fewer lasting effects on the universities than did the tsunamic return of veterans from the wars in Europe, North Africa, Asia, the Atlantic, and the Pacific and the continued engagement and accelerated investment of the federal government in the conduct of academic research.

❋ ❋ ❋

In June 1944, well before the war ended, Congress passed the Servicemen's Readjustment Act, partly to forestall a postwar depression and the potentially volatile demobilization of 15 million servicemen and women into a civilian economy not equipped to absorb them. But the American Legion and other advocates also emphasized that the nation owed the veterans of the largest and costliest war in history all the help it could give—not as charity, but as a solemn obligation. Thus the G.I. Bill of Rights (as the law quickly became known) ensured that returning veterans—of all races, ethnicities, and religions—were offered immediate unemployment compensation for up to a year and a cost-free choice of job training, farm training, high-school completion, or up to four years of higher education in the very best colleges and universities that would take them (and most institutions tipped the scales in their favor).[8] Forty-one percent attended just 38 elite schools; the other 59 percent were spread among 712 accredited but less prestigious institutions. As *Time* magazine archly asked, "Why go to Podunk College when the Government will send you to Yale?" During the ten active years of the program, 2,232,000 vets (including 64,728 women) attended college. Until the G.I. Bill came along, 446,400 of them said they had never dreamed of or planned for college.[9]

8 Michael J. Bennett, *When Dreams Came True: The GI Bill and the Making of Modern America* (Washington, DC: Brassey's, 1996), 255, 261–62.

9 Henry, *Challenges Past*, 63; Keith W. Olson, *The G.I. Bill, the Veterans, and the Colleges* (Lexington: University Press of Kentucky, 1974), 45 (quotation), 48. Many soldiers during the war and before demobilization at its end acquired a taste for higher

Three-quarters of the vet-collegians graduated, so many with high grades that their younger classmates, as at Stanford, dubbed them DARs, "damn average raisers." The *New York Times* good-naturedly accused them of "hogging the honor rolls." Several elite-college presidents, such as Chicago's Robert Hutchins and Harvard's James Conant, gladly retracted their early predictions that the veterans would turn their campuses into "educational hobo jungles" of "the least capable among the war generation." Before the mass readership of *Life* magazine in 1946, Conant admitted that Harvard's vets were "the most mature and promising students Harvard has ever had." They were, he and most faculty and administrators had to admit, mature, seriously motivated, perceptive, and disciplined. Those who were older and those with wives (30 percent) and children (10 percent) were the best students.[10] After having tons of live ammunition thrown at them, they did not flinch at a few professorial questions.

Those high-performing veterans were remarkable for more than steady habits and good grades. On most campuses, particularly large

---

education in military-sponsored correspondence courses (700 offerings), 2,000 Post-Hostility Schools around the world (179 subjects, 25,000 instructors, half-a-million students), and, for one year (1945–46), 4 University Centers in England, Southern France, Italy, and Hawaii. All 3 programs employed faculty from American colleges and universities. The last offered 412 courses to 35,000 American (and hundreds of Allied) men and women of all races and religions. In a forecast of the G.I. Bill, the faculties of the university centers thought their students, many of whom had only high-school diplomas, "the best they ever taught." In addition, the government distributed more than 123 million books (1,180 titles) in paperback Armed Services Editions, fiction and nonfiction. Christopher P. Loss, "'The Most Wonderful Thing Has Happened to Me in the Army': Psychology, Citizenship, and American Higher Education in World War II," *Journal of American History* 92:3 (Dec. 2005), 864–91, at 885. Molly Guptill Manning, *When Books Went to War: The Stories That Helped Us Win World War II* (Boston: Houghton Mifflin Harcourt, 2014). See also Christopher P. Loss, *Between Citizens and the State: The Politics of American Higher Education in the 20th Century* (Princeton, N.J.: Princeton University Press, 2012), chs. 4–5.

10 Suzanne Mettler, *Soldiers to Citizens: The G.I. Bill and the Making of the Greatest Generation* (New York: Oxford University Press, 2005), 64, 70–71; Olson, *G.I. Bill*, 33, 48–56, 75–76; "Remembering the GI Bill," *Newshour with Jim Lehrer*, July 4, 2000, transcript 1–5, at 3 ("hogging"), http://www.pbs.org/newshour/bb/military/july-dec00/gibill_7-4.html.

public ones, they put up with long lines, crowded classes, inadequate housing, and inflation-eroded stipends (even as the Veterans Administration raised them responsively). Serpentine registration and chow lines reproduced the army's "hurry up and wait" ethos. Although vets often received priority for university housing in the fall, their large numbers, family circumstances, and uncertain dates of demobilization made for housing headaches for all concerned. The federal government helped by building "villages" of prefab two-family barracks and metal Quonset huts on the campus outskirts, a few of which are still in use.[11] It also modified surplus military and government buildings for academic use. Former barracks, hospitals, hangars, house trailers, houseboats, and even tugboats were reassigned and retrofitted for student quarters. Government-issue (G.I.) double-deck bunk beds and footlockers saw continued and almost continual use. Whole laboratories, cafeterias, infirmaries, and classrooms were disassembled, moved, and reconstructed on many campuses, accompanied by repurposed furniture, books, vehicles, air conditioners, electronics, chemicals, and medical supplies.[12]

Despite their cramped and hand-me-down living conditions, the gung-ho vets made the most of their educational opportunities with little complaint. Classes, particularly lectures, were oversized and offered little opportunity for discussion. With senior-faculty shortages, graduate assistants (most of whom had escaped the draft) were thrown into the breach.[13] Lab space was in short supply and libraries could never provide the seats in demand. But refresher courses, all-day and evening class schedules, year-round calendars, and—a

11 Princeton's Butler Tract, flimsy ex-army barracks moved to a university polo field in December 1946, was expected to serve for ten years. It was not demolished until 2015, when its mostly married graduate-student residents moved into substantial new quarters elsewhere on campus. "Lakeside Project Delayed," *Princeton Alumni Weekly* (July 9, 2014), 19: W. Barksdale Maynard, "A Wonderful Life," ibid. (July 10, 2013), 28–35. For photos of veteran housing, lines, and classrooms at other universities, see Milton Greenberg, *The GI Bill: The Law That Changed America* (New York: Lickle, 1997), 37–39, 44, 46–49, 52–53; Olson, *G.I. Bill*, between 62–63.

12 Olson, *G.I. Bill*, 66–68, 76–77, 90, 91–93.

13 Between 1940 and 1948, college enrollments grew 75 percent, while the number of faculty rose only 52 percent. Olson, *G.I. Bill*, 72.

FIGURE 25. When the G.I. Bill filled America's campuses to bursting after WW II, the University of Wisconsin housed many of its married veterans and their families in trailer villages near the football stadium. Dubbed Camp Randall after the stadium, the families made do while the vets sought degrees and a return to normalcy.

grace note—exemption from physical education requirements gave most vets what they came for and needed.[14] Although the majority of returning G.I.s chose sub-college education (3.5 million) and training for specific trades (1.4 million) and farm work (700,000), the 2.2 million collegians, particularly those in elite schools, chose fewer courses and majors in directly vocational subjects than in the higher-status liberal arts and engineering, even more so than did their civilian classmates.[15]

The G.I. Bill also launched a series of quiet social changes on America's campuses. The first occurred because the federal government paid the veterans' bills directly to their institutions.[16] Given the loss of tuition income suffered during the war, the colleges could ill afford to turn down veterans who happened to be African-, Asian-, or Hispanic-American, Jewish or Catholic, or from poor or uneducated families, as they had been wont to do before the war. Once the war against fascism and genocidal anti-Semitism had made the U.S. military melting pot melt faster, its veterans had reason to expect equal treatment on America's campuses. Although most black vets chose to return to the South and "historically black colleges and universities" (HBCUs) there, many proceeded to integrate elite colleges—private and public—in the North and West. The navy had been officially desegregated since 1944, but the army delayed until

14 For a close look at veterans' academic life at the University of Iowa, see "Veterans at College," *Life* (April 21, 1947), 105–13. For more elite private schools, see Vance Packard, "Yanks at Yale," *American Magazine* 139 (April 1945), 46–47, and Charles J. V. Murphy, "GIs at Harvard," *Life* 20 (June 17, 1946), 16–22.

15 Olson, *G.I. Bill*, 86–87, 131n14. On the basis of her selective survey of class of 1949 veterans who attended 11 non-elite colleges and universities, Suzanne Mettler emphasized the vets' preference for vocational majors and professional schools. *Soldiers to Citizens*, 68 (table 4.1), 71, 213n60. At more elite universities, such as Wisconsin, the vets chose more prestigious fields in the liberal arts, which drew more takers than all other majors, including engineering. Olson, *G.I. Bill*, 87 (table 5).

16 One key source of revenue for state universities was the Veterans Administration's agreement to pay higher out-of-state tuition for all veterans, even in-state residents. Henry, *Challenges Past*, 131n16.

1948. The G.I. Bill thus accelerated the racial integration of American higher education and, to some extent, society.[17]

A second shift occurred when the influx of war-hardened students in their late twenties and thirties, many married with children of their own, called into question the colleges' long-standing paternalistic policies (*in loco parentis*) and dress codes geared to much younger prep-schooled "gentlemen" of Brooks Brothers tastes. The presence of women—even married ones—in once-all-male environments, particularly the Ivy colleges, furrowed many a decanal brow and gave undergraduates "disturbing" new ideas about coeducation and puritanical parietal rules; those ideas bore the fullest fruit in the late 1960s and early 1970s, after most colleges returned to their prewar restrictions on dress and "dating."[18]

Although most of the Ivies retained or reinstated coat-and-tie dress codes after the war, the veterans' preference and often financial necessity for military leftovers helped push the "casualization" of collegiate—and soon adult—dress.[19] Repatriated fatigue pants, khaki trousers, navy pea coats, double-breasted trench coats, fur-collared flight jackets, and combat boots were ubiquitous signs of the veterans' ascension as the new BMOCs (big men on campus).[20] Even in buttoned-up Harvard, a graduating vet half-bragged that "in 1946, you might as well have been living in an American Legion post as in one of the [university's residential] Houses." That year, 4,000 veterans dominated the record 5,435 students enrolled

17 Mettler, *Soldiers to Citizens*, 72–76; Bennett, *When Dreams Came True*, 247, 249–52, 255, 260–76.

18 Helen Lefkowitz Horowitz, *Campus Life: Undergraduate Cultures from the End of the Eighteenth Century to the Present* (Chicago: University of Chicago Press, 1987), 187; *The Best of PAW: 100 Years of the Princeton Alumni Weekly*, ed. J. I. Merritt (Princeton, N.J.: Princeton Alumni Weekly, 2000), 220, 225.

19 Deirdre Clemente, *Dress Casual: How College Students Redefined American Style* (Chapel Hill: University of North Carolina Press, 2014.

20 James Axtell, *The Making of Princeton University: From Woodrow Wilson to the Present* (Princeton, N.J.: Princeton University Press, 2006), 317–18n15. Although surplus military clothing was sold after the Civil War and WW I, post–WW II was the heyday of "Army-Navy stores" that fed the growing college and youth market for vet-inspired apparel (www.kaufmansarmynavy.com/history).

at Fair Harvard.[21] Those who could not yet afford the expected Ivy uniform made do with military overcoats cut to sport-coat length, service trousers, khaki shirts sans insignia, and an olive-drab or navy-blue tie.[22]

In the same independent spirit, adult veterans had little patience for some of the campus Joe College culture. A fraternity member who thought of paddling or otherwise hazing a battle-hard vet was well advised to think twice. Trying to shave his newly grown freshman head, make him wear a puerile "dink" (beanie with class numerals), or persuade him to sing maudlin college songs on the steps of Old Main was equally fruitless and served to render more than a few hallowed customs obsolete by the 1950s.[23]

❁ ❁ ❁

In addition to its immediate effects, the G.I. Bill left a rich legacy of longer-term influences on American higher education. The first may have been the "halo effect" that spread from the veterans' academic reputations to college students in general (until the noisy and sometimes destructive campus protests of the late 1960s stole the headlines). Related were other positive changes in attitude before Vietnam curdled America's appetite for foreign wars and things military. One was that large numbers of young *non*veterans, who were graduating from high school in growing numbers, came to realize

21 Bennett, *When Dreams Came True*, 252; Murphy, "GIs at Harvard." In September 1947, two-thirds of Princeton's record-breaking enrollments (3,450) were veterans; 160 had previously served in military training programs on the Princeton campus and developed a taste for its liberal arts curriculum. *Best of PAW*, 221. Between 1946 and 1949, veterans comprised well over half of all male students nationally and nearly half of all students in 1946 and 1947. Olson, *G.I. Bill*, 44 (table 1).

22 Bennett, *When Dreams Came True*, 253. T-shirts also made their appearance in warm weather, as they had in the wartime Pacific theater. Clemente, *Dress Casual*, 53–54.

23 Mettler, *Soldiers to Citizens*, 71, 213n59; Olson, *G.I. Bill*, 73–74; Daniel A. Clark, "'The Two Joes Meet—Joe College, Joe Veteran': The G.I. Bill, College Education, and Postwar American Culture," *History of Education Quarterly* 38:2 (Summer 1998), 165–89, at 175 and 175n34.

that higher education was feasible, affordable, and capable of fostering socio-economic mobility better than any other vehicle.

This realization, in turn, put tremendous pressure on the existing 47 state systems of higher education, most of which featured only a single flagship campus, with limited capacity, and teachers colleges. The result was the absorption and repurposing of various public (often military) facilities and private institutions, and later the construction of new branch campuses, throughout the various states. Populous New York State, long dominated by private institutions, did not form a state university system until forced to do so by veteran demand in 1948. Many other states, including Indiana, Illinois, and Pennsylvania, responded to similar imperatives by adding branch campuses.[24] Simultaneously, the engorgement and proliferation of postwar campuses led to the realization that universities were likely to become and remain large places for large student bodies, with the attendant implications for teaching, learning, curricula, and research.

The federal government also came to regard an educated workforce as the key to national prosperity and educated voters as more responsible citizens. Seen for the first time as a truly *national*—not merely personal—benefit, higher education was now regarded as worthy of sustained federal (and state) investment. It became politically acceptable, even laudable, for legislatures to give aid not only to students generally but also to colleges and universities for new facilities, graduate education, and research for peace as well as defense.[25] World War II "placed higher education at the center of American citizenship," and henceforward those citizens ensured that "education would never drift too far from the center of American politics or society again."[26]

When President Harry Truman, only a high-school graduate, received the report of his commission on higher education in 1948,

24 Olson, *G.I. Bill*, 68–72; Henry, *Challenges Past*, 67. New York's Governor Thomas Dewey also backed the state system because New York's private universities discriminated against religious and ethnic minorities in their professional-school admissions. John B. Clark, W. Bruce Leslie, and Kenneth P. O'Brien, eds., *SUNY at Sixty: The Promise of the State University of New York* (Albany: State University of New York Press, 2010), introd. and ch. 1.

25 Henry, *Challenges Past*, 66–68.

26 Loss, "Most Wonderful Thing," 891.

he highly approved its recommendation that "every citizen, youth, and adult is enabled and encouraged to carry his education, formal and informal, as far as his native capacities permit." The commissioners were convinced that half of the population could profit from fourteen years of schooling, and at least a third could complete "an advanced liberal or specialized professional education." To broaden access to higher education, the report recommended doubling enrollments within twelve years; multiplying the number of two-year community, or "junior," colleges; underwriting federal scholarships, fellowships, and aid for general purposes and for physical plants in public institutions; and passing legislation to prevent religious and racial discrimination.[27]

When the Soviet Union stunned the world by launching a satellite into outer space in 1957, America's attention turned quickly to educational quality as well as mass access. As the American Council of Education remonstrated, "The message which this little ball carries to Americans . . . is that in the last half of the 20th century . . . nothing is as important as the trained and educated mind." The following year Congress passed a National Defense Education Act, which linked Cold War preparedness with brainpower by liberally funding student loans, graduate fellowships in a variety of subjects, and support for critical foreign-language and area-studies centers and institutes for advanced study.[28]

❁ ❁ ❁

The search for and development of decisive quanta of brainpower took place—once again—in America's research universities. The deployment of the country's best scientists and engineers in university and government laboratories during WW II set a powerful precedent

27 Henry, *Challenges Past*, 71–72. For key excerpts from the report, see Wilson Smith and Thomas Bender, eds., *American Higher Education Transformed, 1940–2005: Documenting the National Discourse* (Baltimore, Md.: Johns Hopkins University Press, 2008), 84–89. On the advent and implications of mass higher education, see Martin Trow, *Twentieth-Century Higher Education: Elite to Mass to Universal*, ed. Michael Burrage (Baltimore, Md.: Johns Hopkins University Press, 2010), chs. 16–17.

28 Henry, *Challenges Past*, 121–23.

FIGURE 26. A 1958 New Yorker cartoon by Modell captured the impetus behind the U.S. enlistment of academic scientists and facilities in the Cold War contest for intellectual and technological superiority.

for the future pursuit of American research. But the war and its Cold War sequel also taught that "hearts and minds" were as important as military hardware in the winning of war and the prolongation of peace. Therefore higher education in general, not just its science labs, was seen to have a crucial role to play in keeping the U.S. militarily, economically, and intellectually ahead of the rest of the world.

Moreover, the federal government was expected to remain a major partner in underwriting not only university research but also the teaching and learning that preceded and supported that research. By the twenty-first century, the major nations of the world no longer sought only to be ranked top dog in the number of their battleships, long-range bombers, ballistic missiles, or atomic bombs. They also sought top ranking for their research universities, the productivity of their faculties, and the number of their Nobel Prize winners.

The competition had begun urgently and for extremely high stakes in the Second World War. To oversee the recruitment of the country's best minds to meet the military challenge that Hitler and Hirohito had issued, Washington created in 1940 the National Defense Research Committee (NDRC) to build a superior offense and the parallel Committee on Medical Research to handle the inevitable casualties of war. A year later, the well-funded Office of Strategic Research and Development (OSRD) was superimposed lightly upon both, with Vannevar Bush, head of the NDRC and the politically savvy chief of the Carnegie Institution of Washington, as director. Since the army and navy labs were committed to perfecting existing weaponry, the task of the OSRD and NDRC was to enlist universities and the cream of their faculties in finding solutions to new and even unforeseen military threats and challenges.

Bush's shrewd notion was to prevent administrative sclerosis and dangerous delay by writing brief contracts for the work with "universities, research institutes, and industrial laboratories," thus creating a supple pyramid of ample resources, minimal accountability, and maximal invention. His handpicked adjutants were all civilians: the presidents of Harvard (James Conant) and MIT (Karl Compton), the graduate dean at Caltech (Richard Tolman), and the president of the Bell Telephone Laboratories and the American Academy of Science (Frank Jewett), all distinguished scientists who had the administrative experience to guide their assigned, usually multiple, divisions. They, in turn, recruited interdisciplinary teams of scientists and engineers to do the work of giving America's fighting forces the best tools to win the war. By the end of 1940, the NDRC had already written 132 contracts to 32 universities and 19 industrial corporations. At the war's end five years later, the OSRD had signed some 500 contracts worth over $300 million ($3.9 billion in 2015) to just 9 universities. The NDRC had spent a total of $425 million ($5.6 billion in 2015) in its 19 divisions of research.[29]

29 Roger L. Geiger, *Research and Relevant Knowledge: American Research Universities Since World War II* (New York: Oxford University Press, 1993), 31, citing James Phinney Baxter III, *Scientists Against Time* (Boston: Little, Brown, 1946), 456; John Burchard, *Q.E.D.: M.I.T. in World War II* (New York: John Wiley & Sons, 1948), 29.

The bulk of those contracts and dollars went to new research that only America's autonomous universities could have produced in a short time under such pressure. But the development and large-scale production of the professors' inventions was usually handed off to large industrial corporations, many of whose staff members brainstormed in university labs with the academic whitecoats.[30] Together, the scientists and the developers produced a daunting—and ultimately winning—arsenal of weapons and materiel for U.S., and occasionally Allied, forces.

The rush to develop an atomic bomb before Germany did involved more than $2.2 billion (in 2015 dollars) and faculty and crucial machinery from Chicago, Berkeley, Minnesota, Illinois, Columbia, Princeton, and Harvard before and after they were all called to the northern highlands of New Mexico for the top-secret Manhattan Project at Los Alamos. Although the dropping of the A-bomb on two of its major cities forced Japan to surrender, crucial work on microwave radar cost nearly as much ($1.6 billion in 2015 dollars) and contributed to the success of the war effort in nearly all military theaters.[31] MIT's famous Rad Lab (*Radiation* Laboratory to disguise its focus on radar) was a huge enterprise built on 400 contracts worth more than $100 million ($1.3 billion in 2015 dollars). The lab director, Lee DuBridge, came from the University of Rochester; his staff, drawn from 69 universities, included 20 percent of the nation's physicists, among them the future Nobel laureate Isador Rabi (Columbia). In addition to several other dedicated labs,[32] MIT built a mammoth 38,000-square-foot facility behind its signature golden dome

30 The top ten industrial contractors for the OSRD signed nearly 400 contracts worth some $80 million ($1.06 billion in 2015 dollars). Baxter, *Scientists Against Time*, 456–57 (app. C).

31 A week after Pearl Harbor, the MIT student newspaper had affixed to its masthead "Let's Set the Rising Sun." Deborah Douglas, "MIT and War," in *Becoming MIT: Moments of Decision*, ed. David Kaiser (Cambridge, Mass.: MIT Press, 2010, 81–102, at 89.

32 With only two contracts, the Research Construction Company, a model shop to produce small quantities of finished products for urgent use abroad, spent $14 million ($185 million in 2015 dollars), second only to Western Electric's $17 million development tab. Baxter, *Scientists Against Time*, 456–57 (app. C).

for the radar research and its 1,200 personnel. The work resulted in 150 different radar systems, large and small, adapted to different conditions on land, in the air, and on water.[33]

Rad Lab products soon guided night-fighting aircraft, battleships at sea, and anti-aircraft guns. Across town, the Radio Research Laboratory at Harvard, with a staff of 600 directed by Stanford's Frederick Terman, lent help by improving sonar for use in submarine warfare and inventing technologies to block the enemy use of radar. Similar university-based efforts across the country led to efficient amphibious vehicles and landing craft (Berkeley), napalm (Harvard), rockets and guided missiles (Caltech), more accurate ballistics (Penn and Princeton), radio-controlled proximity fuses to detonate bombs at a specified distance above a target to cause maximum damage (Johns Hopkins), jet propulsion to launch carrier planes (Caltech), RDX, an explosive more powerful than TNT (Cornell, Penn State, and Michigan), and new accuracy in aerial bombing (Princeton, Berkeley, and Columbia). The use of sulfa drugs for burns and wounds (UC San Francisco), artificial limbs (Berkeley), dried food for field rations (Berkeley and MIT), and heated aircraft cabins and exterior de-icing (UCLA) were less impressive but no less useful to the war effort.[34]

❁ ❁ ❁

Even before the war ended, President Franklin Roosevelt asked Vannevar Bush to consider the federal government's future role in scientific research. After consulting with other experts, Bush published *Science—The Endless Frontier* in July 1945. His three main arguments were that *basic* research was the source of all technological progress, it required stable long-term funding, and it needed to be insulated

33 Burchard, *Q.E.D.*; Douglas, "MIT and War."

34 Baxter, *Scientists Against Time*; Irvin Stewart, *Organizing Scientific Research for War: The Administrative History of the Office of Strategic Research and Development* (Boston: Little, Brown, 1948); Judith F. Goodstein, *Millikan's School: A History of The California Institute of Technology* (New York: W. W. Norton, 1991), ch. 14; Stadtman, *University of California*, 307–11.

from outside (especially political) dictation or interference. Despite the admiration and credibility that science had earned during the war, the kind of national science foundation Bush envisioned did not gain congressional approval until 1950.[35] But several federal agencies were created that foreshadowed much of the National Science Foundation's anticipated role in promoting university research and would continue to do so long after its creation.

In 1946 two big players entered the field. The Atomic Energy Commission (AEC) began to fund work—conducted mostly in closed labs for fear of Russian spies—on both military and civilian uses of nuclear energy. A richer Maecenas and better friend to university autonomy was the Office of Naval Research (ONR). Run largely by young, idealistic naval officers (most with Ph.D.s) known as Bird Dogs, the ONR visited universities, solicited proposals from scientists, chose and funded many small short-term projects with the advice of scientific experts, and allowed the results to be published. By 1950, it had already spent $20 million a year (c. $197 million in 2015 dollars) on 1,131 projects at 200 institutions. The Korean War kicked its spending up to $30 million a year. During the 1960s, the ONR was supporting basic research to the tune of $50 million annually, with another $30 million going to applied research. But its liberal criteria for choosing projects always included "the probability of ultimate usefulness to the Navy" and not a general concern (like the NSF's) for a national balance of scientific research.[36]

The other services also created offices for research, but they largely sought applied technologies to solve specific military problems and developed less trusting relationships with academic scientists and universities.[37] Only the National Institutes of Health (est. 1947), the research arm of the older Public Health Service, operated like the NSF in relying on expert panels of scientists to award its numerous

35 Geiger, *Research and Relevant Knowledge*, 15–18.

36 Daniel J. Kevles, *The Physicists: The History of a Scientific Community in Modern America* (New York: Alfred A. Knopf, 1978), 353–56; Geiger, *Research and Relevant Knowledge*, 18, 23–25.

37 A year before the Air Force established its own Office of Scientific Research, it spread $84 million among 55 universities, 10 of which got 70 percent. Caltech's Jet-Propulsion Laboratory predictably received the most. Geiger, *Research and Relevant Knowledge*, 23, 25.

grants to researchers, mostly at universities and medical schools. It also remained popular with Congress: its grants budget climbed from only $4 million in 1947 to $1 billion in 1974 ($4.8 billion in 2015 dollars). Today the NIH funds 85 percent of all university research in the health sciences.[38]

The continued importance of the federal government in funding university research and development (R&D) can be glimpsed in a few simple numbers. In 1940 the government contributed $405 million; in 1990, $9 billion. In 2012 the federal investment was almost $66 billion. In 1958–59, at the start of the post-Sputnik "golden age" for research, Harvard received less than 20 percent of its operating income from Washington, none for classified work. But universities that had contracted heavily with the government during WW II still relied on federal largesse and protocols. Caltech drew 84 percent of its funding from Uncle Sam; MIT, 78 percent[39]; Chicago, 55 percent; and Princeton, 54 percent. As late as 2012, 61 percent of all R&D spending by U.S. colleges and universities was federally financed, more than half of it for work in the life sciences. Forty percent (nearly $26.5 billion) went to just 30 universities; the top 8 (six public) spent more than a billion dollars each on R&D; all eight had medical schools, whose research contributed heavily to the institutional expense. The second-largest contribution, from the institutions themselves, totaled not quite 21 percent, a third of the federal investment.[40]

❁ ❁ ❁

Although in 2012 industry contributed only 5 percent to academic R&D, a few universities historically cultivated corporate sources assiduously and successfully.[41] The outstanding example is Stanford,

38 "A Short History of the National Institutes of Health," history.nih.gov/exhibits/history/html.

39 In 1962, the atomic physicist Alvin Weinberg, director of the Oak Ridge National Laboratory, remarked that it had become difficult to tell whether MIT was "a university with many government research laboratories appended to it or a cluster of government research laboratories with a very good educational institution attached to it." Kaiser, "Elephant on the Charles," 108–9.

40 Keller, *Making Harvard Modern*, 187; *CHE Almanac, 2014–15*, 73.

41 *CHE Almanac, 2014–15*, 73.

which—with both military and corporate help—played a decisive role in the entrepreneurial success known as Silicon Valley. Coming out of WW II, Stanford was an unlikely candidate for academic stardom, "the Harvard of the West" as some administrators dreamed. None of its physicists had been called to Los Alamos, and the university, after being given initially only two minor contracts from the NDRC, had to lobby hard in Washington to get 23 more worth $500,000 by the war's end. Before and during the war, Stanford, despite a few strong departments, was on no one's list of top-ten research universities, and some faculty worried about its perceived "mediocrity," comparable to Dartmouth's.[42] Ten years later, the school still suffered from a reputation as a "regional university on the make."[43] It had its eye more on MIT than Harvard and sought to build one nationally recognized department after another with the help of both industry and the military.[44]

The university had two catalysts. One was Fred Terman, who became Stanford's dean of engineering after returning from his wartime direction of Harvard's Radio Lab. The other was Donald Tresidder, a prominent businessman and former chair of Stanford's board of trustees, who had been elected president in 1943. Within a year he made Terman his provost and together they steadily moved

42 In late 1943, Fred Terman, at Harvard for the war effort, wrote to Stanford's general secretary that "we will either consolidate our potential strength and create a foundation for a position in the West somewhat analogous to Harvard in the East, or we will drop to the level of Dartmouth, a well thought of school having about 2 percent as much influence on national life as Harvard." Rebecca S. Lowen, "Transforming the University: Administrators, Physicists, and Industrial and Federal Patronage at Stanford, 1935–49," *History of Education Quarterly* 31:3 (Fall 1991), 365–88, at 377–78.

43 Stuart W. Leslie, *The Cold War and American Science: The Military-Industrial-Academic Complex at MIT and Stanford* (New York: Columbia University Press, 1993), 44; Stephen B. Adams, "Follow the Money: Engineering at Stanford and UC Berkeley during the Rise of Silicon Valley," *Minerva* 47 (2009), 367–90, at 368.

44 Stanford did not emulate MIT's relative disregard for industrial support. In 1950–51, MIT received only 3 percent of its operating budget from industry. Five years later, it changed the title of its Division of Industrial Cooperation to Division of Sponsored Research, from which it received 80 percent of its working capital. Kaiser, "Elephant on the Charles," 106.

postwar Stanford into the big leagues of military contractors and industrial partners.[45]

The Stanford strategy for becoming at least the MIT of the West (although Caltech had a big head start) involved four key tactics: (1) cultivate contacts with the federal government, particularly the armed services, in order to garner research contracts;[46] (2) don't emulate Harvard's "purist" rejection of all classified work if the latter is required to obtain funding that promotes some basic research and contributes to Stanford's national prestige;[47] (3) cultivate industry through an osmotic wall to attract unfettered subsidies rather than subcontracts in order to maintain as much university and faculty independence as possible; and (4) provide ample space for the proximate location of the industries that could develop and produce researchers' inventions, both for the military and the aviation/defense industry that was moving to, or staying put in, California and contributing mightily to its economic prosperity.[48]

The fourth tactic was launched in 1951 when the university set aside 200 acres for the Stanford Industrial Park (renamed *Research* Park in 1974). By 1963, after it had expanded to 700 acres, the park had attracted 42 companies and 12,000 employees.[49] They had convened

45 For a thorough account of Terman's career at Stanford, see C. Stewart Gillmor, *Fred Terman at Stanford: Building a Discipline, a University, and Silicon Valley* (Stanford, Calif.: Stanford University Press, 2004).

46 An attractive feature of military contracts was that they normally paid, without much paperwork or scrutiny, up to 50 percent extra as overhead for the researchers' use of university facilities and utilities. During the war, Stanford spent much of its overhead from the NDRC and ONR on the offices of the deans of students and of women, the registrar, and the director of the summer quarter. Rebecca S. Lowen, *Creating the Cold War University: The Transformation of Stanford* (Berkeley: University of California Press, 1997), 14, 50, 57, 58–63.

47 Stanford did refuse to build an anti-aircraft gun as incommensurate with its idealized mission to the nation.

48 Stuart W. Leslie, "The Biggest 'Angel' of Them All: The Military and the Making of Silicon Valley," in Martin Kenney, ed., *Understanding Silicon Valley: The Anatomy of an Entrepreneurial Region* (Stanford, Calif.: Stanford University Press, 2000), 48–67, 244–45, at 49–50.

49 Lowen, *Creating the Cold War University*, 133. In 2012 the SRP hosted 150 companies. Ken Auletta, "Get Rich U.," *New Yorker* April 30, 2012, 38–47, at 40.

in order to take advantage of Stanford's powers of discovery in fields of commercial interest. But in return for first dibs on Stanford graduates (especially Ph.D.s), early access to Stanford research reports (oral and written), and ready consultation with Stanford faculty-researchers, companies were, through an Industrial Affiliation Program, asked to contribute $5,000 a year for five years. Beginning in 1953 they were also encouraged to send employees to enroll as part-time master's students in the university's Honor Cooperation Program for $10,000 plus tuition; 400 were doing so ten years later. In 1954 Terman was pleased to boast to a General Electric executive that "the penetration of Stanford ideas and principles is really quite far-reaching."[50] With neighbors such as GE, Hewlett-Packard, Litton, Philco, and Kodak, Stanford was well on its way to becoming the alma mater of Silicon Valley.[51]

By 1960, one-third of the $40 million U.S. microwave-tube business was located near the Stanford campus. When Lockheed, another of its neighbors, shifted its emphasis from civilian aircraft to ballistic missiles after Sputnik, Stanford's Division of Aeronautical Engineering picked up contracts worth $460,000 in 1959 alone.[52] When Stanford built the Center for Integrated Systems in 1980 and moved from microwave tubes to solid-state circuitry, it attracted a consortium of microelectronic companies—among them Texas Instruments, Fairchild Semiconductor, Intel, Teletronix—that pledged $15 million for research assistance from the university.[53]

Ever since, Stanford researchers (students included) have been on a sedulous search for discoveries with commercial possibilities.[54] As early as the 1940s, when it teamed up with Sperry Gyroscope to

50 Lowen, *Creating the Cold War University*, 129 (quotation), 130–31, 133.

51 Stuart W. Leslie, "From Backwater to Powerhouse," *Stanford* (March 1990), 55–60, at 60. Silicon was used as a conductive medium in solid-state circuits, as used in computers.

52 Ibid., 58–59.

53 Ibid., 60.

54 By 2013, 26 percent of Stanford's undergraduates majored in computer science or engineering, and 90 percent took at least one course in computer programming. Richard Pérez-Peña, "To Young Minds of Today, Harvard Is the Stanford of the East," *New York Times* (May 30, 2014), A1, A3, at A3.

produce university-inspired microwave tubes and klystrons (linear-beam vacuum tubes used to amplify radio power at ultra-high and microwave frequencies), the university made sure to write contracts that rewarded it handsomely and long term for its ideas. The Office of Technology Licensing opened in 1970 to provide the necessary guidance. Given the plethora of companies spawned by Stanford faculty, students, and ideas—at least 5,000, perhaps as many as 39,900 by 2012—the university not surprisingly has drawn $1.3 billion in royalties from at least 8,000 inventions.[55] That the San Francisco Bay region had and still has an abundance of sunshine and competitive venture capitalists willing to bankroll high-tech start-ups was another key to the singular success of Silicon Valley. Route 128 at some distance from Cambridge and Boston, the Research Triangle well outside Chapel Hill, and other would-be incubators around the country could never develop the close synergy of university, industry, and military that Stanford created and from which it still profits.[56]

55 Congress's Bayh-Dole Act of 1980 also gave the green light to academic entrepreneurship nationwide by allowing universities to profit from the technologies derived from their discoveries financed by federal contracts. Auletta, "Get Rich U.," 40 (5,000); Charles Eesley and William F. Miller (former Stanford provost), "Stanford University's Economic Impact via Innovation and Entrepreneurship" (2012), cited in an ad for the Stanford Graduate School of Business, *Stanford* (Sept.–Oct. 2014)(39,900). When the university sold its stock in Google (it owned the search-technology rights), it cleared $336 million. Yahoo, Cisco, Intuit, LinkedIn, Netflix, and eBay are other Stanford offspring. Many university faculty and administrators have reaped large rewards by investing in local start-ups. Auletta, "Get Rich U.," 42. MIT also profits from its entrepreneurial research. In 2012, its patents produced over $137 million in income, up from nearly $89 million in 2008. *Chronicle of Higher Education* (Sept. 26, 2014), A24.

56 Christophe Lécuyer, *Making Silicon Valley: Innovation and Growth of High Tech, 1930–1970* (Cambridge, Mass.: MIT Press, 2006); Martin Kenney, ed., *Understanding Silicon Valley: The Anatomy of an Entrepreneurial Region* (Stanford, Calif.: Stanford University Press, 2000); Robert Kagan and Stuart Leslie, "Imagined Geographies: Princeton, Stanford, and the Boundaries of Useful Knowledge in Postwar America," *Minerva* 32:2 (June 1994), 121–43; Adams, "Follow the Money"; Leslie, "From Backwater to Powerhouse." On some recent rethinking of the university-related incubator idea, see Paul Basken, "To Lure Workers, Universities Remake Research Parks," *Chronicle of Higher Education* (Oct. 31, 2014), A10.

Stanford and other major research universities that became dependent on federal, especially military, patronage for large parts of their research budgets discovered that Uncle Sam's largesse was not cost free. One cost was some, often significant, loss of university and departmental autonomy to pursue their own academic and intellectual agendas. When strong-minded administrators like Terman sought to build "steeples of excellence" rather than promote inter- and intradepartmental "balance," to put "each tub on its own bottom" by requiring each department to obtain most of its funding from external sources, and to use solely quantitative data to measure each faculty member's "productivity," mostly in terms of grants secured and graduate students graduated, they invariably created dissension between the flush "haves" and the impecunious "have nots" in whose fields federal and military patrons and even foundations seldom offered grants. Usually the less entrepreneurial fields were located in the non-STEM (science, technology, engineering, mathematics) departments: the humanities and the "softer" (less mathematical) social sciences, such as anthropology and geography.[57]

Another casualty of the "steeples" approach was—and still is—equity in the funding of, and balance in faculty attention to, graduate and undergraduate students.[58] Since most graduate students in the easily contracted STEM fields could be supported on contracts and overhead, undergraduates and their instruction were given short shrift. Departmental "tubs" that couldn't pad their own "bottoms" through contracts or other patronage were often reduced to "service" status, deprived of graduate students, and forced to teach large numbers of undergraduates, usually in large lectures.[59]

At the same time, doctoral students dependent on their advisors' research grants often felt pressure to choose dissertation topics that accommodated the granting sponsors' specific agendas rather than

57 Lowen, *Creating the Cold War University*, chs. 3, 6.

58 In 1956, the difference at Stanford between the per-student allocation in Terman's beloved graduate-oriented School of Engineering and the more undergraduate-oriented School of Humanities & Sciences was $255; by 1961, it had grown to $372. Terman was provost from 1955 to 1965. Lowen, *Creating the Cold War University*, 175.

59 Ibid., 159.

their own intellectual curiosity or sense of importance.[60] This tended to reduce *basic* research to *applied*, as well as to corral some projects as classified and therefore unpublishable at a time when "publish or perish" was increasingly the junior faculty's academical imperative. Similarly, splitting between the university and federal paymaster the salaries of researchers, particularly those at semi-independent centers and institutes or (in 1963, fourteen) autonomous national laboratories located at universities, compromised traditional departmental autonomy and created unhelpful divisions between the independent researchers and the tenure-track faculty who did the heavy lifting of teaching, advising, and in-house service as well as their own research.[61]

❁ ❁ ❁

By 1963 the ever-expanding postwar university—the house of Big Science, federal grants, and other large developments—had acquired a new descriptor. In his Godkin Lectures at Harvard, Clark Kerr, the former chancellor of UC-Berkeley and president emeritus of the huge University of California system, described the attributes and

60 Concerned about the large federal impact on higher education, in the early 1960s the Carnegie Foundation for the Advancement of Teaching sponsored self-studies at 23 colleges and universities. William G. Bowen's 335-page report on undergraduate-heavy Princeton, for example, found that only 17 percent of the graduate students in the natural sciences felt that they had been "pulled" to work on either their advisor's or his sponsor's topics. A much larger percentage of graduate students in the humanities and social sciences thought that their fellowships were smaller than those of the scientists and engineers. Graduate-school enrollments had grown noticeably from 15 to 21 percent of the total student body in the 1950s. *The Federal Government and Princeton University: A Report on the Effects of Princeton's Involvements with the Federal Government on the Operations of the University* (Princeton, N.J.: Princeton University, Jan. 1962), ch. 10, at 201 (table 14), 206–10, ch. 11, at 223 (table 17).

61 Lowen, *Creating the Cold War University*, 104, 118, 121, 138, 140–42, 151–55, 182. For a list of the specialized national laboratories and research centers at or operated by major universities in 1963, see Clark Kerr, *The Uses of the University*, 3rd ed. (Cambridge, Mass.: Harvard University Press, 1982 [1963, 1972]), 188–89n3. The individual universities included Harvard, MIT, Caltech, Columbia, Princeton, Johns Hopkins, Penn, Chicago, and Berkeley.

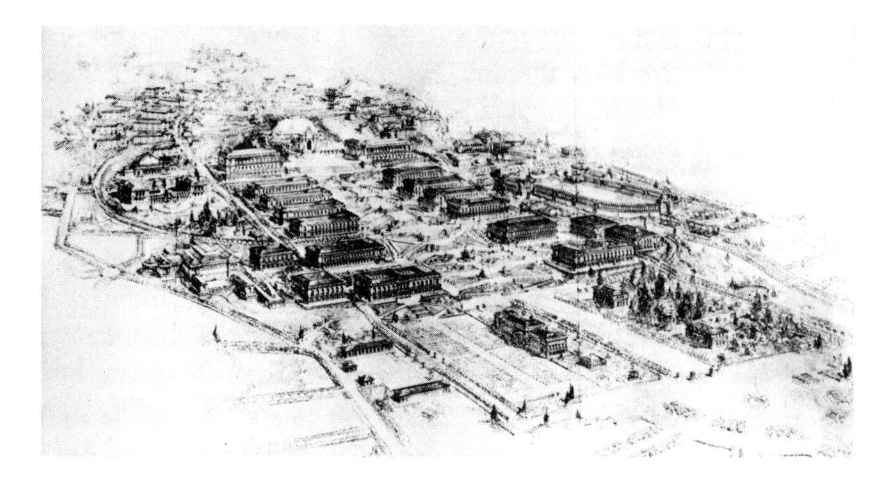

FIGURE 27. In 1899, the prosperous state of California called for a master plan for its academic City of Learning in Berkeley. After an international competition, the fourth-place design was chosen, as was one of its two authors, John Galen Howard, as supervising architect (1901–24). Largely neoclassical with a Beaux-Arts flavor, the Berkeley campus, on its slope overlooking San Francisco Bay, became an apt symbol of what became known in 1963 as the "multiversity."

character of what others had already dubbed the "multiversity."[62] Having taken the pre-war "department store" or "service station" models to greater lengths, each of the evolved research universities was "a whole series of communities and activities" held together largely by "a common name, a common governing board, and related purposes." They more resembled "federal republics" or "city states" of "infinite variety" than unified or unifying "kingdoms." Although they served multiple purposes, centers of power, and clienteles, multiversities had "a unique capacity for riding off in all directions and still staying in the same place." Their primary, unifying, focus was and remains knowledge—its creation, transmission, and application to national needs and global problems. At the center of the

62 Kerr, *Uses of the University*, 136. In 1962, Kerr's own University of California was a *multi*-multiversity, consisting of 6 (now 10) campuses, 40,000 faculty and staff, nearly 100,000 students (200,000 more in extension courses), and an operating budget of nearly $500 million. Ibid., 7–8.

"knowledge industry," they acted as the "producers, wholesalers, and retailers of knowledge," often from semi-autonomous "centers" and "institutes."[63] As such and as the children of "middle-class pluralism," they became "prime instruments of national purpose."[64]

Although the United States experienced much social and political change (some due to the universities' activities), Kerr noted in a 1982 postscript that the approximately 100 American research universities, particularly the 50 elite ones, remained much the same and bore a striking family resemblance. They were "particularly impervious to structural changes, for several reasons. They were nationally indispensable: they turned out essentially the same products—educated citizens and members of the various learned professions, research, and scholarship. With diverse sources of funding and protection from loyal, new, or confirmed upper-class alumni, they preserved a large degree of autonomy from political and economic control. Although they were largely independent entities with room to maneuver, they were also fiercely competitive and therefore shared most of the same goals, purposes, meritocratic standards, and institutional features. Perhaps the most persistent feature was faculty control of the substantial infrastructure: "the teaching, the formation of the curriculum, the research, the public service . . . for love or money."[65]

That last item was key. As Kerr reminded his audience, the research university was "powered by money," as it still is. "Which universities get it in the largest quantities," he safely predicted, "will help determine which of them excel in a decade or two hence." And why? Because "knowledge costs a great deal to produce."[66] Why so?

63 By 2014, Harvard operated 53 research centers, institutes, initiatives, programs, and societies. They ranged from the Aga Khan Program for Islamic Architecture, the Center for Brain Science, and the Korea Institute to the Nanoscale Science and Engineering Center, the South Asia Initiative, and the Ukrainian Research Institute. www.fas.harvard.edu.

64 Kerr, *Uses of the University*, 17, 87, 114, 118, 136.

65 Ibid., 141, 156, 165, 178.

66 The 2013 list of largest university endowments, the 2012 list of the largest research and development (R&D) budgets, and the multiple global rankings of top U.S. research universities show a large overlap of both public and private institutions in the top 30 positions. Thirty-four U.S. universities and one college had endowments of

Because the brightest and most productive researchers, especially scientists, cost the most to hire in the globally competitive marketplace. And they demand the best in labs, libraries, and equipment; low teaching loads; frequent sabbaticals; graduate or postdoctoral assistants; administrative support; high-powered colleagues for stimulation, collaboration, and prestige; and even (as Kerr joked) convenient parking spots—all of which cost the university big extra-salary dollars. "Raids" or "full-court presses" for other universities' "stars" (especially Nobel laureates)—or to prevent one's own from being stolen—were and are especially expensive. But they were sometimes a way to raise the university's national profile and global ranking, a matter of increasing concern for elite and wannabe universities in the last half century.[67]

The acuity of Kerr's observations and predictions was underlined in two books on America's elite universities in 1990 and 2013. The economist Henry Rosovsky, longtime Dean of Arts and Sciences at Harvard (1973–84, 1990–91), published *The University*, what he called "an owner's manual" for the multiversity (primarily the quintessential one in Cambridge).[68] Nearly a quarter century later, the historian John V. Lombardi, former president of the University of Florida and the Louisiana State University System, published an incisive, less personal, guide, *How Universities Work*.[69] Both books document Kerr's main point that elite research universities have changed in essence very little since the multiversity was crowned in the early 1960s. They also second his positioning of them at the top of the worldwide knowledge industry and his emphasis on their meritocratic pursuit of excellence at great expense. Along the way, they

---

over $2 billion; 19 over $5 billion, 6 over $10 billion, and 3 over $20 billion. In 2012, 8 universities spent more than $1 billion on R&D, 22 spent more than $700 million; all U.S. institutions spent nearly $66 billion. *CHE Almanac, 2014–15*, 52, 53.

67 Kerr, *Uses of the University*, 20, 117, 124, 182. On more than one occasion, Kerr thought of the multiversity as "a series of independent faculty entrepreneurs held together by a common grievance over parking" (20).

68 Henry Rosovsky, *The University: An Owner's Manual* (New York: W. W. Norton, 1990).

69 John V. Lombardi, *How Universities Work* (Baltimore, Md.: Johns Hopkins University Press, 2013).

point to developments in the universities' conduct that Kerr wisely predicted and a few that he couldn't foresee.

Kerr's final prediction that "the American research university will be even more essential to American society in 1990 or 2000" than it was in 1982 or 1963 got no argument from his successors, and even a global extension.[70] Rosovsky regarded the top U.S. research universities as "the cutting edge of our national life of the mind." Lombardi saw that since WW II, American higher education had become "an essential industry for the creation of a prosperous middle class and the sustained replication of the elite leaders of business, industry, government, and the arts." It also "became engaged as an active partner as the United States assumed ever-greater responsibility and asserted ever-greater authority in international affairs." Following the American example, many other nations now "see the research university as a powerful base for achieving their national aspirations." Small wonder that in global rankings and regard, America is consistently credited with two-thirds to three-quarters—Rosovsky's estimate—of "the world's leading universities." When international competitors seek to build their own "quality engines," Lombardi asserted, "the model pursued by most . . . is primarily a U.S. model of research university operation."[71] He might have added that nations with authoritarian governments tend to favor economy-building STEM subjects and to eschew the humanities and softer social sciences that universities in democratic Europe and North America also emphasize and support.

❁ ❁ ❁

One key question all three commentators sought to answer was: *why* were American research universities the gold standard in the knowledge industry? Shared answers were the similarity of their goals and

70 Kerr, *Uses of the University*, 184.

71 Rosovsky, *University*, 21, 29, 58; Lombardi, *How Universities Work*, 116, 181. Lombardi's seeming hesitance ("perhaps") to declare that American universities "dominate the global university marketplace" was based more on his criticism of the extant global-ranking methodologies than on any serious doubt that the United States does dominate (ix, 42–44, 180–82).

standards, institutional autonomy in the absence of a federal directorate, intense competition, "lots of money" (as Lombardi preferred to call ample funding), and faculty possessed of specialized expertise, governed by guild discipline, and driven by a constant search for excellence.[72]

Whether they were public or private, with huge or more modest endowments and federal grants, and in spite of their individual independence, research universities, Lombardi noted, "behave in remarkably similar ways" because of the overlap in their "declared values and purpose." "What matters to universities is sustained high performance in both productivity and quality." "Faculty quality," Harvard's dean had emphasized, "is the keystone of university life." "The faculty's degree of excellence . . . determines nearly everything else." To which Lombardi added, "Quality is the main event" because the best universities are quality engines acquiring a disproportionate share of the best-quality students, faculty, and educational and research programs. Since "quality is scarce" the competition for it is "intense," which drives up its cost.[73]

Quality is also specialized. As Rosovsky observed from the Harvard deanery, "Generalists are an endangered species in modern universities; nearly all of us are highly and narrowly specialized." But we are also educated in and acculturated to the particular methodologies and standards of our respective national guilds or disciplines, who claim our primary loyalties.[74] Lombardi emphasized that "although

72 Lombardi, *How Universities Work*, 69.

73 Ibid., 12, 22, 116; Rosovsky, *University*, 183, 229–30. Had he lived to read it, Jacques Barzun, a former Columbia provost, would have applied an astringent footnote to Lombardi's emphasis on "quality" (or excellence). In his 1968 guide, *The American University: How It Runs, Where It Is Going* (New York: Harper & Row), Barzun argued that "excellence is what other people say you have achieved after the work is done. In the doing, the energies should be bent on the task and not on excellence. There are no externals of excellence to be appropriated by going after it or them" (222). See the next paragraph herein for Lombardi's rebuttal.

74 Andrew Abbott, "The Disciplines and the Future," in Steven Brint, ed., *The City of Intellect: The Changing American University* (Stanford, Calif.: Stanford University Press, 2002), ch. 8; Jerry A. Jacobs, *In Defense of Disciplines: Interdisciplinarity and Specialization in the Research University* (Chicago: University of Chicago Press, 2014).

quality is among the most elusive of academic measurements, every university [department] knows what defines quality" because the national discipline of peers "establishes the intellectual standards of their work." It may not always apply those standards consistently or rigorously, but when it doesn't, it cannot help but know that it has fallen short. Few professions produce as many "regular and public judgments about their membership," Rosovsky reminds us. "The pressure to produce [high-] quality research in adequate quantity and to teach well is strong and comes from many directions"—student course evaluators; book reviewers and prize committees; journal editors; grant and fellowship administrators; retention, promotion, and tenure committees; learned and honorary societies; endowed-chair selectors.[75]

According to an extensive 2010 study of elite universities in Europe and the United States, "universities are more productive [of publications and patents] when they are both more autonomous and face more competition."[76] Dean Rosovsky had come to a similar conclusion twenty years earlier. "The American philosophy of governance," he wrote, "is a major factor in explaining the high quality of our universities" because "the combination of competition and independence is a most effective pair of spurs urging us toward even higher levels of excellence." Competition not only "prevented complacency" and promoted "the drive for excellence and change," its benefits extended to virtually all aspects of university life, from endowments, faculty recruitment, and architecture to student admissions, library size, and athletics. In the late 1980s Rosovsky "noticed that at Harvard we worr[ied] more about the lure and power of Stanford than about the attractions of Columbia and Yale." Even the then-chesty salary offers ($100,000-plus) made by the oil-rich University of Texas

75 Rosovsky, *University*, 187, 194, 214; Lombardi, *How Universities Work*, 2, 115, 120.

76 Philippe Aghion, Mathias Dewatripont, Caroline Hoxby, Andreu Mas-Collall, and André Sapir, "The Governance and Performance of Universities: Evidence from Europe and the U.S.," *Economic Policy* 25:61 (Jan. 2010), 7–59. Similar results in a study of 48 national systems of higher education were found in the *Journal of Higher Education Policy and Management* in 2013. Bernard Lane, ""Recipe for Strong Higher Ed," *InsideHigherEd* (Jan. 14, 2014), https://www.insidehighered.com/news/2014/01/14/study-finds-countries-fund-freely-and-regulate-loosely-have-best-higher-ed.

weren't as worrisome to Harvard deans seeking to hold onto their research "stars."[77]

It was a worry well founded—then and now—because Stanford was in the middle of a meteoric rise on just those engines that all three of the above commentators recognized as key. In national rankings of faculty and graduate programs, Stanford rose from a fourteenth–fifteenth place tie in 1957 to a third–fourth tie in five general areas of study, behind only Harvard and Berkeley. By 1983 and again in 1995, only Berkeley ranked higher.[78] With the same momentum, Stanford researchers claimed only 3 Nobel Prizes in the 1950s and '60s, but captured 16 in the next thirty years and another 11 by 2014, not just in STEM fields but also in economics and medicine and physiology.[79]

To help pay for all of this talent, in 1972 Stanford launched a $300 million ($1.7 billion in 2015 dollars) fund-raising campaign, to that date the largest for any university in the world. Fifteen years later, it raised $1.269 billion ($2.7 billion in 2015 dollars), again the largest campaign in U.S. educational history. In 2014 Stanford was so popular with undergraduate applicants—qualified and less so—that the admissions office accepted barely 5 percent.[80] They may not have heard, but their parents might have, that the previous year Stanford received the most private donations ($931 million) of any university in the country, as it had for several years before that. By the end of fiscal year 2014, Stanford's endowment towered at $21.4 billion (the

77 Rosovsky, *University*, 32, 223, 226, 284.

78 Gillmor, *Terman at Stanford*, app. D; *Chronology of Stanford*, 122, 141. On Berkeley's success, see (Provost) George W. Breslauer, "What Made Berkeley Great? The Sources of Berkeley's Sustained Academic Excellence," *Center for Studies in Higher Education (UC-Berkeley), Research & Occasional Paper Series* 3.11 (Jan. 2011), 1–14.

79 http://news.stanford.edu/nobels.

80 Of those few it accepted in 2014, 77 percent chose to enroll, second only to Harvard's 82-percent "yield." *Harvard Magazine* (July-Aug. 2014), 31. In "The Truth Behind College Admission" (*New York Times*, Sunday Review sec., Nov. 30, 2014, p. 2), Kevin Carey reminds us that "it's not that fewer [top] students are accepted; it's that applications [from "long shots and dreamers" armed with the Common Application and abundant application fees] have run riot." "Four out of five well-qualified students who apply to elite schools are accepted by at least one."

third-largest individual fund), up from $18 billion a year earlier.[81] Adding a note of bravado to its challenge, Stanford had won its twentieth consecutive [Athletic] Directors' (formerly Sears) Cups for having won the most league (Pac-12) and NCAA sports championships each year, while keeping their hundreds of student-athletes eligible and graduating in impressive Ivy League–like numbers.[82]

Perhaps most galling of all for Harvard alums and officials was a May 2014 news story in the *New York Times* entitled "To Young Minds of Today, Harvard Is the Stanford of the East."[83] In the current popularity contest, Stanford's tech-savvy, STEM-happy place in the Silicon Valley sun commands a certain amount of media buzz and teenage attention. But Harvard's preeminent endowment ($36.4 billion), Nobel lead (69 to 38), and dominance over the western upstart in all global rankings suggest that the competition is only tightening and will never be over.[84] Nor will it be in ambitious universities below the top few that compete in particular institutional niches, regional rivalries, or the increasingly global agora of research universities.

❁ ❁ ❁

As universities grew larger and more focused on research, they subtly discounted the teaching of undergraduates and devoted more attention to graduate education, which visibly improved. Kerr acknowledged in 1963 that "better facilities, more research assistantships and fellowships, [and] more research projects in which students can work directly with faculty members . . . all result from federal funds." At

81 *Chronology of Stanford*, 108, 127; *Chronicle of Higher Education Almanac, 2014–15* (Aug. 22, 2014), pp. 53–54; news.stanford.edu/news/2014/september/mp-investment-return-092414.html.

82 Mike Antonucci and Kevin Cool, "Game Changer," *Stanford* (Sept.–Oct. 2014), 44–51, at 46.

83 Pérez-Peña, "To Young Minds," *New York Times* (May 30, 2014), A1, A3.

84 Christine Y. Cahill and Matthew Q. Clarida, "Endowment Grows to $36.4B with 15.4 Percent Return," *Harvard Crimson* (Sept. 24, 2014); https://en.wikipedia.org/wiki/List_of_Nobel_laureates_by_university_affiliation. Harvard was able to lure 19 Nobel laureates after they had won elsewhere, Stanford only 4.

the same time, more than one study of the effects of federal aid on higher education found that it "accelerated the long-standing depreciation of undergraduate education at large universities."[85]

Kerr agreed. "Teaching loads and student contact hours have been reduced" as "average class size has been increasing. . . . Faculty members are more frequently on leave or temporarily away from the campus [so] more of the instruction falls to teachers who are not members of the regular faculty." "The best graduate students prefer fellowships and research assistantships to teaching assistantships" and "postdoctoral fellows who might fill the gap usually do not teach." In short, Kerr concluded, "undergraduate education in a large university is more likely to be acceptable than outstanding." But he also noted that "a very few private institutions with long traditions of very high-quality undergraduate instruction have been able to maintain their standards," as Princeton, Yale, Cornell, Duke, Stanford, and Chicago still do.[86]

Rather than join the poor-teaching bandwagon, Dean Rosovsky chose to defend the benefits for undergraduates of the top fifty or so "university colleges." Confessing that "a university college has never consisted of five hundred Mr. Chipses" (neither has any small college), he gave several reasons why undergraduates should want "research-oriented teachers." The first was their "love of learning" because such professors are "people who wish to remain students for

85 The most thorough study was Harold Orlans, *The Effects of Federal Programs on Higher Education: A Study of 36 Universities and Colleges* (Washington, D.C.: The Brookings Institution, 1962), ch. 3.

86 Kerr, *Uses of the University*, 64–65. The high quality of their students also reinforce their attention to undergraduate teaching. No matter the size of their classes, elite university students *demand* the best teaching possible. Having gained admission to some of the most selective—and expensive—institutions in the world, they are not afraid to hold their professors' feet to the fire if faculty are not stimulating, attentive, and effective. In my experience at four U.S. research universities (including Yale and Princeton), professors are much less afraid of student course evaluations, disenrollments, or social media "slams" than they are of not meeting their own high standards and expectations. For a keen expression of teaching engagement at a public flagship (the University of Virginia), see Mark Edmundson, *Why Teach? In Defense of a Real Education* (New York: Bloomsbury, 2013).

the rest of their lives." The second reason was that "persons who have faith in progress and therefore possess an intellectually optimistic disposition—i.e., teacher-scholars—are probably more interesting and better professors." His third reason, of particular importance to an arts-and-sciences dean, was that "a research-oriented faculty is less likely to be the home of intellectual deadwood," whose proportions he reckoned (unscientifically) at less than 2 percent in any major university faculty.[87]

Rosovsky was also convinced that in hiring and tenure decisions, "faculty selection based primarily on research performance leads to fewer mistakes than choices based more on hard-to-define teaching ability. Both talents should be taken into account," he conceded, "but research ability is a better long-term indicator." To clinch his argument for elite universities like Harvard, he posited that "intellectual excitement is enhanced by contact with people who have written books, done major experiments, and held policy positions in government." Still, in the end, he had to admit that research professors "are in large measure judged by the size and quality of their graduate student followings," not their popularity or effectiveness with undergraduates.[88]

More recently, John Lombardi put a different spin on teaching in research universities by underlining the differences in *scale* between places like Caltech (with 950 undergraduates) and Ohio State (with more than 40,000). Although all research universities are committed to the search for new knowledge, we need reminding that "most organize their work from a base in teaching." Despite differences in campus culture and style, "teaching matters in American research universities . . . in almost all cases." And most of it ranges narrowly from "good to very good." Undergraduate curricula are quite similar in their core arts-and-sciences content and disciplinary majors because of competition and regulation. "Competition ensures that each

87 Rosovsky, *University*, 88, 89, 90, 210–11. For several other reasons, see James Axtell, "Twenty-Five Reasons to Publish," *Journal of Scholarly Publishing* 29:1 (Oct. 1997), 3–20, reprinted in Axtell, *The Pleasures of Academe: A Celebration & Defense of Higher Education* (Lincoln: University of Nebraska Press, 1998), ch. 3, esp. 58–66.

88 Rosovsky, *University*, 93, 94, 163.

college and university offers much the same curriculum to a common marketplace of students and parents seeking equivalent products" of high quality. "Regulation reinforces [the] standardization of content through accreditation," a process conducted largely by faculty and administrators from peer or superior institutions.[89]

Leading universities offer a mixture of large and small classes. Upperclassmen and graduate students tend to get the smaller, more personal, more specialized classes; underclassmen are normally acculturated in large lecture courses of several hundred strangers that are often taught by pedagogically talented senior faculty. But increasingly, much undergraduate teaching has been assigned to non-tenure-track, or "contingent" faculty—poorly paid, part-time adjuncts or graduate assistants—as cost-saving measures, even in the face of steadily increasing enrollments.[90] Graduate teaching, in contrast, has remained personal, expensive, and resistant to economies of scale. Because the standard modes of graduate education—seminars, lab-based projects, theses, and dissertations—are research-oriented "handicraft" activities, Lombardi regards scale as the best explanation for "why both public and private research universities appear most similar in their graduate and PhD education and least similar in their undergraduate programs."[91]

The centrality of research in elite universities also explains why teaching is not as prestigious an activity. Lombardi argues that "the quality of university research drives the quality, breadth, and depth of the undergraduate curriculum" (although the reverse might be argued as well).[92] "Teaching delivers the state of current knowledge,"

89 Lombardi, *How Universities Work*, 45–47, 53–54, 121–22.

90 Goldie Blumenstyk, *American Higher Education in Crisis: What Everyone Needs to Know* (New York: Oxford University Press, 2015), 90, 102–104. Brock Read's "Here's the First Mention of an 'Adjunct Professor' in The New York Times" (*Chronicle of Higher Education*, Vitae section, https://chroniclevitae.com/news/624-here-s-the-first-mention-of-an-adjunct-professor-in-the-new-york-times, [July 25, 2014]) offers a revealing graph of mentions of adjuncts, which begins a noticeable ascent in the 1970s. The first mention in the *Times* was to an adjunct professor of law at the University of Virginia in 1855.

91 Lombardi, *How Universities Work*, 50–51, 53–54.

92 A 1977 study of 77 U.S. Nobel laureates in science found that the great majority received their undergraduate education in Ivy League (Harvard, Yale, Princeton,

whereas research "pursues knowledge at the boundaries of our current understanding." Moreover, "teaching talent is more common than research talent" and therefore has to settle for lower salaries. Research is a highly competitive national and international enterprise that is evaluated by rigorous protocols of peer review. Teachers have only local, largely nonportable reputations, partly because of "the national inability to specify the measurable characteristics of quality teaching."[93]

❁ ❁ ❁

Although the personal synergy between professor and student remains essential and familiar, explosions in specialization, content, and technology have even altered the academic landscape in the last few decades. In 1972 Clark Kerr attributed the multiversity's creation to the faculty and their "ever narrower specializations." By 1990, the fissiparous fertility of academic disciplines was no news to Dean Rosovsky. In commenting on the faculty's "extremely demanding and time-consuming" attempts to remain current in their fields, he drew attention to the growth of specialties in biology, his own field of economics, and the literary humanities.[94] He probably wouldn't blanch, twenty-five years later, at the current curriculum in his former Faculty of Arts and Sciences, with its 40 departments and 46 undergraduate "concentrations" (or majors) with such evolved

---

Columbia) or public research (Berkeley) universities, often in the labs of previous Nobel winners. Harriet Zuckerman, *Scientific Elite: Nobel Laureates in the United States* (New York: Free Press, 1977). See also Burton Feldman, *The Nobel Prize: A History of Genius, Controversy, and Prestige* (New York: Arcade Publishing, 2000).

93 Lombardi, *How Universities Work*, 55–57, 123.

94 Kerr, *Uses of the University*, 129, 141; Rosovsky, *University*, 162–63. On the national stage, the members of the American Council of Learned Societies jumped from 13 at its effective founding in 1919 to 72 in 2014. www.acls.org. Thanks to Vice-President Steven Wheatley for a digital copy of the inaugural *Bulletin* (Oct. 1920) and an informative email. The much larger American Association for the Advancement of Science (est. 1848), whose ten million members are divided into 24 "sections" of scientific activity, now has 262 affiliated societies, associations, and academies of science. en.wikipedia.org/wiki/American_Association_for_the_Advancement_of_Science.

titles as Bioengineering, Sanskrit and Indian Studies, and Studies of Women, Gender, and Sexuality.[95]

The content of courses has expanded even more explosively than their titles. The Second World War introduced Americans to many areas of the globe beyond Europe—their peoples, cultures, languages, religions, and politics. After the war the federal government and the Ford Foundation offered liberal grants to universities that would insert the study of those "critical" new places in their curricula and research agendas. Military theaters in the Atlantic and Pacific reminded scholars of the historical importance of oceans, beaches, and coastal economies. America's "peculiar" problem—race—came to the academic fore in the 1960s with the civil rights and Black Pride movements, as did the emergence of women as activists, subjects, and scholars. Non-Caucasian minorities of every hue—and Whites themselves—caught the academic eye as they came into public view. So did gender, sexuality, and their permutations and expressions. Children, the elderly, the "differently abled," and even *non*human species gained scholarly attention. Thanks in part to Earth Day (established as an annual observance on April 22, 1970), the environment finally got its scholarly due, especially as global warming made itself felt and fossil fuels continued to wreak havoc with the air we breathe. History's "losers" also caught a curricular break, particularly America's native peoples, who refused to go away quietly. Like women and African Americans, Native Americans often got their own academic "programs" if they couldn't secure full-fledged departments.[96]

As for reading assignments, books and articles were and are devoted to the history and meaning of virtually everything, major and (arguably no longer) minor: smell- and soundscapes, emotions, pain,

95 www.fas.harvard.edu.

96 David John Frank, Evan Schofer, and John Charles Torres, "Rethinking History: Change in the University Curriculum, 1910–1990," *Sociology of Education* 67:4 (Oct. 1994), 231–42; Lawrence W. Levine, *The Opening of the American Mind: Canons, Cultures, and History* (Boston: Beacon Press, 1996); Sheila Slaughter, "The Political Economy of Curriculum-Making in American Universities," in Brint, ed., *The Future of the City of Intellect*, ch. 10.

body parts, colors, fat, furs, genius, games, gossip, humor, dreams, diseases, clothes (and nudity), poverty, wealth, saltpeter, pearls, booze, (yes) dust, and (my personal favorite) footnotes.[97] Since the scope of study ranges from the most distant galaxies and the Big Bang itself to the subatomic and molecular, professors have no trouble finding engaging assignments and students no lack of research topics, all of which are meant to teach the key methodologies and standards of the sponsoring disciplines.[98]

❁ ❁ ❁

If the fission of the known poses a challenge to liberal arts curricul*a* (there is no single one, nor should there be), the rapid development of new technologies for processing, storing, accessing, "publishing," reproducing, and distributing that knowledge has posed its own challenges to the knowledge industry and its faculty-masters and student-apprentices. There is no doubt that computers, WiFi, the Internet, the Web, email, texting, laser printers, thumb drives, CDs, cloud-storage, smart phones and lecterns, clickers, electronic reserve systems (such as Blackboard), Google, Wikipedia, and electronic readers (Kindle and Nook) have had a considerable impact on learning and teaching. Clearly, many of these inventions save time, frustration, and money and multiply the possibilities for research. At the same time, some uses invite intellectual shortcutting and plagiarism, just as misuse of social media (Twitter, Facebook, Instagram) has the potential to attenuate personal interaction, attention spans, and the social restraint and consideration of face-to-face communication.

Equally disruptive of traditional ways of teaching and learning are new digital experiments, which are intended not only to improve student learning and extend its benefits to nonlocal audiences,

97 I refer to Anthony Grafton's erudite and entertaining *The Footnote: A Curious History* (Cambridge, Mass.: Harvard University Press, 1997). See also Chuck Zerby, *The Devil's Details: A History of Footnotes* (Montpelier, Vt.: Invisible Cities Press, 2002).

98 For a compelling brief for the disciplinary value of historical research for both graduate students and undergraduates, see Anthony Grafton and James Grossman, "Habits of Mind," *American Scholar* 84:1 (Winter 2015), 31–37.

but optimally to produce savings to help ameliorate the "cost disease" that is driving public and private college "sticker prices" above the annual rate of inflation and the budgets of many working- and middle-class families. Two hoped-for solutions are MOOCs (massive open online courses) and the "flipped" classroom. The former resembles a previous phenomenon: educational television (such as Kenneth Clark's popular *Civilization* series), except that the talking expert roamed farther afield—into landscapes, historic homes, and museums—than the familiar academic "sage on the stage" does even in MOOCs. In neither of the two older media, however, does the audience, the "students," get to ask for clarification or to express doubt or disagreement, which are major parts of the learning process. The monologue, however learned or charming it may be, is simply not a dialogue.

The newly dubbed "flipped" classroom was invented to inject more dialogue into even large lectures. In the "flipped," or "blended," classroom, either a local professor or an online MOOC star introduces the essential content of the subject in much less than the traditional 50-minute modules. Each of these is followed by discussion—online or in person—in small groups with or without facilitators ("guides on the side," much like graduate-student TAs in most traditional large lectures) and/or by testing of the module concepts and content. With a module "mastered," the "lecture" and course continue.[99]

Some faculties have resisted the purchase and use of commercial MOOCs taught by "stellar" outsiders, but they often reduce their misgivings when they are able to modify the content, discussion, and testing to suit their particular institutions and student bodies. Nonetheless, everything about online education is experimental and costly in time and treasure, and issues of faculty ownership of courses are difficult to adjudicate. And the jury is still out on

99 Dan Berrett, "Who's the Hardest-Working Person in the Lecture Hall? Maybe It Should No Longer Be the Professor," *Chronicle of Higher Education* (Nov. 21, 2014), A14; Carl Straumsheim, "For Some Research Universities, Flexibility and Modularity Influence Long-Term Plans," *InsideHigherEd*, https://www.insidehighered.com/news/2014/12/02/some-research-universities-flexibility-and-modularity-influence-long-term-plans (Dec. 2, 2014).

whether digital teaching is more intellectually or cost effective than traditional modes.[100]

❁ ❁ ❁

Another educational partner challenged by the digital revolution is the university library. In size and clientele, libraries have grown inexorably to keep up with the growth in enrollments and knowledge. The best-funded universities have, predictably, the largest libraries.[101] America's most extensive university library is Harvard's, with nearly 19 million bound volumes distributed among 73 general and specialized libraries. The University of Illinois and Yale trail by 3 or 4 million volumes. Scrappy Stanford has only half as many as its Cambridge rival, but can also borrow from Berkeley's 11.5 million volumes overnight.[102] The median collection of the 125 members of the Association of Research Libraries (est. 1932) is about 4 million volumes. None of these numbers account for their ability to borrow books and articles through the interlibrary loan system (regularized in 1916),[103] or the millions of digital versions of both now available online. With median budgets of just over $12 million, ARL members spend between 10 and 50 percent for electronic materials and services.[104]

What they get for their money is true progress and tough challenges. An obvious one is space and its configuration. As physical

100 The most thorough and judicious guide to these issues is William G. Bowen, *Higher Education in the Digital Age* (Princeton, N.J.: Princeton University Press, 2013; paperback ed. with additional material and analysis, 2014).

101 A prominent exception is the University of Illinois, whose library is the 5th largest but whose university endowment and library expenditures rank lower (37th and 14th, respectively).

102 "The Nation's Largest Libraries: A Listing by Volumes Held." ALA Library Fact Sheet 22. American Library Association. http://www.ala.org/tools/libfactsheets/alalibraryfactsheet22.

103 Arthur T. Hamlin, *The University Library in the United States: Its Origins and Development* (Philadelphia: University of Pennsylvania Press, 1981), 184–86. In October 2014, 12 elite universities (including 8 Ivies) forged a reciprocal borrowing and personal use agreement, in which borrowed items may be returned at either the lending library or the user's home library. *Cornell Chronicle* (Oct. 1, 2014).

104 Lombardi, *How Universities Work*, 150–53.

FIGURE 28. Harvard's Widener Library, the anchor of the world's largest university library system, was built in 1915 as a memorial to a book-collecting son of the Class of 1907 who was lost with his father on the *Titanic*. Its 10 levels and 50 miles of stacks now hold 3 million of Harvard's nearly 19 million volumes, distributed between 70-some libraries.

collections continue to grow, new shelf space must be found (perhaps off-site for less-used titles and older periodicals) to keep the book-oriented humanists and social scientists happy. But new electronic infrastructures, computer banks, and online collections must also be given "space" and expert staff to accommodate the STEM and medical faculties who rely on more recent experimental data and journals. And students, in timeless search of reading assignments and information for their papers and theses, regard the library as "a service center, a location for group work, and a place to plug into the electronic world and access the materials they need."[105] All users,

105 Ibid., 152–53, at 153. Collaboration (or just socializing) is so common that some libraries reserve "quiet floors" for those who wish to be alone with their books, laptops, or thoughts. Many have loosened their formerly starched rules about the use of pens and consumption of food and drink in the study areas and stacks.

whether in the library or anywhere the Web reaches, resort first to a digital catalog of holdings, *card* catalogs having become relics of the past. Increasingly holdings appear in print (analog) and /or electronic (digital) form. Articles from a huge number of new and old journals and periodicals can be retrieved and read on platforms provided—at a high cost and for an uncertain future—by JSTOR, EBSCO, ProQuest, and other aggregators. Likewise, instead of conning aged black-and-white prints tacked to bulletin boards in the art history department, students can bring up high-resolution color images of the originals on ARTstor.

Existing book holdings of some of the largest research libraries are in the process of being digitized for global consumption—and none too soon for the many titles published well into the twentieth century on cheap acidified paper that, with use, turns to brown flakes. As early as 1971, Project Gutenberg began to digitize and distribute free copies of books in the public domain.[106] Google Books and Hathi Trust made heroic starts in the 1990s but were stymied by authors' copyrights to books published after 1923. Fortunately, their digital copies and catalogue have been incorporated in an equally ambitious but more legal Digital Public Library of America, conceived by Harvard's former library director, the historian Robert Darnton.[107] The Internet Archive (est. 1996), with its sci-fi-sounding "Wayback Machine," seeks eventually to provide free public access to "all knowledge," including books, music, moving images, and evanescent websites. But their e-books, too, are limited to titles in the public domain.[108]

106 https://en.wikipedia.org/wiki/Project_Gutenberg.

107 Robert Darnton, "The National Digital Public Library Is Launched!" *New York Review of Books* (April 25, 2013), 4, 6; Robert Darnton, "Jefferson's Taper: A National Digital Library," *New York Review of Books* (Nov. 24, 2011), 23–25. See also his "The Research Library in the Digital Age," *Bulletin of the American Academy of Arts and Sciences* (Spring 2008), 9–15; "The Library in the New Age," *New York Review of Books* (June 12, 2008), 72–73, 76, 78–80; and "5 Myths of the 'Information Age,'" *Chronicle [of Higher Education] Review* (April 22, 2011).

108 https://en.wikipedia.org/wiki/Internet_Archive. See also Jill Lepore, "The Cobweb: Can the Internet be Archived?" *New Yorker* (Jan. 26, 2015).

The most serious challenge that electronic materials face is guaranteed longevity.[109] Depending on reasonable use, books printed on then acid-free rag paper by Johann Gutenberg in the mid-fifteenth century are as durable, viable, and readable as they were hot off his cold press. E-books and online journals have a fragile, somewhat ethereal, existence, which is complicated by the need to preserve, reconfigure, or supersede the superannuated machines once able to store and produce them on demand. Materials stored on floppy and hard disks, CDs, Blackboard, and thumb drives face the same threat of technological obsolescence or extinction. Since virtually all university presses have adopted acid-free paper, the contents of their books may be expected to survive another, post-Gutenberg 500 years. But whatever form knowledge takes in the future, university libraries will be expected to remain the essential platforms from which researchers dive into the unknown and students learn to swim.

❀ ❀ ❀

The vigorous competition among American research universities has long taken an unusual form that remains an almost total mystery to their global competitors and emulators. With few exceptions, the best universities also compete in intercollegiate athletics, particularly strenuously in the large spectator—"revenue"—sports of football and men's basketball. In so doing, their competitive juices somehow compel them to engage in unsustainably expensive "arms races" to see who can build the biggest and best facilities—stadiums for football, arenas for basketball—and hire the winningest (usually the most expensive) coaches, all to lure the most

109 Steve Kolowich, "Uphill Battle on Digital Preservation," *Inside Higher Ed*, https://www.insidehighered.com/news/2010/04/02/preservation (April 2, 2010), introducing a 116-page report of the Blue Ribbon Task Force on Sustainable Digital Preservation and Access published on Feb. 17, 2010. As corporations, digital bundlers have uncertain shelf lives; universities intent upon operating indefinitely not only do not own the books they license (rent), they cannot be certain that those titles will be available long term when they need them.

proficient "student-athletes" that NCAA-approved "athletic scholarships" can buy.[110]

Those who support big-time sports programs argue that *winning* teams offer universities several benefits: they publicize, often nationally, alma mater's name or 'brand"; they provide bragging rights to students and alumni; they increase donations to the university; they help recruit better-qualified applicants; and their ticket sales, television revenues, and licensed apparel sales not only cover the cost of the athletic department, but often contribute to the educational and general funds for all.[111]

Nearly all of these claims are misleading or false. Beginning with the last, the vast majority of sports programs *lose* money and have to be subsidized, often heavily, by the university ("a direct cost to teaching and research") or by underpublicized student fees, which can cost each student hundreds of dollars.[112] Athletic publicity can cut both ways: in principle, every game has to have a loser. Moreover, teams that cheat academically by hiring "academic advisors" to write their players' papers or take their tests for them,

110 As a result of student-driven legal challenges to the NCAA's monopolistic power and policies, many of the major sports conferences have been forced to raise their athletic scholarships close or equal to the full cost of educating their athletes, to guarantee them for all four years, and to provide better and longer health care. Some of the "revenue" sports have even put aside in trust modest shares of their huge income from ticket and apparel sales and TV appearances.

111 In 2014, "the market for licensed collegiate merchandise [was] worth an estimated $4.5-billion a year." Michael Posner, "Universities Can Put Their Economic Clout to Good Use," *Chronicle of Higher Education* (Nov. 21, 2014), A60.

112 In 2014, only 23 of 228 public Division I universities made more from athletics than they spent, and 16 of those still received university subsidies. Part of the reason was coaches' salaries: in 2013, football coaches at 70 public universities each received more than $1 million (and their many assistants often more than the highest-paid faculty). Athletic budgets in the 13 major sports universities easily exceed $100 million annually; in 2014, 8 of them required student subsidies, 6 in the millions of dollars. For the last decade, athletic spending per athlete has exceeded academic spending per student. Bond issues for large and posh new facilities are often added to the university's overall debt total. Blumenstyk, *American Higher Education in Crisis?* 82–84; Lombardi, *How Universities Work*, 146; *USA Today* (2014), www.usatoday.com/sports/college/schools/finance.

pay recruits under the table, don't graduate their players, or continue to play stars who have committed serious crimes soon pay the price of notoriety and expunged records.[113] Even high-schoolers with somewhat higher SATs and grade-point averages who choose a university largely for its championships or bowl appearances can be dubious recruits for an *educational* institution.[114] By the same token, alumni donations do sometimes rise after conspicuous victories, and go mostly to athletics, but they quickly recede when the feats are not repeated.

Perhaps the greatest scandal in major college sports is that too many athletes are recruited and matriculated as "special admits" who lack the high-school record, native aptitude, or desire to do college-level work, particularly when they are required to spend 30–40 exhausting hours a week in practice, watching game films, conditioning, physical therapy, and often long-distance travel to away games.[115] For such players, graduation rates and life prospects are sadly low, especially when injuries or academic ineligibility puts an end to their annually renewable scholarships.[116] The fairest remedy

113 The long-term academic cheating at UNC-Chapel Hill that was uncovered in 2014 put a serious dent in the flagship university's reputation. Brian Rosenberg, president of Macalester College, argued in a prominent blog that the university should lose its accreditation. "UNC-Chapel Hill Should Lose Accreditation," *Chronicle of Higher Education* (Oct. 24, 2014), blog "The Conversation," http://chronicle.com/blogs/conversation/2014/10/24/unc-chapel-hill-should-lose-accreditation/.

114 Brad R. Humphreys and Michael Mondello, "Intercollegiate Athletic Success and Donations at NCAA Division I Institutions," *Journal of Sports Management* 21 (2007), 265–80.

115 In his freshman year at Ohio State University, a heavily recruited quarterback posted a message on Twitter after taking a sociology exam: "Why should we have to go to class if we came here to play FOOTBALL, we ain't come to play SCHOOL, classes are POINTLESS." Written evidence of his attitude is rare, but the attitude itself, sadly, is widespread. His Twitter message was reproduced in the *New York Times* (Dec. 31, 2014), A1.

116 For the conflicted world of research-university sports, see Charles T. Clotfelter, *Big-Time Sports in American Universities* (New York: Cambridge University Press, 2011); J. Douglas Toma, *Football U.: Spectator Sports in the Life of the American University* (Ann Arbor: University of Michigan Press, 2003); Brian M. Ingrassia, *The Rise of the Gridiron University: Higher Education's Uneasy Alliance with Big-Time*

might be to establish an "academic index" for each NCAA conference in each division, similar to the one the Ivy League installed in the early 1980s, which allows the admission of athletes (and any other specially talented students) with entering high-school grades and standard test scores within one standard deviation below the mean of the previous entering class.[117] It would by no means be a panacea for all that's wrong with the peculiar American situation, but it does have the potential to restore some meaning and integrity to *student* in the NCAA's badly frayed concept of student-athlete.[118]

Our search for the main explanations for America's commanding presence among the leading research universities of the world is not at an end, certainly not with mention only of the financial excesses and moral lapses of big-time college sports. For there are many intercollegiate sports played by truly amateur athletes, male and female, without as well as with athletic scholarships, that do not detract from the students' educational progress, competitive spirit, or integrity.[119] Some of the very best private universities—Harvard, Yale, Princeton, Stanford—field more than 25 or 30 varsity teams and even more "club" and recreational teams to cultivate the ancient

---

Football (Lawrence: University of Kansas Press, 2012); James J. Duderstadt, *Intercollegiate Athletics and the American University: A University President's Perspective* (Ann Arbor: University of Michigan Press, 2000).

117 For the Ivies' AI and some of its operational problems, see James Shulman and William G. Bowen, *The Game of Life: College Sports and Educational Values* (Princeton, N.J.: Princeton University Press, 2001), 13–14, 46; William Bowen and Sarah A. Levin, *Reclaiming the Game: College Sports and Educational Values* (Princeton, N.J.: Princeton University Press, 2003), 176, 263, 268, 343n7, 387nn9, 11.

118 The annual news coverage of the Heisman Trophy for the best college football player is vastly greater than the one-page paid announcement in the *Chronicle of Higher Education* for the William V. Campbell Trophy honoring the best scholar-athlete in college football. See, for example, *CHE* (Dec. 19, 2014), A2, for the latter compared to a Google search for "Heisman."

119 Paul Weiss, *Sport: A Philosophic Inquiry* (Carbondale: Southern Illinois University Press, 1969); Axtell, *Pleasures of Academe*, ch. 7 ("The Making of a Scholar-Athlete"); Shulman and Bowen, *The Game of Life*; Bowen and Levin, *Reclaiming the Game*; Ronald A. Smith, *Pay for Play: A History of Big-Time College Athletic Reform* (Urbana: University of Illinois Press, 2011).

Juvenalian ideal of "a sound mind in a sound body."[120] While winning is an important and the preferred goal, most college coaches know that losing occasionally often teaches more useful lessons in the long run. Unfortunately, as athletic-department publicity machines continue to ballyhoo sport's contributions to player "character," "teamwork," "work ethic," and "school spirit," coaches are hired, fired, and given handsome bonuses solely for the number of games and championships they win.

For the millions of Americans who follow big-time college football and basketball on television or in a packed stadium or arena, there are mere hundreds or handfuls of parents, roommates, and friends seeking a study break who attend the spirited and often deft but seldom brutal contests in field hockey, tennis, soccer, swimming and diving, baseball, water polo, volleyball, golf, rowing, and *touch* (or tag) football. Those sports, too, represent athletics at the leading research universities, but they seldom add to alma mater's national, much less global, reputation. To all appearances, and with good reason, big-time sports are one of the few features of the American research university that the rest of the world, with their own national cultures and pastimes, have little desire to emulate.

❁ ❁ ❁

With that said, we can now get down to gathering up the brass tacks that we've been scattering throughout the previous pages.

120 Juvenal, *The Sixteen Satires*, trans. Peter Green (London: Penguin, 1982), 217: bk. 4, satire 10 (10.356) . Large public universities tend to sponsor fewer varsity teams, perhaps because their big "revenue" sports are profligate investors in the entertainment, rather than the education, business.

EPILOGUE

The Medieval Institution That Ate the World[1]

THE UNIVERSITY IS now more than eight centuries old, but it hasn't shriveled into senescence. Instead of aging, it has in the last century gained new vigor and proliferated progeny not only in the United States but also around the globe. On that basis alone, the latest alarms and hand-wringing over its prospects seem unwarranted.

To many students of social organization, the university is the most versatile institution in contemporary society. American universities in particular serve not only as "crucial sites for the production of knowledge," but as vital "hubs" at the intersection of "multiple institutions" and "social processes that often are regarded as distinct"—everything from the labor market and larger economy (think graduates, placement offices, economics departments, and business and finance schools), the learned professions (graduate and professional schools), and the sciences (all of them) to health care (teaching hospitals, medical and nursing schools), the military (ROTC), government (departments of politics or government and schools of public administration and international relations), high culture (writing programs, art, music, and literature departments), religion (chapels, chaplains, religion departments, and divinity schools), philanthropy (alumni associations and development offices), the family (departments of sociology, psychology, history, and home economics, for starters), and the nation-state (federal funding and regulations). The elite universities at the apex of the higher education system also serve as "sieves" for sorting people, regulating mobility, and credentialing experts; as "incubators" of economic and social capital; and as secular "temples" for the legitimation of official knowledge and

1 Responder "Kieran" to blog post by "jdos23," "The Most Important Thing We Know Least About," orgtheory.wordpress.com/2010/01/13.

new ideas. In modern societies like the United States, "much of the work of class stratification, knowledge production, and legitimation is relegated to the same organizations, universities." Small wonder that "educational credentials serve as primary markers of status."[2] In the United States, college decals on family-car windows and apparel emblazoned with one's own—or one's child's—college name and athletic colors have, until their use spread abroad fairly recently, been unique signs of America's national affection for its colleges and universities and their boost to, or confirmation of, one's social status.[3] As long as contemporary society doesn't im- or ex-plode, there is very little likelihood that the university will lose its complex role at the center of modernity's infrastructure.

Nor is there any great chance, I think, that America's elite universities will cease to crowd the upper reaches of the global rankings of research universities (along with the likes of Oxford, Cambridge, and Imperial College, London); they haven't lost any ground since 2003 when the first rankings were issued from Shanghai. For the elements and conditions that have underwritten U.S. success would have to obtain or be duplicated in competing societies and nations and to decline not only sharply but in unlikely numbers and combinations in the United States. The "secrets" of America's elite-university success are not secrets at all. They have been recognized by scholars and historians, native and foreign, for some time. A quick survey will suggest the large challenge of reproducing them that emulators around the world have had and may continue to have in the future.

2 Mitchell L. Stevens, Elizabeth A. Armstrong, and Richard Arum, "Sieve, Incubator, Temple, Hub: Empirical and Theoretical Advances in the Sociology of Higher Education," *Annual Review of Sociology* 34 (2008), 127–51. See also David Frank and John Meyer, "University Expansion and the Knowledge Society," *Theory and Society* 36:4 (Aug. 2007), 287–311.

3 Paul Fussell, "Schools for Snobbery," *New Republic* (Oct. 4, 1982), 25–26, 28–31; also in Fussell, *Class: A Guide through the American Status System* (New York: Summit Books, 1983), ch. 6. In the past decade or two, even the most reserved British university shops have marketed "brand" sweatshirts and T-shirts (beside the hard-to-decode club ties and college scarves), not only to visiting Americans.

(1) Universities tend to reflect, echo, and codify their national societies and cultures.[4] In a large democracy of considerable economic robustness, national wealth, and educational ambition, the United States has an extensive if "crazily unplanned mix of public and private, religious and secular, small and large, low-cost and expensive institutions"—more than 3,000 four-year institutions alone.[5] This diversity "provides a wealth of environments and opportunities for students to select a school that best matches their needs and capabilities."[6] As a meritocracy (when it functions at its best), the system also allows a person to start at any level and to rise—even to the top—by demonstrating his or her academic or intellectual capacity. Although there is still too strong a correlation between parental income and educational outcome, well-funded elite universities and many other public universities are making progress in admitting and supporting well-qualified students from lower-income and first-generation families. Increases in federal aid programs, such as Pell Grants, are aimed at the same results.

(2) America's academic diversity draws on diverse sources of funding: public and private, federal, state, municipal, corporate, entrepreneurial, and philanthropic.[7] The leading research universities have the ability to garner the most support for their costly research and teaching functions. Most of the best public institutions operate

4 Henry Rosovsky, *The University: An Owner's Manual* (New York: W. W. Norton, 1990), 299; Stevens, Armstrong, and Arum, "Sieve, Incubator, Temple, Hub," 141; Clark Kerr, *The Great Transformation in Higher Education, 1960–1980* (Albany: State University of New York Press, 1991), 41.

5 This figure includes 784 private for-profit institutions, which often lack the usual features of nonprofit colleges and universities, including residential campuses. Hunter R. Rawlings III, "Universities on the Defensive," *Princeton Alumni Magazine* (April 2, 2014), 28–31, at 29; *Chronicle of Higher Education Almanac, 2014–15* (Aug. 22, 2014), 73.

6 Charles M. Vest, *The American Research University from World War II to World Wide Web: Governments, the Private Sector, and the Emerging Meta-University* (Berkeley: University of California Press, 2007), 7–8.

7 American universities, even state-supported ones, have long led the world in cultivating annual and extraordinary support from their alumni. In 2013, the University of California system raised more than $1.6 billion from private, mostly alumni, sources. The University of Texas system was second at $819 million. Private Stanford was by far the largest individual recipient at $931 million. *CHE Almanac 2014–15*, 54.

as quasi-private universities in relying not only on student tuition and annual (if in recent decades steadily declining per student) state support, but on competitive federal grants and contracts (awarded mostly after rigorous peer review), endowments fueled by alumni, corporate, and other donors (encouraged by federal tax policy), and patents and licenses resulting from scientific research and technological innovation.[8]

(3) Most leading universities recognize and cultivate the synergy between teaching and research.[9] With some notable exceptions, such as designated research professors and increasing numbers of adjunct teachers, most tenure-track faculty do both, at least at the graduate level. In term papers, theses, and dissertations, student research is regarded as the best way to teach key disciplinary methods and standards, foster originality, and build well-founded self-confidence. Echoing the American credo, the *Magna Charta Universitatum*, signed by the rectors of 388 European universities in 1988 on the 900th anniversary of the founding of the University of Bologna, declared that "teaching and research in universities must be inseparable if their tuition is not to lag behind changing needs, the demands of society, and advances in scientific knowledge." Accordingly, the "recruitment of teachers, and the regulation of their status" must adhere to that principle.[10]

(4) The structure of American academic departments (framed largely by discipline or sub-discipline) is also a source of faculty quality because departments, particularly in the best universities, trust and encourage junior members to create their own courses, join important committees, and pursue any topics of research and scholarship they choose. Assistant professors assist no one, nor do associate professors. "They are not subservient or apprenticed to

8 Kerr, *Great Transformation*, ch. 3.

9 Vest, *American Research University*, 8; Rosovsky, *University*, 84–94; Rawlings, "Universities on the Defensive," 29; Jonathan R. Cole, *The Great American University: Its Rise to Preeminence, Its Indispensable National Role, Why It Must Be Protected* (New York: Public Affairs, 2009), 112.

10 Kevin Carey, "The Best Idea of the University," *Chronicle of Higher Education* (Oct. 5, 2012) , A32, http://chronicle.com/article/The-Best-Idea-of-the/134758/?cid=at&ut.

senior professors, so they bring to [their] institutions a constant flow of new ideas, passions, and approaches."[11] Whether junior faculty are "home-grown" or imported from rival institutions, they must all survive the tenure gauntlet to remain and become permanent staff. "Up or out" is a tough standard, but it ensures high standards because it is fueled by the intense competition that suffuses the ranks of the top universities. At the same time, the rising tide of adjuncts and part-time faculty, especially in straitened public universities, is a threat to tenure-track stability, quality, and full participation.

(5) The competition for new faculty intensifies when the leading American universities seek senior members to occupy full professorships or endowed chairs. Harvard is the most unabashed in its search for "the best in the world" for each position, but it has plenty of rivals with similar, if quieter, ambitions. Certainly Princeton, Yale, Berkeley, Stanford, Chicago, and a few other elites seek "the best," if not "in the world" at least for their own needs, ambitions, budgets, and bragging rights. None can gainsay the hubris of the tallest ambition, but it *is* a way to set the bar high, to prevent settling for an A- instead of an A+ hire, much less a B+ one, and certainly to avoid the other danger, inbreeding.[12]

(6) Part of America's success in university-building is owed to academe's pursuit of and receptivity to talented foreign students, scholars, and faculty. China may attract more foreigners to its universities than does the United States, but their stays are much shorter and seldom for advanced degrees and faculty positions.[13] The first and

11 Vest, *American Research University*, 8 (quotation); Rosovsky, *University*, 171, 216–18; Christina González, "Can China Build Something Like the University of California?" *InsideHigherEd* (May 31, 2012), https://www.insidehighered.com/views/2012/05/31/can-china-build-something-university-california-essay.

12 Rosovsky, *University*, 31–32, 35, 195–96, 223, 226, 284; Cole, *Great American University*, 5, 186–90; William G. Bowen, *Higher Education in the Digital Age* (Princeton, N.J.: Princeton University Press, 2013; paperback ed. with additional material and analysis, 2014), 12; Kerr, *Great Transformation*, 41; John V. Lombardi, *How Universities Work*, (Baltimore, Md.: Johns Hopkins University Press, 2013), 38, 42, 56; Vest, *American Research University*, 9.

13 Ben Wildavsky, *The Great Brain Race: How Global Universities Are Reshaping the World* (Princeton, N.J.: Princeton University Press, 2010), ch. 3, at 73–74; Ben

most illustrious influx of foreigners came as a gift from Hitler in the 1930s, when the Nazi regime's "racial purity" laws drove hundreds of Jewish scholars and professors from Germany and its Axis conquests. The contributions of such luminaries as Albert Einstein, Erwin Panofsky, Hannah Arendt, John von Neumann, and Hajo Holborn to American research and teaching suggest the magnitude of Hitler's self-inflicted loss.[14] Subsequent additions have brought "a defining quality of intellectual . . . richness" to American universities, particularly in the STEM subjects, but also "cultural richness" in the social sciences, arts, and humanities.[15]

(7) One of the defining features of American higher education is its firm belief in academic freedom for faculty and students alike. Since the creation of the watchdog American Association of University Professors in 1915, universities have sought to secure their essential activities from political, religious, and other kinds of interference.[16] The much-misunderstood institution of tenure, with its familiar trial periods but also its virtually ignored annual or short-term evaluations thereafter, has long been the bulwark of the

---

Wildavsky, "Mea Culpa," *Chronicle of Higher Education* (May 17, 2012), http://chronicle.com/blogs/worldwise/mea-culpa/29574?sid=at&utm.

14 Rosovsky, *University*, 31; Jean Medawar and David Pyke, *Hitler's Gift: The True Story of the Scientists Expelled by the Nazi Regime* (New York: Arcade Publishing, 2000); Donald Fleming and Bernard Bailyn, eds., *The Intellectual Migration: Europe and America, 1930–1960* (Cambridge, Mass.: Harvard University Press, 1969); Laura Fermi, *Illustrious Immigrants: The Intellectual Migration from Europe, 1930–41* (Chicago: University of Chicago Press, 1968); Jarrell C. Jackman and Carla M. Borden, eds., *The Muses Flee Hitler: Cultural Transfer and Adaptation, 1930–1945* (Washington, D.C.: Smithsonian Institution Press, 1983).

15 Vest, *American Research University*, 8.

16 Richard Hofstadter and Walter P. Metzger, *The Development of Academic Freedom in the United States* (New York: Columbia University Press, 1955); Walter P. Metzger, ed., *The American Concept of Academic Freedom in Formation: A Collection of Essays and Reports* (New York: Arno Press, 1977); Louis Menand, ed., *The Future of Academic Freedom* (Chicago: University of Chicago Press, 1996). The *Magna Charta Universitatum* (1988) declared that "freedom in research and training is the fundamental principle of university life." But it was somewhat less forceful when it suggested that "governments and universities, *each as far as in them lies*, must ensure respect for this fundamental requirement." Carey, "Best Idea of the University" (my emphasis).

faculty's freedom to teach and research as their disciplinary guilds advise and allow. In addition to tenure, competition and portable retirement accounts (such as TIAA-CREF) create a kind of "free agency" for top faculty whose mobility is not hamstrung by civil or royal service obligations, as it is in much of Europe, Asia, and the Middle East.[17]

(8) American research universities are especially strong because they are governed similarly and in concert with their strong faculties. Public or private, they rely on "relatively independent" lay boards of trustees, "enlightened and bold" presidential leadership from new-generation "Captains of Erudition," and appointed—and therefore removable—senior and mid-level administrators to reserve to the faculty *almost* sole authority over the curriculum, graduate admissions, research, and faculty hiring, promotion, and firing. Although provosts and academic deans now usually have the deciding vote in senior hires and tenure decisions, as presidents of smaller institutions used to, most came up through the faculty and try to apply its highest standards. These features give the top universities not only flexibility in adapting to "new and changing circumstances," but also large measures of institutional autonomy to guide their own fortunes, free from undue pressure from "political authority and economic power."[18]

(9) The United States has a long tradition of offering undergraduates a broad liberal education for "the whole person," not just for

17 Cole, *Great American University*, 5, 32, 114; Rawlings, "Universities on the Defensive," 29; Kerr, *Great Transformation*, 41.

18 The *growth* of administrative control over budgets (itself not a new phenomenon) also places limits on faculty autonomy in hiring and in some expansions of curriculum. Rosovsky, *University*, 33 (first quotation), 284; Cole, *Great American University*, 5 (second quotation), 115–16; Kerr, *Great Transformation*, 41 (third quotation); *Magna Charta Universitatum*, in Carey, "Best Idea of the University" (fourth quotation); González, "Can China Build;" Lombardi, *How Universities Work*, ch. 14; Larry G. Gerber, *The Rise and Decline of Faculty Governance: Professionalization and the Modern American University* (Baltimore. Md.: Johns Hopkins University Press, 2014); William G. Bowen and Eugene M. Tobin, *Locus of Authority: The Evolution of Faculty Roles in the Governance of Higher Education* (Princeton, N.J.: Princeton University Press and Ithaka, 2015).

technical competence.[19] Its elite research universities have two advantages in providing it. First, professors who work on the frontiers of knowledge know their disciplines deeply and are able to bring their and other researchers' latest findings to bear on class discussion and the choice of topics for research papers and theses. Second, elite-university wealth and low student:faculty ratios enable them to offer "high-touch, individualized" instruction to their highly qualified undergraduates. Even in large public-elite institutions, personalized instruction at the upper levels and in labs, seminars, colloquia, and selective honors programs provide the "high touch" that is a key component of effective and engaged learning.[20] Like our best liberal arts colleges, elite universities offer excellent education, particularly in the humanities and social sciences, the "tried-and-true way," through personalized instruction, careful attention to reading, writing, and mentoring, cultivating passion for intellectual inquiry, and prizing original thought.[21]

(10) In addition to highly talented faculties, U.S. elite universities openly compete for "the best," that is, diversely talented, students from a large international pool. They then admit an often small minority after "holistic" evaluations that go well beyond standardized test scores and high-school GPAs (grade-point averages).[22] In the past century, the United States developed a nationwide elite-applicant pool through the advent of expanded admissions-staff coverage and salesmanship, jet travel that facilitated long-distance visits, Advanced Placement (AP) and International Baccalaureate (IB) high-school courses, Educational Testing Service (College Board)

19 Rosovsky, *University*, ch. 6; Lawrence R. Veysey, *The Emergence of the American University* (Chicago: University of Chicago Press, 1965), ch. 4; Mark Van Doren, *Liberal Education* (New York: Henry Holt, 1943); Michael S. Roth, *Beyond the University: Why Liberal Education Matters* (New Haven, Conn.: Yale University Press, 2014).

20 Lombardi, *How Universities Work*, 179–80.

21 Rawlings, "Universities on the Defensive," 29. A reciprocal benefit is that undergraduate tuition and undergraduate-alumni donations help to underwrite the graduate program and faculty research. Cole, *Great American University*, 32; Joseph Ben-David, *American Higher Education: Directions Old and New* (New York: McGraw-Hill, 1972), 44–45.

22 Vest, *American Research University*, 9; González, "Can China Build."

exams that reported scores to takers' chosen colleges, a (privately financed) National Merit Scholarship program that drew attention to highly qualified students, regional and national competitions in STEM subjects and foreign languages, and an online Common Application that allowed (and technologically encouraged) multiple applications at the touch of a mouse and swipe of a credit card.

Special efforts have also been made in the past decade or two to encourage applications from more top-performing minority, first-generation, and lower-income high-school students. Wealthy universities, especially well-endowed private ones, also practice "need-blind" admissions and offer loan-free financial aid to lower-income admittees in order to reduce the current congruence between socio-economic wealth and favorable admission rates. Elite public universities, with lower "sticker prices" and more obligation to state residents, are working to the same end by energetic fund-raising and endowment building if state legislators prove unresponsive.

(11) An often overlooked characteristic of American universities is their "broad and deep commitment to public service." The clearest manifestation of this imperative was the land-grant university movement in the nineteenth century. But "today a commitment to public service permeates essentially all segments of the university community and has led to strong interactions with [U.S.] business, industry, and government." While public universities exist primarily to serve their own states, private universities also serve the public interest but define it "on their own terms," often quite broadly.[23] As long ago as 1896, when the socially elite College of New Jersey officially became the more serious Princeton University, faculty spokesman Woodrow Wilson endowed the university with the motto "In the Nation's Service," to which was added in 1988 "and in the Service of All Nations." The future Princeton and U.S. president Wilson only articulated what leading American universities have long and increasingly been guided by.[24] Universities that

23 Vest, *American Research University*, 9 (quotations); Cole, *Great American University*, 114–15.

24 James Axtell, *The Making of Princeton University: From Woodrow Wilson to the Present* (Princeton, N.J.: Princeton University Press, 2006), 604; Alexander Leitch,

educate and train large numbers of young people from other nations and seek through their own research to solve large global problems, as do American universities, perform double service to the global public. As more foreign nations realize the modern value of universities as economic and talent "incubators" and try to emulate the elite American research model, as many do, their universities, too, will elevate public service in its many guises on their lists of assets as well as obligations.

(12) A final attribute of elite American universities, which does not figure directly in global rankings, is their generally attractive locations, evocative architecture, and inspiring campuses. Many are located outside congested cities on large parcels of land, or they preceded urban growth and protected their cores. Most have invested in careful landscaping and frequently in accomplished architects. Almost all have created residential campuses, with or without iconic architecture and attractive public spaces, where students can interact daily with each other and with teachers on several levels. For faculty, location "does not necessarily trump the basics: Having the best facilities and resources to get one's work done, and being able to work with colleagues and students of the first rank, can still outweigh geography," but "other things being roughly equal, geographic location matters." America's great geographical (and largely temperate) diversity, each region with its own special attractions, explains in part why foreign and domestic students, scholars, and faculty are drawn to leading U.S. universities such as Harvard, Yale, and Princeton, Berkeley and Stanford, as they are to Oxford and Cambridge. Even if faculty and students eventually do more teaching and learning online, it is a safe bet that the great majority of both will prefer to

---

ed., *A Princeton Companion* (Princeton, N.J.: Princeton University Press, 1978), 385–87; Mark R. Nemec, *Ivory Towers and Nationalist Minds: Universities, Leadership, and the Development of the American State* (Ann Arbor: University of Michigan Press, 2006), esp. chs. 7–9; Nemec, "The Unappreciated Legacy: Wilson, Princeton, and the Ideal of the American State," in James Axtell, ed., *The Educational Legacy of Woodrow Wilson: From College to Nation* (Charlottesville: University of Virginia Press, 2012), 185–206; Adam R. Nelson, "Woodrow Wilson on Liberal Education for Statesmanship, 1890–1910," in ibid., 49–73.

do them on a familiar campus that has gained their loyalty and even affection.[25]

❁ ❁ ❁

In 1982, Clark Kerr, former chancellor of Berkeley and of the University of California, made a now-famous assertion that among the circa "eighty-five institutions in the Western world established by 1520 [that] still exist[ed] in recognizable forms" were the Catholic Church, the British Parliament, and "seventy universities." Amazingly, "these seventy universities . . . [were] still in the same locations" pursuing their "eternal themes of teaching, scholarship, and service, in one combination or another." Although they appeared to outsiders to be "among the least changed of institutions," they had, as insiders knew, "changed enormously in the emphases on their several functions and in their guiding spirits."[26]

Kerr's goal, of course, was to acknowledge the durable lineage of America's fifty or so elite research universities including several of his own University of California campuses. By 2010, when they were last classified by the Carnegie Foundation for the Advancement of Teaching, the number of U.S. universities with "high" or "very high" research activity was over 200, constituting just 4.4 percent of America's institutions of higher education.[27] But he was also saluting the ability of those elite universities to adapt to changing missions and circumstances without forgetting or forgoing their essential purposes. If to date the top U.S. research universities are counted among the most advanced embodiments of

25 Cole, *Great American University*, 114 (quotation); Blumenstyk, *American Higher Education in Crisis?* 147–50, 154; González, "Can China Build"; Richard P. Dober, *Campus Architecture: Building in the Groves of Academe* (New York: McGraw-Hill, 1996); Paul Venable Turner, *Campus: An American Planning Tradition* (Cambridge, Mass.: MIT Press, 1984). For one denizen's appreciation, see "College Towns" in James Axtell, *The Pleasures of Academe: A Celebration & Defense of Higher Education* (Lincoln: University of Nebraska Press, 1998), ch. 10.

26 Clark Kerr, *The Uses of the University*, 3rd ed. (Cambridge, Mass.: Harvard University Press, 1982 [1963, 1972], 152.

27 *Chronicle of Higher Education Almanac 2014–15* (Aug. 22, 2014), 7.

the venerable university model, they owe a great deal to the genetic fortitude of their European ancestors and to the agility of their various American predecessors in taking advantage of the special conditions and opportunities they encountered in their brave new world.

SUGGESTED READING

GENERAL

Cohen, Arthur M., with Carrie B. Kisker. *The Shaping of American Higher Education: Emergence and Growth of the Contemporary System*. 2nd ed. San Francisco: Jossey-Bass, 2010 [1998].

Curti, Merle, and Roderick Nash, *Philanthropy in the Shaping of American Higher Education*. New Brunswick, N.J.: Rutgers University Press, 1965.

Geiger, Roger L. *The History of American Higher Education: Learning and Culture in America from the Founding to World War II*. Princeton, N.J.: Princeton University Press, 2014.

Hamlin, Arthur T. *The University Library in the United States: Its Origins and Development*. Philadelphia: University of Pennsylvania Press, 1981.

Hofstadter, Richard, and Wilson Smith, eds. *American Higher Education: A Documentary History*. 2 vols. Chicago: University of Chicago Press, 1961.

Horowitz, Helen Lefkowitz. *Campus Life: Undergraduate Cultures from the End of the Eighteenth Century to the Present*. New York: Knopf, 1987.

Rudolph, Frederick. *The American College and University: A History. With Introductory Essay and Supplemental Bibliography by John R. Thelin*. Athens: University of Georgia Press, 1990 [1962].

———. *Curriculum: A History of the American Undergraduate Course of Study Since 1636*. San Francisco: Jossey-Bass, 1977.

Tejerina, Fernando, ed. *The University: An Illustrated History*. New York: Overlook Duckworth, 2011.

Thelin, John R. *Essential Documents in the History of American Higher Education*. Baltimore, Md.: Johns Hopkins University Press, 2014.

———. *A History of American Higher Education*. 2nd ed. Baltimore, Md.: Johns Hopkins University Press, 2011 [2004].

Thelin, John R., and Richard W. Trollinger. *Philanthropy and American Higher Education*. New York: Palgrave Macmillan, 2014.

Turner, Paul Venable. *Campus: An American Planning Tradition*. Cambridge, Mass.: MIT Press, 1984.

MEDIEVAL ORIGINS

Catto, J. I., ed. *The Early Oxford Schools*. Vol. 1 of *The History of the University of Oxford*, edited by T. H. Aston. 8 vols. Oxford: Clarendon Press, 1984.

———, ed. *Late Medieval Oxford*. Vol. 2 of *The History of the University of Oxford*, edited by T. H. Aston. 8 vols. Oxford: Clarendon Press, 1992.

Cobban, Alan B. *English University Life in the Middle Ages*. Columbus: Ohio State University Press, 1999.

———. *The Medieval English Universities: Oxford and Cambridge to c. 1500*. Berkeley: University of California Press, 1990 [1988].

———. "Medieval Student Power." *Past & Present*, no. 53 (November 1971), 28–66.

———. *The Medieval Universities: Their Development and Organization*. London: Methuen, 1975.

Courtney, William J. "Inquiry and Inquisition: Academic Freedom in Medieval Universities." *Church History* 58:2 (June 1989), 168–81.

De Ridder-Symoens, H., ed. *Universities in the Middle Ages*. Vol. 1 of *A History of the University in Europe*, edited by Walter Rüegg. Cambridge: Cambridge University Press, 1992.

Karras, Ruth Mazo. "Separating the Men from the Beasts: Medieval Universities and Masculine Formation." In *From Boys to Men: Formations of Masculinity in Late Medieval Europe*, 66–108, 181–94. Philadelphia: University of Pennsylvania Press, 2003.

Lawrence, C[lifford]. H[ugh]. *The Medieval Idea of a University: An Inaugural Lecture*. Bedford College, University of London, June 1972.

Leader, Damien Riehl. *The University to 1546*. Vol. 1 of *A History of the University of Cambridge*, edited by Christopher Brooke, 4 vols. Cambridge: Cambridge University Press, 1988.

Leff, Gordon. *Paris and Oxford Universities in the Thirteenth and Fourteenth Centuries: An Institutional and Intellectual History*. New York: John Wiley & Sons, 1968.

Novikoff, Alex J. "Toward a Cultural History of Scholastic Disputation." *American Historical Review* 117:2 (April 2012), 330–64.

Pedersen, Olaf. *The First Universities*: Studium Generale *and the Origins of University Education in Europe*. Translated by Richard North. Cambridge: Cambridge University Press, 1997.

Rashdall, Hastings. *The Universities of Europe in the Middle Ages*. New ed. by F. M. Powicke and A. B. Emden, 3 vols. Oxford: Oxford University Press, 1936 [1895].

Seybolt, Robert Francis, ed. and trans. *The Manuale Scholarium: An Original Account of Life in the Medieval University*. Cambridge, Mass.: Harvard University Press, 1921.

Thorndike, Lynn, ed. *University Life and Records in the Middle Ages*. New York: Columbia University Press, 1944.

Wagner, David L., ed. *The Seven Liberal Arts in the Middle Ages*. Bloomington: Indiana University Press, 1983.

Wieruszowski, Helene. *The Medieval University: Masters, Students, Learning.* Princeton, N.J.: D. Van Nostrand, 1966.

TUDOR-STUART OXBRIDGE

Charlton, Kenneth. *Education in Renaissance England.* London: Routledge and Kegan Paul, 1965.

Curtis, Mark H. *Oxford and Cambridge in Transition, 1558–1642: An Essay on Changing Relations between the English Universities and English Society.* Oxford: Clarendon Press, 1959.

Feingold, Mordechai. *The Mathematicians' Apprenticeship: Science, Universities, and Society in England, 1560–1640.* Cambridge: Cambridge University Press, 1984.

Goulding, Robert. "Humanism and Science in the Elizabethan Universities." In *Reassessing Tudor Humanism*, edited by Jonathan Woolfson (Basingstoke, UK: Palgrave Macmillan, 2002), 223–42.

Leedham-Green, Elisabeth. "Cambridge Under the Tudors, 1485–1603." In *A Concise History of the University of Cambridge,* 29–65. Cambridge: Cambridge University Press, 1996.

McConica, James. "Humanism and Aristotle in Tudor Oxford." *English Historical Review* 94:371 (April 1979), 291–317.

———, ed. *The Collegiate University.* Vol. 3 of *The History of the University of Oxford*, edited by T. H. Aston, 8 vols. Oxford: Clarendon Press, 1986.

McLean, Antonia. *Humanism and the Rise of Science in Tudor England.* New York: Neal Watson Academic Publications, 1972.

Morgan, Victor, ed. *1546–1750.* Vol. 2 of *A History of the University of Cambridge*, edited by Christopher Brooke, 4 vols. Cambridge: Cambridge University Press, 2004.

O'Day, Rosemary. *Education and Society, 1500–1800: The Social Foundation of Education in Early Modern Britain.* London: Longman, 1982.

Porter, H. C. *Reformation and Reaction in Tudor Cambridge.* Cambridge: Cambridge University Press, 1958.

Sharpe, Kevin, "Archbishop Laud and the University of Oxford." In *History & Imagination: Essays in Honour of H. R. Trevor-Roper*, edited by Hugh Lloyd-Jones, Valerie Pearl, and Blair Worden, 146–64. London: Duckworth, 1981.

Simon, Joan. *Education and Society in Tudor England.* Cambridge: Cambridge University Press, 1966.

Thompson, Craig R. "Universities in Tudor England." In *Life and Letters in Tudor and Stuart England*, edited by Louis B. Wright and Virginia A. LaMar, 337–82. Ithaca, N.Y.: Cornell University Press for the Folger Shakespeare Library, 1962.

Tyacke, Nicholas, ed. *Seventeenth-Century Oxford*. Vol. 4 of *The History of the University of Oxford*, edited by T. H. Aston, 8 vols. Oxford: Clarendon Press, 1997.

COLONIAL AMERICAN COLLEGES

Axtell, James. *The School upon a Hill: Education and Society in Colonial New England*. New Haven, Conn.: Yale University Press, 1974. See ch. 6: "The Collegiate Way."

Broderick, Francis L. "Pulpit, Physics, and Politics: The Curriculum of the College of New Jersey, 1746–1794." *William & Mary Quarterly*, 3rd ser., 6:1 (January 1949), 42–68.

Foster, Margery Somers. *"Out of Smalle Beginings . . .": An Economic History of Harvard College in the Puritan Period (1636 to 1712)*. Cambridge, Mass.: Harvard University Press, 1962.

Gordon, Anne D. *The College of Philadelphia, 1745–1779: The Impact of an Institution*. New York: Garland 1989.

Herbst, Jurgen. "The American Revolution and the American University." *Perspectives in American History* 10 (1976), 279–354.

———. *From Crisis to Crisis: American College Governance, 1636–1819*. Cambridge, Mass.: Harvard University Press, 1982.

———. "*Translatio Studii*: The Transfer of Learning from the Old World to the New." *History of Higher Education Annual* 12 (1992), 85–99.

Hoeveler, J. David. *Creating the American Mind: Intellect and Politics in the Colonial Colleges*. Lanham, Md.: Rowman and Littlefield, 2002.

Hornberger, Theodore. *Scientific Thought in the American Colleges, 1638–1800*. New York: Octagon Books, 1968 [1946].

Humphrey, David C. *From King's College to Columbia, 1746–1800*. New York: Columbia University Press, 1976.

Kraus, Joe W. "The Development of a Curriculum in the Early American Colleges." *History of Education Quarterly* 1:2 (June 1961), 64–76.

McAnear, Beverly. "College Founding in the American Colonies, 1745–1775." *Mississippi Valley Historical Review* 42:1 (June 1955), 24–44.

———. "The Raising of Funds by the Colonial Colleges." *Mississippi Valley Historical Review* 38:4 (March 1952), 591–612.

———. "The Selection of an Alma Mater by Pre-Revolutionary Students." *Pennsylvania Magazine of History and Biography* 73:4 (October 1949), 429–40.

Miller, Howard. *The Revolutionary College: American Presbyterian Higher Education, 1707–1837*. New York: New York University Press, 1976.

Morison, Samuel Eliot. *The Founding of Harvard College*. Cambridge, Mass.: Harvard University Press, 1935.

———. *Harvard in the Seventeenth Century*. 2 vols. Cambridge, Mass.: Harvard University Press, 1935.

———. *Three Centuries of Harvard, 1636–1936*. Cambridge, Mass.: Harvard University Press, 1936.

Morpurgo, J. E. *Their Majesties' Royall Colledge: William and Mary in the Seventeenth and Eighteenth Centuries*. Williamsburg: Endowment Association of The College of William and Mary of Virginia, 1976.

Peckham, Howard H. "*Collegia Ante Bellum*: Attitudes of College Professors and Students toward the American Revolution." *Pennsylvania Magazine of History and Biography* 95:1 (January 1971), 50–72.

Robson, David W. *Educating Republicans: The College in the Era of the American Revolution, 1750–1800*. Westport, Conn.: Greenwood Press, 1985.

Tucker, Louis Leonard. "Centers of Sedition: Colonial Colleges and the American Revolution." *Proceedings of the Massachusetts Historical Society* 91 (1979), 16–34.

Warch, Richard. *School of the Prophets: Yale College, 1701–1740*. New Haven, Conn.: Yale University Press, 1974.

ANTEBELLUM COLLEGES

Allmendinger, David F., Jr. *Paupers and Scholars: The Transformation of Student Life in Nineteenth-Century New England*. New York: St. Martin's Press, 1975.

Beadie, Nancy, and Kim Tolley, eds. *Chartered Schools: Two Hundred Years of Independent Academies in the United States, 1727–1925*. New York: Routledge Fulmer, 2002.

Burke, Colin B. *American Collegiate Populations: A Test of the Traditional View*. New York: New York University Press, 1982.

Coulter, E. Merton. *College Life in the Old South*. Athens: University of Georgia Press, 1983 [1928].

Durrell, Wayne K. "The Power of Ancient Words: Classical Teaching and Social Change at South Carolina College, 1804–1860." *Journal of Southern History* 65:3 (August 1999), 469–98.

Eschenbacher, Herman. "When Brown Was Less than a University but Hope Was More than a College." *Brown Alumni Magazine* (February 1980), 26–33.

Findlay, James. "'Western' Colleges, 1830–1870: Educational Institutions in Transition." *History of Higher Education Annual* 2 (1982), 35–64.

Geiger, Roger L., ed. *The American College in the Nineteenth Century*. Nashville, Tenn.: Vanderbilt University Press, 2000.

———. "The Reformation of the Colleges in the Early Republic, 1800–1820." *History of Universities* 16:2 (2000), 129–82.

Guralnick, Stanley M. *Science and the Ante-Bellum American College*. Memoirs of the American Philosophical Society 109 (Philadelphia, 1975).

Harding, Thomas S. *College Literary Societies: Their Contribution to Higher Education in the United States, 1815–1876*. New York: Pageant Press, 1971.

Henry, James Buchanan, and Christian Henry Scharff. *College as It Is, or, The Collegian's Manual in 1853*. Edited by J. Jefferson Looney. Princeton, N.J.: Princeton University Libraries, 1996.

Herbst, Jurgen. "American Higher Education in the Age of the College." *History of Universities* 7 (1988), 37–59.

Knight, Edgar W., ed. *A Documentary History of Education in the South Before 1860*. 5 vols. Chapel Hill: University of North Carolina Press, 1949–53 . Vol. 3, *The Rise of the State University* (1952). Vol. 4, *Private and Denominational Efforts* (1953).

Naylor, Natalie A. "The Antebellum College Movement: A Reappraisal of Tewksbury's *Founding of American Colleges and Universities*." *History of Education Quarterly* 13 (Fall 1973), 261–74.

Noll, Mark A. *Princeton and the Republic, 1768–1822: The Search for a Christian Enlightenment in the Era of Samuel Stanhope Smith*. Princeton, N.J.: Princeton University Press, 1989.

Pace, Robert F. *Halls of Honor: College Men in the Old South*. Baton Rouge: Louisiana State University Press, 2004.

Potts, David B. *Liberal Education for a Land of Colleges: Yale's* Reports *of 1828*. New York: Palgrave Macmillan, 2010.

Schmidt, George P. *The Old-Time College President*. New York: Columbia University Press, 1930.

Sizer, Theodore R. ed., *The Age of the Academies*. Classics in Education. No. 22. New York: Bureau of Publications, Teachers College, Columbia University, 1964.

Smith, Wilson. "Apologia pro Alma Matre: The College as Community in Ante-Bellum America." In *The Hofstadter Aegis: A Memorial*, edited by Stanley Elkins and Eric McKitrick, 125–53. New York: Alfred A. Knopf, 1974.

Sumner, Margaret. *Collegiate Republic: Cultivating an Ideal Society in Early America*. Charlottesville: University of Virginia Press, 2014.

Winterer, Caroline. *The Culture of Classicism: Ancient Greece and Rome in American Intellectual Life, 1780–1910*. Baltimore, Md.: Johns Hopkins University Press, 2002.

THE GERMAN IMPRESS

Ben-David, Joseph. "The Universities and the Growth of Science in Germany and the United States." *Minerva: A Review of Science, Learning, and Policy* 7:1–2 (Autumn–Winter 1968–69), 1–35.

Clark, William. *Academic Charisma and the Origins of the Research University*. Chicago: University of Chicago Press, 2006.

Conrad, Johannes. *The German Universities for the Last Fifty Years*. Translated by John Hutchison. Glasgow: D. Bryce and Son, 1885 [1884].

Diehl, Carl. *Americans and German Scholarship, 1770–1870*. New Haven, Conn.: Yale University Press, 1978.

Goodchild, Lester F. and Margaret M. Miller, "The American Doctorate and Dissertation: Six Developmental Stages." *New Directions for Higher Education*, no. 99 (Fall 1999), 17–32.

Hart, James Morgan. *German Universities: A Narrative of Personal Experience*. New York: G. P. Putnam's Sons, 1874.

Herbst, Jurgen. *The German Historical School in American Scholarship: A Study in the Transfer of Culture*. Ithaca, N.Y.: Cornell University Press, 1965.

Kohler, Robert E. "The Ph.D. Machine: Building on the Collegiate Base." *Isis* 81:4 (Dec. 1990), 638–62.

Long, Orie William. *Literary Pioneers: Early American Explorers of European Culture*. Cambridge, Mass.: Harvard University Press, 1935.

Mazón, Patricia M. *Gender and the Modern Research University: The Admission of Women to German Higher Education, 1865–1914*. Stanford, Calif.: Stanford University Press, 2003.

McClelland, Charles E. *State, Society, and University in Germany, 1700–1914*. New York: Cambridge University Press, 1980.

Metzger, Walter P. "The German Contribution to the American Theory of Academic Freedom." *Bulletin of the American Association of University Professors* 41:2 (Summer 1955), 214–30.

Paulsen, Friedrich. *The German Universities: Their Character and Historical Development*. Translated by Edward Delavan Perry. New York: Macmillan, 1895.

Reingold, Nathan. "Graduate School and Doctoral Degree: European Models and American Realities." In *Scientific Colonialism*, edited by Nathan Reingold and Marc Rothenberg, 129–49. Washington, D.C.: Smithsonian Institution Press, 1986.

Ryan, W. Carson. *Studies in Early Graduate Education*. Bull. 30 (New York: Carnegie Foundation for the Advancement of Teaching, 1939).

Singer, Sandra L. *Adventures Abroad: North American Women at German-Speaking Universities, 1868–1915*. Westport, Conn.: Praeger, 2003.

Storr, Richard J. *The Beginning of the Future: A Historical Approach to Graduate Education in the Arts and Sciences.* New York: McGraw-Hill, 1973.

———. *The Beginnings of Graduate Education in America*. Chicago: University of Chicago Press, 1953.

Thwing, Charles Franklin. *The American and the German Universities: One Hundred Years of History*. New York: Macmillan, 1928.

Turner, James, and Paul Bernard. "The 'German Model' and the Graduate School: The University of Michigan and the Origin Myth of the American University." *History of Higher Education Annual* 13 (1993), 69–98.

Wellmon, Chad. *Organizing Enlightenment: Information Overload and the Invention of the Modern Research University*. Baltimore, Md.: Johns Hopkins University Press, 2015.

Werner, Anja. *The Transatlantic World of Higher Education: Americans at German Universities, 1776–1914*. New York: Berghahn Books, 2013.

THE NEW UNIVERSITIES

Axtell, James. *The Making of Princeton University: From Woodrow Wilson to the Present*. Princeton, N.J.: Princeton University Press, 2006.

Elliott, Orrin Leslie. *Stanford University: The First Twenty-Five Years*. Stanford, Calif.: Stanford University Press, 1937.

Geiger, Roger L. *To Advance Knowledge: The Growth of the American Research Universities, 1900–1940*. New York: Oxford University Press, 1986.

Goldin, Claudia, and Lawrence F. Katz. "The Shaping of Higher Education: The Formative Years in the United States, 1890 to 1940." *Journal of Economic Perspectives* 13:1 (Winter 1999), 37–62.

Goodspeed, Thomas Wakefield. *A History of the University of Chicago: The First Quarter-Century*. Chicago: University of Chicago Press, 1972 [1916].

Karabel, Jerome. *The Chosen: The Hidden History of Admission and Exclusion at Harvard, Yale, and Princeton*. Boston: Houghton Mifflin, 2005.

Leslie, W. Bruce. *Gentlemen and Scholars: College and Community in the 'Age of the University,' 1865–1917*. University Park, Pa.: Penn State University Press, 1992.

Levine, David O. *The American College and the Culture of Aspiration, 1915–1940*. Ithaca, N.Y.: Cornell University Press, 1986.

Newfield, Christopher. *Ivy and Industry: Business and the Making of the American University, 1880–1980*. Durham, N.C.: Duke University Press, 2003.

Reuben, Julie A. *The Making of the Modern University: Intellectual Transformation and the Marginalization of Morality*. Chicago: University of Chicago Press, 1996.

Roberts, Jon H., and James Turner. *The Sacred and the Secular University*. Princeton, N.J.: Princeton University Press, 2000.

Shils, Edward. "The Order of Learning in the United States: The Ascendancy of the University." In *The Organization of Knowledge in Modern America, 1860–1920*, edited by Alexandra Oleson and John Voss, 19–47. Baltimore, Md.: Johns Hopkins University Press, 1979.

Slosson, Edwin E. *Great American Universities*. New York: Macmillan, 1910.

Stadtman, Verne A. *The University of California, 1868–1968*. New York: McGraw-Hill, 1970.

Stone, James C., and Donald P. DeNeri, eds. *Portraits of the American University, 1890–1910*. San Francisco: Jossey-Bass, 1971.

Storr, Richard J. *Harper's University: The Beginnings*. Chicago: University of Chicago Press, 1966.

Turner, James. *Philology: The Forgotten Origins of the Modern Humanities*. Princeton, N.J.: Princeton University Press, 2014.

Veysey, Laurence R. *The Emergence of the American University*. Chicago: University of Chicago Press, 1965.

GLOBAL ASCENDANCE

Archibald, Robert B., and David H. Feldman. *Why Does College Cost So Much?* New York: Oxford University Press, 2011.

Blumenstyk, Goldie. *American Higher Education in Crisis? What Everyone Needs to Know*. New York: Oxford University Press, 2015.

Bok, Derek. *Higher Education in America*. Princeton, N.J.: Princeton University Press, 2013.

———. *Universities in the Marketplace: The Commercialization of Higher Education*. Princeton, N.J.: Princeton University Press, 2003.

Bowen, William G., and Derek Bok. *The Shape of the River: Long-Term Consequences of Considering Race in College and University Admissions*. Princeton: Princeton University Press, 1998.

Bowen, William G., Matthew M. Chingos, and Michael S. McPherson. *Crossing the Finish Line: Completing College at America's Public Universities*. Princeton, N.J.: Princeton University Press, 2009.

Bowen, William G., Martin A. Kurzweil, and Eugene M. Tobin. *Equity and Excellence in American Higher Education*. Charlottesville: University of Virginia Press, 2005.

Bowen, William G., and Sarah A. Levin. *Reclaiming the Game: College Sports and Educational Values*. Princeton, N.J.: Princeton University Press, 2003.
Bowen, William G., and Eugene Tobin. *Locus of Authority: The Evolution of Faculty Roles in the Governance of Higher Education*. Princeton, N.J.: Princeton University Press, 2015.
Brint, Steven, ed. *The City of Intellect: The Changing American University*. Stanford, Calif.: Stanford University Press, 2002.
Charles, Camille Z., Mary J. Fischer, Margarita A. Mooney, and Douglas S. Massey. *Taming the River: Negotiating the Academic, Financial, and Social Currents in Selective Colleges and Universities*. Princeton, N.J.: Princeton University Press, 2009.
Clotfelter, Charles T. *Big-Time Sports in American Universities*. New York: Cambridge University Press, 2011.
———. *Buying the Best: Cost Escalation in Elite Higher Education*. Princeton, N.J.: Princeton University Press, 1996.
Cole, Jonathan R. *The Great American University: Its Rise to Preeminence, Its Indispensable National Role, Why It Must Be Protected*. New York: Public Affairs, 2009.
Espenshade, Thomas J., and Alexandria Walton Radford. *No Longer Separate, Not Yet Equal: Race and Class in Elite College Admission and Campus Life*. Princeton, N.J.: Princeton University Press, 2009.
Geiger, Roger L. *Knowledge and Money: Research Universities and the Paradox of the Marketplace*. Stanford, Calif.: Stanford University Press, 2004.
———. *Research and Relevant Knowledge: American Research Universities Since World War II*. New York: Oxford University Press, 1993.
Gerber, Larry G. *The Rise and Decline of Faculty Governance: Professionalization and the Modern American University*. Baltimore, Md.: Johns Hopkins University Press, 2014.
Graham, Hugh Davis, and Nancy Diamond. *The Rise of American Research Universities: Elites and Challengers in the Postwar Era*. Baltimore, Md.: Johns Hopkins University Press, 1997.
Henry, David D. *Challenges Past, Challenges Present: An Analysis of American Higher Education Since 1930*. San Francisco: Jossey-Bass, 1975.
Kerr, Clark. *The Uses of the University*. 3rd ed. Cambridge, Mass.: Harvard University Press, 1982.
Kirp, David L. *Shakespeare, Einstein, and the Bottom Line: The Marketing of Higher Education*. Cambridge, Mass.: Harvard University Press, 2003.
Levine, Arthur. "Higher Education as a Mature Industry." In *In Defense of American Higher Education*, edited by Philip G. Altbach, Patricia J.

Gumport, and D. Bruce Johnstone, 38–58. Baltimore, Md.: Johns Hopkins University Press, 2001.

Lombardi, John V. *How Universities Work*. Baltimore, Md.: Johns Hopkins University Press, 2013.

Rhode, Deborah L. *In Pursuit of Knowledge: Scholars, Status, and Academic Culture*. Stanford, Calif.: Stanford University Press, 2006.

Rosovsky, Henry. *The University: An Owner's Manual*. New York: W. W. Norton, 1990.

Shulman, James L., and William G. Bowen. *The Game of Life: College Sports and Educational Values*. Princeton, N.J.: Princeton University Press, 2001.

Smith, G. Kerry, ed. *1945–1970: Twenty-Five Years*. San Francisco: Jossey-Bass, 1970.

Smith, Wilson, and Thomas Bender, eds. *American Higher Education Transformed, 1940–2005: Documenting the National Discourse*. Baltimore, Md.: Johns Hopkins University Press, 2008.

Vest, Charles M. *The American Research University from World War II to World Wide Web: Governments, the Private Sector, and the Emerging Meta-University*. Berkeley: University of California Press, 2007.

Wildavsky, Ben. *The Great Brain Race: How Global Universities Are Reshaping the World*. Princeton, N.J.: Princeton University Press, 2010.

INDEX

Note: Pages in bold indicate text in figures.